Evidence for Criminal Justice

Evidence for Criminal Justice

Cliff Roberson
Robert Winters

Carolina Academic Press
Durham, North Carolina

Library of Congress Cataloging-in-Publication Data

Roberson, Cliff, 1937- author.
  Evidence for criminal justice / Cliff Roberson and Robert Winters.
    pages cm
  Includes bibliographical references and index.
  ISBN 978-1-61163-669-7 (alk. paper)
  1. Evidence, Criminal--United States. I. Winters, Robert C., author. II. Title.

  KF9660.R59 2015
  345.73'06--dc23

                        2015034441

Carolina Academic Press
700 Kent Street
Durham, NC 27701
Telephone (919) 489-7486
Fax (919) 493-5668
www.cap-press.com

Printed in the United States of America

Cliff Roberson
To Elena

Robert Winters
To Sue, my wife, and Mike, my son, for your unfailing support, encouragement and inspiration.

Contents

Preface

Evidence for Criminal Justice is designed for criminal justice professionals who want or need a better understanding of the rules of evidence. In addition to explaining the rules, we have presented information to help the reader understand the reasons behind the rules. The rules of evidence in state and federal courts are designed to ensure a fair trial. In the criminal justice area, they are designed to ensure that both the defendant and the prosecutor can present admissible evidence in a fair and efficient manner to the jury or, in the case of a judge alone, to the trial judge. The U.S. Constitution guarantees the accused and the government a fair trial. Not a perfect trial, but a fair one.

In both state and federal courts, the trial judge makes decisions of law and the jury makes findings of fact. Accordingly when dealing with evidence issues, the question of whether or not certain evidence is admissible is a decision made by the trial judge. The weight to place on admitted evidence is the decision of the fact-finders, the jury in a jury trial.

The text is subdivided into eleven chapters. Each chapter is designed as a stand-alone subject. But to obtain a clear understanding of the rules of evidence, every chapter needs to be examined. Included as Appendix A is the Federal Rules of Evidence. Included as Appendix B is a journal article on Locard's principle. His principle is that every contact leaves traces. This principle is basic to anyone reviewing a crime scene. For a better understanding of his principle, read the journal article.

Finally, while we are listed as the only authors, we could not have completed the text without the help and assistance of many professionals, including our editor Beth Hall, Tim Colton in the production department, and Tasha Clark, who served as our contract coordinator and production editor. Please notify us with any suggestions, recommendations for improvement, or errors at either cliff.roberson@washburn.edu or rwinters@kaplan.edu.

Evidence for Criminal Justice

Chapter 1

Introduction to the Study of Evidence

Chapter Objectives

What you should know and understand after studying this chapter:

- Purpose of the rules of evidence
- Difference between circumstantial and direct evidence
- The background on the Federal Rules of Evidence
- The types of evidence
- The divisions of responsibilities among court personnel
- The general evidentiary principles

Chapter Outline

Introduction
Federal Rules of Evidence
Types of Evidence
Direct or Circumstantial Evidence
Guilt or Innocence
Division of Responsibility
Evidentiary Policies
Practicum
Summary
Questions in Review
Key Terms
Endnotes

Introduction

The primary purpose of the rules of evidence is to help ensure a fair trial.

Evidence is generally defined as any matter of fact that a party to a lawsuit offers to prove or disprove an issue in the case. Evidence consists of a system of rules and standards that is used to determine which facts may be admitted, and to what extent a judge or jury may consider those facts, as proof of a particular issue in a lawsuit. The study of evidence is the study of the collection of rules and regulations involving the proof of facts and the inferences and arguments that arise from such proof in the trial of a lawsuit. In this text for the most part we will restrict our discussion of evidence to only criminal trials. In this chapter, we will introduce many evidentiary concepts. Generally these concepts will be briefly discussed in this chapter but treated in more detail later in the book.

Why do we restrict the evidence that is admissible in American courts? As noted above, to ensure a fair trial for all parties to the trial. In a criminal trial, this means that both the accused and the state or federal government have a right to a fair trial. Or stated another way, the rules of evidence are designed to regulate that portion of the trial process that pertains to evidence so that proceedings can be fair for all involved. These rules also are used to assist the judge or jury in determining the facts involved. Another important function of the rules of evidence is as guidelines that determine how evidence should be handled. The guidelines help determine what evidence is admissible, when it is admissible, and who is entitled to present it.

In this text, we will discuss the various rules of evidence and explain how they work in actual criminal cases. The reader should keep in mind that the rules of evidence are used when it is necessary to establish certain facts in the trial courts. In both the federal and state systems, most cases are disposed of by guilty pleas. Generally only about ten percent of the cases are actually tried in a trial court. The rest are disposed of by guilty pleas and many of the guilty pleas are the results of plea bargains between the government and the defense.

There are fifty state court systems and one federal court system operating in the United States. However, most criminal cases are tried in state trial courts based on violations of the state criminal code or criminal laws.

There is no one set of rules regarding the admissibility of evidence in the United States. In the federal courts there are the Federal Rules of Evidence (FRE) (Appendix A). Each state has separate rules of evidence. But the vast majority of states have patterned their evidentiary rules after the federal rules. While there are minor differences among the states, for the most part, the policies set forth in the federal rules apply.

Federal Rules of Evidence

In March 1961, the Judicial Conference of the United States approved a proposal to start an Advisory Committee on Rules of Evidence. Prior to that as early as 1938, former Attorney General William D. Mitchell suggested that an "advisory committee should tackle the task of revising the rules of evidence and composing them into a new set of rules to be promulgated by the Supreme Court." In 1958, the House of Delegates of the

American Bar Association (ABA) recommended the formulation of uniform rules. Also in 1958, the Judicial Conference established a Committee on Rules of Practice and Procedure. It was not until 1975 that the first version of the rules was adopted. As an interesting historical note, the approval of the federal rules by the senate was delayed because the senate was busy dealing with Watergate scandal.

Until 1933, federal courts trying a criminal case used the rules of evidence governing the state in which the federal court sat. However, they were required to apply the state rules as they existed in 1789, when the federal courts were created. For the states that joined the union after 1789, the courts utilized the state evidence law as it existed when the state joined the union.[1] After 1933 and prior to the adoption of the federal rules, the courts based their evidentiary rulings primarily on common law policies.

The first version of the Federal Rules of Evidence was adopted in 1975. In drafting the 1975 rules, the committee relied heavily on the California Evidence Code and the Uniform Rules of Evidence that had been drafted by the National Conference of Commissioners on Uniform State Laws that was published in 1953. The rules as amended have not varied greatly from what was regarded as the better-reasoned ruling found previously under the common law system.

The rules were extensively revised in 2012. The U.S. Judicial Conference Advisory Committee on the Federal Rules of Evidence, which drafted the 2012 version of the rules, stated that the purposes of the comprehensive revisions were to simplify, clarify, and make more uniform all of the federal rules of practice, procedure, and evidence. As noted in Federal Rule 102, the rules should be interpreted to help ensure a fair trial and to eliminate unjustifiable expense and delay.

The U.S. Supreme Court in *Bourjaily v. United States*[2] stated that in interpreting and applying the rules it will generally look to their plain meaning unless such a result would be absurd. Often the Court has used common law principles, legislative history, and the Advisory Committee's Notes as guides to interpret the rules.

> **Federal Rules of Evidence, Rule 102. Purpose**
> These rules should be construed so as to administer every proceeding fairly, eliminate unjustifiable expense and delay, and promote the development of evidence law, to the end of ascertaining the truth and securing a just determination.
> (As amended Apr. 26, 2011, eff. Dec. 1, 2011.)

Currently, the rules encompass 68 separate rules addressing topics from hearsay to attorney-client privilege, relevancy of evidence, and expert testimony. The rules are individually numbered and divided among the following 11 articles:

General Provisions
Judicial Notice
Presumptions in Civil Actions and Proceedings
Relevancy and Its Limits
Privileges
Witnesses
Opinions and Expert Testimony
Hearsay

Authentication and Identification
Contents of Writings, Recordings, and Photographs
Miscellaneous Rules

Photo 1-1

Appomattox Court House, Virginia, in April 1865.
Photo courtesy of the Library of Congress.

Evidence in Action

Procedure for Enacting New Amendments and Rules of Evidence

Under the Rules Enabling Act, the Supreme Court normally prescribes Federal Rules of Evidence. Pursuant to 28 U.S.C. § 2074, the Supreme Court transmits to Congress (not later than May 1 of the year in which a rule prescribed under section 2072 is to become effective) a copy of the proposed rule. The rule takes effect no earlier than December 1 of the year in which the rule is transmitted unless otherwise provided by law. (Occasionally, Congress has enacted legislation amending the rules rather than accepting recommendations from the Judicial Conference and Supreme Court. Congress has also reserved the right to enact any changes to the rules involving privileges.)

Federal Rules of Criminal Procedure

In federal courts involving criminal cases, the Federal Rules of Criminal Procedure (FRCP) are used in conjunction with the Federal Rules of Evidence (FRE). The FRCP were first enacted in the 1940s and have been amended numerous times. The last revision was in December 2013. Most states have similar rules. While there are minor variations among the jurisdictions, the rules of criminal procedure within the states and federal governments are substantially similar.

Several of the FRCP rules have an impact on when or if certain evidence may be admitted in a criminal trial. For example, if the defense intends to introduce evidence of an alibi defense, the defense must provide notice of the intent to introduce this evidence pursuant to FRCP Rule 12.1. Generally this notice must be given at least 14 days prior to the start of the trial, but the time limit may be modified by the trial judge.

FRCP Rule 12.2 requires the defense to provide advance notice of an insanity defense and set forth the procedures for mental examinations. The rule also governs the admissibility of statements made by a defendant during the required mental examinations.

FRCP Rule 16 requires that the government disclose various types of evidence to the defense. The rule also indicates that certain types of information in the custody of the government are not subject to disclosure. For example, the disclosure of material prepared by a government attorney in connection with the prosecuting of the case is generally not subject to disclosure.

Local Rules of Court

In both state and federal jurisdictions, courts have established local rules of for the trial of criminal cases. The example set forth in the Evidence in Action Box is a copy of a local rule issued by the U.S. District Court for the Western District of Oklahoma. FRCP Rule 57 provides that each district court may enact local rules. The local rules may not be enforced in a manner that causes a party to lose rights because of an unintentional failure to comply with the requirement. The local rules are designed to regulate in any manner consistent with the applicable law. In addition, the local rules must be consistent with and not duplicative of statutes or jurisdiction-wide rules.

Evidence in Action

The United States District Court For The Western District of Oklahoma, Local Rule 39.3

Rule 39.3: Use of Electronic Devices, Photographs, or Tape Recorders at Trial.

(a) The taking of photographs and operation of tape recorders and radio or television broadcasting in the courthouse during the progress of or in connection with judicial proceedings, including proceedings before a United States Magistrate Judge, whether or not court is actually in session, is prohibited.

(b) A judge may, however, permit the use of electronic or photographic means for the presentation of evidence or the perpetuation of a record, and the broadcasting, televising, recording, or photographing of investitive, ceremonial, or naturalization proceedings.

(c) The court prohibits the use of cellular telephones, pagers, or other electronic communication devices in the courtroom. Such devices may be carried on the person within a courtroom only if the device is turned off or non-auditory.

Types of Evidence

Evidence may be divided into five traditional types of evidence:

- real,
- demonstrative,
- documentary,
- testimonial, and
- judicially noticed evidence.

Real evidence frequently refers to physical objects. For example, a bullet taken from the body of a murder victim is considered real evidence. The wrecked automobile at the scene of an automobile accident case is also real evidence. In civil proceedings where a person is suing or being sued for failure to fulfill the terms of the contract, the actual contract is real evidence.

Real evidence may be defined as the thing, the existence or characteristics of which are relevant and material. It is usually evidence that is directly involved in some event in the case.

Demonstrative evidence is evidence that demonstrates or illustrates the testimony of a witness. For example, a diagram of the building where the crime occurred is considered demonstrative evidence. A photo of the crime scene is also considered demonstrative evidence. The purpose of demonstrative evidence is to illustrate testimony. Before demonstrative evidence is admissible it must be authenticated. The authentication is usually done by a witness who is familiar with the area being shown or depicted in the evidence and who can testify that the evidence is a fair representation of the area. Note a photograph or video of an individual committing a crime is real evidence, whereas the picture or video of the scene where a crime has been committed is demonstrative evidence.

Documentary evidence is a document such as a gun registration form that indicates that the murder weapon at one time belonged to the accused. Documentary evidence may also be considered real evidence. A birth certificate is an example of documentary evidence. If an accused is being tried for providing false information to a law enforcement officer, the written statement containing the false information is both real evidence and documentary evidence. A report of a blood alcohol test is frequently both real and documentary evidence.

Testimonial evidence is probably the most basic form of evidence. It is the only form of evidence that does not require authentication as a prerequisite for its admissibility. Testimonial evidence consists of what is stated in court proceedings by a competent witness. Generally to be a competent witness, the witness must take the oath to tell the truth or a substitute. Unless the witness is an expert witness, he or she generally must have personal knowledge about the subject of the testimony. The witness must remember what he or she perceived and be able to communicate what the witness perceived. There are other rules of competence that relate to special circumstances which are discussed later in the text.

There two classifications of witnesses to testify in court; lay witnesses and expert witnesses. A lay witness is a witness who is testifying as to matters in which he or she has a personal knowledge. For the most part, a lay witness may testify only to matters to which he or she has personal knowledge. An exception to this general rule is that a lay witness may testify in the form of opinions or inferences which are:

- rationally based on perception of the witness and
- helpful to a clear understanding of the witness' testimony or the determination of a fact in issue.[3]

Under the above restrictions on giving opinion testimony by a lay witness, a lay witness could probably testify in court that she saw the defendant driving very fast in a school zone and that she estimates his speed was in excess of 50 miles per hour. The defense may cross examine her on why she estimated that the speed was in excess of 50 miles per hour.

In all American court jurisdictions, expert witnesses are granted more latitude to testify regarding opinions and inferences if their scientific, technical, or other specialized knowledge will assist the trier of fact (judge or jury) to understand the evidence or to determine a fact issue.[4] The expert's testimony must assist the trier of fact, if scientific it must be reliable, and the expert must have sufficient specialized knowledge regarding the issues that the expert is testifying on. An expert witness may not testify on the ultimate issue in a trial. In other words, the expert witness may not testify that in his or her opinion the defendant committed the act or is guilty.

A common restriction with testimonial evidence is the prohibition against using hearsay evidence. Even law students have difficulty in determining what constitutes hearsay and its exceptions. Hearsay may be defined as testimonial evidence presented in court, or written evidence of a statement made out of court, where the statement is offered to show the truth of the matter stated. For example, a witness on the stand states that she heard John state that he was going to the Browns' residence. This is a type of hearsay if admitted for the purpose of establishing that John went to the Browns' residence. Note there are numerous exceptions to the prohibition against entering hearsay evidence that will be discussed later in the text. For example if a defendant brags at a bar that he killed the victim, a person who overheard that statement may testify that the defendant made that statement in an attempt to establish defendant's guilt. Evidence that a defendant made an admission or confession is usually admissible as an exception to the hearsay rule because it is an admission against the interests of the defendant.

Judicially Noticed Evidence

Judicial notice is a shortcut that dispenses with the need to present evidence on the issue. July 4 of each year is Independence Day in the United States. It is also a national holiday, and therefore the courts are not open for regular business. Why do we need to present evidence that July 4 is a national holiday when everybody in the United States knows that? The trial judge may take judicial notice without the need for evidence on the issue.

Judicially noticed evidence is defined in FRE 201. The rule provides that the court may take judicial notice of facts that are not subject to reasonable dispute. For example, a trial judge may take judicial notice of the fact that the City of Los Angeles is located in the State of California without any evidence being presented on this issue. Under certain situations, a trial court may take judicial note of the statutes of another jurisdiction. For example in a case being tried in the State of New York, the trial judge may under certain circumstances take judicial notice of a New Jersey statute.

Prior to the Federal Rules of Evidence and the Federal Rules of Criminal Procedure, co-author Cliff Roberson prosecuted a federal case in Honolulu, Hawaii. The main issue in the case was the admissibility of testimony taken in a prior case against the defendant. The witness who presented the original testimony was unavailable because he was somewhere in Mexico. At the time the rules of admissibility for such testimony were that the witness was in a different jurisdiction and at least 100 miles from the place where the present trial was being held. The conviction was reversed on appeal because Roberson failed to enter evidence that Mexico was at least 100 miles from Honolulu. Under the present rules of evidence, the trial judge could have taken judicial notice of this fact without the necessity of proving it.

To be judicially noticed without the introduction of evidence, the fact must be one that is not subject to a reasonable dispute, generally known with the trial court's jurisdiction, and can be accurately and readily determined from sources whose accuracy cannot reasonably be questioned.

The trial court may take judicial notice on its own; or it must take judicial notice if a party requests it, and the court is supplied with the necessary information. The court may take judicial notice at any stage of the proceeding. On timely request, a party is entitled to be heard on the propriety of taking judicial notice and the nature of the fact to be noticed. If the court takes judicial notice before notifying a party, the party, on request, is still entitled to be heard. In a criminal case, the court must instruct the jury that it may or may not accept the noticed fact as conclusive.

The general rules of admissibility apply to all five types of evidence. Other rules apply only to certain types of evidence. These issues will be discussed in later chapters.

Direct or Circumstantial Evidence

A famous case and one that illustrates the difference between direct and circumstantial evidence was the 1850 case of *Commonwealth v. Webster*. The victim was Dr. George Parkman, a prominent Bostonian. He was a doctor of medicine of the University of

Aberdeen and a member of the Massachusetts Medical Society. The accused Dr. John Webster was also a prominent man of Boston's society and a doctor of medicine at Harvard University. He was also a member of the Massachusetts Medical Society and was connected with the American Academy of Arts and Sciences.

The evidence in the Webster case indicated that Dr. Parkman left his home on the afternoon of November 23, 1849, that he was in good health and was seen going toward the medical college. On the next day, an extensive but unsuccessful search was made for Dr. Parkman. On November 30, parts of his body were found in a furnace. The artificial teeth found in the furnace were identified as belonging to Dr. Parkman. Evidence was also presented that defendant Webster was indebted to Dr. Parkman and Parkman was trying to collect the debt. Evidence established that Parkman had an appointment with defendant Webster on the day he disappeared.

The defendant had no means of paying the debt which was evidenced by a note in the possession of Dr. Parkman on the day he disappeared. Afterwards the note was found in possession of the defendant. The defendant John Webster, a professor of chemistry in the medical college in Boston, was found guilty of the murder of Parkman based on circumstantial evidence. He was hanged on August 30, 1850.

As noted in the case by Chief Justice Shaw of the Supreme Judicial Court of Massachusetts in 1850,[5] the distinction between direct and circumstantial evidence is that direct or positive evidence is when a witness can be called to testify to the precise fact which is the subject of the issue on trial; that is, in a case of homicide, that the party accused did cause the death of the deceased. Whatever may be the kind or force of the evidence, this is the fact to be proved. But suppose no person was present on the occasion of the death, and of course that no one can be called to testify to it; is it wholly unsusceptible of legal proof? Experience has shown that circumstantial evidence may be offered in such a case; that is, that a body of facts may be proved of so conclusive a character as to warrant a firm belief of the fact quite as strong and certain as that on which discreet men are accustomed to act in relation to their most important concerns. It would be injurious to the best interests of society if such proof could not avail in judicial proceedings. If it was necessary always to have positive evidence, how many criminal acts committed in the community, destructive of its peace and subversive of its order and security, would go wholly undetected and unpunished?

Chief Justice Shaw noted that the necessity, therefore, of resorting to circumstantial evidence, if it is a safe and reliable proceeding, is obvious and absolute. Crimes are secret. Most men, conscious of criminal purposes and about the execution of criminal acts, seek the security of secrecy and darkness. It is therefore necessary to use all other modes of evidence besides that of direct testimony, provided such proofs may be relied on as leading to safe and satisfactory conclusions; and, thanks to a beneficent providence, the laws of nature and the relations of things to each other are so linked and combined together, that a medium of proof is often thereby furnished, leading to inferences and conclusions as strong as those arising from direct testimony.

Guilt or Innocence

The first presumption is that a defendant is not guilty unless and until the government proves beyond a reasonable doubt each element of the offense charged. (Associate Supreme Court Justice David Souter in *Clark v. Arizona*[6])

The right to trial by jury and proof beyond a reasonable doubt is a given and all legislative policymaking—good and bad, heartless and compassionate—must work within the confines of that reality. (Associate Supreme Court Justice Antonin Scalia in *Oregon v. Ice*[7])

Under our American system of justice, before an individual may be legally convicted of a crime, the prosecution must establish each and every element of the charged crime beyond a reasonable doubt. In civil law cases, the party that has the burden of proof only need establish the facts by a preponderance of the evidence.

An example of the difference between the civil and criminal burdens of proof is illustrated by the O.J. Simpson cases. Orenthal James "O.J." Simpson was the first National Football leader to rush for more than 2,000 yards in a season, a mark he set in 1973. Simpson was elected to the Pro Football Hall of Fame in 1985. After retiring from professional football, Simpson had a career as a football broadcaster and actor.

In 1995, O.J. was acquitted of the 1994 murder of his former wife Nicole Brown Simpson and Ronald Goldman after a lengthy and internationally publicized criminal trial, the *People v. Simpson*. The jury in the case apparently decided that the prosecution had not established his guilt beyond a reasonable doubt.

After the verdict of not guilty, the Goldman family sued O.J. for the wrongful death of Ronald Goldman. In 1997, a civil court awarded a $33.5 million judgment against Simpson for the death of Ronald Goldman. How do you explain the fact that the criminal court jury found him not guilty while a civil court found that he had caused the wrongful death of Ronald Goldman? In the criminal trial, the government's burden of proof was to establish the guilt by proof beyond a reasonable double. In the civil law suit, the Goldman family's burden was to establish the wrongdoing by only a preponderance of evidence—a far lesser degree of proof.

What constitutes proof beyond a reasonable doubt is a catchy phrase but one that the courts have struggled to define. The trial judge, when instructing a jury prior to the jury's deliberations, will instruct the jury members on the elements of the crime, the elements of any lesser included offences, any defenses raised by the evidence, and on the burden of proof.

In defining the phrase "proof beyond a reasonable doubt," often a judge will state to the jury one of the following definitions:

- A real doubt is a doubt based upon reason and common sense after careful and impartial consideration of all the evidence, or lack of evidence, in a case.
- Proof beyond a reasonable doubt, therefore, is proof of such a convincing character that you would be willing to rely and act upon it without hesitation in the most important of your own affairs. However, it does not mean an absolute certainty.

Photo 1-2

When juries are deliberating, they are usually segregated to prevent anyone from influencing them. The above photo shows a segregated jury going to lunch during their deliberations in the Becker-Rosenthal murder trial in a Green Car Sight Seeing Company vehicle, driving past the Manhattan Criminal Courts Building in New York City on May 14, 1919. Photo courtesy of the Library of Congress.

Evidence in Action

Excerpts from In Re Winship 397 U.S. 358 (1970)
and
United States v. Comstock 560 U.S. 126 (2010)

The *In Re Winship* case involved juvenile delinquency proceedings. The Family Court, Bronx County, New York adjudged the juvenile to be a juvenile delinquent. He appealed. The New York Supreme Court, Appellate Division affirmed the family court decision. The case was then appealed to the U.S. Supreme Court. The U.S. Supreme Court held that the reasonable-doubt standard of criminal law has constitutional stature and that juveniles, like adults, are constitutionally entitled to proof beyond reasonable doubt when juveniles are charged with violations of criminal law.

Associate Supreme Court Justice William J. Brennan, Jr. delivered the opinion of the Court. On page 360 he stated:

> The requirement of proof beyond a reasonable doubt has this vital role in our criminal procedure for cogent reasons. The accused during a criminal prosecution has at stake interest of immense importance, both because of

the possibility that he may lose his liberty upon conviction and because of the certainty that he would be stigmatized by the conviction. Accordingly, a society that values the good name and freedom of every individual should not condemn a man for commission of a crime when there is reasonable doubt about his guilt.... There is always in litigation a margin of error, representing error in fact-finding, which both parties must take into account. Where one party has at stake an interest of transcending value—as a criminal defendant his liberty—this margin of error is reduced as to him by the process of placing on the other party the burden of persuading the factfinder at the conclusion of the trial of his guilt beyond a reasonable doubt. Due process commands that no man shall lose his liberty unless the Government has borne the burden of convincing the factfinder of his guilt. To this end, the reasonable-doubt standard is indispensable, for it impresses on the trier of fact the necessity of reaching a subjective state of certitude of the facts in issue.

Compare the *In Re Winship* case with the *United States v. Comstock* case.

In *United States v. Comstock* (560 U.S. 126, 2010), the government sought civil commitment of federal prisoners, who would otherwise be released from prison, as sexually dangerous persons pursuant to the Adam Walsh Child Protection and Safety Act. The prisoners moved to dismiss petitions on the basis that this was a criminal proceeding and should require proof beyond a reasonable doubt.

The Court held that the federal statute, enacted as part of the Adam Walsh Child Protection and Safety Act, allowed a district court to order the civil commitment, beyond the date the prisoner would otherwise be released, of a sexually dangerous federal prisoner. The Court stated that the requirement that the Government prove its claims by "clear and convincing evidence" was constitutional. The Court noted that Congress could have reasonably concluded that federal inmates who suffered from a mental illness that caused them to have serious difficulty in refraining from sexually violent conduct would pose an especially high danger to the public if released, and Congress could also have reasonably concluded that a reasonable number of such individuals would likely not be detained by the States if released from federal custody.

Question: The Court has held that juvenile proceedings accusing a juvenile of a criminal act are criminal in nature and requires proof beyond a reasonable doubt. The Court has also held that proceedings to hold sexually dangerous federal prisoners beyond their normal release date are a civil proceeding and require only proof by clear and convincing evidence. **Is there a reasonable justification for the distinction between the two cases?**

If in a criminal trial the prosecutor fails to establish beyond a reasonable doubt the guilt of the accused, does this mean that the accused is innocent? Frequently in press statements you will hear the accused state, "The court found me innocent of the charges."

Even judges and attorneys make the same mistake. That is a clear misstatement of the results. A jury verdict of "not guilty" simple means that the government failed to establish the accused guilt beyond a reasonable doubt. It does not mean that the accused is innocent. For example in the earlier discussed case involving O.J. Simpson, most people thought he was guilty but that the government had failed to prove his guilt beyond a reasonable doubt.

Division of Responsibility

Judicial Review

In our government, theoretically it is the duty of Congress and the president, the two elected branches of government, to make public policy. It is the duty of the courts (judges who are generally appointed) to interpret and apply the law. In actual practice, judges make policy and establish rules when interpreting and applying the laws. Many researchers contend that the policy-making function of the courts is its greatest power. For example, the Supreme Court in establishing the requirement that law enforcement officers give a Miranda warning when questioning in-custody suspects is a clear example of the Court's policy-making function.[8]

Judicial review is the authority of the courts to determine whether acts of Congress, the executive branch, and the states are constitutional. The authority for judicial review is not found in the U.S. Constitution, but was established by the Court in the famous case of *Marbury v. Madison*.[9] This is another example of the Court's policy-making power and probably the most important decision in Supreme Court history.

In the *Marbury* case, after President John Adams lost his bid for reelection and Thomas Jefferson was elected in 1800, the Federalists (Adams's party) controlled Congress. Congress authorized an increase in the number of circuit courts. Adams, shortly before he left office, appointed judges to these new positions that were favorable to his party. Some of his "Midnight" appointments were not delivered before Jefferson took office. Jefferson immediately stopped their delivery. One of the justices of the peace, William Marbury, filed a writ of mandamus demanding Secretary of State James Madison deliver the appointments. The Supreme Court, led by John Marshall, denied the request citing part of the Judiciary Act of 1789 as unconstitutional.

In *Marbury v. Madison*, the Supreme Court announced for the first time the principle that a court may declare an act of Congress void if it is inconsistent with the Constitution. Chief Justice John Marshall, writing for the Court, denied the petition and refused to issue the writ. He noted that the petitioners were entitled to their commissions, but that the Constitution did not give the Supreme Court the power to issue writs of mandamus. The Court determined that Section 13 of the Judiciary Act of 1789, which provided that such writs might be issued, was inconsistent with the Constitution and thus unconstitutional.

While the immediate effect of the decision was to deny power to the Court, its long-run effect was to establish the right of the Court as the final arbiter of the constitutionality of congressional legislation.

Duties of a Trial Judge

Chief Judge Casey Rodgers, U.S. District Court for the Northern District of Florida, listed five basic tasks of a trial judge.[10] The trial judge presides over the trial from a desk, called a bench, on an elevated platform. The five basic tasks are listed below:

- The first is simply to preside over the proceedings and see that order is maintained.
- The second is to determine whether any of the evidence that the parties want to use is illegal or improper.
- Third, before the jury begins its deliberations about the facts in the case, the judge gives the jury instructions about the law that applies to the case and the standards it must use in deciding the case.
- Fourth, in bench trials (trial by judge alone), the judge must also determine the facts and decide the case.
- The fifth is to sentence convicted criminal defendants.

While there may be some variances in state proceedings, the tasks are similar. Generally the judge makes decisions regarding which laws to apply to the case. The jury determines the facts involved. Thus the trial judge is the law finder and the jury the fact-finder. If there is no jury as in a trial by judge alone, the judge performs both functions.

What is a question of law and what is a question of fact? In ruling on legal issues, the trial judge has sole responsibility. A question of fact is a question addressing fact issues such as, was the accused the one who committed the murder? If an accused has confessed to a murder, the trial judge will rule as to whether or not the confession is admissible. The jury will then rule on whether or not the confession is true or if the accused confessing to something he or she did not do. The trial judge will also rule on whether or not the confession may be entered into evidence.

Duties of the Prosecutor

Duties of a prosecutor are not to convict a defendant, but to ensure justice. The American Bar Association's (ABA) Model Rules of Professional Conduct, Rule 3.8 states that a prosecutor has the responsibility of a minister of justice and not simply that of an advocate. This responsibility carries with it specific obligations to see that the defendant is accorded procedural justice, that guilt is decided upon the basis of sufficient evidence, and that special precautions are taken to prevent and to rectify the conviction of innocent persons.

If a prosecutor knows of new, credible and material evidence creating a reasonable likelihood that a person outside the prosecutor's jurisdiction was convicted of a crime that the person did not commit, the prosecutor should make prompt disclosure to the court or other appropriate authority, such as the chief prosecutor of the jurisdiction where the conviction occurred. If the conviction was obtained in the prosecutor's jurisdiction, the prosecutor is required to examine the evidence and undertake further investigation to determine whether the defendant is in fact not guilty or make reasonable efforts to cause another appropriate authority to undertake the necessary investigation, and to promptly disclose the evidence to the court and, absent court-authorized delay, to the defendant. Any such disclosure to a represented defendant must be made through the defendant's counsel, and, in the case of an unrepresented defendant, would ordinarily be accompanied by a request to a court for the appointment of counsel to assist the defendant in taking such legal measures as may be appropriate.

Duties of the Defense Counsel

The National Legal Aid & Defenders' Association (NLADA) has established guidelines as to the role of a defense counsel in a criminal case. The NLADA guideline 1.1 states that the paramount obligation of criminal defense counsel is to provide zealous and quality representation to their clients at all stages of the criminal process. Attorneys also have an obligation to abide by ethical norms and act in accordance with the rules of the court.

The defense counsel is an officer of the court. As an officer of the court, the counsel may not present false or misleading information or evidence to the court. A frequent situation occurs when an accused admits to his or her counsel that he or she committed the crime and then testifies on the stand that he or she did not commit the crime. The defense counsel cannot correct the testimony because of the attorney-client privileges that are discussed later in the text, but neither can the attorney willfully allow a defendant to present false evidence.

The general consensus regarding this situation is that if the attorney is aware of this testimony before it is presented, the attorney should advise the defendant against committing perjury and if the accused insists on so doing, the attorney should request permission to withdraw from the case. In requesting withdrawal from the case, the attorney generally needs to provide the trial judge with a reason for the request. In such cases, the attorney should merely inform the judge that because of ethical conflict he or she cannot continue as counsel without revealing the nature of the conflicts. A similar procedure should be followed if the accused commits perjury without first informing the counsel of the facts.

Students frequently ask the authors, "Would you rather defend a guilty or innocent person?" The standard answer to this question is that attorneys generally feel more comfortable defending guilty persons. It is very nerve-wracking to defend a person that you think is innocent and worry about him or her going to prison for a mistake you made. When defending a guilty person, your job as counsel is to get the best deal for the defendant. If the best deal is an acquittal because the prosecutor cannot establish his or her guilt, that is not your fault. Generally the best deal includes getting reduced punishment for the defendant. Note that about 90 percent of all criminal trials that are completed are based on guilty pleas.

The NLADA guidelines provide that defense counsel should inform the defendant of any tentative negotiated agreement reached with the prosecution, and explain to the client the full content of the agreement, and the advantages and disadvantages and the potential consequences of the agreement. The decision to enter a plea of guilty rests solely with the client, and defense counsel should not attempt to unduly influence that decision.

The NLADA guidelines states that defense counsel should be fully informed as to the rules of evidence, and the law relating to all stages of the trial process, and should be familiar with legal and evidentiary issues that can reasonably be anticipated to arise in the trial.

In addition, defense counsel should decide if it is beneficial to secure an advance ruling on issues likely to arise at trial (e.g., use of prior convictions to impeach the defendant), and, where appropriate, counsel should prepare motions and memoranda for such advance rulings. The defense counsel should endeavor to establish a proper record for appellate review. As part of this effort, counsel should request, whenever necessary, that all trial proceedings be recorded.

Defense counsel should advise the client as to suitable courtroom dress and demeanor. If the client is incarcerated, counsel should be alert to the possible prejudicial effects of the client appearing before the jury in jail or other inappropriate clothing. Defense counsel should plan with the client the most convenient system for conferring throughout the trial. Where necessary, defense counsel should seek a court order to have the client available for conferences. During pretrial proceedings and throughout preparation and trial, defense counsel should consider the potential effects that particular actions may have upon sentencing if there is a finding of guilt.

Duties of the Bailiff

The duties of a bailiff or marshall may vary by jurisdiction. Generally the bailiff maintains order in the courtroom during trial and protects the jury from outside contact. Other duties generally include:

- Checking the courtroom for security and cleanliness.
- Enforcing courtroom rules of behavior and warning persons not to smoke or disturb court procedure.
- Collecting and retaining unauthorized firearms from persons entering the courtroom.
- Preventing people from entering the courtroom while the judge is instructing the jury.
- Providing jury escort to restaurant and other areas outside of the courtroom to prevent jury contact with public.
- Guarding lodging of sequestered jury.
- Reporting need for police or medical assistance to sheriff's office.
- Announcing the entrance of the judge.

Duties of the Court Clerk

The duties of a court clerk vary according to jurisdiction. Some of the general duties include:

- Being the primary point of contact for the public seeking to obtain information about scheduling, forms, documentation and procedures.
- Communicating effectively and exercising patience with the county's constituency, as legal matters can be confusing and frustrating.
- Filing, preparing and producing documents that pertain to the court's function, such as affidavits, written statements, case files and consent forms. The court clerk ensures the security of these documents by following local or federal guidelines regarding release of information and privacy.
- Taking official minutes of court proceedings, which includes notes of what is taking place during a deposition, meeting or case.

Evidentiary Policies

There are certain evidentiary policies that are standard within the federal and state jurisdictions. Some of the most common are briefly discussed in this section. They are also discussed in greater detail in later sections of the text.

Judicial Discretion

Under the federal rules and all state evidentiary rules or laws, the trial judge is granted a wide latitude of discretion. For example, FRE 403 provides that the trial judge has discretion to exclude relevant evidence if its probative value is substantially outweighed by a danger of one or more of the following: unfair prejudice, confusing the issues, misleading the jury, undue delay, wasting time, or needlessly presenting cumulative evidence.

FRE 611 provides that the trial judge should exercise reasonable control over the mode and order of examining witnesses and presenting evidence so as to:

- make those procedures effective for determining the truth;
- avoid wasting time; and
- protect witnesses from harassment or undue embarrassment.

FRE 611 also directs that the trial judge should control cross-examinations and should not allow them to go beyond the subject matter of the direct examination and matters affecting the witness's credibility. The judge may allow inquiry into additional matters as if on direct examination.

While the discretion of the trial judge is wide, it is not unlimited. Frequently the question on appeal is whether or not the trial judge abused his or her discretion in ruling on certain evidence issues.

Rule of Admissibility

Under the common law system, jurors are the primary fact-finders. As the jury system developed in England, there was a distrust of jurors. In order to control jurors, numerous restrictions were placed on the admissibility of evidence. Jurors were considered as incapable of sorting out good evidence from bad evidence. Prior to the enactment of the Federal Rules of Evidence, the study of evidence was primarily a study of the rules of exclusion.

Starting with the federal rules, the policy changed. In both federal and state systems, more trust is now placed in jurors, and the rules currently allow broader accessibility to the relevant facts. The rules in both federal and state systems have been codified to favor admissibility.

Under the concept of admissibility, generally if an item of evidence is admissible for one reason and inadmissible for other reasons the item may be admitted at the discretion of the trial judge. Frequently the trial judge will give instructions for the jurors to consider the evidence for a limited purpose only. Accordingly, if I offer into evidence an item and the offer is refused by the judge, generally this does not prevent me from re-offering the same item into evidence on different grounds. For example, I offer into evidence the fact that the defendant in a robbery case has previously been convicted of robbery in order to establish that the defendant is a bad person. The trial judge would clearly reject this evidence. But I probably could enter into evidence the fact that the defendant has been convicted of a robbery that was conducted under similar unusual circumstances to help establish that the same person committed both robberies and that the defendant is that person. In the latter case, the judge would need to instruct the jury that the evidence of the prior robbery was entered only for the purposes of trying to establish the identity of the robber.

Right of Confrontation

The Sixth Amendment of the U.S. Constitution provides that a person accused shall have the right to be confronted with the witnesses against him or her. In addition, the Fifth and Fourteenth Amendments' due process clauses have been interpreted to include the right of confrontation. Basically this right includes, with a few exceptions, the right to cross-examination of any witnesses against an accused. The present approach used by the U.S. Supreme Court was stated in the case of *Crawford v. Washington*.[11] In *Crawford*, the Court indicated that all statements of declarants who do not take the stand are banned for use against an accused if the statement is entered for the truth of the statement. Note: *Crawford* did not ban the use of a statement used for purposes other than trying to prove the truth of the statement. Accordingly, a statement that is not offered as a testimonial statement may be admissible on other grounds.

Need to Object

The general rule is that before a trial judge's ruling or decision on an evidence issue may be appealed, that the opposing party must have objected to its admissibility. Generally the objection must be specific and state the basis on which the objection is based. Accordingly, in most jurisdictions not only must the opposing party object to the introduction of the item, the party must also state a valid grounds for the objection before the ruling will be reversed on appeal.

Character Evidence

For the most part, the character of the defendant may not be introduced into evidence to establish that he or she is a bad person and therefore likely to have committed the act. FRE 404(b) and most state rules provide that evidence of a person's character or character trait is not admissible to prove that on a particular occasion the person acted in accordance with the character or trait.

There are numerous exceptions to this rule. The following exceptions apply in a criminal case:

- a defendant may offer evidence of the defendant's pertinent trait, and if the evidence is admitted, the prosecutor may offer evidence to rebut it;

- a defendant may offer evidence of an alleged victim's pertinent trait, and if the evidence is admitted, the prosecutor may: offer evidence to rebut it; and offer evidence of the defendant's same trait; and in a homicide case, the prosecutor may offer evidence of the alleged victim's trait of peacefulness to rebut evidence that the victim was the first aggressor.

Evidence of a witness's character may be admitted. Evidence of a crime, wrong, or other act is not admissible to prove a person's character in order to show that on a particular occasion the person acted in accordance with the character. Character evidence may be admissible for another purpose, such as proving motive, opportunity, intent, preparation, plan, knowledge, identity, absence of mistake, or lack of accident.

Practicum

Practicum One

In the *North Carolina v. Alford* case,[12] Henry Alford was indicted for first-degree murder. Although there was no eyewitness to the crime, the testimony indicated that, shortly before the killing, Alford took his gun from his house, stated his intention to kill the victim, and returned home with the declaration that he had carried out the killing. Alford took the stand, denied the murder and testified that he does not remember what happened that evening, but that he was pleading guilty because he faced the threat of the death penalty if he did not do so.

How would you describe the evidence against Alford? Was it direct or circumstantial? What if Alford had confessed to the murder, would his confession be direct or circumstantial evidence? Would it be documentary evidence? Would the confession be direct evidence?

Practicum Two

Assume that you are a defense counsel and you are questioning the jury panel in an attempt to select a jury that is friendly to your side. You ask a jury member the following question: "If before receiving any evidence in this case the trial judge asks you to vote either guilty or not guilty, how would you vote?" The prospective jury member states that she could not vote either way. On what ground would you challenge this jury member?

Practicum Three

The defendant is on trial for statutory rape of a female under the age of 16 years old. He confesses to the police. At the time the prosecutor offers the confession into evidence, the defense objects stating that the defendant was not properly warned prior to being interrogated, that the defendant had requested to speak to an attorney before he confessed, and finally that the confession was forced and was not true.

Which of these issues would the trial judge rule on and which would the jury determine?

Summary

- The primary purpose of the rules of evidence is to help ensure a fair trial.
- Evidence is generally defined as any matter of fact that a party to a lawsuit offers to prove or disprove an issue in the case.
- Evidence consists of a system of rules and standards that is used to determine which facts may be admitted, and to what extent a judge or jury may consider those facts, as proof of a particular issue in a lawsuit.
- There are fifty state court systems and one federal court system operating in the United States. However, most criminal cases are tried in state trial courts based on violations of the state criminal code or criminal laws.
- The first version of the Federal Rules of Evidence was adopted in 1975. In drafting the 1975 rules, the committee relied heavily on the California Evidence Code and the Uniform Rules of Evidence that had been drafted by the National Conference of Commissioners on Uniform State Laws that was published in 1953.
- The U.S. Supreme Court has stated that in applying the rules it will generally look to their plain meaning unless such a result would be absurd. Often the Court has used common law principles, legislative history, and the Advisory Committee's Notes as guides to interpret the rules.
- In both state and federal jurisdictions, courts have established local rules for the trial of criminal cases.
- Evidence may be divided into five traditional types of evidence: real, demonstrative, documentary, testimonial, and judicially noticed evidence.
- Judicial notice is a shortcut that dispenses with the need to present evidence on the issue.
- The distinction between direct and circumstantial evidence is that direct or positive evidence is when a witness can be called to testify to the precise fact which is the subject of the issue on trial; that is, in a case of homicide, that the party accused did cause the death of the deceased.
- Under our American system of justice, before an individual may be legally convicted of a crime, the prosecution must establish each and every element of the charged crime beyond a reasonable doubt. In civil law cases, the party that has the burden of proof only need establish the facts by a preponderance of the evidence.
- In our government, theoretically it is the duty of Congress and the president, the two elected branches of government, to make public policy. It is the duty of the courts (judges who are generally appointed) to interpret and apply the law. In actual practice, judges make policy and establish rules when interpreting and applying the laws.
- Duties of a prosecutor are not to convict a defendant, but to ensure justice.
- The paramount obligation of criminal defense counsel is to provide zealous and quality representation to their clients at all stages of the criminal process. Attorneys also have an obligation to abide by ethical norms and act in accordance with the rules of the court.
- The defense counsel is an officer of the court. As an officer of the court the counsel may not present false or misleading information or evidence to the court.

- Under the federal rules and all state evidentiary rules or laws, the trial judge is granted a wide latitude of discretion.
- The rules in both federal and state systems have been codified to favor admissibility.
- The Sixth Amendment of the U.S. Constitution provides that a person accused shall have the right to be confronted with the witnesses against him or her.
- The general rule is that before a trial judge's ruling or decision on an evidence issue may be appealed, that the opposing party must have objected to its admissibility.
- For the most part, the character of the defendant may not be introduced into evidence to establish that he or she is a bad person and therefore likely to have committed the act.

Questions in Review

1. Explain the different burdens of proof.
2. What is required before a trial court may legally find the defendant guilty in a criminal case?
3. What is the standard of proof required in juvenile proceedings where the juvenile is accused of stealing money?
4. The federal government wants to retain a prisoner beyond his normal release date because the government officials believe that he is a sexually dangerous offender. What level of proof does the government need to establish continued confinement?
5. What constitutes circumstantial evidence?
6. When may evidence of an accused's character be admitted into evidence?

Key Terms

Circumstantial Evidence: Evidence from which the proof of a fact may be inferred.

Clear and Convincing Proof: The evidence presented must be highly and substantially more probable to be true than not and the trier of fact must have a firm belief or conviction in its factuality.

Common Law: The legal rules that have evolved first in England and now in the United States based on prior court decisions.

Direct Evidence: Evidence which establishes the fact in question without the need for inferences.

Preponderance of the Evidence: The standard required in most civil cases. This is also the standard of proof used in grand jury indictment proceedings. The standard is met if the proposition is more likely to be true than not true. The standard is satisfied if there is greater than a 50 percent chance that the proposition is true.

Proof Beyond a Reasonable Doubt: A real doubt is a doubt based upon reason and common sense after careful and impartial consideration of all the evidence, or lack of evidence, in a case. Proof beyond a reasonable doubt, therefore, is proof of such a convincing character that you would be willing to rely and act upon it without hesitation in the most important of your own affairs. However, it does not mean an absolute certainty.

Endnotes

1. Judicial Conference of the United States' Committee on Rules of Practice and Procedure, (1962) Rules of Evidence; A Preliminary Report on the Advisability and Feasibility of Developing Uniform Rules of Evidence for the U.S. District Courts. Republished by the American Bar Association (1978). Available at http://apps.americanbar.org/litigation/litigationnews/. Accessed on August 29, 2014.

2. 483 U.S. 171 (1987).

3. FRE 701

4. FRE 702.

5. Commonwealth v. Watkins, 59 Mass. 295 (1850).

6. Clark v. Arizona, 548 U.S. 735 (2006).

7. Oregon v. Ice, 555 U.S. 160 (2009).

8. Miranda v. Arizona, 384 U.S. 436 (1966).

9. 5 U.S. 137 (1803).

10. Website of the U.S. for the Northern District of Florida at http://www.flnd.uscourts.gov/jurors/courtParticipants.cfm. Accessed on September 1, 2014.

11. 541 U.S. 36 (2004).

12. 400 U.S. 25 (1970).

Chapter 2

Restrictions on the Use of Evidence

Chapter Objectives

What you should know and understand after studying this chapter:

- How evidence is used to determine the guilt or innocence of a defendant
- The restrictions on the admissibility of evidence
- Purpose of the exclusionary rule
- The main enforcement mechanism of the U.S. Constitution
- The rationale behind the fruit of the poisonous tree doctrine
- Exceptions to the warrant requirements for searches

Chapter Outline

Introduction
The Exclusionary Rule
Fruit of the Poisonous Tree
The Warrant Requirement
Police Misconduct
The Right of Confrontation
Conclusion
Practicum
Summary
Questions in Review
Key Terms
Endnotes

Introduction

Because evidence is the heart of any criminal prosecution, it is the fulcrum on which the determination of guilt or innocence hinges. As such, the courts have taken great pains over the years to ensure that evidence introduced into the courtroom was not obtained in a manner that violates the constitutional protections of the accused. While the employment of evidence is the responsibility of attorneys, its collection is the primary responsibility of the investigator, so law enforcement officers must understand the limitations on what evidence is acceptable in the courtroom and what is not.

The admissibility of evidence from a constitutional standpoint stems from three main sources: the restrictions on search and seizure found in the Fourth Amendment, the restrictions on self-incrimination found in the Fifth Amendment, and the right to counsel found in the Sixth Amendment.

The Exclusionary Rule

The Exclusionary Rule is one of the main enforcement mechanisms of the constitutional protections outlined at the beginning of the chapter. While the U.S. Constitution establishes these protections, it does not specify how these protections are to be fulfilled or enforced. As we will see in this section, such mechanisms arose later from court decisions. While there are alternative protections, in practice they are difficult to execute and rarely used.

In theory, a law enforcement officer (or other government employee or agent) could be subject to criminal prosecution for an illegal search or seizure. Some states have statutes criminalizing procurement of a search warrant without probable cause, as does the Federal Criminal Code, but the offense is typically a misdemeanor. Even fewer states have criminalized the improper execution of a valid warrant, the execution of an invalid warrant, or conducting a search without a warrant.[1] More practically, the entire point of procuring a warrant is to require law enforcement to appear before a magistrate and present probable cause for the warrant, so improperly procured or invalid warrants should be rare absent outright falsification of the facts. In any event, criminal prosecution for these offenses has been rare.

Another possibility is civil action, as a person subjected to an illegal search and/or seizure has a tort claim under common, state, or federal law. In particular, officers at the state or local level are subject to federal civil rights statutes, and in *Bivens v. Six Unknown Federal Narcotics Agents*,[2] the U.S. Supreme Court extended an implied right for relief in federal court against federal officers even though they are not directly subject to those same statutes.[3] However, there are several practical reasons civil actions are also rare.

Law enforcement officers have two main defenses. The first is qualified immunity. Designed to balance "two important interests—the need to hold public officials accountable when they exercise power irresponsibly and the need to shield officials from harassment, distraction, and liability when they perform their duties reasonably," according to the opinion in *Pearson et al. v. Callahan*,[4] qualified immunity protects government officials from tort claims brought against them as individuals.[5] Because the immunity "is an entitlement not to stand trial, not a defense from liability," courts are encouraged to make a ruling "early in the proceedings so that the cost and expenses of trial are avoided."[6]

The *Pearson* decision unanimously overturned the mandatory use of the formal test of qualified immunity created by *Saucier v. Katz*.[7] The *Saucier* test required a court considering a claim of qualified immunity to determine whether the facts alleged or shown by the plaintiff constitute a violation of a constitutional right, whether that right was "clearly established" at the time of the defendant's alleged misconduct, and if so whether a "reasonable officer" would have believed that the defendant's conduct in violating that right was lawful.[8] However, the high court did not rule out continued use of the *Saucier* test, only its mandatory application in all qualified immunity cases.

Since an officer may well encounter the *Saucier* test should a suspect attempt to bring a tort claim, it is worth taking time to consider the circumstances of the *Pearson* case in order to understand the mechanics of the test. Callahan, the respondent, had been convicted of drug possession and distribution in a Utah court based on his sale of drugs to a confidential informant after he voluntarily allowed the informant to enter his home. Officers entered and searched his home without a warrant once the sale had been completed. Their actions were based on the "consent-once-removed" doctrine, which allows police to enter a home without a warrant after consent to enter has previously been granted to an undercover officer who then observes contraband in plain view. Moreover the federal district court where Pearson's action was originally filed held that their reliance on this justification was reasonable.

On appeal, the Tenth Circuit reversed the district court's summary judgment in favor of the petitioners (the officers) based on the *Saucier* test. The judges did not want to see the consent-once-removed doctrine extended to include informants, as existing precedent involved entry only by undercover officers. As for the respondent's right to be free from unreasonable searches and seizures in his home, that was a principle long established at the time of the arrest. The officers knew this and, in the opinion of the Tenth Circuit, could not reasonably have assumed their actions to be reasonable since the exigent circumstances exception did not apply, they knew that they had no warrant, the respondent had not consented to their entry into his home, and—the crux of the issue—that his voluntary admission of the informant into his home could not reasonably be construed as extending to them.[9]

The U.S. Supreme Court in turn reversed the Tenth Circuit and reinstated the district court's determination of qualified immunity. In writing the unanimous opinion, Justice Samuel Alito concluded,

> Petitioners are entitled to qualified immunity because it was not clearly established at the time of the search that their conduct was unconstitutional. When the entry occurred, the consent-once-removed doctrine had been accepted by two State Supreme Courts and three Federal Courts of Appeals, and not one of the latter had issued a contrary decision. Petitioners were entitled to rely on these cases, even though their own Federal Circuit had not yet ruled on consent-once-removed entries.[10]

This case should demonstrate the value of keeping abreast of significant constitutional law decisions even in other jurisdictions, since absent a relevant ruling in one's own jurisdiction, those decisions can be relied on when choosing a course of action in the field.

The final alternate method for enforcing constitutional search and seizure protections is discipline by the officer's own department and/or a police review board. Critics often claim that incidents of discipline for illegally obtaining evidence are extremely rare,[11] but the truth of this (and how much of a deterrent internal discipline actually is) will vary from agency to agency.

In the end, the surest method in the eyes of the courts for upholding constitutional protections is the Exclusionary Rule—prohibiting the use of illegally obtained evidence against a suspect. As previously mentioned, the rule does not come from the U.S. Constitution. Rather, it has been developed through years of precedent.

The earliest foundation of the Exclusionary Rule was established by *Boyd v. United States* in 1886.[12] Following the confiscation of a shipment of plate glass by federal customs agents, the defendants were ordered by the judge in the subsequent prosecution to produce documents verifying the details of the shipment. The defendants argued that being compelled to produce evidence to be used against them would constitute self-incrimination, which is prohibited by the Fifth Amendment.[13] The U.S. Supreme Court concurred, although the majority opinion held the production of those documents to have been a violation of the unreasonable search and seizure prohibition of the Fourth Amendment; Justice Samuel Miller concurred with the opinion but held that the Fifth Amendment had been violated.[14] In either event, the evidence so produced was ordered to be excluded from consideration at retrial.

However, *Boyd* was construed rather narrowly, and for another decade courts continued to rely on the common law principle that evidence was admissible no matter how it had been acquired.[15] The Exclusionary Rule has its origin in *Weeks v. U.S.*[16] The respondent, Weeks, had been convicted based on evidence—some of it consisting of private papers analogous to those in *Boyd*—seized from his home during two searches, both conducted without warrants. In excluding that evidence from the retrial, the Supreme Court made its position very clear:

> If letters and private documents can thus be seized and held and used in evidence against a citizen accused of an offense, the protection of the Fourth Amendment, declaring his right to be secure against such searches and seizures, is of no value, and, so far as those thus placed are concerned, might as well be stricken from the Constitution. The efforts of the courts and their officials to bring the guilty to punishment, praiseworthy as they are, are not to be aided by the sacrifice of those great principles established be years of endeavor and suffering which have resulted in their embodiment in the fundamental law of the land.[17]

It is important to understand that the Fourth Amendment was not considered to restrict the actions of officers at the state (or lower) level; it was applicable only to federal law enforcement. The first step toward applying the Exclusionary Rule to the states was *Wolf v. Colorado*.[18] The ruling held that the Fourth Amendment's restrictions on search and seizure were extended to the states by the Due Process Clause of the Fourteenth Amendment. However, the Supreme Court did not go so far as to require use of the Exclusionary Rule in state courts, reasoning that the states had other means of deterring illegal search and seizure by police. "Granting that in practice the exclusion of evidence may be an effective way of deterring unreasonable searches," the majority opinion stated, "it is not for this Court to condemn as falling below the minimal standards assured by the Due Process Clause a State's reliance upon other methods which, if consistently enforced, would be equally effective."[19]

Over the next several years the Supreme Court did reject the admissibility of evidence in state courts under specific circumstances that it found particularly egregious—for example, evidence of narcotics possession that "had been obtained by forcible administration of an emetic at a hospital after officers had been unsuccessful in preventing [the suspect] from swallowing certain capsules" in *Rochin v. California*[20] (characterized by Justice Felix Frankfurter as "methods too close to the rack and screw").[21] But in general it held to the standard established in *Wolf*, as in *Irvine v. California*,[22] in which a man convicted of bookmaking was convicted in part based on recordings from a microphone that police placed by entering his home without a warrant and subsequently moved multiple times during warrantless re-entries. Though the decision was a narrow 5-4, the majority refused to order the evidence barred or to vacate Irvine's conviction.[23]

Photo 2-1

A picture of the sculpture "Majesty of Justice" located in the Great Hall, 2nd Floor, Department of Justice, Washington, D.C. The aluminum sculpture was made in 1935 by Carl Paul Jennewein. Its dimensions are 12 foot 6 inches by 41 inches. Photo courtesy of the Library of Congress.

It was *Mapp v. Ohio* in 1961 that finally overturned *Wolf* and applied the Exclusionary Rule universally to the states.[24] The opinion addressed the faulty rationale of alternatives to excluding evidence propounded in that case, noting "The obvious futility of relegating the Fourth Amendment to the protection of other remedies has, moreover, been recognized by this Court since *Wolf*." Reasoning that the Fourth Amendment had already been deemed enforceable against the states by the Due Process Clause (in *Wolf*),

Justice Tom Clark succinctly laid out in the majority opinion the Court's rationale as well as its view of the utility of the Exclusionary Rule:

> Therefore, in extending the substantive protections of due process to all constitutionally unreasonable searches—state or federal—it was logically and constitutionally necessary that the exclusion doctrine—an essential part of the right to privacy—be also insisted upon as an essential ingredient of the right newly recognized by the *Wolf* case. In short, the admission of the new constitutional right by *Wolf* could not consistently tolerate denial of its most important constitutional privilege, namely, the exclusion of the evidence which an accused had been forced to give by reason of the unlawful seizure. To hold otherwise is to grant the right but, in reality, to withhold its privilege and enjoyment. Only last year, the Court itself recognized that the purpose of the exclusionary rule is to deter—to compel respect for the constitutional guaranty in the only effectively available way—by removing the incentive to disregard it.[25]

The case implied by the phrase "only last year" in the foregoing passage was *Elkins et al. v. United States.*[26]

The *Elkins* case arose after James Elkins and Raymond Clark were convicted in Oregon on wiretapping charges based in part on recordings and a recording machine seized by state law enforcement officers in violation of the Fourth Amendment. In this case the trial was in federal court, but the evidence was admitted since federal law enforcement had played no part whatsoever in seizing the evidence in question. The majority opinion walked in some detail through the cases that developed the Exclusionary Rule, including *Weeks* and *Irvine v. California*, ultimately concluding that a double standard regarding evidence illegally seized by state and federal officers would create an unacceptable temptation:

> Free and open cooperation between state and federal law enforcement officers is to be commended and encouraged. Yet that kind of cooperation is hardly promoted by a rule that implicitly invites federal officers to withdraw from such association and at least tacitly to encourage state officers in the disregard of constitutionally protected freedom. If, on the other hand, it is understood that the fruit of an unlawful search by state agents will be inadmissible in a federal trial, there can be no inducement to subterfuge and evasion with respect to federal-state cooperation in criminal investigation. Instead, forthright cooperation under constitutional standards will be promoted and fostered.[27]

In *Elkins* the Supreme Court thus took the next logical step of excluding from federal proceedings illegally obtained evidence even when such evidence had been procured by state officers with no federal involvement. *Mapp* took the final step of applying the Exclusionary Rule universally.

As we saw in the introduction to this chapter, it is not merely evidence obtained in violation of the Fourth Amendment that is subject to exclusion, although in practice the majority of cases have devolved from Fourth Amendment issues. The Fifth Amendment, which prohibits self-incrimination, and the Sixth Amendment, which guarantees the right to counsel, can also trigger the Exclusionary Rule. (In fact, as you may recall, the *Boyd* case of 1886 discussed at the beginning of this section was viewed as a Fifth

Amendment issue by the court.) The heart of the Exclusionary Rule in the context of the Fifth and Sixth Amendments comes from what is arguably the most famous U.S. Supreme Court case to date, at least in the arena of criminal law: *Miranda v. Arizona.*[28]

While law enforcement officers are generally familiar with the circumstances of Miranda, we will avoid assumptions and present a summarized review of the circumstances. Ernesto Miranda was arrested and ultimately charged with the kidnap and rape of an 18-year-old mentally challenged woman in Arizona in 1963. Under police interrogation, he confessed to the crime. However, at no time did police inform him that he did not have to answer their questions nor that he was entitled to have an attorney present during questioning. His defense counsel attempted to have the confession excluded in a pretrial motion but was overruled.

When the case reached the Supreme Court in 1966, it was actually one of four cases with similar circumstances reviewed simultaneously (*Vignera v. New York*, *Westover v. United States*, and *California v. Stewart* being the other three). Prior to *Miranda*, the presumption was that it was the responsibility of the suspect to be aware of his constitutional rights and that as such the police had no duty to inform him. The majority opinion, written by Chief Justice Earl Warren, explored in detail various interrogation techniques published in police manuals and in wide use at the time, as well as historical abuses. Chief Justice Warren answered those who contended that "the third degree is necessary to get the facts" by quoting Lord Sankey, Lord Chancellor of England: "It is not admissible to do a great thing by doing a little wrong.... It is not sufficient to do justice by obtaining a proper result by irregular or improper means."[29] Echoing the deterrent effect of the Exclusionary Rule envisioned in various Fourth Amendment cases, the opinion predicted, "Unless a proper limitation upon custodial interrogation is achieved—such as these decisions will advance—there can be no assurance that practices of this nature will be eradicated in the foreseeable future."[30]

The direct result of the case was the Miranda warning: a formal recitation of a suspect's Fifth Amendment right against self-incrimination and Sixth Amendment right to legal counsel. The format of the warning actually arose from a question asked by one of the justices during the oral arguments of the case about the practices of the FBI at that time when performing interrogations. Chief Justice Warren sent a list of questions to the FBI director after the hearing and included his answers in the opinion. The director responded that "The standard warning long given by Special Agents of the FBI to both suspects and persons under arrest is that the person has a right to say nothing and a right to counsel, and that any statement he does make may be used against him in court," adding that "After passage of the Criminal Justice Act of 1964, which provides free counsel for Federal defendants unable to pay, we added to our instructions to Special Agents the requirement that any person who is under arrest ... must also be advised of his right to free counsel if he is unable to pay."[31]

Chief Justice Warren also inquired about the timing of the warning ("at the very outset of the interview" and "may be given to a person arrested as soon as practicable after the arrest") and FBI procedure in the event an individual under interrogation requested to consult with counsel ("the interview is terminated at that point," although "It may be continued, however, as to all matters other than the person's own guilt or innocence"). He went on to compare the practices of other countries such as England, Scotland (which barred "use in evidence of most confessions obtained through police interrogation"), India, Ceylon (both former colonial possessions that inherited much of their legal system from England), and the Uniform Code of Military Justice, all of which provided similar protections.[32]

To better understand the Supreme Court's standards in this matter, it is useful to consider certain details of the circumstances of these cases. In *Miranda*, the suspect signed a written confession on a form that included "a typed paragraph stating that the confession was made voluntarily, without threats or promises of immunity and 'with full knowledge of my legal rights, understanding any statement I make may be used against me.'" The Court held, however, that "The mere fact that he signed a statement which contained a typed-in clause stating that he had 'full knowledge' of his 'legal rights' does not approach the knowing and intelligent waiver required to relinquish constitutional rights."[33]

In *Vignera*, the matter was much more straightforward. Vignera made an oral confession to the detective who questioned him. When the defense asked the detective during trial whether he had warned the suspect of his right to counsel, the prosecution objected and the trial judge sustained the objection, so the question was not answered in open court. Vignera subsequently provided a written statement to an assistant district attorney in a session transcribed by a court reporter, and the transcript contained no warnings provided by the ADA. Nevertheless, the trial judge instructed the jury, "The law doesn't say that the confession is void or invalidated because the police officer didn't advise the defendant as to his right. Did you hear what I said? I am telling you what the law of the State of New York is." The Court held that the evidence "indicates that Vignera was not warned of any of his rights before the questioning by the detective and by the assistant district attorney. No other steps were taken to protect these rights."[34]

In *Westover*, the suspect was arrested and interrogated on the night of his arrest and the following morning by Kansas City police. The FBI arrived and began questioning him around midday about an unrelated bank robbery in Sacramento. Around mid-afternoon he signed a written confession that included a declaration that "the agents advised Westover that he did not have to make a statement, that any statement he made could be used against him, and that he had the right to see an attorney." One of the interrogating agents also testified that they had advised him of these rights. The Court held that despite the fact that he was interrogated by two separate agencies, in effect what he experienced was a near-continuous period of questioning during the 14-plus hours he had been in custody, and in any event there was no evidence of any warning of his rights being provided prior to the arrival of the FBI. " ... From Westover's point of view, the warnings came at the end of the interrogation process. In these circumstances, an intelligent waiver of constitutional rights cannot be assumed."[35]

(As a matter of historical interest, especially for those who are concerned by the balancing of individual rights with society's right to effective law enforcement, it is interesting to consider the ultimate fate of Ernesto Miranda. While his conviction was overturned by the Supreme Court and the state of Arizona was ordered to retry him, this time absent the illegally obtained confession, he was nevertheless convicted a second time on the strength of other evidence. After serving his sentence and being released from prison, he was killed in a bar fight in 1976.)[36]

While the Exclusionary Rule might seem harsh and unbending at first glance, keep in mind that it is a court-created remedy and deterrent, not an independent constitutional right. It arose not from the language of the Constitution but from subsequent court opinions. Writing for the majority in the fairly complex case of *Illinois v. Gates*,[37] Justice William Rehnquist noted, "The exclusionary rule is 'a judicially created remedy designed to safeguard Fourth Amendment rights generally,' and not 'a personal constitutional right of the party aggrieved,'" here quoting from *United States v. Calandra*.[38] In other words, it is a tool the courts may employ to curb what they determine to be abuses of the government's power to search and seize, not an automatic penalty imposed on the prosecution.[39] At present the courts continue to try to balance the protection of individual rights with the need for effective law enforcement. In *United States v. Leon*,[40] the ruling stated in part, "The [exclusionary] rule is not an individual right and applies only where its deterrent effect outweighs the substantial cost of letting guilty and possibly dangerous defendants go free."[41]

Photo 2-2

The Santa Clara County Courthouse in 1997, located in San Jose, California.
Photograph courtesy of the Library of Congress.

Because the Bill of Rights regulates the actions of the government, it has no application to civil matters, so by extension the Exclusionary Rule also does not apply in civil proceedings. This includes deportation hearings, a precedent established by *INS v. Lopez-Mendoza*.[42] The holding in *Lopez-Mendoza* was in several respects narrowly focused on legal aspects particular to deportation hearings, such as the fact that such hearings are designed to prevent an ongoing violation of the law (*i.e.*, the continued presence of an individual who has entered the country illegally) and the very low burden of proof required in these hearings (identity and alienage, and the identity of a defendant is never suppressible).[43]

One final word on the Exclusionary Rule and direct evidence: Evidence gathered in violation of constitutional restrictions can still be used to impeach a witness (that is, to call their credibility into question), even though it cannot be used to establish the defendant's guilt. The intent is to prevent perjury. This exception was established by *Walder v. United States*.[44]

Walder had been indicted in 1950 for possession of heroin. He claimed that the evidence had been unlawfully seized and successfully petitioned to have it barred under the Exclusionary Rule. Walder was arrested again in 1952 on multiple narcotics charges. He was the only witness in his defense, and under direct examination repeatedly claimed that he had never sold, possessed, or transferred narcotics at any time. The prosecution then introduced the testimony of one of the officers who had conducted the search and seizure in the 1950 case as evidence that Walder was blatantly lying. The judge specifically instructed the jury that the evidence illegally obtained in 1950 could not be used in determining Walder's guilt or innocence, but only in considering the reliability of his testimony. In its opinion, the Supreme Court noted,

> Of his own accord, the defendant went beyond a mere denial of complicity in the crimes of which he was charged and made the sweeping claim that he had never dealt in or possessed any narcotics. Of course, the Constitution guarantees a defendant the fullest opportunity to meet the accusation against him. He must be free to deny all the elements of the case against him without thereby giving leave to the Government to introduce by way of rebuttal evidence illegally secured by it, and therefore not available for its case in chief. Beyond that, however, there is hardly justification for letting the defendant affirmatively resort to perjurious testimony in reliance on the Government's disability to challenge his credibility.[45]

The impeachment exception was fairly narrowly constructed. The *Walder* opinion contrasted the circumstances in that case with those of *Agnello v. United States*.[46] Agnello had been arrested in a bust that followed a cocaine purchase by two undercover officers. Following his arrest, officers searched his home—which was several blocks away—without a warrant and discovered a can of cocaine in his bedroom. The can was barred from admission since the permissible warrantless search of an individual and his immediate surroundings incident to arrest does not extend to a dwelling located a significant distance away. At trial, Agnello testified that he had received the packages from one of his co-defendants but was not aware of their contents and would not have carried them if he had been.[47]

Under cross-examination by the prosecution, Agnello testified that he had never seen narcotics. The prosecutor produced the can found in Agnello's bedroom and asked whether he had seen it; Agnello answered that he had not and had never seen it in his house. The prosecution was permitted to enter the can into evidence as a rebuttal of Agnello's testimony.[48] The distinction that caused the Supreme Court to hold this use of illegally obtained evidence impermissible was that

> In his direct examination, Agnello was not asked and did not testify concerning the can of cocaine. In cross-examination, in answer to a question permitted over his objection, he said he had never seen it. He did nothing to waive his constitutional protection or to justify cross-examination in respect of the evidence claimed to have been obtained by the search.[49]

Such distinctions may seem very narrow and technical indeed, and as a practical matter the determination of whether and how such evidence might be used at trial is the purview of prosecutors, not law enforcement officers, but it is nevertheless important to understand the scope and limits of the Exclusionary Rule.

Fruit of the Poisonous Tree

The Exclusionary Rule has ramifications beyond evidence obtained directly in violation of the Fourth, Fifth, or Sixth Amendment. Logically, evidence discovered indirectly thanks to the original illegally obtained evidence is also barred from admission at trial. This doctrine is known as "fruit of the poisonous tree."

The doctrine originally arose from the Supreme Court ruling in *Silverthorne Lumber Co., Inc. v. United States*.[50] Silverthorne and his father had been subpoenaed and ordered to produce company documents for production before a grand jury. They refused and were subsequently arrested at their homes. While they were detained, federal agents raided the company's offices, seizing all documents found there, without a warrant, and also took or summoned all employees to the U.S. District Attorney's office.[51]

The Silverthornes petitioned the court for the return of the documents. While the district attorney did return them, agents first made photos or copies of all of them and retained those copies. Based on the information in the copied documents, the district attorney issued revised subpoenas for the original documents, with "a new indictment ... framed based upon the knowledge thus obtained." In describing the actions taken, the Supreme Court opinion noted (with some measure of sarcasm) that "although, of course, its seizure was an outrage which the Government now regrets, it may study the papers before it returns them, copy them, and then may use the knowledge that it has gained to call upon the owners in a more regular form to produce them...."[52]

A clearer example of the doctrine comes from *Wong Sun v. United States*.[53] In this case the two petitioners had been convicted of possession and transportation of heroin, but both warrantless arrests were held to have been illegal because they were "not based on 'probable cause' within the meaning of the Fourth Amendment nor 'reasonable grounds' within the meaning of the Narcotics Control Act of 1956."[54] The defense had objected to the admission of three pieces of evidence as "fruits of the illegal arrests": "(1) statements made orally by petitioner Toy in his bedroom at the time of his arrest; (2) heroin surrendered to the agents by a third party as a result of those statements; and (3) unsigned statements made by each petitioner several days after his arrest...."[55]

Walking through the Supreme Court's analysis of each of these points is informative as to the construction of the fruits of the poisonous tree doctrine. First, "the statements made by Toy in his bedroom at the time of his unlawful arrest were the fruits of the agents' unlawful action, and they should have been excluded from evidence." Next, "The narcotics taken from a third party as a result of statements made by Toy at the time of his arrest were likewise fruits of the unlawful arrest, and they should not have been admitted as evidence against Toy." Finally,

> In view of the fact that, after his unlawful arrest, petitioner Wong Sun had been lawfully arraigned and released on his own recognizance and had returned voluntarily several days later when he made his unsigned statement, the connection between his unlawful arrest and the making of that statement was so attenuated that the unsigned statement was not the fruit of the unlawful arrest and, therefore, it was properly admitted in evidence.[56]

There are four exceptions to the fruit of the poisonous tree doctrine. The first is when there is an independent source for knowledge of the evidence apart from the illegal search or seizure.[57] For example, a document exists that indicates illegal activity by a suspect. If the police seize the document during an illegal search, but a few days later a confidential informant e-mails one of the officers that same document, it is admissible since the same evidence came from a separate source.

The second exception is inevitable discovery.[58] Say that police conduct an illegal search of a suspect's home and find a map that shows the location of an illegal marijuana field that happens to be located in an open field behind a nearby shopping center. Ordinarily the discovery of the marijuana field would not be admissible as evidence since it was located with a map obtained by an illegal search. However, in this case the field is located in close proximity to a heavily trafficked public area and is not concealed. Its eventual discovery is inevitable, so the field is admissible as evidence. (Linking the field to the suspect might be problematic, however, since the map retrieved from his house cannot be used for that purpose.) However, inevitability is a strong concept, and the court must be satisfied that discovery of the evidence would truly have occurred even absent the illegal search.

The third exception is good faith. If an officer or agent conducts a search or seizure that he genuinely believes to be legal, even if it subsequently is found to be illegal, any evidence obtained will be admissible.[59] (Note that good faith is an exception to the Exclusionary Rule in general, not merely to the fruit of the poisonous tree doctrine.) This exception can take two basic forms. The first is when the officer believes no warrant is necessary for the search or seizure. The second is when the officer executes a warrant that is invalid but does not know (and could not reasonably be expected to know) that this is the case. For example, the judge issuing the warrant might have reached an incorrect finding of probable cause—exactly as we will see in a moment. However, another important consideration regarding invalid warrants is that a warrant be "precise on its face." This concept will be explored later in this chapter in the section *Police Misconduct*.

The good faith exception originated with *United States v. Leon*.[60] Following an extensive investigation into suspected drug trafficking activities, the Burbank Police Department applied for a warrant to search several residences and vehicles. The warrant application was reviewed by multiple deputy district attorneys and ultimately approved by a state court judge. The evidence thus obtained was challenged by the defense at trial, and while the district court that conducted the evidentiary hearing agreed that the officers had acted in good faith, it determined that the affidavit failed to properly establish probable cause for a number of reasons, including staleness of the information and the lack of credibility of the informants providing it, none of which were remedied by the police investigation prior to requesting the warrant.[61]

The lower courts rejected the state's claim that evidence obtained by officers acting in good faith on an invalid warrant should not be subject to the Exclusionary Rule. The Supreme Court, however, disagreed, observing that " ... the exclusionary rule is designed to deter police misconduct, rather than to punish the errors of judges and magistrates" and that

> In the ordinary case, an officer cannot be expected to question the magistrate's probable cause determination or his judgment that the form of the warrant is technically sufficient. Once the warrant issues, there is literally nothing more the policeman can do in seeking to comply with the law, and penalizing the of-

ficer for the magistrate's error, rather than his own, cannot logically contribute to the deterrence of Fourth Amendment violations.[62]

The opinion does note that this reliance on the accuracy of the warrant must be constrained by reasonableness:

> A police officer's reliance on the magistrate's probable cause determination and on the technical sufficiency of the warrant he issues must be objectively reasonable. Suppression remains an appropriate remedy if the magistrate or judge in issuing a warrant was misled by information in an affidavit that the affiant knew was false or would have known was false except for his reckless disregard of the truth, or if the issuing magistrate wholly abandoned his detached and neutral judicial role. Nor would an officer manifest objective good faith in relying on a warrant based on an affidavit so lacking in indicia of probable cause as to render official belief in its existence entirely unreasonable. Finally, depending on the circumstances of the particular case, a warrant may be so facially deficient—i.e., in failing to particularize the place to be searched or the things to be seized—that the executing officers cannot reasonably presume it to be valid.[63]

Another version of the good faith exception to the Exclusionary Rule applies when an officer conducts a search and/or seizure acting in reliance on a statute that is later held to be unconstitutional. The source of this exception is *Illinois v. Krull et al.*[64] A detective entered an auto salvage yard and requested access to vehicle purchase records. He was told that the records could not be located and was instead provided with a list of several purchases. Upon examining the vehicles, he determined that three had been stolen and found that the VIN had been removed from a fourth. Krull and two others were arrested and charged with various offenses.[65]

The officer had acted based on a 1981 Illinois statute that required motor vehicle and vehicle parts dealers to provide state officials access to certain records on demand. The day after the search of Krull's salvage yard, a federal court held that the statute in question was unconstitutional, and on that basis the state district court and Illinois Supreme Court ruled the evidence inadmissible. The U.S. Supreme Court overturned those rulings since the officer's actions had been legal at the time the search was conducted. The majority opinion noted, "Officers conducting such searches are simply fulfilling their responsibility to enforce the statute as written. If a statute is not clearly unconstitutional, officers cannot be expected to question the judgment of the legislature that passed the law," adding subsequently that in this specific case, "The detective's reliance on the Illinois statute was objectively reasonable. Even assuming that the statute was unconstitutional because it vested state officials with too much discretion, this constitutional defect would not have been obvious to a police officer acting in good faith."[66]

As with officers acting in good faith on invalid warrants, however, the Supreme Court once again imposed constraints of reasonableness: "Under the exception to the exclusionary rule recognized here, a statute cannot support objectively reasonable reliance if, in passing it, the legislature wholly abandoned its responsibility to enact constitutional laws, or if the statutory provisions are such that a reasonable law enforcement officer should have known that the statute was unconstitutional."[67]

The final exception occurs when there is "attenuation between the illegal activity and the discovery of the evidence."[68] A simple example already considered here was the statement given by Wong Sun after his arrest which was ruled admissible despite its origin in an unlawful arrest since several days had passed between the arrest and his provision of the statement, and Wong Sun had not been detained in the meantime.

The notion of standing means that one must have an actual dispute based on harm suffered or the potential to suffer harm as a result of a statute or act by agents of the government (for purposes of this discussion, searches or seizures conducted by law enforcement). The U.S. Supreme Court has gradually modified this concept as it affects the Exclusionary Rule, moving toward an emphasis on the reasonable expectation of privacy that originated with *Katz v. United States*[69] and away from reliance on ownership of goods seized by an illegal search or presence in a premises that is searched unlawfully.

Significant cases that modified the concept of ownership were *United States v. Salvucci* and *Rawlings v. Kentucky*.[70] In *Salvucci*, police had seized stolen checks during an illegal search of Salvucci's mother's apartment. Because Salvucci had no interest in the premises—that is, he was not a party to the lease or a resident of the apartment—the Supreme Court held that he had no standing to petition for the exclusion of the evidence in question.[71]

In *Rawlings*, police had entered a house to execute an arrest warrant on one of the residents. A second resident and four visitors were present. Police searched the house for Marquess, the arrestee, and while they did not locate him, they did detect the smell of marijuana smoke and observed marijuana seeds. Based on this, two officers left to obtain a search warrant while the remaining officers detained the occupants. Once the officers returned with the search warrant, they read the warrant to the occupiers and provided Miranda warnings as well. A female visitor was ordered to empty her purse, which was found to contain illegal drugs. Rawlings immediately claimed ownership of the drugs, and a search of his person produced $4,500 in cash and a knife.[72]

The U.S. Supreme Court refused to bar the drugs or the cash under the Exclusionary Rule. The money had been discovered by a lawful search incident to arrest, and as for the drugs, Rawlings had no expectation of privacy in a purse that he did not own, even though he claimed ownership of them. In noting that " 'arcane' concepts of property law do not control the ability to claim the protections of the Fourth Amendment," the opinion referred to *Rakas v. Illinois*.[73]

In *Rakas*, police had stopped a vehicle on the suspicion that it was the getaway vehicle from a robbery. During a search of the vehicle, a weapon was discovered under the front seat, along with ammunition in the glove compartment. The petitioners—who did not own the car—were convicted of armed robbery and moved to suppress the evidence under the Exclusionary Rule. The trial court denied the petition since they "lacked standing to object to the lawfulness of the search because they concededly did not own either the car or the rifle and shells," a ruling that was upheld by the Illinois Appellate Court, and the U.S. Supreme Court affirmed those decisions. The ruling noted that "a person aggrieved by an illegal search and seizure only through the introduction of damaging evidence secured by a search of a third person's premises or property has not had any of his Fourth Amendment rights infringed."[74]

The Warrant Requirement

In order to ensure that searches and seizures by law enforcement are compliant with constitutional protections, courts generally require that any search and/or seizure be conducted in accordance with a warrant issued by a judge. The rationale is that the warrant process provides the opportunity for an objective third party to determine whether probable cause does in fact exist.

There are three main types of warrants. The first is the **knock-and-announce warrant**, which imposes the requirement for officers to knock, announce and identify themselves, and provide the occupant time to answer the door. Interestingly, in 2006 the U.S. Supreme Court ruled in *Hudson v. Michigan*[75] that the failure of law enforcement to knock or announce when relying on a knock-and-announce warrant does not automatically activate the exclusionary rule. The ruling identified several interests protected by the knock-and-announce procedure:

> … human life and limb (because an unannounced entry may provoke violence from a surprised resident), property (because citizens presumably would open the door upon an announcement, whereas a forcible entry may destroy it), and privacy and dignity of the sort that can be offended by a sudden entrance.

However, Justice Scalia continued, " … the rule has never protected one's interest in preventing the government from seeing or taking evidence described in a warrant. Since the interests violated here have nothing to do with the seizure of the evidence, the exclusionary rule is inapplicable."[76]

The logical counterpart to the knock-and-announce warrant is the **no-knock warrant**. As the name suggests, these warrants allow law enforcement to enter a premises without prior notification. They are typically issued only when there is a reasonable expectation that the occupant could destroy the evidence sought in the time allowed by a knock-and-announce warrant.[77]

Least common is the **anticipatory warrant**, which is issued to authorize a search or seizure justified by a condition which does not yet exist but is reasonably expected to exist at some point in the future. The U.S. Supreme Court upheld this form of warrant as not violating the warrant clause of the Fourth Amendment in *United States v. Grubbs*.[78] In that particular case, police had obtained a warrant with an affidavit that explained that it would not be executed until a parcel—expected to contain child pornography that Grubbs had ordered from an undercover postal inspector—arrived at his residence.[79]

While the rule itself is fairly straightforward, the associated complexity arises from the multitude of exceptions to the warrant requirement. There are in fact a number of exceptions to the Fourth Amendment warrant requirement for searches. Following are the major ones.

Plain View Doctrine: No warrant is required for an officer to seize any item in plain view if the officer has probable cause to believe that the item is involved in a criminal act.[80]

Open Fields Doctrine: No warrant is required to search an open field or other outdoor area, even if such area is on private property, as there is no reasonable expectation of privacy in an open outdoor area. (Consider the concept of inevitable discovery discussed previously as an exception to the fruit of the poisonous tree doctrine.) However, this exception does not extend to **curtilage**, which is the area immediately surrounding a private dwelling and is legally considered to be part of the dwelling.[81] Based on the Supreme Court ruling in *United States v. Dunn*,[82] the courts consider four factors in defining what constitutes curtilage and what constitutes an open field (in legal terms, everything else):

- The proximity of the area in question to the dwelling;
- Whether the area falls within an enclosure that surrounds the dwelling;
- The customary use of the area; and
- What actions, if any, the resident has taken to protect the area from access or observation by passers-by.[83]

Adjuncts to the Open Fields Doctrine are Supreme Court rulings holding that the erection of a fence (particularly one not specifically designed to provide privacy) in an open field does not create a reasonable expectation of privacy and that it is permissible to shine a flashlight into a protected area even without probable cause.[84]

Search incident to a lawful arrest: Upon making a lawful arrest, a police officer may search the arrestee's person and the area immediately around him without a warrant or consent. Even if the officer mistakenly but in good faith arrests the wrong person and in the course of the post-arrest search discovers contraband, that evidence is permissible.[85]

Exigent circumstances: This principle applies to situations in which obtaining a warrant is impractical, usually because of time constraints. There are two main variations. One is when an officer has reasonable belief that there exists an immediate danger to his life or that of others or to private property, or otherwise faces a compelling need to take official action, and in taking such action does not have the primary intent of arresting or seizing evidence, no warrant is required. Typical situations that fall into this category are the fresh pursuit (a.k.a. "hot pursuit") of a suspect, the need to prevent the escape of a suspect, and the need to protect public safety or welfare.[86]

It should not be assumed, however, that even circumstances that on initial review appear to clearly justify the exigent circumstances exception will be viewed that way by the courts. The case of *Michigan v. Fisher*[87] is informative. These are the circumstances:

> Police officers responded to a complaint of a disturbance near Allen Road in Brownstown, Michigan. Officer Christopher Goolsby later testified that, as he and his partner approached the area, a couple directed them to a residence where a man was "going crazy." Upon their arrival, the officers found a household in considerable chaos: a pickup truck in the driveway with its front smashed, damaged fenceposts along the side of the property, and three broken house windows, the glass still on the ground outside. The officers also noticed blood on the hood of the pickup and on clothes inside of it, as well as on one of the doors to the house. (It is disputed whether they noticed this immediately upon reaching the house, but undisputed that they noticed it before the allegedly unconstitutional entry.) Through a window, the officers could see respondent, Jeremy Fisher, inside the house, screaming and throwing things. The back door was locked, and a couch had been placed to block the front door.
>
> The officers knocked, but Fisher refused to answer. They saw that Fisher had a cut on his hand, and they asked him whether he needed medical atten-

tion. Fisher ignored these questions and demanded, with accompanying pro-
fanity, that the officers go to get a search warrant. Officer Goolsby then pushed
the front door partway open and ventured into the house. Through the window of the open door he saw Fisher pointing a long gun at him. Officer Goolsby
withdrew.[88]

Fisher was subsequently charged with assault with a dangerous weapon and possession of a firearm during the commission of a felony. Goolsby's entry into the house
would seem to be an obvious case of exigent circumstances. Yet the trial court suppressed the evidence (*i.e.*, Goolsby's statement regarding Fisher's actions), holding that
"mere drops of blood were insufficient to establish a belief of serious injury within the
house," and the Michigan Court of Appeals affirmed the decision. The Michigan Supreme
Court declined to hear the case, which ultimately reached the U.S. Supreme Court.
The Supreme Court did overturn the exclusion and allow admission of Goolsby's testimony, noting that "they [the officers] did see Fisher screaming and throwing things,"
and as such, "It would be objectively reasonable to believe that Fisher's projectiles might
have a human target (perhaps a spouse or a child), or that Fisher would hurt himself
in the course of his rage."[89]

It is worth considering, however, some of the facts underlying the trial court's decision to exclude the officer's testimony, which are cited in the dissent by Justices Stevens
and Sotomayor:

> He [the trial judge] found the police decision to leave the scene and not re-
> turn for several hours—without resolving any potentially dangerous situation
> and without calling for medical assistance—inconsistent with a reasonable be-
> lief that Fisher was in need of immediate aid. In sum, the one judge who heard
> Officer Goolsby's testimony was not persuaded that Goolsby had an objectively
> reasonable basis for believing that entering Fisher's home was necessary to
> avoid *serious* injury.[90]

Clearly, exigent circumstances may not always be so clear-cut as the situation might
initially indicate.

The second is the need to prevent immediate destruction of evidence. This justification can embrace a vast range of possible circumstances, and has even been used to
justify warrantless, non-consensual blood draws to determine the blood alcohol content of DUI arrestees since the body is constantly metabolizing alcohol and thereby destroying evidence. (That particular exigency was overturned in *Missouri v. McNeely*[91]
for routine DUI cases.)

A good examination of the exigent circumstances principle can be obtained from
Kentucky v. King.[92] In October 2005, Lexington, Kentucky, police officers were pursuing
a suspect identified by an undercover officer who had just completed a drug buy from
the individual and directed the uniformed officers to a specific breezeway of a nearby apartment complex. The officers heard a door slam in the breezeway just before they arrived
and detected a strong odor of marijuana emanating from the back left door of the breezeway. They knocked on the door and announced themselves. The door was not opened,
but the officers heard sounds from the apartment that led them to believe evidence was
being destroyed. At that point they forced entry, where they discovered several individ-

uals in possession of drugs and drug paraphernalia. The original suspect was subsequently located in the apartment through the back right door of the breezeway.[93]

The exigent circumstances exception does not exist when it is police conduct that creates those circumstances, and this was the claim Hollis made in moving to suppress the evidence obtained after the warrantless entry. In affirming Hollis's claim the Kentucky Supreme Court used a two-part test: first, whether police had deliberately created the exigent circumstances (which is an act of bad faith), and if not, whether it was reasonably foreseeable that their conduct would do so. The Kentucky Supreme Court held in essence that the initial "knock and announce" by the officers created the exigent circumstances. In overturning this ruling, the U.S. Supreme Court countered that the standard must be one of reasonableness, and if prior police conduct has been lawful—that is, not in violation or threatened violation of the Fourth Amendment—then it has not created the exigency.[94] This ruling finally clarified the confusion arising from various police-created exigency tests (such as the one applied by the Kentucky Supreme Court) that had arisen in various state and lower federal courts.[95]

Emergency entry: If an officer enters a dwelling in the course of responding to an emergency such as a fire or medical emergency and discovers evidence of a crime in plain view (or in the course of actions reasonably necessary to that response), the Fourth Amendment has not been violated. The warrantless entry was made for reasons of public safety, not to procure evidence, and is therefore acceptable.

An interesting variation on this exception arose in Massachusetts in 2011 when a woman notified police of two dead dogs and a third "emaciated" dog in her neighbor's yard. Unable to obtain any response from the owner of the house, the officers climbed up on a snowbank in order to observe the yard over the privacy fence surrounding it and observed what the neighbor had described. They then contacted the fire department to remove the padlock on the gate so that they could enter the yard.

The owner was subsequently charged with three counts of animal cruelty. She filed to suppress evidence obtained by police entry into her yard on the grounds that it was a warrantless search, thereby raising the question of whether the emergency exception extends to the welfare of animals. The Supreme Judicial Court of Massachusetts ultimately ruled in *Commonwealth v. Duncan*[96] that it does, although this precedent is valid only in Massachusetts.[97]

Searches at or near the border: Although an extremely particular and geographically limited circumstance, the conduct of warrantless searches at the national border requires no additional justification, not even probable cause or reasonable suspicion. The ruling in *United States v. Ramsey*, 431 U.S. 606, 616 (1977) stated, "That searches made at the border, pursuant to the longstanding right of the sovereign to protect itself by stopping and examining persons and property crossing into this country, are reasonable simply by virtue of the fact that they occur at the border, should, by now, require no extended demonstration." Once an individual departs the border, however, even by a few miles, this exception no longer applies.[98]

Motor vehicle searches: An example of new technology not foreseen by the Constitution, automobiles became a Fourth Amendment issue in the early twentieth century, particularly given their use for smuggling during Prohibition. SCOTUS was fairly forgiving when it came to automobile searches. Because the mobility of the automobile provided a means to quickly remove evidence from police jurisdiction and possibly facilitate its destruction, obtaining a warrant for a vehicle search was seen as impractical. Because they are used on public thoroughfares in plain view, not generally used as a repository for personal items, and do not serve as a residence, the courts associate a reduced expectation of privacy with motor vehicles.[99] Given its significance and frequency of occurrence, this exception will be explored more fully in the subsequent section *The Fourth Amendment and Motor Vehicles*.

Vessel searches: With a rationale closely related to that of border searches, seagoing vessels may be stopped and boarded without a warrant even in the absence of any suspicion of criminal activity in order to inspect documentation. The extensive freedom of movement available to vessels—beyond even that of motor vehicles—is considered to justify this degree of latitude.[100]

Consent search: If an individual agrees that the officer may conduct a search without first obtaining a warrant, such a consent search does not violate the Fourth Amendment. Naturally, there are conditions: consent must be given intelligently, specifically, and unequivocally, and it must not arise from duress or coercion, whether implicit or explicit.[101] Also, since the individual has granted consent for the search, he has full authority over the location to be searched and may choose to limit the scope of that search.[102]

If the search involves a physical premises with two or more residents and one of them consents to a search but the other one objects, the objecting resident's rights take precedence, and no consent search may be conducted. However, if a consent search does take place and evidence that potentially incriminates another resident of the premises who was not present to give or withhold consent, that evidence will be admissible.[103]

Landlords are not entitled to grant permission to search a leased premises. Similarly, an employer may consent to a search of its place of business but is not entitled to grant permission for a search of spaces specifically assigned to an employee.[104]

Police Misconduct

By now it should be clear that the Exclusionary Rule is envisioned by the courts as a deterrent against police misconduct. The rationale is that if illegally obtained evidence cannot be used to prosecute a suspect, there will be no motivation for police to engage in search or seizure activities that contravene the Fourth, Fifth, or Sixth Amendments. In *Elkins v. United States*, the Supreme Court declared that the "basic postulate of the exclusionary rule ... is ... to prevent, not to repair. Its purpose is to deter—to compel respect for the constitutional guaranty in the only effectively available way—by removing the incentive to disregard it."[105]

In practice the Exclusionary Rule is really aimed at no other group besides law enforcement. In *United States v. Leon* we saw the Court hold that " ... the exclusionary rule is designed to deter police misconduct, rather than to punish the errors of judges and magistrates."[106] In *Leon* and *Illinois v. Krull et al.* we saw the Court discuss constraints of reasonableness even as in both cases it upheld the admissibility of evidence based on the good faith exception.[107]

The main issue related to police misconduct in the collection of evidence that we have not yet addressed in detail is the procurement of warrants. While acting on a faulty warrant is not the fault of police, a warrant must be "precise on its face." That is, police cannot have presented vague or incomplete facts in order to obtain a warrant that is superficially valid but in truth (and with full knowledge of the officers) circumvents the establishment of probable cause and/or the specification of the areas to be searched and the items to be sought. Consider the following example:

> Judge E. Doe issues a warrant based on Officer Ellay's sworn testimony that he saw Al Bronco removing stolen shoes from his trunk and carrying them into his home in Big Town, California. The warrant is made out for "that property owned by Mr. Al Bronco in Big Town, California." Unbeknownst to Judge E. Doe, Al owns several houses in Big Town, one in which his mother lives and the others which he rents out. Officer Ellay is aware of this, and executes the search of the intended home. Because the warrant is not "precise on its face…," Officer Ellay's search cannot be said to be in good faith and this exception to the Exclusionary Rule will not apply.[108]

The courts are wary of attempts to make end-runs around the warrant requirement or to create good faith exceptions where none actually exist, and the penalties for knowingly filing a false affidavit can significantly exceed watching a suspect walk for lack of evidence.

The Right of Confrontation

The Sixth Amendment governs the rights of the accused in criminal prosecutions. We have already seen the amendment's impact on evidence collection resulting from the right to have counsel present during police questioning. However, another clause in this amendment is significant for the use of evidence at trial: the Confrontation Clause. With the Constitution's typical brevity, the clause makes up only eight words of the amendment, which is quoted here in its entirety with the Confrontation Clause emphasized:

> In all criminal prosecutions, the accused shall enjoy the right to a speedy and public trial, by an impartial jury of the state and district wherein the crime shall have been committed, which district shall have been previously ascertained by law, and to be informed of the nature and cause of the accusation; **to be confronted with the witnesses against him;** to have compulsory process for obtaining witnesses in his favor, and to have the assistance of counsel for his defense.[109]

The purpose of the clause was summed up in *Mattox v. United States*[110] as ensuring that "the accused has an opportunity not only of testing the recollection and shifting the conscience of the witness, but of compelling him to stand face to face with the jury in order that they may look at him, and judge by his demeanor upon the stand and the manner in which he gives his testimony whether he is worthy of belief."[111]

For many years enforcement of the Confrontation Clause was closely related to the hearsay rule in federal courts. Legally, hearsay is "the prior out-of-court statements of a person, offered affirmatively for the truth of the matters asserted, presented at trial either orally by another person or in written form."[112] Various applications of and exceptions to the hearsay rule evolved through precedent:

- "Evidence given at a preliminary hearing could not be used at the trial if the absence of the witness was attributable to the negligence of the prosecution."[113]
- If, however, the "witness's absence had been procured by the defendant, testimony given at a previous trial on a different indictment could be used at the subsequent trial."[114]
- Dying declarations are admissible.[115]
- "Testimony given at a former trial by a witness since deceased" is admissible.[116]
- The prosecution may not "use a judgment of conviction against other defendants on charges of theft in order to prove that the property found in the possession of defendant now on trial was stolen."[117] Also, generally speaking the courts frown on confessions of accomplices if the accomplice cannot be cross-examined by the defendant, such as when the accomplice refuses to testify based on the Fifth Amendment right against self-incrimination or when the accomplice has moved to another state by the time of the trial and the prosecution makes no effort to return him to be available for cross-examination.[118] In short, the Supreme Court views "accomplices' confessions that incriminate defendants" as "presumptively unreliable."[119] Generally speaking, the Confrontation Clause is satisfied so long as there is an opportunity to cross-examine the witness with the aid of counsel, even if such cross-examination does not occur during the trial. For example, in *California v. Green*, witness statements were admitted because although they had been given at a pretrial hearing, they were sworn testimony, the defendant was represented by counsel, and the defense had the opportunity to cross-examine the witness.[120]

Although at times the Supreme Court has subscribed to a literal interpretation of the principle that the accused must be able to confront a witness against him—as in have the witness physically face-to-face—a significant exception has been the testimony of victims in child sex abuse cases. The state's interest in protecting the welfare of children, substantiated by a significant body of research showing the "psychological trauma suffered by child abuse victims," outweighs the right of the defendant to physically confront the witness. The Supreme Court has upheld alternatives, such as in *Maryland v. Craig*, which validated Maryland's practice of having the child witness testify by closed-circuit television so that he or she was visible to the defendant, judge, and jury but could not see the accused.[121] Interestingly, the Court had previously rejected the use of a one-way screen around the witness box that served essentially the same purpose with its ruling in *Coy v. Iowa*, but the significant difference between the two cases was that Iowa mandated use of the screen by statute in *all* child sex abuse cases—creating a "statutory presumption of trauma"—whereas Maryland required case-by-case evaluation to determine whether the child witness would be likely to suffer "serious emotional distress" if required to face the defendant.[122]

Conclusion

The rules governing the admissibility of evidence are fairly few and straightforward. It is the exceptions that prove challenging and have engaged the attention of the courts over the years. Over time the general trend of rulings toward or away from increased protection of constitutional rights in the face of the state's interest in combating crime has changed periodically as a result of social values, the political climate, and the makeup of the various courts.

To place this trend in proper perspective, it should be remembered that the steadily increasing crime rates would not begin to level out until the end of the decade, and many Americans were strongly concerned about violent crime and the rate at which it was growing.

Such changes, however, are generally evolutionary; that is how the American legal system is designed. While the details of exactly what may be admitted at trial and how an argument may be framed based on precedent is the responsibility of attorneys, law enforcement officers nevertheless need a general understanding of the principles that guide the enforcement of constitutional protections and how those principles impact the day-to-day activities of criminal investigation.

Practicum

Evaluate the following scenarios to determine whether the Exclusionary Rule would apply and why or why not.

Practicum One

Detective Watson has been investigating James Green for some time and believes that Green is distributing methamphetamine from his business, an auto body shop, acting as a middleman between wholesale producers and a network of dealers. Because he provides the dealers only with the amount of product they can be expected to move in a day or two, the quantities involved in each transaction are small. However, the only criminal activity for which Watson has sufficient evidence to establish probable cause is the operation of a "chop shop," selling parts from stolen automobiles. Watson prepares an affidavit in which he presents his evidence of dealing in stolen goods, claiming that Green is trafficking in jewelry. Police execute the warrant and in the course of the search of the body shop discover small bundles of one-gram packets of methamphetamine. Green is arrested on narcotics charges, and his defense attorney moves to have the drugs barred under the Exclusionary Rule.

Practicum Two

Albert Jordan is suspected of various financial scams constituting wire fraud. A warrant has been issued allowing investigators to intercept his telephone and e-mail traffic, but thus far the tap has produced no evidence of value. An officer conducting surveillance of Jordan's home sees Jordan leave and conducts an illegal search of the residence, copying the contents of a flash drive that contains documents demonstrating Jordan's guilt. That night Jordan e-mails some of those documents to an accomplice, and they are intercepted. Prior to his trial, Jordan's defense counsel moves to have all documents copied from the flash drive excluded from evidence.

Practicum Three

Steve Johnson is arrested following a motor vehicle accident for which he is at fault after he shows obvious signs of intoxication and fails a field sobriety test. While he is at the hospital receiving care for minor injuries, police obtain a warrant authorizing them to procure a blood sample from Johnson. The sample is analyzed at the state forensic lab by technician David Horton. Two months later Johnson comes to trial. The prosecution announces that Horton will not be testify because he is on unpaid leave and instead has Hector Gonzales, another technician from the forensic lab, testify regarding the BAC determined from Johnson's blood sample. Johnson's defense counsel moves to bar the forensic evidence based on the Confrontation Clause.

Practicum Four

Police file an affidavit to obtain a warrant to search the home of Peter Osborne, a suspected murderer. Detective Foster prepares an affidavit listing the pieces of evidence he hopes to find at Osborne's home. The local court is closed for the weekend, and Foster is unable to find a new warrant form, so he fills out an older version of the form instead. He takes this form and the affidavit to the residence of the presiding judge and tells the judge the form requires revision and approval. The judge returns the form with his approval but does not list the pieces of evidence from the affidavit on the warrant. Police find items from the affidavit in Osborne's home and charge him with first-degree murder. During Osborne's trial, the judge states that the warrant did not conform to Fourth Amendment standards because it did not describe the items to be seized. On appeal to the state supreme court, Osborne's defense counsel argues that the trial judge should have suppressed the evidence since no good-faith exception existed for admitting evidence obtained on a faulty warrant.

Summary

- Because evidence is the heart of any criminal prosecution, it is the fulcrum on which the determination of guilt or innocence hinges.
- The admissibility of evidence from a constitutional standpoint stems from three main sources: the restrictions on search and seizure found in the Fourth Amendment, the restrictions on self-incrimination found in the Fifth Amendment, and the right to counsel found in the Sixth Amendment.
- The Exclusionary Rule is one of the main enforcement mechanisms of the constitutional protections. While the U.S. Constitution establishes these protections, it does not specify how these protections are to be fulfilled or enforced.
- Another possibility is civil action, as a person subjected to an illegal search and/or seizure has a tort claim under common, state, or federal law. In particular, officers at the state or local level are subject to federal civil rights statutes, and in *Bivens v. Six Unknown Federal Narcotics Agents*.
- The final alternate method for enforcing constitutional search and seizure protections is discipline by the officer's own department and/or a police review board.

- It was *Mapp v. Ohio* that finally overturned *Wolf* and applied the Exclusionary Rule universally to the states.
- The Exclusionary Rule has ramifications beyond evidence obtained directly in violation of the Fourth, Fifth, or Sixth Amendment. Logically, evidence discovered indirectly thanks to the original illegally obtained evidence is also barred from admission at trial. This doctrine is known as "fruit of the poisonous tree."
- There are four exceptions to the fruit of the poisonous tree doctrine.
- In order to ensure that searches and seizures by law enforcement are compliant with constitutional protections, courts generally require that any search and/or seizure be conducted in accordance with a warrant issued by a judge. The rationale is that the warrant process provides the opportunity for an objective third party to determine whether probable cause does in fact exist.
- There are a number of exceptions to the Fourth Amendment warrant requirement for searches.
- The Exclusionary Rule is envisioned by the courts as a deterrent against police misconduct. The rationale is that if illegally obtained evidence cannot be used to prosecute a suspect, there will be no motivation for police to engage in search or seizure activities that contravene the Fourth, Fifth, or Sixth Amendments.

Questions in Review

1. What are the exceptions to the warrant requirement for searches?
2. Explain the meaning of "open fields." Does it include areas that are not open?
3. What is the purpose of the exclusionary rule?
4. What are the three main sources from a constitutional point that the admissibility of evidence rests on?
5. Explain the "fruit of the poisonous tree" doctrine.

Key Terms

Abandoned Property: Property left behind in such a manner that the owner relinquishes possessory interest in it. Abandonment also ends that individual's reasonable expectation of privacy regarding the item or items.

Admissible Evidence: Evidence which may be introduced into court proceedings. To be admissible, evidence must either be relevant or imply the greater or lesser probability of some fact which is material to the case.[123] (A simple example of the latter is evidence used to impeach the credibility of a witness, which while it may not be directly relevant to the proceedings nevertheless by implication lessens the probability that his or her testimony about facts directly related to the case are accurate or truthful.)

Excluded Evidence: Evidence which while neither irrelevant nor inadmissible is not admitted in the court proceeding in question and may not be considered in the resolution of the case.[125] (Excluded evidence is distinct from inadmissible evidence.)

Good Faith: A sincere belief which lacks any malice or intent to defraud and could be held by a reasonable person in similar circumstances. The concept of good faith is determined from the totality of the circumstances rather than from any formal rule.[126]

Objective Test of Privacy Expectation: The objective test is fulfilled when in similar circumstances, a reasonable person would have likewise expected privacy.

Probable Cause: A reasonable basis exists to believe that a crime may have been committed and, in the case of a search, that evidence of that crime is likely to be present in the location to be searched.

Qualified Immunity: Protection from lawsuits enjoyed by government officials acting in an official capacity, so long as their actions are reasonable.[127]

Reasonable Suspicion: Under a given set of circumstances and based on specific and articulable facts, a reasonable person would suspect that a crime may have been committed.

Relevant Evidence: Evidence which directly contributes to confirming or denying (1) a fact material to the case or (2) a fact that is otherwise significant to the resolution of the case.

Search: An agent or employee of the government infringes an individual's expectation of privacy, assuming that such expectation is considered reasonable by society. Note that a private individual not acting on behalf of the government is exempt from Fourth Amendment restrictions.

Seizure (person): An agent or employee of the government (1) uses physical force to restrain an individual or (2) creates such a situation that a reasonable person experiencing the same or similar circumstances would not feel free to leave the scene.

Seizure (property): An agent or employee of the government interferes with an individual's possessory interest in a piece of property. A seizure is unreasonable when the property owner had a reasonable expectation of privacy regarding the item or items. However, the previous owner of a piece of abandoned property has no standing to claim unreasonable seizure.

Standing (formally, *locus standi*): The right to bring suit in a court regarding a given matter. For federal (and in particular constitutional) matters, an individual must have an actual dispute, having sustained or having the potential to sustain direct injury or harm; simply disagreeing with a federal law or government action is not sufficient. In Fourth Amendment matters, the plaintiff must have had a legitimate expectation of privacy at the searched location that was violated.

Subjective Test of Privacy Expectation: The subjective test is fulfilled when the individual in question genuinely and actually expected privacy.

Endnotes

1. Edwards, Richard A. (June 1955). Criminal Liability for Unreasonable Searches and Seizures. *Virginia Law Review* (41:5), pp.621–25. Accessed online at http://www.jstor.org/discover/10.2307/1070343?uid=3739688&uid=2134&uid=2484316563&uid=2&uid=70&uid=3&uid=2484316553&uid=3739256&uid=60&sid=21104715835653. (Accessed on January 20, 2015).

2. Bivens v. Six Unknown Federal Narcotics Agents, 403 U.S. 388 (1971).

3. Justia (n.d.). Alternatives to the Exclusionary Rule. Accessed online at http://law.justia.com/constitution/us/amendment-04/30-exclusionary-rule.html. (Accessed on January 20, 2015).

4. Pearson et al. v. Callahan, 555 U.S. 223 (2009).

5. Legal Information Institute (n.d.). Pearson et al. v. Callahan. Ithaca, NY: Cornell University Law School. Accessed online at http://www.law.cornell.edu/supct/html/07-751.ZS.html#content. (Accessed on January 20, 2015).

6. Legal Information Institute (n.d.). Saucier v. Katz. Ithaca, NY: Cornell University Law School. Accessed online at http://www.law.cornell.edu/supremecourt/text/533/194.

7. Saucier v. Katz, 533 U.S. 194 (2001). (Accessed on January 22, 2015).

8. Ibid.

9. Legal Information Institute (n.d.). Pearson et al. v. Callahan.

10. Ibid.

11. Justia (n.d.). Alternatives to the Exclusionary Rule.

12. Boyd v. United States, 116 U.S. 616 (1886).

13. Casebriefs, LLC (n.d.). Boyd v. United States. Accessed online at http://www.casebriefs.com/blog/law/criminal-procedure/criminal-procedure-keyed-to-israel/investigation-by-subpeona/boyd-v-united-states/.(Accessed on January 21, 2015).

14. Casebriefs, LLC (n.d.). Boyd v. United States. Accessed online at http://www.casebriefs.com/blog/law/criminal-procedure/criminal-procedure-keyed-to-israel/investigation-by-subpeona/boyd-v-united-states/2/.(Accessed on January 20, 2015).

15. Legal Information Institute (n.d.). Fourth Amendment: Search and Seizure. Ithaca, NY: Cornell University Law School. Accessed online at http://www.law.cornell.edu/anncon/html/amdt4frag5_user.html. (Accessed on January 23, 2015).

16. Weeks v. U.S., 232 U.S. 383 (1914).

17. Justia (n.d.). Weeks v. United States. Accessed online at https://supreme.justia.com/cases/federal/us/232/383/case.html. (Accessed on January 20, 2015).

18. Wolf v. Colorado, 338 U.S. 252 (1949).

19. Wolf v. Colorado. Fayetteville, AR: University of Arkansas Law School. Accessed online at http://law.uark.edu/documents/Wolf_v_Colorado.pdf. (Accessed on January 22, 2015).

20. Rochin v. California, 342 U.S. 165 (1952).

21. Legal Information Institute (n.d.). Fourth Amendment: Search and Seizure.

22. Irvine v. California, 347 U.S. 128 (1954).

23. The Oyez Project (n.d.). Irvine v. California. Chicago: Illinois Institute of Technology Kent College of Law. Accessed online at http://www.oyez.org/cases/1950-1959/1953/1953_12. (Accessed on January 20, 2015).

24. Mapp v. Ohio, 367 U.S. 643 (1961).

25. Legal Information Institute (n.d.). Mapp v. Ohio. Ithaca, NY: Cornell University Law School. Accessed online at http://www.law.cornell.edu/supremecourt/text/367/643.

26. Elkins et al. v. United States, 364 U.S. 206 (1960). (Accessed on January 20, 2015).

27. Legal Information Institute (n.d.). James Butler ELKINS and Raymond Frederick CLARK, Petitioners, v. UNITED STATES of America. Ithaca, NY: Cornell University Law School. Accessed online at http://www.law.cornell.edu/supremecourt/text/364/206.

28. Miranda v. Arizona, 384 U.S. 436 (1966). (Accessed on January 23, 2015).

29. Legal Information Institute (n.d). Miranda v. Arizona. Ithaca, NY: Cornell University Law School. Accessed online at http://www.law.cornell.edu/supremecourt/text/384/436. (Accessed on January 23, 2015).

30. Ibid.

31. Ibid.

32. Ibid.

33. Ibid.

34. Ibid.

35. Ibid.

36. Walenta, Craig (1995–2010). The Miranda Warning. U.S. Constitution Online. Accessed online at http://www.usconstitution.net/miranda.html. (Accessed on January 20, 2015).

37. Illinois v. Gates, 462 U.S. 213 (1983).

38. United States v. Calandra, 414 U.S. 338, 348 (1974).

39. Legal Information Institute (n.d.). Illinois v. Gates. Ithaca, NY: Cornell University Law School. Accessed online at http://www.law.cornell.edu/supremecourt/text/462/213#writing-USSC_CR_0462_0213_ZO. (Accessed on January 25, 2015).

40. United States v. Leon, 468 U.S. 897 (1984).

41. Legal Information Institute (n.d.). United States v. Leon. Ithaca, NY: Cornell University Law School. Accessed online at http://www.law.cornell.edu/supremecourt/text/468/897. (Accessed on January 20, 2015).

42. INS v. Lopez-Mendoza, 468 U.S. 1032 (1984).

43. The Oyez Project (n.d.). INS v. Lopez-Mendoza. Chicago: Illinois Institute of Technology Kent College of Law. Accessed online at http://www.oyez.org/cases/1980-1989/1983/1983_83_491. (Accessed on January 27, 2015).

44. Walder v. United States, 347 U.S. 62 (1954).

45. Legal Information Institute (n.d.). Walder v. United States. Ithaca, NY: Cornell University Law School. Accessed online at http://www.law.cornell.edu/supremecourt/text/347/62. (Accessed on January 20, 2015).

46. Agnello v. United States, 269 U.S. 20 (1925).

47. Justia (n.d.). Agnello v. United States. Accessed online at https://supreme.justia.com/cases/federal/us/269/20/case.html. (Accessed on January 21, 2015).

48. Ibid.

49. Ibid.

50. Silverthorne Lumber Co., Inc. v. United States, 251 U.S. 385 (1920).

51. Justia (n.d.). Silverthorne Lumber Co., Inc. v. United States. Accessed online at https://supreme.justia.com/cases/federal/us/251/385/case.html. (Accessed on January 20, 2015).

52. Ibid.

53. Wong Sun v. United States, 371 U.S. 471 (1963).

54. Justia (n.d.). Wong Sun v. United States. Accessed online at https://supreme.justia.com/cases/federal/us/371/471/case.html. (Accessed on January 20, 2015).

55. Ibid.

56. Ibid.

57. National Paralegal College (2003–2007). The Exclusionary Rule. Constitutional Law & Criminal Procedure. Accessed online at http://nationalparalegal.edu/conlawcrimproc_public/ProtectionFromSearches&Seizures/ExclusionaryRule.asp. (Accessed on January 27, 2015).

58. Ibid.

59. Ibid.

60. United States v. Leon, 468 U.S. 897 (1984).

61. Legal Information Institute (n.d.). United States v. Leon. Ithaca, NY: Cornell University Law School. Accessed online at http://www.law.cornell.edu/supremecourt/text/468/897. (Accessed on January 20, 2015).

62. Ibid.

63. Ibid.

64. Illinois v. Krull et al., 480 U.S. 340 (1987).

65. Legal Information Institute (n.d.). ILLINOIS, Petitioner v. Albert KRULL, George Lucas and Salvatore Mucerino. Ithaca, NY: Cornell University Law School. Accessed online at http://www.law.cornell.edu/supremecourt/text/480/340. (Accessed on January 30, 2015).

66. Ibid.

67. Ibid.

68. Legal Information Institute (n.d.). Fruit of the Poisonous Tree. Ithaca, NY: Cornell University Law School. Accessed online at http://www.law.cornell.edu/wex/fruit_of_the_poisonous_tree. (Accessed on January 30, 2015).

69. Katz v. United States, 389 U.S. 347 (1967).

70. United States v. Salvucci, 448 U.S. 83 (1980) and Rawlings v. Kentucky, 448 U.S. 98 (1980).

71. Legal Information Institute (n.d.). Enforcing the Fourth Amendment: The Exclusionary Rule. Ithaca, NY: Cornell University Law School. Accessed online at http://www.law.cornell.edu/anncon/html/amdt4frag5_user.html#fnb228. (Accessed on January 20, 2015).

72. Legal Information Institute (n.d.).—L.Ed.2d—RAWLINGS v. KENTUCKY. Ithaca, NY: Cornell University Law School. Accessed online at http://www.law.cornell.edu/supremecourt/text/448/98. (Accessed on January 20, 2015).

73. Rakas v. Illinois, 439 U.S. 128 (1978).

74. Legal Information Institute (n.d.). RAKAS et al. v. ILLINOIS. Ithaca, NY: Cornell University Law School. Accessed online at http://www.law.cornell.edu/supremecourt/text/439/128. (Accessed on January 28, 2015).

75. Hudson v. Michigan, 547 U.S. 586 (2006).

76. Legal Information Institute (n.d.). Hudson v. Michigan. Ithaca, NY: Cornell University Law School. Accessed online at http://www.law.cornell.edu/supct/html/04-1360.ZS.html. (Accessed on January 20, 2015).

77. Legal Information Institute (n.d.). Fourth Amendment. Ithaca, NY: Cornell University Law School. Accessed online at http://www.law.cornell.edu/wex/fourth_amendment. (Accessed on January 20, 2015).

78. United States v. Grubbs, 547 U.S. 90 (2006).

79. Legal Information Institute (n.d.). United States v. Grubbs. Ithaca, NY: Cornell University Law School. Accessed online at http://www.law.cornell.edu/supct/html/04-1414.ZS.html. (Accessed on January 25, 2015).

80. 4th Amendment in everyday life (n.d.). Accessed online at http://www.revolutionary-war-and-beyond.com/4th-amendment.html. (Accessed on January 20, 2015).

81. Ibid.

82. United States v. Dunn, 480 U.S. 294 (1987).

83. Legal Information Institute (n.d.). Curtilage. Ithaca, NY: Cornell University Law School. Accessed online at http://www.law.cornell.edu/wex/curtilage. (Accessed on January 20, 2015).

84. Legal Information Institute (n.d.). United States v. Dunn. Ithaca, NY: Cornell University Law School. Accessed online at http://www.law.cornell.edu/supremecourt/text/480/294. (Accessed on January 23, 2015).

85. Legal Information Institute (n.d.). Fourth Amendment. Ithaca, NY: Cornell University Law School. Accessed online at http://www.law.cornell.edu/wex/fourth_amendment.

86. 4th Amendment in everyday life (n.d.). Accessed online at http://www.revolutionary-war-and-beyond.com/4th-amendment.html. (Accessed on January 30, 2015).

87. Michigan v. Fisher, 130 S. Ct. 546 (2009).

88. Michigan v. Jeremy Fisher. Fayetteville, AR: University of Arkansas Law School. Accessed online at http://law.uark.edu/documents/Michigan_v._Jeremy_Fisher.pdf. (Accessed on January 30, 2015).

89. Ibid.

90. Ibid.

91. Missouri v. McNeely, 133 U.S. 832 (2013).

92. Kentucky v. King, 131 U.S. 1849 (2011).

93. Legal Information Institute (n.d.). Kentucky v. King. Ithaca, NY: Cornell University Law School. Accessed online at http://www.law.cornell.edu/supct/cert/09-1272. (Accessed on January 20, 2015).

94. Legal Information Institute (n.d.). Fourth Amendment: Exigent Circumstances. Ithaca, NY: Cornell University Law School. Accessed online at http://www.law.cornell.edu/supct/cert/case_summary/2011/fourth_amendment_exigent_circumstances. (Accessed on January 24, 2015).

95. Pettry, Michael T. The Exigent Circumstances Exception After Kentucky v. King. FBI Law Enforcement Bulletin. Washington, D.C.: Federal Bureau of Investigation. Accessed online at http://www.fbi.gov/stats-services/publications/law-enforcement-bulletin/march-2012/the-exigent-circumstances-exception-after-kentucky-v.-king. (Accessed on January 20, 2015).

96. Commonwealth v. Duncan, SJC-11373 (2014).

97. Commonwealth v. Duncan (2014). Accessed online at http://law.justia.com/cases/massachusetts/supreme-court/2014/sjc-11373.html.

98. Border Searches (n.d.). Accessed online at http://law.justia.com/constitution/us/amendment-04/18-border-searches.html. (Accessed on January 20, 2015).

99. Vehicular Searches (n.d.). Accessed online at http://law.justia.com/constitution/us/amendment-04/15-vehicular-searches.html. (Accessed on January 23, 2015).

100. Vessel Searches (n.d.). Accessed online at http://law.justia.com/constitution/us/amendment-04/16-vessel-searches.html.

101. Legal Information Institute (n.d.). Fourth Amendment. Ithaca, NY: Cornell University Law School. Accessed online at http://www.law.cornell.edu/wex/fourth_amendment. (Accessed on January 20, 2015).

102. Neil, Richard (n.d.). Search & Seizure Law Update [PowerPoint presentation]. Slide 85. Accessed online at http://www.leotrainer.com/pptsearchupdate.ppt. (Accessed on January 22, 2015).

103. Legal Information Institute (n.d.). Fourth Amendment. Ithaca, NY: Cornell University Law School. Accessed online at http://www.law.cornell.edu/wex/fourth_amendment. (Accessed on January 27, 2015).

104. Ibid.

105. Legal Information Institute (n.d.). Enforcing the Fourth Amendment: The Exclusionary Rule.

106. Legal Information Institute (n.d.). United States v. Leon.

107. Ibid and Legal Information Institute (n.d.). ILLINOIS, Petitioner v. Albert KRULL, George Lucas and Salvatore Mucerino.

108. National Paralegal College (2007). The Exclusionary Rule.

109. Legal Information Institute (n.d.). Sixth Amendment. Ithaca, NY: Cornell University Law School. Accessed online at http://www.law.cornell.edu/constitution/sixth_amendment. (Accessed on January 20, 2015).

110. Mattox v. United States, 156 U.S. 237 (1895).

111. Legal Information Institute (n.d.). Sixth Amendment: Rights of Accused in Criminal Prosecutions: Confrontation. Ithaca, NY: Cornell University Law School. Accessed online at http://www.law.cornell.edu/anncon/html/amdt6frag6_user.html#fnb145. (Accessed on January 20, 2015).

112. Ibid.

113. Motes v. United States, 178 U.S. 458 (1900).

114. Reynolds v. United States, 98 U.S. 145 (1879).

115. Kirby v. United States, 174 U.S. 47 (1899) and Robertson v. Baldwin, 165 U.S. 275 (1897).

116. Mattox v. United States, 156 U.S. 237 (1895).

117. Kirby v. United States, 174 U.S. 47 (1899) and Dowdell v. United States, 221 U.S. 325 (1911).

118. Douglas v. Alabama, 380 U.S. 415, (1965) and Pointer v. Texas, 380 U.S. 400 (1965).

119. Lee v. Illinois, 476 U.S. 530 (1986) and Lilly v. Virginia, 527 U.S. 116 (1999).

120. California v. Green, 399 U.S. 149 (1970)

121. Maryland v. Craig, 497 U.S. 836 (1990)

122. Ibid.

123. National Paralegal College (2007). The Exclusionary Rule. *Constitutional Law and Criminal Procedure*. Accessed online at http://nationalparalegal.edu/conlawcrimproc_public/ProtectionFromSearches&Seizures/ExclusionaryRule.asp (Accessed on January 22, 2015).

124. Ibid.

125. Ibid.

126. Ibid.

127. Legal Information Institute (n.d.). Qualified immunity. Ithaca, NY: Cornell University Law School. Accessed online at http://www.law.cornell.edu/wex/qualified_immunity. (Accessed on January 90, 2015).

Chapter 3

Nature of Real Evidence

Chapter Objectives

What you should know and understand after studying this chapter

- What constitutes real evidence
- The fundamental principles of physical evidence
- The requirements for authentication of the evidence
- How evidence should be preserved
- The use of physical evidence in criminal trials
- The requirements of materiality

Chapter Outline

Introduction

Perhaps no aspect of police investigative work so fascinates the general public as that of forensics. From an army of Sherlock Holmes-like detectives armed with magnifying glasses found in literature to the popularity (and proliferation) of the various *CSI* television shows and others like them, people tend to be fascinated with the role of physical evidence in solving crimes. Professional investigators know all too well that identifying suspects (and in many cases making available physical evidence have value in court by finding a suspect to which it can be linked) has more to do with good interviewing (and lots of it). After all, most forensic or physical evidence submitted for analysis is intended to establish associations. It is important to note that physical evidence is generally not very effective at identifying a culprit when one is not already known. Typically the identity of the culprit is developed in some other way and then physical evidence is used to help establish proof of guilt.[1] (Fingerprints are the major exception to this principle, but even then a fingerprint found at a crime scene must already be in a database in order to produce a match; otherwise, it can only provide confirmation after the fact.)

Once it is time to take a case to court, however, forensics will play a key role. In fact, physical evidence is often referred to as **forensic evidence** (or less commonly **scientific evidence**) since some form of analysis is usually necessary to make physical evidence usable in a prosecution. But for that evidence to be useful in the courtroom, it must have been properly handled from the moment an officer arrives at the crime scene.

Physical or real evidence can take numerous forms. The National Forensic Science Technology Center of the U.S. Department of Justice identifies just a few examples:

- Biological material—blood, semen, or saliva
- Fibers
- Paint chips
- Glass
- Soil and vegetation
- Accelerants
- Fingerprints
- Hair
- Impression evidence—shoe prints, tire tracks, or tool marks
- Fracture patterns—glass fragments or adhesive tape pieces
- Narcotics[2]

Because of its objectivity and reliability (if properly collected, preserved, and analyzed)—especially compared to eyewitness testimony—physical evidence is therefore often referred to as the silent witness.[3]

Here we will consider first the legal rules governing whether physical evidence is admissible in court or not. We will then look at how physical evidence must be collected and secured in order to preserve its value and admissibility.

Materiality

In Chapter 2 we defined some of the legal terms associated with evidence and its use. You may recall that admissible evidence must be either relevant or imply the greater or lesser probability of some fact which is material to the case, such as through its use to impeach a witness. Relevance is in turn based on **materiality**, and though the two

Photo 3-1

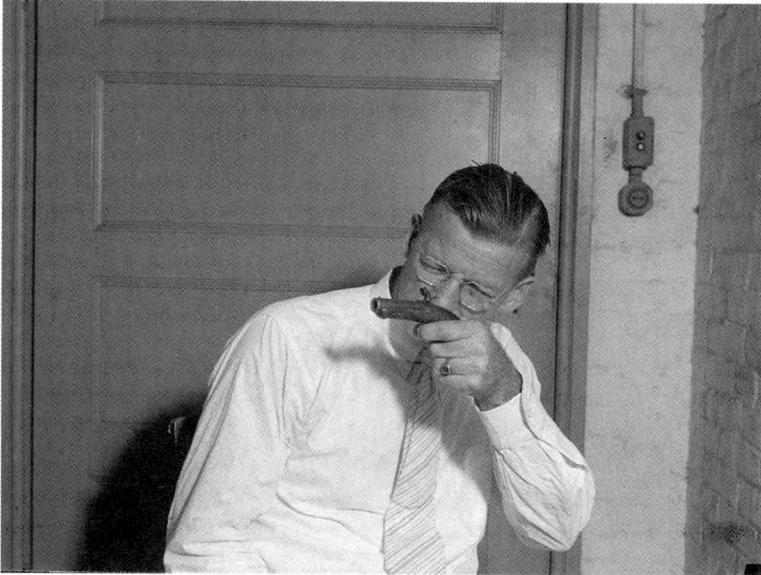

The gun being held by Edwin Pitts in 1937 is an example of real evidence.
This gun was used by John Wilkes Booth to kill President Abraham Lincoln in 1865.
Photo courtesy of the Library of Congress.

terms tend to be used interchangeably, they have slightly different shades of meaning. In Rule 1 of the Model Code of Evidence developed by the American Law Institute, relevant evidence is defined as having any tendency in reason to prove any material matter and includes opinion evidence and hearsay evidence.[4] Similarly, Rule 401 of the Federal Rules of Evidence states that "relevant evidence means evidence having any tendency to make the existence of any fact that is of consequence to the determination of the action more probable or less probable than it would be without the evidence."[5] Where the rule reads "any fact that is of consequence to the determination of the action," it is safe to substitute "any material fact."

For criminal matters, material physical evidence accomplishes at least one of three possible purposes. First, it may aid the investigator in solving the case. For example, evidence might help to disprove (or prove) an alibi offered by a suspect, identify or further develop a suspect, confirm or eliminate connections between one suspect and one or more others, identify stolen property or other contraband, help to determine a *modus operandi* (MO) or identify similarities in MO between the current case and others, or simply provide leads to the investigator.[6]

Second, it may prove or help to prove one or more elements of the crime. For example, glass fragments, wood splinters, or paint chips found on a suspect's clothing might help to prove forced entry. Blood, semen, hair, or skin might provide DNA evidence linking a suspect to an assault, rape, or homicide. Bullets recovered from the body of a homicide victim or his surroundings might be matched by ballistics comparison to a weapon in the possession of a suspect.[7]

Finally, physical evidence might provide support for a particular theory regarding a crime. For example, auto paint found on the clothing of a victim might show that a vehicle impact was the cause of injury. (The color of that paint might then provide a lead, and subsequent chemical analysis might prove that it originated from a particular model of vehicle—all elements of aiding in solving the case.) The presence of footprints might demonstrate that at least two perpetrators were present at the scene. In the absence of a body, shell casings at the scene might show that a victim was shot rather than stabbed or beaten.[8]

Rule 402 of the Federal Rules of Evidence states plainly, "Evidence which is not relevant is not admissible." However, the converse of that principle—that is, that all relevant evidence is admissible—is not always true. Rule 402 states initially, "All relevant evidence is admissible, except as otherwise provided by the Constitution of the United States, by Act of Congress, by these rules, or by other rules prescribed by the Supreme Court pursuant to statutory authority."[9] The "except as otherwise provided" provision covers a significant amount of legal ground, and evidence affected by it becomes **excluded evidence**—evidence which is neither irrelevant nor inadmissible but is not admitted in the criminal proceeding and may not be considered in adjudicating the case.

There are numerous rules for determining relevancy and admissibility, and significant cases will typically have one or more hearings specifically regarding the admissibility of evidence. Many of these rules affect evidence types other than physical evidence, such as documentary evidence or witness testimony, and those will be addressed in the appropriate chapters later in this text. Rule 403 of the Federal Rules of Evidence describes the broad categories fairly succinctly:

- Although relevant, evidence may be excluded if its probative value is substantially outweighed by the danger of unfair prejudice,
- confusion of the issues, or
- misleading the jury, or
- by considerations of undue delay, waste of time, or needless presentation of cumulative evidence.[10]

The first category is **prejudicial evidence**. Common examples are photographs of a crime scene and/or the bodies of victims that are particularly gruesome, or a bloody teddy bear or other toy in a child homicide case. Typically, such evidence has little probative value—that is, it cannot prove anything significant. In the case of gruesome photos, they prove little other than that the victims are truly deceased—something rather rarely at issue in a homicide trial—or perhaps the manner of death—evidence the medical examiner can provide quite efficiently by testimony. The problem is that jurors, having had the horror of the crime shoved in their faces, as it were, will tend to look to punish someone for what was done, and the only someone available is the defendant. Yet the photographs probably show only what was done, not any evidence of who did it.[11]

The second category is evidence with the potential to confuse or mislead the jury. During O.J. Simpson's homicide trial, many commentators noted that the prosecution presented complex DNA and other scientific evidence in a manner that often left jurors with little understanding of what had been demonstrated, making that evidence easily countered by the defense. Scientific evidence often falls into this exclusion category, particularly if the science in question is new or has little support in the scientific or academic community. Aside from the potential to confuse the jury with unfamiliar scientific concepts, such novel scientific concepts tend to have no shortage of detractors, meaning the defense can easily produce expert witnesses to counter the evidence being produced. This has the potential to divert the proceedings into a debate over the validity of the technique used to produce the evidence, which further muddles things for the jury and wastes the court's time.[12]

The notion of wasting the court's time leads us into the third category of undue delay and waste of time, which generally comes in the form of needless presentation of cumulative evidence. This issue is less common with physical evidence; it is more commonly seen in the form of a parade of witnesses each testifying to essentially the same fact, or document after document produced for a similar purpose. But introducing multiple pieces of physical evidence intended to prove the same fact is no different. Judges frown on such performance, and aside from being prohibited by the rules of evidence, such tactics can actually backfire: the jury may well begin to wonder why the prosecution (or defense, for that matter) feels the need to so desperately prove a particular fact, or the prosecution may simply be seen as bullying the defendant—beating a dead horse, as the saying goes. The best strategy is to pick a handful of pieces of evidence that out of all those available best prove the fact in question and leave it at that.[13]

Finally, note that physical evidence may represent either **direct evidence** or **circumstantial** (indirect) **evidence**. Despite a notion that seems widely held among the general public that circumstantial evidence is inadmissible, in the majority of cases most if not all physical evidence will be circumstantial. In the introduction we noted that physical evidence must usually be analyzed in order to serve as evidence. Such analysis merely draws inferences from known facts, which is precisely what circumstantial evidence is.[14] A suspect may confess that he shot the victim with a particular weapon, or an eyewitness may testify to those facts—that confession or testimony is direct evidence. If instead a bullet is recovered from the victim's body and subsequently matched by ballistics testing to a weapon registered to the suspect and in his possession at the time of the crime, it can be inferred that the suspect's weapon discharged the fatal shot and (even more indirectly) that it was the suspect who fired the weapon.

Yet despite being produced by reliable, scientific techniques, this information alone can never prove conclusively that the suspect shot the victim. Rather, most successful criminal prosecutions rest in part on the collection of numerous pieces of circumstantial evidence—physical or otherwise—that paint a common picture of the circumstances surrounding the crime in question. It is for this reason that the careful collection, handling, safeguarding, and processing of all available physical evidence at a crime scene is so important.

Fundamental Principles of Physical Evidence

The first systematic use of factual information to aid in law enforcement is generally credited to Alphonse Bertillon, a clerk in the Paris police force. In 1879 he joined the Premier Bureau of the Prefecture of Police, where he began organizing the huge number of existing files based on a system used by his father, an anthropologist. The file system placed all of an individual's distinguishing characteristics, including body measurements, onto a single card, and as the science of photography advanced he later added photos to the cards. This system, eventually named Bertillonage, created the first law enforcement database to aid criminal investigations.[15]

By 1891 the new science of fingerprint identification all but replaced Bertillonage, but Bertillon made contributions to other aspects of criminal investigation. His use of photography was not limited to his database of prior offenders. More significantly, he pioneered its use in crime scene documentation and introduced the concept of including a measuring scale in each photo for reference purposes. Previously crime scenes were documented by a combination of sketches and notes—assuming they were documented at all. Bertillon photographed not only victims but also their relationship to other pieces of evidence and any other items of interest at the scene such as footprints, stains, tool marks, and points of entry.[16]

Bertillon's influence on forensics continued through his students, including Edmond Locard. Locard furthered Bertillon's basic concept of applying scientific methods and logic to criminal investigation and identification and gave us a fundamental principle of forensic science: Locard's Exchange Principle. This principle holds that

> [w]hen any person comes into contact with an object or another person, a cross-transfer of physical evidence occurs. By recognizing, documenting, and examining the nature and extent of this evidentiary exchange ... criminals could be associated with particular locations, items of evidence, and victims. The detection of the exchanged materials is interpreted to mean that the two objects were in contact. This is the cause and effect principle reversed; the effect is observed and the cause is concluded.

Furthermore, forensic scientists also recognize that the nature and extent of this exchange can be used not only to associate a criminal with locations, items, and victims, but with specific actions as well.[17] Appendix B is a reprinted copy of a journal article by Chisum and Turvey which explains in detail Locard's exchange principle.

Advocates of forensic science tended to speak strongly in its favor, especially as it transformed criminal investigation in the late nineteenth and early twentieth centuries. Hans Gross, an Austrian professor of criminology and former magistrate, exemplified this attitude when he declared, "The progress of criminology means less trust in witnesses and more in real proofs."[18] Half a century later, Paul Kirk, a professor of criminalistics at the University of California at Berkeley, similarly asserted that

> ... the utilization of physical evidence is critical to the solution of most crime. No longer may the police depend upon the confession, as they have done to a large extent in the past. The eyewitness has never been dependable, as any experienced investigator or attorney knows quite well. Only physical evidence is infallible, and then only when it is properly recognized, studied, and interpreted.

However, these proponents and others recognized that assumptions about the infallibility of conclusions based on evidence analysis are all too common. The physical evidence is (at least usually, as we will see) what it is, and the techniques used to analyze and evaluate it are straightforward and objective. The complication arises when the investigator or forensic analyst develops a premise based on the observations generated by evidence analysis. As John Thornton, a professor of forensic science at the University of California at Berkeley and a student of Paul Kirk, put it:

> Induction is a type of inference that proceeds from a set of specific observations to a generalization, called a premise. This premise is a working assumption, but it may not always be valid. A deduction, on the other hand, proceeds from a generalization to a specific case, and that is generally what happens in forensic practice. Providing that the premise is valid, the deduction will be valid. But knowing whether the premise is valid is the name of the game here; it is not difficult to be fooled into thinking that one's premises are valid when they are not.

It is helpful to understand the difference between induction and deduction (or inductive and deductive reasoning), since recognizing which process he or she is using can be vital to an investigator. Induction is the process of inferring a general law or principle from observation of particular instances, or adducing (pulling together) a number of separate facts, particulars, etc. especially for the purpose of proving a general statement.[19] Deduction, on the other hand, is to draw a conclusion from something known or assumed, or inference by reasoning from generals to particulars.[20] In short, induction takes a set of specific observations and uses them to arrive at a generalization; deduction takes accepted generalizations and from that arrives at an assumption about a specific case.

To paraphrase Karl Popper, a twentieth-century philosopher of science and critic of induction, inductive reasoning would say that since we have observed one hundred crows and all of them were black, then it follows that all crows are black. Yet unless we observe every crow in existence and verify that it is in fact black—an obvious impossibility—we cannot generalize with perfect surety that all crows are black.[21] (You may have heard the principle that it is impossible to prove a negative. Applying that here, we cannot prove that no crows are white; the fact that we have never seen one does not necessarily mean they do not exist.) Deductive reasoning would say that since it is an accepted fact that crows are black, if we should come across a crow, it will be black.

To return to Thornton's assertion quoted previously, induction uses a set of observations—in our case, generated from evidence analysis—to arrive at a working assumption that he calls a premise, which in science is called a hypothesis. It is important for the forensic analyst and the investigator both to recognize that a hypothesis is not fact; it is an assumption, and it is necessary to then attempt to confirm or deny that hypothesis (and to do so objectively!) with additional facts. Deductive reasoning can look powerful and flawless at first glance, since it does not make assumptions. The problem is that deductive reasoning is based on its own set of premises, and if any of those premises are flawed, so too will be the deduction. In the previous paragraph we demonstrated deductive reasoning by saying that given the premise that all crows are black, we can confidently conclude that any crow we find will be black. But what is the basis for our starting premise that all crows are black? How do we know that it is valid?

Photo 3-2

Physical evidence must be kept secure by law enforcement. The above photograph was taken in October, 1938. It shows a secret service agent checking a locker that contains confiscated currency in a pending case. Photo courtesy of the Library of Congress.

The truth is that induction is powerful and a commonly used tool in science. A hypothesis is developed based on a set of observations and then tested for validity. For that matter, humans unconsciously use induction every day as we learn and build a body of experience. But induction can also give rise to prejudice, which is simply *pre-judging* based on assumptions about a group. To give a crude example using a common prejudice in early twentieth-century American society, "Irishmen are drunkards [the premise]. This man is Irish. Therefore, he is a drunkard [the deduction]." The key—whether in daily life or in criminal investigation—is to recognize the limitations of a hypothesis created by induction. As Thornton put it, " … too often a hypothesis is declared as a deductive conclusion, when in fact it is a statement awaiting verification through testing."[22] It is also crucial that the investigator analyze facts objectively to test the hypothesis rather than selectively choosing and/or interpreting the evidence that supports his or her hypothesis—a psychological trap that can be hard to avoid.

There is another potential flaw in reliance on physical evidence—what Chisum and Turvey refer to as the assumption of integrity:

> The process of crime reconstruction is often built on the assumption that evidence left behind at a crime scene, which has been recognized, documented, collected, identified, compared, individuated, and reconstructed, is pristine. This assumption involves the belief that the process of taping off an area, limiting access, and setting about the task of taking pictures and making meas-

urements ensures the integrity of the evidence found within. Subsequently, any conclusions reached through forensic examinations and reconstructions of that evidence are assumed to be a reliable lens through which to view the crime. This assumption is not always accurate.[23]

Rather, investigators must account for the effects of evidence dynamics in investigating and reconstructing a crime.

> Even though a reliable *chain of evidence* may be established, physical evidence may have been altered prior to or during its collection and examination. Unless the integrity of the evidence can be reliably established, and legitimate evidentiary influences accounted for, the documentation of a chain of evidence, by itself, does not provide acceptable ground upon which to build reliable forensic conclusions.[24]

Chisum and Turvey define evidence dynamics as any influence that changes, relocates, obscures, or obliterates physical evidence, regardless of intent, and begins as evidence is being transferred, and ends when the case is ultimately adjudicated.[25]

Avoiding the introduction of evidence dynamics—at least by those causes that are controllable by the investigator—is vital to preserving the best possible set of physical evidence to aid in investigation and prosecution. For that reason, we will next consider procedures for the preservation of physical evidence.

Photo 3-3

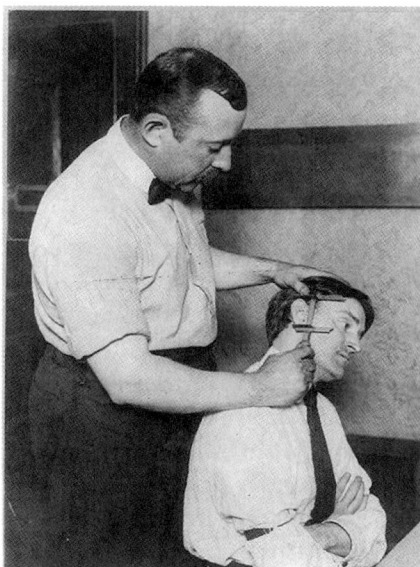

Prior to the use of fingerprints for identification, police used the Bertillon method of identification which consisted of measuring various parts of the body. In the above 1908 photograph a New York City police inspector McCafferty is measuring Deputy Woods at the Tenderloin station house is using Bertillon system of measuring prisoners. Photo courtesy of the Library of Congress.

Preservation of Real Evidence

The key to preserving physical evidence is the proper handling of the crime scene. In 1998 the National Institute of Justice, at the request of U.S. Attorney General Janet Reno, established the 44-member Technical Working Group on Crime Scene Investigation (TWGCSI) to develop guidelines for crime scene management. While most law enforcement agencies have their own internal policies for crime scene management and evidence collection, the TWGCSI guide provides an outline of the general steps to take that will be applicable across nearly all jurisdictions.

1. The initial responding officer(s) shall promptly, yet cautiously, approach and enter crime scenes, remaining observant of any persons, vehicles, events, potential evidence, and environmental conditions.[26] The first responders must balance a set of demanding responsibilities: maintaining situational awareness of any persons or vehicles still present at the scene or leaving it and assessing the scene while assuming that a crime is ongoing until demonstrated otherwise and generally taking steps to ensure officer safety. Because the site must be assumed to be a crime scene until proved otherwise, responders must be particular in their actions so as to minimize the risk of damaging, destroying, or adulterating evidence.

2. The initial responding officer(s) arriving at the scene shall identify and control any dangerous situations or persons.[27] Officers must identify any potential threats to their safety or that of bystanders, ranging from hazardous materials to dangerous persons, and call for backup or supervisory assistance as appropriate while maintaining control of the scene.

3. The initial responding officer(s) shall ensure that medical attention is provided with minimal contamination of the scene.[28] The well-being of victims is the first priority, so medical personnel must be summoned. However, balancing medical care with evidence preservation is delicate. Responders should guide arriving medical personnel to the victims and point out any potential evidence both along the route to the victim and on the victim himself, such as bullet holes, tears, or other damage to clothing. They should document all items or persons moved by medical personnel and ensure that no items are removed or altered in the course of treatment. Any statements by victims (including dying declarations), witnesses, bystanders, or suspects should be documented as well. If at all possible, an officer should accompany any victims transported for medical treatment to ensure the preservation of evidence at the hospital.

4. The initial responding officer(s) shall identify persons at the crime scene and control their movement.[29] If numerous people are present at the scene, this step will be more easily accomplished once backup arrives. Both suspects and witnesses must be secured and separated as soon as possible, while bystanders who are not witnesses must be removed from the scene in order to avoid jeopardizing evidence. Likewise, the victim and any family members or friends must also be controlled, albeit in a compassionate manner. The access and movements of any responding personnel such as paramedics must be controlled, and all unauthorized or nonessen-

tial persons (including members of the media, other law enforcement personnel not working the case, and politicians) must be excluded.

5. The initial responding officer(s) at the scene shall conduct an initial assessment to establish and control the crime scene(s) and its boundaries.[30] The scene boundaries must be determined by the responder, working outward from the focal point of the incident to ensure the boundaries include any entry and egress points used by the suspects and witnesses as well as locations to or from which the victim or evidence may have been moved. Physical barriers must be placed as available and appropriate, and once boundaries are established, the entry and exit of all persons to and from the scene must be documented. Measures must be taken as needed to protect evidence from weather or other environmental factors (such as lawn sprinkler systems) and from damage or destruction by vehicle movement or foot traffic. Any victim or object that is moved must be documented. Finally, officers must monitor their own behavior and that of others present to avoid adulterating the scene:

> Persons should not smoke, chew tobacco, use the telephone or bathroom, eat or drink, move any items including weapons (unless necessary for the safety and well-being of persons at the scene), adjust the thermostat or open windows or doors (maintain scene as found), touch anything unnecessarily (note and document any items moved), reposition moved items, litter, or spit within the established boundaries of the scene.[31]

6. The initial responding officer(s) at the scene shall provide a detailed crime scene briefing to the investigator(s) in charge of the scene.[32] Once the assigned investigator arrives, the responders should brief him or her and continue to assist in controlling the scene while turning over responsibility for the documentation of entry and exit by persons. The responders should not depart until formally relieved.

7. Documentation must be maintained as a permanent record.[33] The responders must document all observations of the crime scene upon arrival, any information gained from suspects, victims, or witnesses, and both their own actions and those of others. This documentation becomes part of the case file.

Once the assigned investigator arrives at the scene, a new set of recommended guidelines takes effect.

1. The investigator(s) in charge shall identify specific responsibilities, share preliminary information, and develop investigative plans in accordance with departmental policy and local, state, and federal laws.[34] This step includes the investigator's side of the crime scene briefing included in the guidelines for first responders. The investigator is also responsible for further evaluating any safety issues for personnel at the scene, as well as following up the work of the first responders: evaluating the scene boundaries they established, identifying and prioritizing scenes if there are multiple sites, and determining an entry/exit route for all personnel entering and leaving the scene. The investigator must also evaluate any search and seizure issues involved in securing further evidence. Secure areas near the scene must be selected for equipment staging and consultation and for temporary evidence storage. Once these measures are in place, the initial investigative work begins: identifying and documenting witnesses, requesting additional investigative re-

sources as needed, executing a canvass of the surrounding area, and beginning the process of documenting and photographing the scene.

2. The investigator(s) in charge shall conduct a walk-through of the scene. The walk-through shall be conducted with individuals responsible for processing the scene.[35] In addition to providing an opportunity for initial documentation of the scene, the walk-through lets the investigator identify evidence that may be fragile, perishable, or otherwise subject to contamination, damage, or destruction by environmental factors. Any such vulnerable evidence should immediately be documented prior to taking steps to preserve it.

3. The investigator(s) in charge shall assess the scene to determine specialized resources required.[36] At this time the investigator commences the processing of the crime scene. The first step is to determine what resources are necessary, such as additional personnel to deal with multiple scenes, multiple victims, a large number of witnesses, and so forth. Qualified personnel are assigned to evidence collection tasks, and forensic technicians are summoned as needed, with all assignments documented.

4. The investigator(s) in charge shall require all personnel to follow procedures to ensure scene safety and evidence integrity.[37] This is the contamination control step, which means enforcing scene and evidence collection control measures. Access and access routes must continue to be controlled, and collection personnel must use appropriate personal protective equipment to avoid contamination of the scene or of themselves (as in the case of potential bloodborne pathogens). All tools and equipment must be sanitized between collections, and in the case of biological evidence, single-use collection kits must be used. In some cases it may be advisable to collect elimination samples from first responders, which allow evidence originating from them to be identified and ruled out.

5. The investigator(s) in charge shall ensure documentation of the scene.[38] The investigator is responsible for determining what forms of documentation are needed at a given scene. These include photographs, video, sketches, and notes. All methods used should be thorough; for example, photography should cover far, medium, and close-up views; evidence both with and without measurement scales and identifiers; people including victims, suspects, witnesses, and bystanders as well as vehicles present; and alternate perspectives such as the point of view of any witnesses at the time they observed the crime or the ground or floor beneath the victim once the body has been moved.

6. The investigator(s) in charge and team members shall determine the order in which evidence is collected.[39] The prioritization of collection must take into account all forms of evidence which may exist even if they have not yet been observed. Generally speaking, collection should proceed from open areas to out-of-view areas, from least intrusive to most intrusive collection methods, and from most transient evidence to least transient. Searches for evidence should be conducted in a systematic manner, and collection methods must not compromise any subsequent collection methods used on the same evidence source. Of course, environmental risks to evidence are among the first considerations.

7. The team member(s) shall ensure the effective collection, preservation, packaging, and transport of evidence.[40] The collection process must be systematic. Each piece of evidence must be identified with its location at the scene, the date of collection, and the identity of the collector. Chain of custody must be established. It is advisable to obtain control samples from the scene, as well as elimination samples in some circumstances. Electronically recorded evidence must be secured as soon as possible. Evidence must be packaged so as to avoid cross-contamination. The initial condition of firearms should be recorded prior to rendering them safe for transport and storage.

8. Law enforcement personnel and other responders shall participate in or initiate a crime scene debriefing to ensure the crime scene investigation is complete and to verify post-scene responsibilities.[41] The debriefing should include all investigators and evidence collectors, as well as first responders if they are available. The debriefing identifies evidence collected and outlines preliminary assessments of the scene, as well as forensic testing to be conducted. It is an opportunity to ensure all necessary evidence collection has been performed before the scene is released.

9. The investigator(s) in charge shall direct a walk-through at the conclusion of the scene investigation and ensure that the scene investigation is complete.[42] At this point a final visual inspection of the scene is performed to ensure that all equipment and materials from the investigation have been removed and that no hazardous conditions remain. The investigator verifies that all evidence collected has been accounted for.

10. The investigator(s) in charge shall ensure that reports and other documentation pertaining to the crime scene investigation are compiled.[43] The case file must include all documentation originating from the scene, from the reports of the first responders to the results of any forensic analysis conducted, as well as any associated legal documents such as search warrants.

Not surprisingly, outdoor crime scenes are the most vulnerable to loss or adulteration of evidence resulting from the various processes of evidence dynamics discussed previously. Weather is generally the most prominent threat, followed by access by unauthorized individuals. Depending on the size, location, and nature of the scene, securing it can be a significant challenge—consider the differences between an alleyway and an open field in a large city park.

If weather is a threat, the best strategy is to collect vulnerable evidence as quickly as possible without compromising its integrity. Unlike a building that can probably be locked, securing an outdoor scene will almost always require keeping personnel present. Obviously, given a crime scene that is partially indoors and partially outdoors, investigators should prioritize handling of the outdoor portion.

Processing a scene at night is particularly challenging. No matter how well-lit the scene may be, the probability of overlooking evidence is high. The best strategy is to secure the scene for processing during daylight—assuming, of course, that factors such as weather or the ability to secure the scene do not create an even greater risk of evidence loss or adulteration.[44]

While indoor crime scenes are protected from weather and easier to secure, it is still necessary to limit as much as possible access to the site even by authorized personnel.

Especially in the case of biological trace evidence that may be used in DNA analysis, the more people who access the scene, the greater the probability of contamination. First responders, EMTs, crime scene technicians, and medical examiners all have legitimate reasons to be present, but access should be kept to a minimum, and personnel present should be supervised to ensure they are not tainting evidence.[45]

A hybrid of the indoor and outdoor crime scenes is the conveyance—a vehicle that is involved in (or is the scene of) the commission of a crime. Like indoor sites they tend to be easier to secure, and in many cases a vehicle can be impounded and transported to secure storage, but like outdoor sites they are more vulnerable to weather since evidence may be present on the exterior of the conveyance as well as the interior. It is also important to remember that additional evidence is likely to be found surrounding the vehicle, such as footprints created or items dropped as a suspect fled. This portion of the site is little different from an outdoor scene in its handling.[46]

Securing usable, untainted physical evidence from a scene requires what the National Forensic Science Technology Center (NFSTC) describes as a deliberate, methodical, disciplined approach to collection and preservation of evidence. This is particularly true with biological material that may yield DNA evidence. While DNA analysis is powerful, it is also subject to contamination by anyone who is present at the scene and/or handles physical evidence.

The collection process should be informed by all available information about the crime and crime scene that are available, typically as initially gained from first responders, witnesses, and/or victims. A good understanding of the circumstances of the crime can guide the investigator to the areas that should be prioritized in the search for evidence. For a crime involving forced entry, for example, the first search would be of the entry point, where the suspect may have left clothing fibers, fingerprints, paint from a tool, or even blood during the process of gaining entry. Also, samples of glass, wood, metal, paint, and other materials present at the entry point should be collected for possible matching against any such evidence discovered on the clothing of a future suspect. Next, the areas around the entry point should be examined for footprints, dropped items, and other possible material, including soil and vegetation samples for anything that might have been deposited on the offender's clothing.[47]

A violent crime such as an assault or rape is likely to leave the most possible evidence on the victim and suspect themselves. Fingerprints, fibers, hair, cosmetics, tissue, and bodily fluids such as blood, semen, saliva, and vaginal fluid may be found on both the body and clothing of either party or both. The assailant could well have injuries from the victim's defensive efforts such as bite marks or scratches that leave tissue fragments under the victim's fingernails, and the same sorts of evidence may be found on the suspect as well.[48]

Fragile evidence such as trace transfers and biological material should be collected first and packaged in such a manner that protects the evidence from environmental effects and cross-contamination. Collectors should use full protective equipment including Tyvek body suits, gloves, shoe covers, and hair nets particularly when dealing with biological samples vulnerable to contamination. It may be necessary to employ oblique lighting and alternate light sources such as ultraviolet (UV) to detect some trace evidence.[49]

Specific collection methods vary according to the type of evidence and the nature of the substrate (the surface on which the evidence is found). The table below shows the methods recommended by the NFSTC.[50]

Trace evidence is often vital to establishing or proving a connection between an individual and a particular location or another individual. Here we will consider some common forms of trace evidence, their uses and limitations, and collection methods.

Table 3-1. Blood & Other Body Fluids

Type of Collection	Procedure
Cuttings	Removal of a section of the item containing the stain using a sterile or clean cutting device.
Wet Absorption	A sterile swab, gauze pad, or threads are slightly moistened with sterile distilled water. An effort should be made to concentrate the stain in a localized portion of the swab or pad. For example, when using a swab, the stain should be concentrated on the tip. The collection medium is concentrated into the stain and allowed to air dry. Some laboratories recommend following the first moistened swabbing with a second dry swabbing to ensure thorough sample collection. Both swabs are retained and submitted for analysis.
Scraping Method	Using a clean razor blade or scalpel, the sample is scraped into a clean piece of paper that can be folded and packaged in a paper envelope or other appropriate packaging.
Lifting with Tape	For dried blood stains on a non-absorbent surface, fingerprint lifting tape may be placed over the stain and lifted off. The stain is transferred to the adhesive side of the tape, which may then be secured on a clear piece of acetate for submission to the laboratory.

Table 3-2. Hair & Fiber Collection

Type of Collection	Procedure
Visual Collection	On some surfaces, hairs and fibers can be seen with the naked eye. Using clean forceps and trace paper, the sample can be removed from the surface and placed into a clean piece of paper that can be folded and packaged in a paper envelope or other appropriate packaging.
Tape Lifting	Water- or methanol-soluble tapes are available for the collection of trace hair and fiber evidence. The tape is applied to the location of the suspected sample, removed, and packaged.
Vacuuming Method	The area where the suspected samples are located are vacuumed up and caught in a filtered trap attached to the vacuum. These samples are packaged in clean trace paper or submission to the laboratory. Vacuuming is the least desirable collection method because there is a risk of cross contamination if the equipment is not properly cleaned between each use.

Hair: A single hair can be identified as human or animal, and for human hair analysis can determine from what part of the body the hair originated. Testing can determine chemical composition, color, shape, and in many cases the race of the person from which it originated. Should the hair include the follicle, DNA testing is possible, but otherwise hair is normally used only for comparison to exclude a suspect. Control samples are collected from a suspect for comparison with evidentiary samples and should come from all parts of the body (multiple locations on the head, the body, and the pubic area).[51]

Fibers: Fibers originate from fabric or similar textiles like carpet. They are broadly classified as natural (wool, silk, cotton, etc.), synthetic (entirely manmade, such as nylon and polyester), or manufactured (based on natural materials but reorganized, such as rayon). On one hand fiber evidence can be extremely useful. Fibers are distinctive, and they are also very mobile and cling easily to shoes, clothing, hair, and so forth. A person entering a carpeted room, for example, will almost certainly leave with carpet fibers on their shoes. However, this mobility is also a liability, as fibers can easily be brushed away or become airborne, meaning fiber evidence can be very perishable. Collection is normally by tweezers for larger fibers. An area can also be vacuumed with the sample obtained separated later at the laboratory. Fiber evidence may be collected with tape, but the destructive effects of the adhesive make this a less-preferred option.[52]

Glass: Glass commonly plays a role in evidence collection by acting as a depository surface for fingerprints or blood. However, tiny fragments of broken glass may linger in clothing, shoes, skin, or hair. Analysis can determine the origin and nature of a glass sample, as window glass is markedly different from windshield glass, which is in turn different from a vase, drinking glass, or bottle. Tweezers or tape can be used to collect fragments identified with a magnifying glass, but as with fibers tape is less preferred because of the effects of the adhesive.[53]

Paint: Among forms of trace evidence, paint is one of the most valuable. One reason is that it is found in so many places. Another is that its color provides an easy starting point for investigation. A third is that it has physical and chemical properties that make it possible to identify very specifically—in the case of automotive paint, for example, it can be used to identify the make, model, and sometimes even year of the vehicle from which it originated. Paint also tends to transfer relatively easily under violent conditions—think of a vehicle striking another vehicle, a pedestrian, or a building, or of a tool used to force entry. Samples are normally collected from an original surface by scraping down to the metal or other substrate in order to capture all layers, or from a surface where it has been deposited by careful scraping that does not disturb any underlying paint original to the depository surface. For vehicle collisions in particular, preserving the edges of transferred paint chips is important to enable fracture matching against the originating surface.[54]

A significant advancement in the analysis of trace evidence is the development of databases of commonly used substances. The FBI, for example, maintains the National Automotive Paint File, a compilation of over 45,000 samples of automotive paint dating back to the 1930s. Standards databases make it possible to trace carpet fiber to a specific manufacturer once its chemical composition is known.[55] This makes matching or identifying the origin of a sample obtained from a crime scene a relatively simple matter. A list of databases useful in forensic analysis along with a description of their utilization, abilities, and limitations can be found in the *National Institute of Justice Journal* available at http://www.nij.gov/journals/258/Pages/forensic-databases.aspx.

Despite what television shows and movies involving criminal investigations might have us believe, however, trace evidence is not all-powerful. As explained previously with hair, for example, absent a follicle that enables DNA testing a hair sample can only be used conclusively to exclude a suspect. A match does not establish that the hair in question came from a particular individual, although it may represent a piece of circumstantial evidence used to construct a case. In fact, when it comes to confirming rather than excluding, trace evidence can offer only levels of certainty. While there is no universally accepted formal scale for measuring certainty, the FBI Laboratory Scientific Working Group for Material Analysis proposed a conclusion scale in 2009 intended to quantify the level of certainty resulting from evidence analysis.[56]

Table 3-3. Level of Certainty Resulting from Evidence Analysis

Identified (Type I Association)	A positive identification; an association in which items share **individual** characteristics that show with reasonable scientific certainty that the items were once from the same source.
Very Strong Support	An association in which items are consistent in all measured physical properties or chemical properties and share **highly unusual** characteristic(s) that are unexpected in the population of this evidence type.
Strong Support (Type II Association)	An association in which items are consistent in all measured physical properties or chemical properties and share **unusual** characteristic(s) that are unexpected in the population of this evidence type.
Moderately Strong Support (Type III Association)	An association in which items are consistent in all measured physical properties or chemical properties and could have originated from the same source. Because similar items have been manufactured or could exist in nature and could be indistinguishable from the submitted evidence, an individual source cannot be determined.
Moderate Support (Type IV Association)	An association in which items are consistent in all measured physical properties or chemical properties and so could have originated from the same source. This sample type is commonly encountered in our environment and may have limited associative value.
Limited Support (Type V Association)	An association in which some minor variation exists between the known and questioned items that could be due to factors such as sample heterogeneity, contamination of the sample(s), or the quality of the sample. The items may be associated, but other sources exist with the same level of association.
Inconclusive	No conclusion can be reached regarding the association between the items.
Elimination	The items are dissimilar in physical properties or chemical composition and did not originate from the same source.

It is important to understand that this scale will not necessarily be accepted in every court, but it does provide a point of reference in determining how strongly a given piece of evidence supports the theory of the crime under investigation.

Chain of Custody and Authentication

The integrity of physical evidence—and its admissibility in a criminal proceeding—is tied directly to the chain of custody. Just as a chain with a single broken link is unable to function, failure at any point along the chain of custody to maintain its integrity will render evidence useless. For evidence to be reliable, it must be possible to confirm that (1) the evidence being presented or analyzed is the same evidence that was collected at the crime scene and (2) all access to the evidence was both controlled and documented to ensure that it was not tainted either deliberately or inadvertently.[57]

As evidence is gathered, it must be properly packaged and labeled. Labeling procedures will vary from jurisdiction to jurisdiction but typically include the name of the person collecting the evidence and the date, time, and location of its collection at a minimum; a case number and the names of the victim and/or defendant are also commonly included. Packaging standards vary according to the type of evidence. The *Physical Evidence Manual* of the Oregon State Police provides us with several examples.

Arson evidence: Because arson crimes frequently involve accelerants that are volatile and will therefore evaporate if exposed to open air, arson evidence is to be sealed in airtight containers, preferably metal cans. Heat-sealable plastic bags are acceptable if specifically manufactured to contain flammable evidence but, if used, must be accompanied by an unused bag to serve as a control.[58]

Biological evidence: This type of evidence can take many forms, but packaging guidelines are generally similar. Wet or moist evidence should never be placed in plastic packaging since the trapped moisture can accelerate natural decay processes and cause the sample to degrade. Rather, such evidence should be dried and placed in paper or cardboard packaging. This includes the collection of large quantities of liquid blood, which should be collected on sterile cotton swabs which are then allowed to air-dry. On surfaces that permit it, such as upholstery or carpeting, the section containing the bloodstain can be cut out in its entirety. Sources of saliva evidence can often be collected and submitted whole—cigarette butts, chewing gum, drinking containers, and the like. If not, samples are collected in a manner similar to blood. In all cases, biological samples must be packaged separately to avoid cross-contamination.[59]

Controlled substances: Live plants or plant material and all other damp or wet evidence must be dried prior to packaging, with the exception of fresh khat which is frozen and must not be placed in airtight packages. A substance suspected to contain LSD must be kept away from direct light. Liquid samples from clandestine drug laboratories should be placed in glass vials and then packaged in an outer plastic container filled with an absorbent substance in the event of breakage during transportation.[60]

Again, the preceding examples are specific to the Oregon State Police forensics laboratory; exact procedures may vary from jurisdiction to jurisdiction. However, they should provide some idea of considerations all labs will face in handling evidence.

Any chain of custody system must identify (1) all persons who have possessed the evidence (called custodians) beginning with its collection and (2) "any changes to the state or condition of the item" or else documentation that its condition has not been materially altered.[61] Chain of custody records normally include information about the person who initially observed or collected the object, documentation of the possession of the object by that person, its transportation to a laboratory, its possession by laboratory technicians, its retrieval from the laboratory, its deposit into secure storage, and its final transport to court.

Some forms of evidence are considered self-authenticating under the Federal Rules of Evidence, but most of these are documentary in nature, not physical. Per rule 901(b)(4), a piece of physical evidence may be self-authenticating based on its appearance, contents, substance, internal patterns, or other distinctive characteristics of the item, taken together with all the circumstances.[62] However, for physical evidence the issue is less about identity than relevance.

> A chain of custody may be required to authenticate an object of physical evidence that has no unique identifying characteristic. It is always required where the object's relevance is not based on simple authentication, as where the condition of the object speaks for itself, but is instead based on characteristics which require explanation by an expert who has tested it. In this instance, the chain of custody is required not only to authenticate the object, but to document the fact that it was not materially altered before the expert examined it.[63]

Unique characteristics include obvious ones such as serial numbers noted upon evidence collection; as a note of historical interest, this was the means used at trial to identify the rifle used by Lee Harvey Oswald. They also include common police practices such as initials placed on the object in an indelible fashion, if the witness can later identify his initials.[64]

However, even evidence possessed of "distinctive characteristics" is normally subject to chain of custody procedures, and this is a sound practice, particularly for evidence that may prove crucial to the trial. A firearm will normally have a serial number, but if the presence of the suspect's fingerprints on that weapon is important to the case, the chain of custody is necessary to authenticate that aspect of the evidence. Moreover, even in cases where an object of physical evidence has distinctive characteristics, it is still prudent to document the chain of custody because the issue of authentication will remain as a matter of credibility.[65] In other words, a defense attorney will be perfectly justified in raising doubt in the minds of jurors regarding that particular piece of evidence. Also, the lack of a well-documented chain of custody will provide defense counsel with a ready-made issue for appeal.[66]

Since excluding damaging physical evidence makes the job of defense counsel much easier, it is important for investigators to understand typical defense strategies for attacking physical evidence.

- Argue that the object is unduly prejudicial to the defendant.[67] In the "Materiality" section earlier in this chapter, we discussed this notion, particularly as it relates to crime scene photographs that are especially gory. The "gruesome objects" balancing test weighs the prejudicial effect against the defendant versus the value of the evidence to the jury in deciding the case. Precedent has held that crime scene photographs "are admissible at trial even if they are gory, gruesome, horrible, or revolting so long as they are used by a witness to illustrate his testimony and so long as an excessive number of photographs are not used solely to arouse the passions of the jury."[68]

- Argue that the person collecting the object was prejudiced towards the defendant and had planted the evidence.[69] The main defense against this tactic is careful adherence to crime scene analysis procedures. Sound procedures and a high level of professionalism in executing them make this charge harder for the jury to believe and in any event minimize the opportunities for fraudulent introduction of evidence.
- Try to show that the object is not relevant.[70] Again, under the Federal Rules of Evidence relevance is key to admissibility.
- Argue that the officer cannot positively identify the object as the same object that the officer had recovered at the crime scene.[71] This attack is best countered by careful adherence to evidence-marking procedures.
- Try to prove that the object was tampered with.[72] The chain of custody must be rigorously documented to defend against this charge.
- Argue that it is contaminated in such a way that the object no longer can prove the fact intended.[73] Again, this is the reason for chain of custody and evidence handling and storage procedures.
- Argue that the evidence was collected by an incompetent investigator.[74] Your professionalism, training, adherence to procedures, and demeanor on the witness stand are best used to block this attack.

The last thing any investigator wants is to see his or her careful work in compiling a case wasted because of sloppiness in handling, processing, or storing evidence. Procedures exist for a reason, and they definitely matter.

Physical Evidence and Defense Counsel

For the law enforcement officer who works the opposing side of the American adversarial system of justice, the question of how a suspect's defense attorney would handle physical evidence might never arise. Yet the possibility that an attorney could come into possession of evidence not discovered by police is a very real one—so much so that the American Bar Association has promulgated guidelines for defense attorneys to handle such circumstances. In order that investigators fully understand the responsibilities of defense counsel, we will consider those guidelines here.

Situations that might seem clear-cut to the law enforcement officer can be fraught with questions for a defense attorney. The potential conflict is between the attorney's duty of competence, confidentiality, and loyalty and the obligation to serve the best interests of clients despite the clients' unpopularity or the heinous nature of the defendants' alleged crimes on the one hand, and the legal requirement to act within the bounds of the law in carrying out the duty to zealously protect and pursue a client's legitimate interests on the other.[75]

Attorneys face a variety of sources that provide generalized guidance or (less frequently) specific rules for dealing with such situations. They are

- The Model Rules of Professional Conduct of the American Bar Association (ABA);
- Section 119 of Restatement (Third) of the Law Governing Lawyers;
- ABA Standard 4-4.6;
- In some jurisdictions, state statutes; and
- Various legal precedents established by courts at all levels, particularly the state.

The Model Rules of Professional Conduct are probably the most general and therefore least helpful. The *Preamble* to the Model Rules emphasizes that an attorney must always act within the bounds of the law when protecting a client's interests, but as Uphoff notes, "The bounds of the law, however, are not always easily determined."[76]

According to Model Rule 8.4, an attorney may not commit a criminal act, engage in dishonest or deceitful conduct, or engage in conduct prejudicial to the administration of justice. Model Rule 3.4(a) specifies that an attorney may not unlawfully obstruct another party's access to evidence or unlawfully alter, destroy, or conceal a document or other material having potential evidentiary value nor counsel or assist another person to do any of these forbidden acts. However, Uphoff points out that not all conduct that obstructs, alters, destroys, or conceals evidence violates Rule 3.4 based on its use of the word "unlawfully."[77] Yet the net effect of this rule is to direct the attorney back to the laws of the jurisdiction in which he or she is operating, which may or may not specify the bounds of allowable conduct in such matters.

Unfortunately, moving to an examination of state laws does not do much to clarify the situation. Uphoff quotes Joy and McMunigal in describing the criminal law relating to obstruction of justice as complicated, ambiguous, and subject to considerable jurisdictional variations.[78] Some jurisdictions do exempt attorneys from at least some of the criminal obstruction of justice statutes, but this is uncommon. Generally there are no safe harbor provisions for defense counsel. On occasion courts have interpreted such statutes in such a way that defense attorneys deemed to have acted in good faith were not subject to criminal prosecution or disciplinary action, but reliance on an assumption that specific conduct will after the fact be determined to have been in good faith is risky, and the mere threat of criminal prosecution or disciplinary sanctions may well chill some defense lawyers from taking action that a zealous advocate ought to be willing to take in defending a client.[79]

Such court decisions have run the gamut. A small sampling follows.

***Commonwealth v. Stenhach*, 517 Pa. 589; 534 A. 2d 769; 1987 Pa.:** While incriminating physical evidence is not protected by any privilege, and defense counsel has a duty to deliver it to the prosecution immediately after a reasonable time for examination, meaning the public defenders charged in this case acted wrongly, these (Pennsylvania obstruction of justice) statutes do not provide enough notice for what might constitute a crime in these kinds of circumstances.[80] In other words, defense counsel should have turned the evidence in their possession over to police, but they were not guilty of violating the law because the relevant Pennsylvania statutes were far from clear.

***In re* Original Grand Jury Investigation, 89 Ohio St. 3d 544, 733 N.E. 2d 1135 (2000):** An attorney was deemed obligated by law to turn over to the grand jury an incriminating letter written by his client. In this case a subpoena had been issued, but ethically an attorney is required to turn over physical evidence even in the absence of a court order.[81]

State *ex rel.* **Hyder v. Superior Court of Maricopa County, 128 Ariz. 253, 625 P.2d 316 (1981):** The duty of non-disclosure covers the periods prior to and subsequent to the creation of the attorney-client relationship as well as during the duration of the relationship.[82]

Commonwealth v. Hughes, **380 Mass. 583, 404 N.E. 2d 1239,** *cert. denied*, **449 U.S. 900 (1980):** A defendant charged with assault with a deadly weapon was ordered to produce a pistol registered in his name after a police search turned up neither the pistol nor any related evidence. The defendant refused and was held in contempt.[83] The upshot of the obvious Fifth Amendment issue created here is that by extension, mandatory disclosure rules imposed on attorneys potentially may enable the government to obtain from defense counsel voluntarily what it cannot constitutionally obtain from a defendant by use of a subpoena.[84]

Dean v. Dean, **607 So. 2d 494 (1992):** Florida's Fourth District Court of Appeal recognized that it promoted public policy to permit a lawyer to return stolen property to the police without being compelled to identify the client.[85] (This is one of the alternatives available under some interpretation of various rules in cases where the possession of stolen property is an issue.)

People v. Belge, **372 N.Y.S. 2d 788 (Onondaga Co. 1975):** This decision in this case, affirmed twice on appeal, held that confidential communications between a client and an attorney are subject to attorney-client privilege. The particulars of this case involved a homicide allegedly committed by Robert F. Garrow, Jr. Francis R. Belge was one of the attorneys assigned to Garrow who, based on information provided by Garrow, located the body of Alicia Hauck in a cemetery. At that time he inspected the body and confirmed to his satisfaction that it was in fact the body of the individual Garrow claimed to have murdered. When this examination was subsequently revealed during trial as part of Garrow's insanity defense, Belge was indicated by the county grand jury for two violations of New York law: failing to provide a "decent burial" to the dead and failing to report the death of any person without medical attendance to the authorities.[86] An *amicus curiae* brief supplied by the National Association of Criminal Defense Lawyers and cited by the decision referred to *Leary v. United States*,[87] which asserted that the defendant may not be obligated to provide a significant link in a chain of evidence tending to establish his guilt and that by extension. The client's Fifth Amendment rights cannot be violated by his attorney.[88]

Magill v. Superior Court, **103 Cal. Rptr. 2d 355 (2001):** This California case reached the opposite conclusion of New York's *People v. Belge*. Magill, an attorney, had been contacted by an individual who wanted him to photograph a van owned by the individual and a trailer that he had rented and provide those photographs to the California Highway Patrol (CHP) in order to determine whether law enforcement was seeking that particular vehicle in connection with a hit-and-run accident that had occurred a short time previously. Ultimately the CHP sought and obtained a warrant to seize the photographs, some of which included the license plate of the vehicle. Magill petitioned for exclusion of the photographs, claiming that they were protected by attorney-client privilege. The court disagreed, though noting that the circumstances of the case were "unusual."[89]

Henderson v. State, 962 S.W. 2d 544 (Tx. Ct. of Crim. App. 1998): During the course of an interview with a woman accused of murdering a baby she was babysitting, Hall, a federal public defender, had the defendant draw a detailed map showing where she had buried the baby. Hall provided the map to the woman's Texas attorneys (she had been arrested in Kansas), and subsequently the Texas authorities successfully subpoenaed the map and used it to locate the infant's remains—which needless to say were crucial to the prosecution—although the map itself was not introduced at trial. The Texas Court of Criminal Appeals found that while the map was indeed a privileged document under attorney-client privilege, in this case that privilege was subordinated to the strong public interest of protecting a child from death or serious bodily injury. While the rationale might be sound, some observers found its application in this specific case particularly strained given the remote possibility that the baby was alive.[90]

Physical Evidence in Criminal Prosecutions

While theoretical discussions of physical evidence in criminal investigation and prosecution are all well and good, and certainly necessary, it can be helpful to see how forensics have factored into real-world cases. Following are ten high-profile criminal cases of the twentieth century—dating as far back as 1932—that were significantly impacted by the use of physical evidence.

One of the most famous criminal cases of the 1930s was the kidnapping of Charles Lindbergh's 20-month-old son in March 1932. Although the Lindberghs paid a ransom of $50,000, Charles Lindbergh, Jr. was never returned. The child's body was discovered in May 1932 not far from his home. Law enforcement tracked serial numbers of the currency used to pay the ransom, which led them to Bruno Hauptmann. Hauptmann still had over $14,000 from the ransom payment in his possession. Two key pieces of forensic evidence were used to convict Hauptmann. One was analysis of the handwriting in the ransom note, which matched that of Hauptmann. The other was comparison of the wood from Hauptmann's attic, which matched that used in the construction of a ladder used in the kidnapping.[91]

Another famous kidnapping of the 1930s was that of Oklahoma oilman Charles Urschel. He was kidnapped in July 1933 by George "Machine Gun" Kelly, who demanded a ransom of $200,000 dollars—the largest ransom ever paid up to that time. Urschel was extremely attentive during his kidnapping and provided details of his environment that enabled the FBI to identify the location in which he was held. The main evidence used to conduct Kelly, however, was forensic: Urschel was careful to place as many of his fingerprints as possible throughout the house during his captivity.[92]

In 1970 Clifford Irving and Richard Suskind approached publisher McGraw-Hill with letters supposedly from eccentric billionaire recluse Howard Hughes. The men claimed that Hughes had agreed to allow them to write his biography, under the condition that he would correspond only with them. McGraw-Hill paid $765,000 for rights to the book. When news of the biography became public, however, Hughes denounced it as a fraud. He would only speak to reporters by telephone, so forensic experts conducted a spectrographic voiceprint analysis to confirm that the speaker was indeed

Hughes. (Another type of forensic analysis had fallen short, however; handwriting analysis had failed to identify the letters that Irving and Suskind had presented as forgeries.) The two men eventually confessed to the hoax and served time in prison. (Irving, ironically enough, subsequently wrote a book about the scheme to forge the will, and in 2008 his story was even made into a motion picture.)[93]

In early 1970, the pregnant wife and two children of Jeffrey MacDonald, an Army physician, were stabbed to death in what MacDonald reported had been a home invasion by four men. MacDonald survived with minor wounds. Investigators immediately suspected the doctor, but the Army, which originally had jurisdiction over the case, eventually dropped the prosecution because the investigative techniques used had been so poor. MacDonald was subsequently brought to trial in a civilian court, however, and there a forensic scientist testified that a key piece of evidence—the doctor's pajama top, which he claimed to have used in defending himself against the intruders— almost certainly could not have been damaged as a result of self-defense. Rather, it was clear that the top, which had 48 knife holes, had been folded four times and placed on the body of MacDonald's wife, who had been stabbed exactly 21 times. The crime scene reconstruction provided by forensic analysts was the major factor in MacDonald's conviction on three counts of murder.[94]

The notorious serial killer Ted Bundy proved extremely difficult to tie to his murders. Arrested in 1975, he was convicted only of kidnapping because of a lack of physical evidence linking him to any of the 30 or more murders he is believed to have committed. He escaped from jail in Colorado while standing trial for murder in 1977 and fled to Florida, where he killed another three victims in 1978. Recaptured in February 1978, Bundy was eventually convicted for the murder of Lisa Levy based on a match between his very distinctive dental patterns and a bite mark on Levy's buttock, as well as for the murder of 12-year-old Kimberly Leach based on fibers found in his van that were matched to the girl's clothing.[95]

The "BTK Killer" who operated in the Wichita, Kansas area between 1974 and 1991 was so named because he liked to bind, torture, and kill his victims. He was also an egotistical attention hound and constantly sent letters to the media to taunt police. Responsible for 10 murders, the killer disappeared for several years and then began communicating with the media again in 2004. It was this new communication that led to his identification, because he chose to send a computer floppy disk to a local newspaper. Forensic analysts used deleted data recovered from the disk to link it to someone named Dennis at a Wichita church, leading investigators to Dennis Rader, who confessed and was convicted for nine murders.[96]

A serial killer operating in the Atlanta area strangled 29 victims, mostly children, between 1979 and 1981. The killer dumped a number of the bodies in a local river, so police staked out the river and eventually arrested Wayne Williams as he drove away from a location where police had heard a splash. Williams had not actually been seen dumping a body, but the arrest led to the collection of an extensive array of fiber evidence that tied victims to the suspect's home, vehicles, and dog. He was eventually convicted for the murders of two adults, although police were confident that he was also the perpetrator of at least most of the child murders.[97]

In 1983 two boys were murdered in Omaha, Nebraska. One body was found bound with an unusual type of rope that police were unable to identify. Acting on a report of a suspicious individual who appeared to be watching a local school, investigators traced the license plate of the reported vehicle to John Joubert, who was stationed at a nearby Air Force base. A search turned up more of the same unusual rope in Joubert's possession, and its rarity—Joubert had obtained it while in Korea—was sufficient to prompt a confession from the suspect. Hair from one of the boys was also discovered in his vehicle. Police subsequently tied Joubert to a third murder in Maine in 1982 when his dental patterns were matched to bite marks on that boy.[98]

Another highly publicized serial killer was the Night Stalker of Southern California, who broke into homes during the night and murdered or assaulted the occupants. He killed 13 and injured many others between June 1984 and August 1985. A report of a suspicious vehicle in a neighborhood that happened to be near the site of a recent attack eventually led police to an abandoned vehicle. Forensic technicians were able to recover a fingerprint from the car, which was matched to Richard Ramirez. Police widely publicized pictures of Ramirez, who was identified and arrested a week later.[99]

The Green River Killer, who specialized in prostitutes, killed 48 (and possibly as many as 90) women in Washington in the 1980s and 1990s, with most of the murders occurring in 1982 and 1983. Investigators had named Gary Ridgway as a person of interest in 1983 because of prior conduct with prostitutes, but DNA samples collected in 1987 were inconclusive as the technology was still in its early stages. Improved DNA analysis techniques led to new testing in 2001 that linked Ridgway to the killings, and he eventually confessed. He was convicted of 48 of the murders and subsequently claimed to have committed even more.[100]

These historical examples demonstrate how forensic analysis of physical evidence can be used to break cases and convict perpetrators. However, it should be noted as well that traditional investigative techniques were also crucial, in many cases leading investigators to the key evidence—tips from the public in the case of Joubert and Ramirez or the profiling of known offenders in the case of Ridgway. Forensic analysis is not a magic wand, and as we noted in the introduction, generally speaking a suspect is identified through traditional investigation, and only then is physical evidence used to confirm that suspect's association with the crime.

Conclusion

Physical evidence can be the defining feature of a criminal prosecution, the "smoking gun," bloodstain, fingerprint, or fiber sample that convinces the jury to convict. However, physical evidence is not all-powerful. First, it often has no value until traditional investigative techniques lead to a suspect. Second, it must be collected, handled, and analyzed with care in order to preserve its admissibility and value in a court of law. Understanding the constraints under which attorneys operate in dealing with physical evidence is important for the investigator or even for the first responder, who may be the first one at a crime scene and responsible for protecting and preserving the evidence that is present there. Failure at any step along the way can make the otherwise most convincing piece of evidence useless for the prosecutor.

Practicum

Evaluate the following circumstances (all of which are based on real-world cases) and identify potential causes of evidence dynamics and the impact on crime scene reconstruction. (All scenarios are drawn from "Evidence Dynamics: Locard's Exchange Principle & Crime Reconstruction" in the *Journal of Behavioral Profiling*, cited previously.)

Practicum One

The body of a female rape-homicide victim is discovered. The victim had been sexually assaulted and had her throat cut. Crime scene photographs show distinctive bloodstain patterns on her clothing, including possible handprints on her panties. However, the coroner refuses to allow the removal of the victim's clothing prior to removal of the body, and the remains are placed in a body bag for transport to the laboratory.

As investigator on the scene, what would you recommend?

Practicum Two

The body of a deceased elderly man is found in his bed by investigators upon their arrival. However, examination reveals ligature marks on his neck. No source of the marks is apparent.

How would you as the lead detective on the scene handle the situation?

Practicum Three

The body of an adolescent female is discovered on a couch in her home, which she shares with her mother and brother. She is determined to have died from strangulation and is wearing only a shirt and bra. Physical examination shows evidence of prior sexual abuse, including the absence of her hymen and anal scarring. The victim also had a history of promiscuity. At the laboratory, semen is found on her perineum, and the DNA matches one of her mother's lovers. However, the mother and the suspect had previously had sexual relations on the couch where the victim was found, as well as in the mother's bed, where the victim had played earlier with her brother. In addition, video from the crime scene shows several evidence technicians moving evidence on and around the couch as well as touching the victim's body; some were gloved and some were not.

What conclusions would you draw from the above information?

Practicum Four

A young man is stabbed multiple times by rival gang members. He flees to his home but collapses on the sidewalk outside. Photographs taken by first responders show a blood trail and the victim lying face down. Paramedics arrive and roll the youth onto his back as they render medical assistance.

What steps would you take to preserve the crime scene?

Summary

- Perhaps no aspect of police investigative work so fascinates the general public as that of forensics.
- It is important to note that physical evidence is generally not very effective at identifying a culprit when one is not already known.
- Typically the identity of the culprit is developed in some other way and then physical evidence is used to help establish proof of guilt.
- Fingerprints are the major exception to this principle, but even then a fingerprint found at a crime scene must already be in a database in order to produce a match; otherwise, it can only provide confirmation after the fact.
- For that evidence to be useful in the courtroom, it must have been properly handled from the moment an officer arrives at the crime scene.
- Physical or real evidence can take numerous forms.
- Relevant evidence is defined as "having any tendency in reason to prove any material matter and includes opinion evidence and hearsay evidence."
- Rule 402 of the Federal Rules of Evidence states plainly, "Evidence which is not relevant is not admissible."
- The first systematic use of factual information to aid in law enforcement is generally credited to Alphonse Bertillon, a clerk in the Paris police force.
- The key to preserving physical evidence is the proper handling of the crime scene.
- The integrity of physical evidence—and its admissibility in a criminal proceeding—is tied directly to the chain of custody.
- As evidence is gathered, it must be properly packaged and labeled.
- Some forms of evidence are considered self-authenticating under the Federal Rules of Evidence, but most of these are documentary in nature, not physical.

Questions in Review

1. What constitutes physical evidence?
2. Why is it important to handle physical evidence in prescribed ways?
3. Explain how evidence is authenticated at trial time.
4. What is meant by the term the "integrity of physical evidence"?
5. What are the keys to preserving physical evidence?

Key Terms

Chain of Custody: The term chain of custody, in legal contexts, refers to the chronological documentation or paper trail, showing the seizure, custody, control, transfer, analysis, and disposition of physical or electronic evidence.

Materiality: Materiality is a legal term. When speaking of facts, the term generally means a fact which is significant to the issue or matter at hand.

Physical Evidence: Physical evidence usually involves objects found at the scene of a crime. Physical evidence may consist of all sorts of prints such as fingerprints, footprints, handprints, tidemarks, cut marks, tool marks, etc.

Trace Evidence: Trace evidence is created when objects contact. Material is often transferred by heat or induced by contact friction.

Endnotes

1. (2014). Police: Criminal Investigations—Sources of Information and Evidence in Criminal Investigations. Accessed online at http://law.jrank.org/pages/1656/Police-Criminal-Investigations-Sources-information-evidence-in-criminal-investigations.html. (Accessed on February 12, 2015).

2. (2007). Types of Evidence. Largo, FL: National Forensic Science Technology Center. Accessed online at http://www.nfstc.org/pdi/Subject01/pdi_s01_m01_01.htm. (Accessed on February 12, 2015).

3. Ibid.

4. Nemeth, Charles P. (2011). Law and Evidence: A Primer for Criminal Justice, Criminology, Law and Legal Studies, p. 7. Burlington, MA: Jones & Bartlett Learning. Accessed online at http://samples.jbpub.com/9780763766610/CH01.pdf. (Accessed on February 12, 2015).

5. Ibid.

6. Ibid, p. 9.

7. Ibid.

8. Ibid.

9. Ibid.

10. Ibid, p. 10.

11. Ibid.

12. Ibid, pp. 10–11.

13. Ibid, p. 11.

14. Ibid, pp. 16–17.

15. Chisum, W. J. and Turvey, B. (January 2000). Evidence Dynamics: Locard's Exchange Principle & Crime Reconstruction. Journal of Behavioral Profiling (1:1). Accessed online at http://www.profiling.org/journal/vol1_no1/jbp_ed_january2000_1-1.html. (Accessed on February 12, 2015).

16. Ibid.

17. Ibid.

18. Ibid.

19. Rothchild, Irving (2006). Induction, Deduction, and the Scientific Method: An Eclectic Overview of the Practice of Science. Cleveland, OH: Case Western Reserve University School of Medicine, pp. 2–3. Accessed online at http://www.ssr.org/sites/ssr.org/files/uploads/attachments/node/16/rothchild_scimethod.pdf. (Accessed on February 14, 2015).

20. Ibid, p. 3.

21. Ibid.

22. Chisum and Turvey.

23. Ibid.

24. Ibid.

25. Ibid.

26. Technical Working Group on Crime Scene Investigation (January 2000). Crime Scene Investigation. Washington, D.C.: National Institute of Justice, p. 11. Accessed online at http://www.fbi.gov/about-us/lab/forensic-science-communications/fsc/april2000/twgcsi.pdf. (Accessed on February 17, 2015).

27. Ibid, p. 12.

28. Ibid, p. 13.

29. Ibid, p. 14.

30. Ibid, p. 15.

31. Ibid, p. 16.

32. Ibid, p. 17.

33. Ibid.

34. Ibid, p. 19.

35. Ibid, p. 20.

36. Ibid, p. 22.

37. Ibid, p. 24.

38. Ibid, p. 25.

39. Ibid, p. 26.

40. Ibid, p. 27.

41. Ibid, p. 29.

42. Ibid, p. 30.

43. Ibid, p. 31.

44. (2007). Crime Scenes: Outdoor. Largo, FL: National Forensic Science Technology Center. Accessed online at http://www.nfstc.org/pdi/Subject01/pdi_s01_m01_02_a.htm. (Accessed on February 12, 2015).

45. (2007). Crime Scenes: Indoor. Largo, FL: National Forensic Science Technology Center. Accessed online at http://www.nfstc.org/pdi/Subject01/pdi_s01_m01_02_b.htm. (Accessed on February 12, 2015).

46. (2007). Crime Scenes: Conveyance. Largo, FL: National Forensic Science Technology Center. Accessed online at http://www.nfstc.org/pdi/Subject01/pdi_s01_m01_02_c.htm. (Accessed on February 12, 2015).

47. (2007). Location & Collection of Evidence. Largo, FL: National Forensic Science Technology Center. Accessed online at http://www.nfstc.org/pdi/Subject01/pdi_s01_m01_03.htm. (Accessed on February 12, 2015).

48. Ibid.

49. Ibid.

50. (2007). Collection Techniques. Largo, FL: National Forensic Science Technology Center. Accessed online at http://www.nfstc.org/pdi/Subject01/pdi_s01_m01_05.htm. (Accessed on February 19, 2015).

51. (n.d.). A Simplified Guide to Trace Evidence. Largo, FL: National Forensic Science Technology Center. Accessed online at http://www.crime-scene-investigator.net/SimplifiedGuideTrace Evidence.pdf. (Accessed on February 18, 2015).

52. Ibid.

53. Ibid.

54. Ibid.

55. Ibid.

56. Ibid.

57. (2007). Preservation of Evidence. Largo, FL: National Forensic Science Technology Center. Accessed online at http://www.nfstc.org/pdi/Subject01/pdi_s01_m01_04.htm. (Accessed on February 12, 2015).

58. Forensic Services Division (May 2002, revised December 13, 2011). Physical Evidence Manual. Salem, OR: Oregon State Police, pp. 5-1–5-2. Accessed online at http://www.crime-scene-investigator.net/Phys_Evid_Manual_OR.pdf. (Accessed on February 1, 2015).

59. Ibid, pp. 6-2–6-4.

60. Ibid, pp. 7-1–7-4.

61. (n.d.). Chain of Custody. Getting Your Hands on the Evidence. American Legal Institute, p. 41. Accessed online at http://files.ali-cle.org/thumbs/datastorage/skoob/articles/BK38-CH05_thumb.pdf. (Accessed on February 15, 2015).

62. Legal Information Institute (n.d.). Rule 901: Authenticating or Identifying Evidence. Federal Rules of Evidence. Ithaca, NY: Cornell University Law School. Accessed online at http://www.law.cor-

nell.edu/rules/fre/rule_901. (Accessed on February 15, 2015).

63. Chain of Custody, p. 41.

64. Ibid, p. 43.

65. Ibid, p. 44.

66. Ibid.

67. (n.d.). Physical Evidence [PowerPoint presentation]. Bakersfield, CA: Bakersfield College, slide 15. Accessed online at https://www.google.com/url?sa=t&rct=j&q=&esrc=s&source=web&cd=9&ved=0CFgQFjAI&url=http%3A%2F%2Fwww2.bakersfieldcollege.edu%2Fcfeer%2FLaw%2520of%2520Evidence%2FEvidence-Physical%2520Evidence.ppt&ei=mSRhVLixM5f6oQSPkIGYAw&usg=AFQjCNFt5j80zt6k5QrMMTL85vMjNH4t_Q&sig2=2fwybUm-Jqrj9oqyiLOLlQ&bvm=bv.79189006,d.cGE&cad=rja. (Accessed on February 12, 2015).

68. Ibid, slides 51–52.

69. Ibid, slide 15.

70. Ibid.

71. Ibid, slide 16.

72. Ibid.

73. Ibid.

74. Ibid, slide 17.

75. Uphoff, Rodney J. (2011). Handling Physical Evidence: Guidance Found in ABA Standard 4-4.6. Criminal Justice (2:2), Summer 2011. Accessed online at http://www.americanbar.org/content/dam/aba/publications/criminal_justice_magazine/cjsu11_uphoff.authcheckdam.pdf. (Accessed on February 13, 2015).

76. Ibid.

77. Ibid.

78. Ibid.

79. Ibid.

80. (2014). Commonwealth v. Stenhach. Casebriefs, LLC. Accessed online at http://www.casebriefs.com/blog/law/ethics/ethics-keyed-to-hazard/relationship-of-law-lawyers-and-ethics/commonwealth-v-stenhach/2/.(Accessed on February 13, 2015).

81. Legal Information Institute (n.d.). Ohio Legal Ethics Narrative: III Advocate. Ithaca, NY: Cornell University Law School. Accessed online at http://www.law.cornell.edu/ethics/oh/narr/OH_NARR_3.4.HTM. (Accessed on February 12, 2015).

82. Legal Information Institute (n.d.) Arizona Legal Ethics. Ithaca, NY: Cornell University Law School. Accessed online at http://www.law.cornell.edu/ethics/az/narr/AZ_NARR_1_06.HTM. (Accessed on February 15, 2015).

83. Justia (n.d.). Goldsmith v. Superior Court (People) (1984). Accessed online at http://law.justia.com/cases/california/court-of-appeal/3d/152/76.html. (Accessed on February 12, 2015).

84. Uphoff.

85. Ibid.

86. (2014). People v. Belge. Leagle.com. Accessed online at http://leagle.com/decision/197526983Misc2d186_1233.xml/PEOPLE%20v.%20BELGE. (Accessed on February 17, 2015).

87. Leary v. United States, 395 U.S. 6 (1969).

88. Ibid.

89. Ardaiz, P. J. (January 10, 2001). Charles F. Magill et al., Petitioners, v. The Superior Court of the County of Madera et al., Respondents. Court of Appeal, Fifth District of California. Accessed online at http://scholar.google.com/scholar_case?case=13386783466858246048&q=magill+v.+superior+court&hl=en&as_sdt=8000006&as_vis=1. (Accessed on February 16, 2015).

90. Uphoff.

91. (n.d.). 10 Famous Criminal Cases Cracked by Forensics. Criminal Justice Schools Blog. Accessed online at http://www.criminaljusticeschools.org/blog/10-famous-cases-cracked-by-forensics/. (Accessed on February 12, 2015).

92. Ibid.

93. Ibid.

94. Ibid.
95. Ibid.
96. Ibid.
97. Ibid.
98. Ibid.
99. Ibid.
100. Ibid.

Chapter 4

Documentary Evidence

Chapter Objectives

What you should know and understand after studying this chapter:

- The issues involved with documentary evidence
- The best evidence rule
- The issues involved in the different types of documentary evidence
- The admissibility tests for different types of documentary evidence
- The authentication of different types of documentary evidence
- Issues regarding the admission of business records

Chapter Outline

Introduction

Whereas real evidence typically refers to objects that had an actual role in a crime, documentary evidence is usually introduced to establish what allegedly did or did not happen. Of course, evidence covers such a wide range of possible forms that these lines can easily become blurred. For example, photographs or maps of a crime scene are documents but also serve as real evidence, with the caveat that these are normally used

Photo 4-1

In this 1930 photograph, E.K. Thode, chief of the National Division of Identification and Information, U.S. Department of Justice, displays a reconstructed fingerprint from verbal descriptions received by telephone and telegraph. Photograph courtesy of the Library of Congress.

to explain or to illustrate testimony. Explanatory diagrams, photos, and the like are not normally admitted into evidence even when they are presented at trial.

A more straightforward (if less informative) definition is that "documentary evidence consists of any information that can be introduced at trial in the form of documents."[1] Of course, technology has taken us well beyond simple writing or printing on paper, and today "documents" can include photographs, films and video recordings, microfiche, X-rays, and the many forms of electronic media such as e-mails, word processing or spreadsheet files, Web pages, and the multitudinous varieties of social media.

Documentary evidence is far more prevalent in civil law, as reflected in the tactic occasionally employed by large corporate defendants of burying their opponents in paper, whether the matter at hand is as simple as a contested will or as complex as a contract dispute, intellectual property claim, or medical malpractice suit. However, there are instances in which documentary evidence is an issue in a criminal prosecution, and here we will examine the various rules governing its use and methods of authentication, with special attention to increasingly prevalent electronic media.

Admissibility: Identification and Authentication

In many respects, the admissibility test for documentary evidence is similar or identical to that for real evidence, which will stand to reason once we examine the various tests. The first basic standard is relevance, which will be explored below in connection with identification and authentication. The second standard, just as with real evidence, is the passing of the various exclusion tests. These include the danger of unfair prejudice or surprise; confusion of the issues, or potential to mislead the jury; if it is cumulative; or if it is otherwise excludable by virtue of the federal or state constitutions or statutes.[2]

The first test of admissibility is the identification and authentication of the evidence. In practice, identification is less an issue than authentication, and the two terms are somewhat interchangeable. In federal courts this aspect is addressed by Rule 901 of the Federal Rules of Evidence, Authenticating or Identifying Evidence. In technical terms, identification and authentication speak to relevance. If the authenticity of a piece of documentary evidence cannot be confirmed, logically there is no way to establish that it has any relevance to the matter at hand. As noted in Chapter 3, relevancy (or materiality) means that a piece of evidence serves at least one of three purposes:

- It aids the investigator in solving the case.
- It proves or helps to prove one or more elements of the crime.
- It provides support for a particular theory regarding a crime.

Evidence is also relevant if it tends to make the existence of any material fact of the case more or less probable than it would otherwise be; the classic example is evidence used to impeach a witness.[3]

The following authentication methods are drawn directly from Section b of Rule 901, which cautions that these are examples only—not a complete list—of evidence that satisfies the requirement of identification and authentication.[4]

1. **Testimony of a witness with knowledge.** The most common application of this test is testimony from an individual who was present at the signing of a document. It can also be applied to chain of custody documentation to establish that a piece of real evidence is in fact the one taken from the crime scene.

2. **Non-expert opinion about handwriting.** Verification of handwriting need not be made by a handwriting expert. A witness who is familiar with the handwriting of the alleged author of a document may testify to its authenticity. Such familiarity may come from habitually seeing that person write, exchanging correspondence with him or her, or similar means. However, the witness cannot testify to handwriting if he is a layperson and gained familiarity with the handwriting in question only for the purposes of the litigation; that ability is reserved to handwriting experts. An alternate version of the non-expert handwriting opinion is allowing the jury to compare the documentary evidence to handwriting samples.[5]

3. **Comparison by an expert witness or the trier of fact.** In some cases the testimony of a handwriting expert may be used. The evolution of the principles governing the validation of handwritten documents through English common law and subsequently in the statutes of the various U.S. states is long, tortuous, and burdened with an unusually high level of caution compared to many other forms of evidence. The Federal Rules of Evidence remedy that situation by setting no higher standard for handwriting specimens.[6] In doing so the rules cite language from 28 U.S.C. §1731: "The admitted or proved handwriting of any person shall be admissible,

for purposes of comparison, to determine genuineness of other handwriting attributed to such person."[7] It is easy to see how a handwriting expert might well be used by the party attempting to deny the authenticity of a given document, not establish it.

4.   **Distinctive characteristics and the like.** This refers to the appearance, contents, substance, internal patterns, or other distinctive characteristics of the item, taken together with all the circumstances.[8] This method can be applied to a number of different situations. Examples provided by Rule 901 include:

   • A document or telephone conversation may be shown to have emanated from a particular person by virtue of its disclosing knowledge of facts known peculiarly to him.[9]
   • A letter may be authenticated by content and circumstances indicating it was in reply to a duly authenticated one.[10]
   • Language patterns may indicate authenticity or its opposite.[11]

5.   **Opinion about a voice.** The standards for authenticating a voice are much lower and comparable to visually identifying a person. Since unlike with handwriting there is no expert standard for aural voice identification, testimony need not even come from a witness who previously knew the speaker; anyone may compare voice samples to determine whether they come from the same person. This applies to speech heard firsthand, recorded, or transmitted.

6.   **Evidence about a telephone conversation.** A telephone conversation may be authenticated in the obvious way — by the caller's testimony that he recognized the other person's voice. In addition, authentication may be achieved if the witness can testify that the person to whom he spoke had knowledge of facts of which only a particular person would have been aware, he called a specific person's number and the individual answering self-identified as that person, or he called a business and discussed matters relevant to the business with the individual who answered the phone. (For clarity, authentication in this case is meant to establish that a given telephone call was placed to a particular number.)

7.   **Evidence about public records.** Public records are authenticated by proof that (1) a document was recorded or filed in a public office as authorized by law or (2) the record or statement in question is from the office where records of its kind are normally kept. Such proof of custody is generally sufficient, even with electronic records, although in some cases copies of public records may need to be certified by the issuing office.

8.   **Evidence about ancient documents or data compilations.** Despite the use of the word "ancient," documentary evidence need not be on par with the Dead Sea scrolls in order to meet this standard. Rather, authentication is achieved when it is established that the document is in a condition that raises no suspicion regarding its authenticity, was located in a place where it would likely and reasonably be if it were authentic, and it is at least 20 years old when presented. The common law standard for ancient documents was originally 30 years, based mostly on the point at which witnesses would probably be unavailable. Today's shorter standard has less to do with witness unavailability than with the low likelihood that a documentary fraud would still be viable after so much time. Also, given the increasing prevalence of electronic record storage, the condition of the document is now less important than its custody or location where found.

9. **Evidence about a process or system.** The main burden here is to prove that the process or system in question will reliably produce an accurate result. X-rays are an older example; today computer systems are the primary object of this standard, especially in regards to data mining or otherwise extracting records from large, complex databases.
10. **Methods provided by a statute or rule.** This is an open-ended allowance for any authentication method that may be permitted by federal statute or prescribed by a rule promulgated by the U.S. Supreme Court. Specific existing examples include official record authentication methods prescribed by Civil Procedure Rule 44 and Criminal Procedure Rule 27, court reporter record authentication methods prescribed by 28 U.S.C. §753(b) and Civil Procedure Rule 80(c), and deposition authentication methods prescribed by Civil Procedure Rule 30(f).[12]

The standards in Rule 901 (and in various state rules of evidence) comprise three broad categories of authentication: direct, indirect, and self-authentication. *Direct authentication* is achieved by the testimony of a witness with direct knowledge. It may also occur procedurally when a party admits to a document's existence and/or execution in the pleadings, responses to interrogatories, deposition testimony, stipulation, or testimony at trial, that admission will be sufficient to authenticate the document.[13]

Indirect authentication is accomplished through circumstantial evidence, as outlined in Rule 901(b)(4). References within a document to information that only a particular individual would know qualify under this standard, and even a speech or writing style that has distinctive characteristics can be authenticating which dealt with correspondence found on a computer hard drive.[14] Also, if an individual took action based on a document, such as taking steps directed in an e-mail or letter that action can serve to authenticate the correspondence (as well as proving that the individual received it).

Finally, several types of documentary evidence are *self-authenticating*. Ancient documents as outlined in Rule 901(b)(8) fall into this category, and Federal Rule of Evidence 902, Evidence That Is Self-Authenticating, provides a number of others.[15]

1. **Domestic public documents that are sealed and signed.** This refers to a document that bears a seal purporting to be that of the United States; any state, district, commonwealth, territory, or insular possession of the United States; the former Panama Canal Zone; the Trust Territory of the Pacific Islands; a political subdivision of any of these entities; or a department, agency, or officer of any entity named above; and a signature purporting to be an execution or attestation.
2. **Domestic public documents that are not sealed but are signed and certified.** This is primarily an exception for documents that do not bear a formal seal but otherwise bear the signature of an officer or employee of an entity named in Rule 901(1) and that of another public officer who has a seal and official duties within that same entity who certifies under seal—or its equivalent—that the signer has the official capacity and that the signature is genuine.
3. **Foreign public documents.** This is a document that purports to be signed or attested by a person who is authorized by a foreign country's law to do so. The document must be accompanied by a final certification that certifies the genuineness of the signature and official position of the signer or attester—or of any foreign official whose certificate of genuineness relates to the signature or attestation or is in a chain of certificates of genuineness relating to the signature or attestation. The cer-

tification may be made by a secretary of a United States embassy or legation; by a consul general, vice consul, or consular agent of the United States; or by a diplomatic or consular official of the foreign country assigned or accredited to the United States. If all parties have been given a reasonable opportunity to investigate the document's authenticity and accuracy, the court may, for good cause, either order that it be treated as presumptively authentic without final certification or allow it to be evidenced by an attested summary with or without final certification.

4. **Certified copies of public records.** A copy of an official record—or a copy of a document that was recorded or filed in a public office as authorized by law—is self-authenticating if the copy is certified as correct by the custodian or another person authorized to make the certification or by a certificate that complies with Rule 902(1), 902(2), or 902(3); a federal statute; or a rule prescribed by the Supreme Court.

5. **Official publications.** This includes any document issued by a public agency.

6. **Newspapers and periodicals.** Because they exist in the public domain as well as in multiple copies, these documents are self-authenticating.

7. **Trade inscriptions and the like.** This includes any inscription, sign, tag, or label purporting to have been affixed in the course of business. The main use of such evidence is to indicate origin, ownership, or control.

8. **Acknowledged documents.** These are accompanied by, or sealed with, a certificate of acknowledgment by a qualified third party, most often a notary public. (In some states a notary public is not required to actually affix, imprint, or emboss a physical seal; so long as governing state law is followed, the requirements of this rule are considered to have been met.)

9. **Commercial paper and related documents.** Commercial paper refers to unsecured short-term (generally less than 270 days) promissory notes issued by corporations, along with any accompanying documentation. Obviously, such documents will very rarely be at issue in a criminal trial.

10. **Presumptions under a federal statute.** Federal law may establish that a specific type of document other than those listed here is self-authenticating.

11. **Certified domestic records of a regularly conducted activity.** The original or a copy of a domestic record that meets the requirements of Rule 803(6)(A)-(C), as shown by a certification of the custodian or another qualified person that complies with a federal statute or a rule prescribed by the Supreme Court. Rule 803 is Exceptions to the Rule Against Hearsay; Section (6)(A)-(C) specifies that the record of a regularly conducted activity must (1) be made at or near the time of the act, event, condition, opinion, or diagnosis by someone with direct knowledge or based on information transmitted by someone with direct knowledge; (2) be kept in the course of a regularly conducted activity of a business, organization, occupation, or calling, whether or not for profit; and (3) be kept as a regular practice of that activity.[16] Before the trial or hearing, the proponent must give an adverse party reasonable written notice of the intent to offer the record—and must make the record and certification available for inspection—so that the party has a fair opportunity to challenge it.

12. **Certified foreign records of a regularly conducted activity.** This is the original or a copy of a foreign record that meets the requirements of Rule 902(11), modified as follows: the certification, rather than complying with a federal statute or Supreme Court rule, must be signed in a manner that, if falsely made, would subject the

maker to a criminal penalty in the country where the certification is signed. The proponent must also meet the notice requirements of Rule 902(11). Documents of this type are at issue almost solely in civil cases.

Photo 4-2

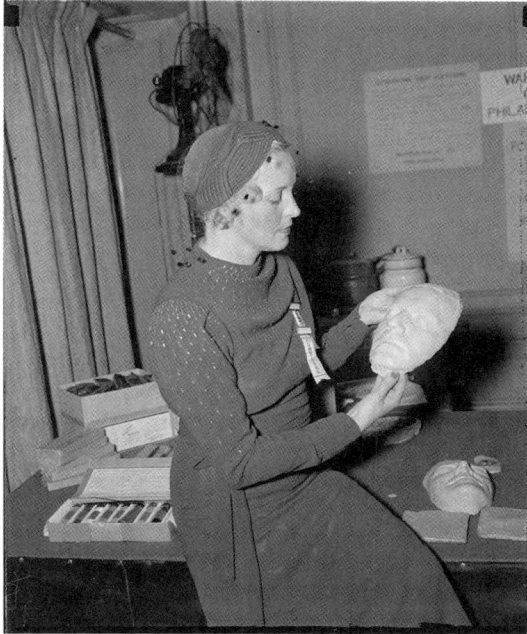

In the 1930s, police departments often used death masks of criminals for identification purposes. The above photograph is of a Mrs. Clark Schilder, wife of the Chief of the Division of Identification, Federal Bureau of Identification, inspecting a death mask on September 29, 1937, at the Annual Convention of the International Association for Identification. Photograph courtesy of the Library of Congress.

Admissibility: Best Evidence Rule

The best evidence rule can be somewhat misleading, as it has nothing to do with the objective quality of evidence. Rather, it requires that when introducing documentary evidence, the proponent must produce the original document unless a valid reason exists not to do so. Federal Rule of Evidence 1002, Requirement of the Original, states simply, "An original writing, recording, or photograph is required in order to prove its content unless these rules or a federal statute provides otherwise."[17] The purpose behind the rule is to ensure that the trier of fact has the actual language contained in a document whenever that language (the content of the document) is at issue. When the content of the document is at issue, neither a witness's description nor a copy that may have been altered are considered as reliable as the original document.[18] Note that for purposes of this rule, originals include the first copy of a document, as well as duplicate originals, such as a contract executed in duplicate, both of which are considered originals. Also, it is not acceptable for a witness to merely testify as to what he or she re-members the contents or language of a document to be. This is a safeguard against ac-cidental or unintentional faulty recollection of the facts, as well as outright fraud or selective presentation of a document's contents.[19]

The Federal Rules of Evidence establish particular definitions regarding documen-tary evidence. Under Rule 1001(d), an original of a writing or recording means the writing or recording itself or any counterpart intended to have the same effect by the person who executed or issued it. For electronically stored information, original means any printout—or other output readable by sight—if it accurately reflects the infor-mation. The notes to the rule add further refinement:

> A carbon copy of a contract executed in duplicate becomes an original, as does a sales ticket carbon copy given to a customer. While strictly speaking the original of a photograph might be thought to be only the negative, practical-ity and common usage require that any print from the negative be regarded as an original. Similarly, practicality and usage confer the status of original upon any computer printout.[20]

Conversely, Rule 1001(e) defines a "duplicate" as a counterpart produced by a me-chanical, photographic, chemical, electronic, or other equivalent process or technique that accurately reproduces the original. The notes distinguish "copies" produced by methods possessing an accuracy which virtually eliminates the possibility of error. Copies thus produced are given the status of originals in large measure. Copies subsequently produced manually, whether handwritten or typed, are not within the definition. It should be noted that what is an original for some purposes may be a duplicate for oth-ers. Thus a bank's microfilm record of checks cleared is the original as a record. How-ever, a print offered as a copy of a check whose contents are in controversy is a duplicate.[21]

The best evidence rule is not always as restrictive as it may initially seem, however. The first question is what the documentary evidence in question is intended to prove. Obvi-ously, if specific aspects of a document's contents are at issue, then producing the docu-ment itself will clearly be necessary. However, in many cases the question may instead be more straightforward. If a prosecutor is using a writing to prove specific facts—that a contract was written, a deed was delivered, or a conversation took place—that could also be proved by a witness who observed those events taking place. The witness's testimony in that case would not be prohibited just because a writing memorialized those facts.[22]

Second, the best evidence rule is one of preference, rather than exclusion. More often than not, a copy of a document is acceptable so long as there is a valid reason that the original cannot be produced. Typically, the requirement for an original is most rigid when there is either a genuine question about the authenticity of the copy or there is some reason that it would be unfair to admit the copy over the original, a standard expressed in Federal Rule of Evidence 1003. In short, copies are acceptable so long as the document contents are not in dispute, and in practice the attorneys on both sides of a case typically agree beforehand as to what documentary evidence may be admit-ted as a copy rather than an original.[23]

Federal Rule of Evidence 1004, Admissibility of Other Evidence of Content, estab-lishes four specific conditions under which an original need not be produced:

1004(a): All the originals are lost or destroyed, and not by the proponent acting in bad faith.

1004(b): An original cannot be obtained by any available judicial process. Typically this occurs when the original is in the possession of a third party and a subpoena is impractical, as in when the holding party is outside the jurisdiction of the court, or has not succeeded in procuring the document.

1004(c): The party against whom the original would be offered had control of the original; was at that time put on notice, by pleadings or otherwise, that the original would be a subject of proof at the trial or hearing; and fails to produce it at the trial or hearing. The rationale here is that if the party wishes to dispute the authenticity of a copy introduced into evidence, it has the ability to produce the original at will.

1004(d): The writing, recording, or photograph is not closely related to a controlling issue.[24]

The special nature of public records dictates special treatment under these rules as well. As the notes to Rule 1005 explain, removing them from their usual place of keeping would be attended by serious inconvenience to the public and to the custodian. As a consequence judicial decisions and statutes commonly hold that no explanation need be given for failure to produce the original of a public record. Rule 1005 itself states,

> The proponent may use a copy to prove the content of an official record— or of a document that was recorded or filed in a public office as authorized by law—if these conditions are met: the record or document is otherwise admissible; and the copy is certified as correct in accordance with Rule 902(4) or is testified to be correct by a witness who has compared it with the original. If no such copy can be obtained by reasonable diligence, then the proponent may use other evidence to prove the content.[25]

To clarify, the evidence standards still require some form of certification even for public records in order to protect the interests of the party against whom they are introduced.

Modern records—particularly in the case of complex litigation or cases involving large companies—may be what Federal Rule of Evidence 1006 refers to as "voluminous." It is entirely possible for business or other records to run to literally millions of pages of printed material. As such, Rule 1006 provides that the proponent may use a summary, chart, or calculation to prove the content of voluminous writings, recordings, or photographs that cannot be conveniently examined in court. There are conditions, however; the proponent must make the originals or duplicates available for examination or copying, or both, by other parties at a reasonable time and place. And the court may order the proponent to produce them in court.[26]

Finally, much like the exceptions to the hearsay rule permitted under Rule 801(d)(2), an original need not be provided when the content of a document has been proved by the opposing party against whom the evidence is offered. Rule 1007, Testimony or Statement of a Party to Prove Content, states specifically, "The proponent may prove the content of a writing, recording, or photograph by the testimony, deposition, or written statement of the party against whom the evidence is offered. The proponent need not account for the original."[27] However, since even the opposing party could produce an inaccurate recounting of a document's contents from memory, the rule limits such admissions to those made in the course of sworn testimony or in writing.

The application of most of the foregoing rules is typically the function of the court (that is, the judge), as determinations of admissibility especially regarding secondary documents are procedural matters. In the language of Rule 1008, Functions of the Court and Jury, "Ordinarily, the court determines whether the proponent has fulfilled the factual conditions for admitting other evidence of the content of a writing, recording, or photograph under Rule 1004 or 1005." However, "in a jury trial, the jury determines — in accordance with Rule 104(b) — any issue about whether (a) an asserted writing, recording, or photograph ever existed; (b) another one produced at the trial or hearing is the original; or (c) other evidence of content accurately reflects the content."[28]

The underlying rationale is best explained by an example provided in the notes to Rule 1008:

> Questions may arise which go beyond the mere administration of the rule preferring the original and into the merits of the controversy. For example, plaintiff offers secondary evidence of the contents of an alleged contract, after first introducing evidence of loss of the original, and defendant counters with evidence that no such contract was ever executed. If the judge decides that the contract was never executed and excludes the secondary evidence, the case is at an end without ever going to the jury on a central issue. *Levin, Authentication and Content of Writings*, 10 Rutgers L.Rev. 632, 644 (1956). The latter portion of the instant rule is designed to insure treatment of these situations as raising jury questions. The decision is not one for uncontrolled discretion of the jury but is subject to the control exercised generally by the judge over jury determinations.[29]

In other words, judges must take care in the exercise of the rules, such that the jury is not deprived of the opportunity to hear and make decisions about those issues of documentary evidence that are central, or at least crucial, to the arguments of the case.

When determining what documentary evidence to submit and whether originals will be required, attorneys work through a process of laying a foundation. The first step is to determine whether the best evidence rule applies or not. As Querijero explains, the distinction is "whether you are trying to prove something within the specific language of the document itself (*e.g.*, the allegedly defamatory statement at issue in the case) or whether you are trying to prove a fact related to a document (*e.g.*, that your client learned of the statement when he or she read it published in the newspaper)." If the document addresses an issue that is collateral to the case, the best evidence rule is not applicable.[30] The next step is to ascertain whether any of the automatic exceptions to the requirement for the production of the original apply, such as a statutory or public records exception. Normal procedure is for opposing counsels to agree on what documents may be admitted as copies by mutual agreement as part of the pretrial process. If there are no automatic or mutually agreed exceptions to original production and the original is not available, the challenge of justifying admission of a copy begins.

Where the original document is lost or destroyed, it must first be established that the document existed and in the case of loss that a diligent search has been conducted but the original could not be located. In the case of destruction, proof of destruction is most easily accomplished through the testimony of a witness who observed its destruction, assuming that is an option. In either case, it must be established that the party did not deliberately lose or destroy the original in order to avoid its production. A common example particularly in the case of business records is a document control policy that dictates the digital storage of scanned copies with deliberate destruction of the originals. It would be necessary to produce the company's policy, possibly backed up by testimony from an appropriate individual from the organization, and demonstrate that the original was duplicated and destroyed in accordance with that policy and routine procedure (rather than, for example, inexplicably destroyed a year early).[31]

For originals that are located outside the court's jurisdiction, it should first be established that the document is in fact located there. Next, it must be demonstrated that attempts were made to subpoena the document but were unsuccessful or that no legal channel was available to compel production of the original.[32]

For originals that are in the possession of the opposing party, the process is fairly straightforward. The first step is to establish that the opponent possesses the document, and the second is to prove that adequate notice was provided to produce it. Such notice typically comes from the pleading itself, routine discovery requests, or a subpoena duces tecum.[33]

Special Forms of Documentary Evidence

Having considered general rules of documentary evidence admissibility, we will now look at some specific considerations for particular types of records.

Business records appear commonly and extensively in the courtroom, and while they are most prevalent in civil litigation, there are many instances in which they may appear in criminal cases, such as money laundering, receiving stolen property, and various forms of fraud to name just a few. Business records receive an automatic exception to the hearsay rule thanks to the inherent trustworthiness of records created and maintained in the course of doing business.[34]

Exactly what constitutes a "business" in legal terms for purposes of defining business records varies from jurisdiction to jurisdiction, so it is important to be familiar with relevant state law in your jurisdiction. Querijero outlines the standards of Connecticut law. Connecticut General Statute §52-180(d) and the Connecticut Code of Evidence §8-4 define business to include business, profession, occupation, and calling of every kind.[35] Additionally, precedent established in Connecticut courts has extended the definition still further to include bank records,[36] medical records,[37] police records,[38] and reports of various professionals,[39] which addressed the reports of social workers specifically. The main exclusions (in general, not limited to Connecticut law) are activities that are not conducted for commercial or public purposes.

Photocopies of business records are admissible under 28 U.S.C. §1732. In order to qualify for the business record exception, there are three main criteria under Federal Rule of Evidence 803(6): the record was made (a) at or near the time of the act described in the record by or based on information transmitted by someone with knowledge; (b) in the course of a regularly conducted activity of a business, organization, occupation, or calling, whether or not for profit; and (c) as a regular practice of that activity.[40] Under Federal Rules of Evidence 902(11), business records can be established as authentic without the testimony of a live witness so long as an appropriate custodian certifies the records as accurate. Opposing counsel, however, must have an opportunity to review both the certification and the underlying record.[41]

The major complication that can arise with business records is content that includes hearsay. Often careful analysis is required to make this determination, especially with complex records. Querijero offers the example of *State v. George*,[42] in which a victim of child sexual abuse reported to a staff member (not named in the record) at an institution for troubled youths the names of witnesses who could verify the defendant's sexual abuse of the victim. As she summarizes it, even though the record was admissible as a business record, and even though the staff member had a duty to report information on the record, the fact that the reported information came from another individual not required to report rendered it hearsay and, thus excludible under the hearsay rule.

State v. William C. provides a contrasting example. In this case a report submitted by a social worker investigating child abuse allegations was at issue.[43] The report was deemed to fall under the hearsay exception since it was entirely the product of the social worker's professional obligation to investigate and report, unlike the child sexual abuse victim in the previous example who had no organizational responsibility to make statements to the staff member and had not made those statements under oath.

Finally, if an opinion is included within a business record, it is admissible as evidence only if the speaker would be qualified to give the opinion in oral testimony. In other words, placing the opinion within the context of a document lends it no more weight than it would have if spoken by a witness under oath in open court, and as such it must be carefully extracted from the record in question.

Although they are normally at issue in civil proceedings such as tort claims, medical bills and records may occasionally enter into a criminal case. In federal court such records are subject to essentially the same standards as other business records, meaning that they must be certified as true and accurate by the custodian or another qualified person and that they must have been made in the regular course of business by someone with firsthand knowledge.

However, standards in state courts may vary materially, so it is advisable to become familiar with local rules. Connecticut, for example, made all signed medical records and bills from treating medical providers admissible without the testimony of a live witness as of October 1, 2001, but such automatic admissibility applies only to civil actions. The burden to challenge the qualification of any particular record as admissible under these standards is on the opposing party.

We have already examined the self-authenticating nature of public records. The main caveat is that as with business records, a document may contain statements that qualify as hearsay. For example, a police report may include witness statements, and since such statements are made by persons with no official duty to report and are not made under oath, they constitute hearsay. (It would be necessary to subpoena those individuals so that they might provide statements in a deposition, testify in open court, and be cross-examined in order to introduce their observations regarding an incident.)

It is also important to understand that status as a public record does not automatically convey the imprimatur of authority. Querijero cites the example of *Barlow v. Dep't of Pub. Health, Connecticut*,[44] where a state investigator's report lost the presumption of reliability afforded to public records once it was established that the report was based in part on several hearsay statements and had not even been finalized. The district court noted that the court was entitled to consider

(1) the timeliness of the investigation;

(2) the special skill or experience of the official;

(3) whether a hearing was held and the level at which it was conducted; and

(4) any motive of the investigator inconsistent with accuracy in determining whether to accept such a document.[45]

The smart investigator will ensure that his or her work leaves no gaps that might be exploited in such a manner.

Electronic Evidence

It should come as a surprise to no one that various forms of electronic media are rapidly becoming the prevalent form of documentation. Moreover, the nature of digital recordkeeping means that the sheer volume of documented information has swollen by multiple orders of magnitude. Also, the speed with which technology now changes can easily outstrip the pace of legal changes, which were always intended to be evolutionary rather than revolutionary. The Federal Rules of Evidence that we have examined thus far have generally adapted to the nature of modern documents, but technology has also created entirely new forms of records that were not contemplated even a few decades ago.

First, it is necessary to distinguish evidence that has been created from electronic data from that which is merely stored in a computer system. Many businesses have taken archives of paper records dating back many years and scanned them into electronic storage. Such systems generally produce copies that are acceptable under existing rules, particularly for business records. However, increasingly, documents are created from stored data. A simple example is a report generated from a database—the basis of most modern electronic records systems—which can easily contain millions, or tens or hundreds of millions, of separate pieces of data. Given such a huge mass of data, the software that searches for, identifies, extracts, and collates relevant data must be reliable because there is no practical way to manually verify the accuracy of a report it generates. Yet the layperson has no hope of evaluating the accuracy of any given database, software package, or resultant report, and even computer technology experts cannot always vouch for their reliability—else every piece of software we use would be flawless.

Courts at all levels have come to recognize this fact. Querijero points out that over the years both state and federal courts have expressed concern that computer-generated records may not possess sufficient indicia of reliability to be admissible. In *American Oil Co. v. Valenti*, the court declared that business records that are generated by computers present structural questions of reliability that transcend the reliability of the underlying information that is entered into the computer. Computer machinery may make errors because of malfunctioning of the hardware ... or defects in the software.[46] *State v. Swinton* went into even more detail:

> [R]eliability problems may arise through or in: (1) the underlying information itself; (2) entering the information into the computer; (3) the computer hardware; (4) the computer software (the programs or instructions that tell the computer what to do); (5) the execution of the instructions, which trans-

forms the information in some way—for example, by calculating numbers, sorting names, or storing information and retrieving it later; (6) the output (the information as produced by the computer in a useful form, such as a printout of tax return information, a transcript of a recorded conversation, or an animated graphics simulation); (7) the security system that is used to control access to the computer; and (8) user errors, which may arise at any stage.[47]

Connecticut evidence rules require that a party seeking to admit computer-generated information in state court must demonstrate the basic reliability of the computer system and process involved in creating the evidence. According to *American Oil Co. v. Valenti*, this means testimony by a person with some degree of computer expertise, who has sufficient knowledge to be examined and cross-examined about the functioning of the computer.[48] However, this does not automatically mean a computer programmer, nor does it require the individual who actually input data into the system.

Rather, the standard is that the witness be familiar with the method used to create the evidence and the technology supporting it and must be able to be cross-examined by opposing counsel on those methods. Establishing a foundation for admissibility of computer-generated documents in Connecticut requires meeting six basic standards set forth in *State v. Swinton*:

(1) the computer equipment is accepted in the field as standard and competent and was in good working order, (2) qualified computer operators were employed, (3) proper procedures were followed in connection with the input and output of information, (4) a reliable software program was utilized, (5) the equipment was programmed and operated correctly, and (6) the exhibit is properly identified as the output in question.[49]

The Connecticut courts have extrapolated from these standards to establish computer-generated evidence as acceptable in a number of different circumstances:

- Images of bite marks on a murder victim were digitally enhanced to display detail that would not be visible to the naked eye, and others had images of the defendant's teeth superimposed.[50]
- Computer-generated maps were deemed admissible based on testimony from a technician regarding the mapping process and its accuracy.[51]
- Job cost details related to a construction project were deemed admissible based on testimony from a construction professional who testified to the process and data involved.[52]
- A summary of mortgage data for a group of foreclosures was admitted based on testimony from the bank manager who had prepared the report.[53]

Federal standards are actually less stringent than the examples given here for Connecticut, not differing significantly from the standards for non-computerized records. Still, federal courts have not extended *carte blanche* to computer-generated documents. For example, in *Potamkin Cadillac Corp. v. B.R.I. Coverage Corp.*, the court excluded a computer-generated accounting history because the data on which it was based contained a number of uncorrected errors—a condition not remedied by virtue of being computer-generated.[54] Yet witness testimony regarding the reliability of methods used to collect and maintain a database used to generate a report was sufficient to permit admission of that document in *Health Alliance Network, Inc. v. Continental Casualty Co.*[55]

Electronic messages—a category that once comprised mostly e-mail but now includes mobile phone text messages and messages sent directly from social media applications—carry their own set of authentication challenges. The problem is that the fact that a message originated from a particular account is not in and of itself sufficient proof that the owner of that account actually sent the message. Aside from not-uncommon and well-documented "hacks" of e-mail and social network accounts, the simple fact that many people leave such accounts logged in on devices such as mobile phones, tablets, and laptop and desktop computers means they are accessible to others.

Consequently, the standards for authenticating electronic messages have evolved in jurisdictions across the country. In this case the old ways are still reliable, and "distinctive characteristics" or appropriate circumstantial evidence can be the simplest and most direct method for establishing authorship. Following are some examples of such authentication applied in various state and federal cases.

- For letters found on a computer hard drive, the mode of expression of the writing, detailed references to the defendant's finances, and circumstantial evidence linking the defendant's presence at home with the time the letters were created on his home computer.[56]
- For e-mails, the inclusion of specific facts known to the defendants.[57]
- For a chat room message, the author's subsequent appearance at a meeting that had been arranged through that message.[58]
- For e-mails, a discussion of various identifiable personal and professional matters.[59]
- For text messages, the inclusion of details known to only a small number of people.[60]

Another authentication method that has been used multiple times in federal court is testimony from an individual who was included in an e-mail chain or chat message regarding the accuracy of the transcripts. Finally, bear in mind that communications of this type will frequently contain hearsay statements, so they must be evaluated carefully for admissibility.

Web pages are authenticated much in the manner of other documents. Printed copies of government websites, for example, are considered self-authenticating, while others can be authenticated in much the same way as other documents in the same category. In some courts a simple affidavit from the individual who downloaded and printed the copy of the page is sufficient.

One challenge of Web pages, however, is that many of them change, and sometimes frequently. Given the timeframes that are common in the legal system, a page may have changed substantially by the time documentary evidence has to be gathered. Printed copies of Web pages are typically date-stamped, although there is no reason this alone should be sufficient.

An interesting exploration of this issue arose in *United States v. Bansal*.[61] The case involved the introduction of images of archived Web pages collected by a service called the Wayback Machine, which catalogs and stores pages from across the Internet. Based on witness testimony as to how the service functions, archived images were accepted by the court as authentic.

Practical Application: Documentary Evidence in Stalking Cases

We have considered an extensive number of rules and principles used in determining the admissibility of documentary evidence. As has been stated more than once, for the most part these rules are the concern of attorneys. However, it may be helpful to consider the use of both physical (hard copy) and electronic documents in the prosecution of a specific criminal offense: stalking or harassment.

Electronic communication records: These tend to be among the most frequently seen in stalking cases given the nature of the offense. Typical sources will be telephone call records, copies of emails sent and/or received, and Internet usage records. Unfortunately, authentication standards can surprisingly make such documents difficult to introduce in court, since normally a qualified records custodian will have to testify to make such documents admissible into evidence. For example, for telephone records the records custodian could be an employee of the servicing telecommunications company who may well be located in another state. That fact may make appearance in court financially impractical for either the prosecution or the defense. As such, in practice such evidence is actually used fairly rarely.

For that reason, the more common usage of such documents is to refresh a witness's recollection—usually the victim's—regarding the frequency of various electronic communications and the dates and times associated with them. When these records are used for this purpose, the actual electronic communication records themselves are not introduced into evidence. Instead, they are shown only to the witness during his or her testimony as a means of assisting their recollection. However, once recollection has been aided, the witness must testify from memory, rather than relying heavily on or outright reading from the documents. In other words, this technique cannot be used as a "backdoor" method to relay the contents of the documents to the jury.[62]

"Hard copy" communications: In addition to (or more rarely instead of) electronic communications, the victim may have received handwritten letters, notes, drawings, or similar means of communication. For such items to be admissible, the witness who received the material would have to testify as to the authenticity of the items, the circumstances under which they came into his or her possession, and the basis for determining that the items were produced by the defendant.[63]

Medical records: Such records might be used to show the emotional impact of the alleged stalking or harassment on the victim and/or any physical manifestations that resulted from the distress caused by the alleged patterns of behavior. While in some jurisdictions an appropriate custodian of such records would have to testify to lay the proper foundation for their admission into evidence, in others medical records would have a lower threshold of authentication to meet.[64]

Domestic violence orders of protection: In many cases stalking may be alleged to have been performed by an estranged spouse or significant other. If the charge of aggravated stalking alleges that the defendant knowingly violated such an order, it would be normal to introduce the order into evidence to prove its contents as part of showing how the defendant's conduct was a violation of its provisions, and possibly to help demonstrate a pattern of behavior. Since public records are self-authenticating, this type of document is normally quite straightforward.[65]

Court order regarding conditions of release and bond: Much as with protective orders, a previous abuser may have violated conditions of release through the alleged stalking. It would be similarly appropriate to introduce the order into evidence to prove its contents as part of showing how the defendant's conduct was a violation of its provisions and how the alleged offense was a continuation of a prior pattern of behavior.[66]

Video surveillance records: Depending on the circumstances of the stalking, it is possible that video footage might be available from a private business or public institution to show the defendant's identity and the frequency of his or her presence at that location. A somewhat more complicated example would be if the victim independently used video equipment on his or her own to identify the defendant and document that the harassment or stalking was taking place. Conversely, the same sort of video surveillance records could be used by the defendant to show his or her presence elsewhere at the time of the alleged stalking or harassment. In any of these cases, an appropriate foundation from the custodian of such records would be necessary for such material to be actually introduced into evidence.[67]

Conclusion

Documentary evidence tends to be extensive and complex, though less so in criminal proceedings than in civil ones. For the most part dealing with such evidence will be the province of attorneys. However, it is helpful for the investigator to understand what sorts of documents will be most helpful and usable for the prosecutor and what will and will not be admissible when it is time to allocate limited time and resources to investigating and pursuing evidence.

Practicum

Practicum One

The standards for ancient documents have changed from the original common law rules. Explain why the 30-year standard once existed, why 20 years is now the accepted standard, and why the passage of time is considered to reduce the necessity for authentication.

Practicum Two

The investigative report of a detective is to be introduced into evidence at a criminal trial. Describe three ways in which the defense might attempt to have the report excluded as inadmissible.

Practicum Three

A series of e-mails alleged to have been written by the defendant in a criminal case are to be introduced into evidence. The defense asserts that the e-mails, while coming from the defendant's account, were not actually written by him. How might the prosecution establish that the defendant did in fact write them?

Summary

- Whereas real evidence typically refers to objects that had an actual role in a crime, documentary evidence is usually introduced to establish what allegedly did or did not happen.
- A more straightforward (if less informative) definition is that "documentary evidence consists of any information that can be introduced at trial in the form of documents."
- In many respects, the admissibility test for documentary evidence is similar or identical to that for real evidence.
- The first test of admissibility is the identification and authentication of the evidence.
- Indirect authentication is accomplished through circumstantial evidence, as outlined in FRE Rule 901(b)(4).
- Several types of documentary evidence are self-authenticating.
- The best evidence rule can be somewhat misleading, as it has nothing to do with the objective quality of evidence. Rather, it requires that when introducing documentary evidence, the proponent must produce the original document unless a valid reason exists not to do so.
- The best evidence rule is one of preference, rather than exclusion.
- It is important to understand that status as a public record does not automatically convey the imprimatur of authority.
- Electronic messages—a category that once comprised mostly e-mail but now includes mobile phone text messages and messages sent directly from social media applications—carry their own set of authentication challenges.
- Documentary evidence tends to be extensive and complex, though less so in criminal proceedings than in civil ones.

Questions in Review

1. Explain the best evidence rule.
2. How are e-mails authenticated?

3. What is meant by direct authentication?
4. Define documentary evidence.
5. What are the key issues in admitting business records?

Key Terms

Best Evidence Rule: Best evidence rule requires that when introducing documentary evidence, the proponent must produce the original document unless a valid reason exists not to do so.

Direct Authentication: Direct authentication is achieved by the testimony of a witness with direct knowledge.

Documentary Evidence: Documentary evidence consists of any information that can be introduced at trial in the form of documents.

Electronic Messages: Electronic messages are a category that once comprised mostly e-mail but now includes mobile phone text messages and messages sent directly from social media applications.

Indirect Authentication: Indirect authentication is accomplished through circumstantial evidence.

Official Publications: Official publications include any document issued by a public agency.

Endnotes

1. Querijero, Michelle L. (n.d.). A Practical Guide to Evidence in Connecticut. Hartford, Connecticut: Shipman & Goodwin, LLP, p. 9–1. Accessed online at http://www.shipmangoodwin.com/files/19628_Chapter09Final.pdf. (Accessed on April 11, 2015).

2. Ibid, pp. 9–4 and 9–5.

3. Legal Information Institute (n.d.). Rule 401: Test for Relevant Evidence. Ithaca, NY: Cornell University Law School. Accessed online at http://www.law.cornell.edu/rules/fre/rule_401. (Accessed on April 11, 2015).

4. Legal Information Institute (n.d.). Rule 901: Authenticating or Identifying Evidence. Ithaca, NY: Cornell University Law School. Accessed online at http://www.law.cornell.edu/rules/fre/rule_901. (Accessed on April 11, 2015).

5. (n.d.). Documentary Evidence. Palo Alto, CA: Stanford Law School. Accessed online at https://www.law.stanford.edu/sites/default/files/child-page/181856/doc/slspublic/evidencelongol-chill.doc. (Accessed on April 13, 2015).

6. Legal Information Institute. Rule 901: Authenticating or Identifying Evidence.

7. Ibid.

8. Ibid.

9. Globe Automatic Sprinkler Co. v. Braniff, 89 Okl. 105, 214 P. 127 (1923).

10. California Evidence Code § 1420.

11. People v. Nichols, 378 Ill. 487, 23 N.E.2d 766 (1942); McGuire v. State, 200 Md. 601, 92 A.2d 582 (1952); and State v. McGee, 336 Mo. 1082, 82 S.W.2d 98 (1935).

12. Legal Information Institute. Rule 901: Authenticating or Identifying Evidence.

13. Querijero, p. 9–4.

14. *State v. John L.*, 85 Conn. App. 291, 302–202 (2004).

15. Documentary Evidence.

16. Legal Information Institute (n.d.). Rule 803: Exceptions to the Rule Against Hearsay. Ithaca, NY: Cornell University Law School. Accessed online at http://www.law.cornell.edu/rules/fre/rule_803. (Accessed on April 11, 2015).

17. Legal Information Institute (n.d.). Rule 1002: Requirement of the Original. Ithaca, NY: Cornell University Law School. Accessed online at http://www.law.cornell.edu/rules/fre/rule_1002. (Accessed on April 21, 2015).

18. Querijero, p. 9–8.

19. Ibid.

20. Legal Information Institute (n.d.). Rule 1001: Definitions That Apply to This Article. Ithaca, NY: Cornell University Law School. Accessed online at http://www.law.cornell.edu/rules/fre/rule_1001. (Accessed on April 11, 2015).

21. Querijero, p. 9–8.

22. Ibid, pp. 9–8 and 9–9.

23. Ibid, p. 9–9.

24. Legal Information Institute (n.d.). Rule 1004: Admissibility of Other Evidence of Content. Ithaca, NY: Cornell University Law School. Accessed online at http://www.law.cornell.edu/rules/fre/rule_1004. (Accessed on April 14, 2015).

25. Legal Information Institute (n.d.). Rule 1005: Copies of Public Records to Prove Content. Ithaca, NY: Cornell University Law School. Accessed online at http://www.law.cornell.edu/rules/fre/rule_1005. (Accessed on April 12, 2015).

26. Legal Information Institute (n.d.). Rule 1006: Summaries to Prove Content. Ithaca, NY: Cornell University Law School. Accessed online at http://www.law.cornell.edu/rules/fre/rule_1006. (Accessed on April 13, 2015).

27. Legal Information Institute (n.d.). Rule 1007: Testimony or Statement of a Party to Prove Content. Ithaca, NY: Cornell University Law School. Accessed online at http://www.law.cornell.edu/rules/fre/rule_1007. (Accessed on April 11, 2015).

28. Legal Information Institute (n.d.). Rule 1008: Functions of the Court and Jury. Ithaca, NY: Cornell University Law School. Accessed online at http://www.law.cornell.edu/rules/fre/rule_1008. (Accessed on April 17, 2015).

29. Ibid.

30. Querijero, p. 9–11 and 9–12.

31. Ibid, p. 9–11.

32. Ibid, pp. 9–11 and 9–12.

33. Ibid, p. 9–12.

34. Ibid, p. 9–14.

35. Ibid.

36. State v. Lawler, 30 Conn. App. 827, 832 (1993).

37. Gil v. Gil, 94 Conn. App. 306, 321 (2006).

38. Paquette v. Hadley, 45 Conn. App. 577, 581 (1997).

39. State v. William C., 267 Conn. 686, 701 (2004).

40. Legal Information Institute. Rule 803.

41. Querijero, p. 9–15.

42. State v. George, 280 Conn. 551, 594 (2006).

43. State v. William C., 267 Conn. 701.

44. Barlow v. Dep't of Pub. Health, Connecticut, 319 F. Supp. 2d 250, 258 (D. Conn. 2004).

45. Ibid.

46. American Oil Co. v. Valenti, 179 Conn. 349, 358–59 (1979).

47. State v. Swinton, 268 Conn. 781, 813 (2004).

48. American Oil Co. v. Valenti, 179 Conn. at 359.

49. State v. Swinton, 268 Conn. at 811–812.

50. State v. Swinton, 268 Conn. at 814.

51. State v. Polanco, 69 Conn. App. 169, 184 (2002).

52. Duplissie v. Devino, 96 Conn. App. 673, 697 (2006).

53. F.D.I.C. v. Carabetta, 55 Conn. App. at 376.

54. Potamkin Cadillac Corp. v. B.R.I. Coverage Corp., 38 F.3d. 627.

55. Health Alliance Network, Inc. v. Continental Casualty Co., 245 F.R.D. 121, 130 (S.D.N.Y. 2007).

56. State v. Eleck, 130 Conn. App. at 641.

57. United States v. Siddiqui, 235 F.3d 1318, 1322–23 (11th Cir. 2000).

58. United States v. Tan, 200 F.3d 627, 630–31 (9th Cir. 2000).

59. United States v. Safavian, 435 F.Aup.2d 36, 40 (D. D.C. 2006).

60. Dickens v. State, 175 Md. App. 231, 237–41 (2007).

61. United States v. Bansal, 663 F.3d 634, 667–668 (3d Cir. 2011).

62. Judicial Education Center (2015). Documentary or Physical Evidence. Albuquerque, NM: University of New Mexico Law School. Accessed online at http://jec.unm.edu/education/online-training/stalking-tutorial/documentary-or-physical-evidence. (Accessed on April 11, 2015).

63. Ibid.

64. Ibid.

65. Ibid.

66. Ibid.

67. Ibid.

Chapter 5

Demonstrative Evidence

Chapter Objectives

What you should know and understand after studying this chapter:

- What constitutes demonstrative evidence
- The purpose of using demonstrative evidence
- Standards for using scientifically based demonstrative evidence
- Techniques for presenting and using demonstrative evidence
- When demonstrative evidence is relevant

Chapter Outline

Introduction

Thus far in this text we have looked at various aspects of real (often called substantive) evidence. Marks describes substantive evidence as that which is adduced for the purpose of proving a fact in issue.[1] Demonstrative evidence, by contrast, is that evidence addressed directly to the senses without intervention of testimony.[2] Typically demonstrative evidence is used to explain or clarify some fact at issue, particularly one that is complex or otherwise potentially difficult for the jury to understand.

A court case is often filled with complex facts, and a trial may last several days. Psychological research provides us with several relevant facts. First, people learn roughly three-quarters of what they know from visual media. Second, on average people retain 20 percent of information they see and only about ten percent of information they hear after 72 hours, but if they both see and hear information presented, the retention rate rises to about 65 percent.[3] For an attorney faced with presenting a complex case, the ability to do something other than "talk at the jury" will clearly be important—and demonstrative evidence is often the key. In this chapter we will examine the nature of various forms of demonstrative evidence and how it may be employed at trial, as well as the rules governing such use.

Nature of Demonstrative Evidence

Unlike real and documentary evidence, demonstrative evidence is the tool of the attorney. The detective, law enforcement officer, or investigator generally has little association with it except to the extent that such evidence must be based on data gathered at a crime scene. It generally takes the form of charts and graphs, video, reconstruction, or computer animation.

In most cases such forms of evidence only illustrate the testimony of a witness—particularly that of an expert witness on complex issues—or summarize a large number of important facts. It does not by itself prove anything. As mentioned in the introduction to this chapter, demonstrative evidence is distinguished from substantive evidence. Perhaps surprisingly, the term "demonstrative" is not used at all in the body of the Federal Rules of Evidence and merits only a single mention in the Advisory Committee Notes to those rules.[4] This has on occasion posed problems for the courts, because no clear, formal definition exists (at least at the federal level—we will consider some state-level jurisprudence later in this chapter).

In tackling this issue from a legal scholarship standpoint, Professor Robert Brain opened a legal studies paper with this overview of the state of demonstrative evidence:

> … Demonstrative evidence has largely become the forgotten stepchild of evidence scholarship. As a result, no one has yet developed a satisfactory theory explaining the relevance of demonstrative evidence. No one has correctly denoted the characteristics of demonstrative evidence that distinguish it from other forms of trial evidence. No one has proposed a uniform treatment concerning its admissibility or a consistent methodology regarding how such exhibits are to be treated at trial or even whether they should be viewed by jurors during their deliberations. Perhaps most surprisingly, there is not even a settled definition of the term.[5]

Professor Brain was writing in 1992; as we will see later in this chapter, the federal appeals courts (particularly the Seventh Circuit) have since addressed some of the open items he poses. But as we will also see, the courts have not always treated those issues consistently.

For what is probably the most basic definition available, we first turn to *Black's Law Dictionary*, which defines demonstrative evidence thus: "That evidence addressed directly to the senses without intervention of testimony. Real (thing) evidence such as the gun in a trial of homicide or the contract itself in the trial of a contract case. Evidence apart from the testimony of witnesses concerning the thing. Such evidence may include maps, diagrams, photographs, models, charts, medical illustrations, X-rays."[6] The problem with this definition is that it is misleading in some respects: the term "real evidence" can be construed to imply that it is substantive evidence.

An example of the challenges arising from the lack of clear definitions of demonstrative evidence can be seen in *Baugh v. Cuprum*,[7] though fortunately this is also one of the cases in which the appellate court handed down some clear guidance in the matter. The case was a product liability suit that originated when a ladder manufactured by Cuprum collapsed while the plaintiff, John Baugh, was using it to clean out his gutters, resulting in severe brain injury. The plaintiff alleged negligence and defective design. Complicating the plaintiff's case were the facts that there were no eyewitnesses to the accident and that the plaintiff could not testify because of his brain injury.[8]

An expert witness called by the defense used an "exemplar" ladder—a newly made ladder of an identical model to the one used by the plaintiff. The plaintiff's counsel objected to the admission of the ladder as evidence, in part because discovery in the case had closed two years previously and the defense had not previously proposed submitting the ladder. Defense counsel argued that "the ladder would be simply a demonstrative exhibit that we'll use during the direct examination of [Cuprum's expert]." And these exhibits are demonstrative. They are not substantive evidence. They are not to be admitted for substantive evidence. It's just simply to demonstrate and help the jury understand his testimony.[9] The trial judge consented to admission of the ladder despite the plaintiff's objection and the late disclosure specifically because it was intended to be only demonstrative.

The defense's expert witness used the exemplar ladder in a video that accompanied his testimony and showed him testing the strength and stability of the ladder as well as performing other tests that included jumping on the ladder as if it were a pogo stick and tipping the ladder in different positions.[10] In addition, the ladder was present in the courtroom. However, since it was only a demonstrative exhibit, it was not provided to the jury during their deliberations.

The problem arose when during the second day of jury deliberations, the jurors asked to see the exemplar ladder. The plaintiff's counsel objected, and initially the judge agreed, even stating that demonstrative evidence is normally not sent back to the jurors. But in response to a query from the judge about allowing the ladder into the jury room, the plaintiff's counsel noted that as a matter of practice demonstrative evidence is not provided to the jury during deliberations and that furthermore he would have had his own experts test the ladder had he known it would be given to the jury.[11]

Overruling the plaintiff, the trial judge initially decided that the jury could come into the courtroom to view the ladder and so notified the jury, specifying in her note to them that "The exemplar ladder is a demonstrative evidence. It was not admitted in evidence." Somewhat oddly, despite being given permission to view the ladder, the jury did not examine it that day. However, the second day the jury once again asked about the ladder, and the plaintiff's counsel once again objected. This time the judge pressured the plaintiff to specify the harm that would result if the ladder were provided to the jury: "Again, apart from the fact that this is not what you were expecting or planned for, I want to know what the prejudice is. How is your client prejudiced?" At a minimum, the plaintiff responded, he would have consulted with his own experts "if I knew the individuals were going to be playing with exemplar ladders and so forth in the courtroom."[12]

The judge overruled the objection, and the jury was allowed into the courtroom to view the ladder. But less than half an hour later, the jury returned with yet another request: they wanted to be able to step on the ladder. Yet again, the plaintiff's counsel objected on much the same basis as he had before, as well as raising "additional objectives regarding potential juror reconstruction of the accident." The following day the judge allowed the ladder into the jury room, though she included a warning that "under no circumstances are you to endeavor to reconstruct the occurrence." Less than four hours later, the jury returned a verdict in favor of the defendant, which the plaintiff appealed.[13]

The issue, of course, was the provision of the unadmitted ladder to the jury during its deliberations. In its opinion the appellate court first addressed the very issue we are considering: the ambiguous meaning of the term "demonstrative evidence." As a starting point, "in its broadest and least helpful use, the term 'demonstrative' is used to describe any physical evidence." The court noted that "when the term is used in this way, demonstrative exhibits may range from Shakespeare's version of Marc Antony's funeral oration displaying the bloody toga in *Julius Caesar* … to the knife in *Twelve Angry Men*." Moreover, "as jurors have become more visually oriented, counsel in modern trials seek to persuade them with an ever-expanding array of objects, maps, charts, displays, summaries, video reconstructions, computer simulations, and so on." The end result is that "courts sometimes get hopelessly confused in their analysis."[14]

The appellate panel then very succinctly noted that "without the consent of all parties, a deliberating jury may not consider exhibits not actually admitted into evidence." It moved on in the following section of its ruling to employ the term "demonstrative exhibits," which it described as "a persuasive, pedagogical tool created and used by a part as part of the adversarial process to persuade the jury." One key factor is that since such exhibits "are meant to 'illustrate or clarify a party's position,' and they are by definition 'less neutral in [their] presentation' and thus are not properly considered evidence."[15]

It is important to recall here the purpose of the Federal Rules of Evidence as stated in Rule 102: "to administer every proceeding fairly, eliminate unjustifiable expense and delay, and promote the development of evidence law, to the end of ascertaining the truth and securing a just determination."[16] Under Rule 403, "the court may exclude relevant evidence if its probative value is substantially outweighed by a danger of one or more of the following: unfair prejudice, confusing the issues, misleading the jury, undue delay, wasting time, or needlessly presenting cumulative evidence."[17] It stands to reason that an exhibit that is deliberately selected to enhance one party's presentation of the facts of a case is not neutral and could prejudice the jury. In fact, Stephen Lindsay, who is a faculty member of the National Criminal Defense College and frequent lecturer on criminal defense practice, offers his own definition of demonstrative evidence: "Demonstrative evidence is anything and everything, regardless of whether admissible or even offered as evidence, including attorney/client/witness demeanor in the courtroom, which tends to convey to and evoke from the jury a 'sense impression' that will benefit our case, whether through advancing our case in chief or diminishing the prosecution's case."[18] Clearly, this is not something intended to be neutral.

Photo 5-1

The above photograph was used in an arson trial in the early 1900s to establish the extent of the damages to the building. Photo courtesy of the Library of Congress.

That is not necessarily wrong or negative; after all, our system of justice is adversarial. Neither prosecution nor defense will choose to knowingly introduce evidence that is harmful to its case, nor are they required to do so (although if such evidence exists, doubtless the opposing side will do its best to ensure that it makes its way into court). While we sometimes hear people decry "tricks and technicalities" that set criminals (well, strictly speaking, alleged criminals) free, those "technicalities" are based for the most part on established, well-known rules, and it is the responsibility of the trial judge to ensure the professional and appropriate behavior of the attorneys on both sides of a case.

The appellate panel stated in its analysis of the case, "The general rule is that materials not admitted into evidence simply should not be sent to the jury for use in its deliberations."[19] The judges went on to cite three specific examples:

Bankcard America, Inc. v. Universal Bancard Systems, Inc.[20]: In this case, which had also been appealed to the Seventh Circuit, 43 exhibits were provided to the jury during its deliberations, and of those 24 had not been admitted into evidence. However, the appellate panel found that "The 21 exhibits that should not have gone to the jury … consisted mostly of innocuous letters, boilerplate contract language, meaningless fax cover sheets, and pages of cryptic business records." Moreover, "All of these documents were cumulative of testimony given during the trial and of other documents that were properly admitted into evidence," and though none had been admitted, "all of them probably would have been admitted upon request." The net result was that "Though submitting these exhibits to the jury was a mistake, it was not plain or prejudicial error that warranted a new trial."[21]

Artis v. Hitachi Zosen Clearing, Inc.[22]: In another case heard before the Seventh Circuit, this one involving a claim of racial discrimination in employment practices, "a large piece of cardboard printed with the damages [the plaintiff's counsel] proposed" that had been used during the attorney's summation but was not an admitted piece of evidence "somehow … went into the jury room anyway, and one juror said that she found it 'helpful.'" The appellate panel held that the exhibit was unlikely to have affected the verdict and that the subject matter it addressed—proposed damages—was already stipulated.[23]

United States v. Holton:[24] In this case the issue was the provision of transcripts of tape recordings that were provided to the jury to assist them as they listened to recordings that had been admitted into evidence, although the transcripts had not. The court noted that to protect jury deliberations from improper influence, we ordinarily restrict the jury's access only to exhibits that have been accepted into evidence and consideration by the jury of documents not in evidence is in error[25] (citing *United States v. Treadwell,*[26] (1985)).

In limited instances, some courts have permitted demonstrative exhibits to be provided to the jury during deliberations. The most notable, mentioned in the Seventh Circuit opinion in *Baugh,* was the Tenth Circuit interstate automobile theft case, *United States v. Downen* (1974).[27] There the judges upheld on appeal the provision of chart used by the prosecution that organized the different stolen vehicles, dates, and counts of the indictment to the jury. The panel's rationale was that so long as papers, documents, or articles, whether or not admitted in evidence were accompanied by careful cautionary instructions as to their use and limited significance when provided to the jury, such actions are within the discretion accorded the Trial Court in order that it may guide and assist the jury in understanding and judging the factual controversy.[28]

The Seventh Circuit clearly did not espouse this line of reasoning, describing the decision (along with a Fifth Circuit decision in *Big John, B.V. v. Indian Head Grain Co.* (1983))[29] as departing from longstanding practice and having only the most tenuous support. Given that demonstrative exhibits are acknowledged to be specifically intended to present the case of one side or the other in the most positive possible light, it is difficult to understand how any court could assume that merely providing stern instructions to the jury about how much weight to give a particular exhibit could be effective. No matter how well-intentioned the jury members might be, the influence created by such an exhibit could easily be unconscious. There is a reason the rules exist that exclude, for example, excessively gory pictures of a crime scene or victim that do not serve any other evidentiary purpose. Needless to say, it is the Seventh Circuit's position that in general holds sway in the American legal system.

So with all of these issues considered, we will embrace the Seventh Circuit's use of the more accurate term "demonstrative exhibits," or as an alternative "demonstrative aids." Because a demonstrative exhibit can in fact be substantive evidence—something we will examine in a moment—the phrase "demonstrative evidence" is unclear and potentially misleading. For our purposes in this text demonstrative evidence has been admitted; a demonstrative exhibit or demonstrative aid has not. It is important to remain aware, however, that many if not most others may continue to use unclear terminology.

Standards for Scientifically Based Demonstrative Evidence

We have now established that not every demonstrative exhibit is purely demonstrative. Some are substantive evidence in and of themselves, such as a computer simulation or reconstruction of an accident where scientific and other factual data is entered into a computer that processes the data and generates a visual image of how the accident must have occurred.[30] Because such simulations stand as evidence on their own, the standards imposed by the courts for their admissibility are high. The simulation is dependent on the application of scientific principles and mathematical calculations, and the courts treat them like other scientific tests that require proof of those scientific principles and data when making determinations of admissibility.[31]

Demonstrative evidence depends for its probative value on the testimony of the witness, so while the evidence may recreate an event, the validity of the conclusion does not depend on the proper application of scientific principles.[32] However, a computer or other video animation of an event in particular can be powerful for a jury, and it is human nature to assign more weight to such a recreation of events than might be warranted. For that reason, the opposing party in a case must be given plenty of notice and opportunity to review (and possibly object to) any demonstrative evidence—particularly any type of computer animation—intended to be used at trial; absent that notice, it is quite likely that the court will exclude the evidence, or at a minimum relegate it to the status of a demonstrative exhibit. Judges must also carefully instruct juries regarding how such evidence is to be construed and weighted in their deliberations.

There is one narrow set of circumstances in which computer animations are generally held to be self-authenticating and almost automatically relevant and therefore admissible: aircraft accident reconstruction. The National Transportation Safety Board (NTSB) has extensive expertise in such matters, and the science and methodology underlying its computer animations are nearly unassailable, though even they must be backed by the testimony of an expert witness with personal knowledge of both the simulation methodology in general and the data used to generate the specific simulation at issue.[33] Of course, aircraft accidents are rarely criminal matters and not the sort of thing routinely investigated by law enforcement agencies. But understanding why NTSB animations of accidents carry such weight as substantive evidence in court helps illuminate the general criteria used to judge such evidence.

We will specifically address scientific evidence later in this text. However, here we will briefly consider demonstrative evidence that is based on science in order to understand the threshold for acceptance by the courts. The standards by which scientific evidence are judged have evolved along with scientific understanding through the twentieth and into the twenty-first centuries. The original standard, known as the common law *Frye* rule or simply the *Frye* rule, dates from the 1923 Supreme Court case *Frye v. United States*.[34] The case involved the attempted introduction of evidence based on a systolic blood pressure measurement to test for deception—a crude lie detector, in other words. The lower court ultimately refused to admit that evidence despite expert testimony from the scientist who had conducted the test. On appeal the U.S. Supreme Court affirmed, noting in part,

Just when a scientific principle or discovery crosses the line between the experimental and demonstrable stages is difficult to define. Somewhere in this twilight zone the evidential force of the principle must be recognized, and while courts will go a long way in admitting expert testimony deduced from a well-recognized scientific principle or discovery, the thing from which the deduction is made must be sufficiently established to have gained general acceptance in the particular field in which it belongs.[35]

The *Frye* rule, then, set general acceptance in the scientific community as a prerequisite for admitting scientific evidence in court.[36] Needless to say, this established a fairly high bar, and the *Frye* rule was considered restrictive. In the 1975 version of the Federal Rules of Evidence, Rule 702 imposed a more liberal standard whereby expert scientific or technical opinions are admissible in evidence if they are relevant and helpful to the judge or jury in determining the facts of the case.[37] Unfortunately, this leaves much to the judge's discretion while providing little in the way of guidance for establishing a standard.

What is generally considered the landmark case in scientific evidence admissibility standards came in 1993 with *Daubert v. Merrell Dow Pharmaceuticals, Inc.* (1993).[38] This was a product liability case in which two children with birth defects and their parents sued the manufacturer of Bendectin, a widely used treatment for morning sickness in pregnant women. Filing in California, the plaintiffs presented statistical evaluations of existing epidemiological studies because no specific causal link between the drug and birth defects had been identified, leaving indirect evidence as the only option—but evidence arguably admissible under the 1975 Federal Rules of Evidence. Merrell Dow countered that under the *Frye* rule, no generally accepted scientific evidence proved that its drug had caused the birth defects. The lower courts held to the *Frye* rule and ruled against the plaintiffs, who appealed to the U.S. Supreme Court.

The case thus placed the more stringent *Frye* rule face-to-face with the more liberal Federal Rules of Evidence, setting the stage for the Supreme Court to establish exactly what the admissibility standards for scientific evidence would be going forward. Given both the importance of the case and its technical nature, several groups filed *amicus curiae* (friend of the court) briefs in support of one side or the other. Of those, the most influential group supporting the Dauberts was headed by Professor Ronald Bayer and came to be known as the Bayer group; its counterpart supporting Merrell Dow was headed by Professor Nicolaas Bloembergen and similarly came to be known by his name.[39]

The Bayer group made five main arguments:

- First was that in the group's view, the Ninth Circuit (which had rendered an appellate decision) was wrong in its categorical exclusion of research deemed to be at odds with the prevailing wisdom, as this did not adequately reflect the nature of the scientific endeavor as they understood it.[40]
- Second, they rejected what they presumed to be the Ninth Circuit's view of good science as only that held as consensus within the scientific community and so demonstrated by publication in peer-reviewed journals. Rather than what it characterized as the continuous accumulation of objective, irrefutable truths, the Bayer group contended that scientific progress is actually revolutionary, that a new theory is seldom or never just an increment to what is already known. Rather,

its assimilation requires the reconstruction of prior theory and the reevaluation of prior fact.[41]

- Third, in the words of Stephen Jay Gould, one of the group's members, scientific facts should not be viewed as "unsullied, pristine bits of truth because culture influences what we see and how we see it."[42]

- Fourth, the group argued that scientific conclusions are not as certain as the courts assume. One criticism of the epidemiologically based statistical evidence presented by the Dauberts was that it could be manipulated to produce varying or even contradictory conclusions. The comparison the group offered for the plaintiffs' statistical re-analysis of existing data was auditing a previously completed financial report or submitting medical records and complex tests to another physician to obtain a second opinion. Furthermore, they argued, simply because research to date had not produced a link between Bendectin and birth defects, that did not mean that no study ever would and thus the matter was closed.[43]

- Finally, the Bayer group suspected that the courts wanted what it colorfully described as "a quick and easy Good Housekeeping Seal of Approval" on science, and that they had seized upon peer-reviewed publication as an appropriate litmus test for admissibility.[44] But the group rejected that standard and argued for more liberal standards such as those found in the 1975 Federal Rules of Evidence.

The Bloembergen group argued directly against the proposals of the Bayer group. While acknowledging that peer-reviewed publication is no panacea, they insisted that the scientific scrutiny afforded by peer review and publication is a necessary, although not sufficient, requirement for establishing what is good science.[45] The group likewise agreed that scientific truth is neither absolute nor constant, but reminded the justices of a basic principle of science: a hypothesis can be disproved by a single experiment or piece of data, but no matter how many experiments or how much data confirms it, it cannot, ultimately, be proven true because knowledge is always incomplete, and scientific statements or theories are never final and are always subject to revision or rejection.[46]

In this regard the Bloembergen group pointed to a fundamental difference between the legal and scientific worlds: a court of law seeks to establish the truth beyond the shadow of a doubt in criminal matters, but it is the nature of science that no scientific fact can ever be considered "absolute truth," because in a month or a year or a hundred years new information could overturn a hypothesis that had until that time been confirmed repeatedly.[47] (Consider for how many centuries the earth was considered to be the center of the universe.)

Science and the law employ different methodologies and seek "truth" in different manners. Science seeks "descriptive general theories based on particular data," whereas the law needs "a system of normative general rules that are individualized to apply to particular cases"—working in opposite directions, as it were. Science also works to predict future events, while the legal system attempts to discover facts about unique past events.[48]

The Bloembergen group agreed once more with the Bayer group that science does not "automatically exclude a piece of evidence just because it is deemed unorthodox at the time." But again, science and the law have different purposes, they argued. Scientific facts are introduced into the courtroom in support of one side or the other in a legal dispute, so the criteria used to judge evidence in the laboratory are not appropriate in that setting, and more restrictive standards should be applied.[49]

Finally, the Bloembergen brief proposed that the peer-reviewed publication standard widely espoused by the courts was a reasonable and appropriate one. However, it noted that the purpose of the peer review process is to judge the methodology and underlying principles of the research, "but not the conclusions reached."[50] In short, the group supported the continued use of the *Frye* rule.

The Supreme Court in a majority opinion written by Justice Blackmun struck a balance between the *Frye* rule and the 1975 Federal Rules of Evidence, though at first glance it might not seem so: the justices unanimously held that the Federal Rules of Evidence should supersede the *Frye* rule. However, the Bloembergen brief strongly influenced much of what followed in the opinion.

Justice Blackmun proposed that lower court judges should serve as "gatekeepers" tasked with ensuring "the reliability of scientific evidence." However, he specifically directed that in doing so, judges should "evaluate reliability in terms of the validity of the scientific methodology involved, not on the general acceptance of the conclusions generated," and went a step further in stating that scientific conclusions used in court must be testable. He accepted what the Bayer group had asserted and ruled that peer review can be one indicator of reliability but cannot solely determine it.[51]

What Blackmun took from the Bloembergen brief was predominantly the differences between science and the law. He agreed that "scientific conclusions are subject to perpetual revision. Law, on the other hand, must resolve disputes finally and quickly." Consequently, "it may be useful to consider a wide range of information in the scientific process, but not necessarily in the legal process."[52] Blackmun praised "the balance struck by Rules of Evidence designed not for the exhaustive search for cosmic understanding but for the particularized resolution of legal disputes."[53]

While much of this legal rationale applies to direct scientific evidence, it also indirectly impacts the science on which simulations and other such demonstrative evidence is based. This is an important consideration given how quickly simulation and other computer technology is evolving. It may also draw the line between a computer *animation* that illustrates the prosecution's or defense's version of events and a computer *simulation* that uses available factual data to reconstruct an event. It may well be quite difficult for the jury to distinguish between the two, so it will fall to the judge to make that determination based on the rules for admitting scientific evidence discussed here. The standards are, after all, significantly lower for unadmitted exhibits: " … Because an animation merely illustrates and is based on the witness's testimony, instead of math and science, it is not substantive evidence, and thus there are no *Daubert*, *Frye*, or Rule 702 implications."[54]

Techniques for Use of Demonstrative Evidence

Stephen Lindsay, the previously quoted criminal defense attorney who often serves as a federal public defender and writes and speaks extensively on the topic, asserts that cultural changes have actually made demonstrative exhibits (Lindsay uses "demonstra-

Photo 5-2

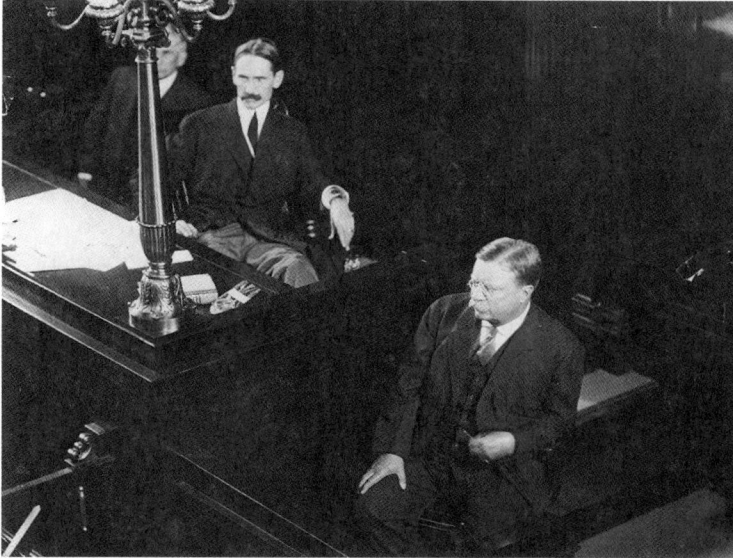

Colonel Theodore Roosevelt testifying before a jury in the Roose Libel case in the court house at Marquette, Michigan, in 1913. Photograph courtesy of the Library of Congress.

tive evidence," but we will remain consistent in our previously established use of terminology) more important in the modern courtroom. He identifies two major factors that have made this so.

The first is what he calls the "diminishing ability to use imagination" that he asserts is prevalent among today's jury pools. He points to older techniques that relied on "verbal gymnastics, fancy speeches, and a big dose of charisma during closing arguments," something most of us have probably seen repeatedly in television and movie portrayals of trials.[55] Lindsay attributes this change to two causes.

One is that television has advanced significantly (to say nothing of visual effects in movies). For the previous generation, television shows "tended to be black and white ... and were filmed using one or two cameras." Consequently, viewers were forced to "fill in" many aspects of the scene that were not presented to them on the screen. But modern television "has become multi-dimensional. Programs are filmed using ten or fifteen cameras giving the viewer a complete perspective of everything that is going on. There is little room, if any room at all, for the viewer to make use of his or her imagination."[56] Another similar generational factor that Lindsay does not identify is that books were a much more common form of entertainment in the past, and of course books demand far more from the reader's imagination than the most primitive television show ever did.

Lindsay next identifies the changes in music experienced by the "MTV Generation." He notes that in the days before music videos, "each listener used his or her imagination to decide what the song was about." Now, thanks to music videos, "the listeners (viewers) are told what the song means, in vivid color, with stereophonic sound, and from every available camera angle." As a result, he asserts, listeners are now told what a song means rather than having to use their imagination to figure that out.[57] Although Lindsay was writing recently, it could be argued that music has shifted yet again. Because so many listeners now consume digital music from a mobile device rather than sitting in front of a television, the music video is less influential than it was during its heyday in the 1980s when, as many have commented, "MTV actually showed music videos." Granted, new distribution channels such as YouTube make music videos readily available, but both now and in the "MTV years" music videos often seemed to have little to do with the lyrics of the song and left much open to interpretation. So in some respects Lindsay's arguments carry less weight than they might have twenty years ago.

Nevertheless, his central point seems sound: that modern jury pools are made up of people who for the most part have been "media-trained to avoid using imagination."[58] It is difficult to dispute the proposition that the public today is highly visually oriented and thanks to modern special effects and computer graphics expects to see everything laid out before their eyes. If the evening (or online) news can provide a computer animation of the latest crime or tragedy, why can't an attorney?

Lindsay's other factor is that, in his words, "prosecutors have figured out the power and persuasiveness of demonstrative evidence and are actively using it against us." Indeed, to repeat an earlier quote from the Seventh Circuit decision in *Baugh*, "as jurors have become more visually oriented, counsel in modern trials seek to persuade them with an ever-expanding array of objects, maps, charts, displays, summaries, video reconstructions, computer simulations, and so on."[59] In short, demonstrative exhibits are no longer an edge in the courtroom; they are now necessary just to "keep up with the competition," as it were.

As we have stated multiple times in this chapter, demonstrative exhibits are the responsibility of the attorney, not the law enforcement officer. Typically they are based on evidence gathered through traditional collection methods, on the results of investigation, or both. Nevertheless, it is worth understanding how these tools may be employed in the courtroom, and Lindsay provides examples and suggestions to his readers that should prove informative.

One example, which he uses to drive home his point that prosecutors are now wise to the use of demonstrative exhibits, involved the kidnapping, rape, and murder of a young female jogger. Her assailant abducted her and took her to a remote forested area where he assaulted her, tying her to a tree before killing her. The jury quickly returned a conviction, but during the sentencing phase the prosecutor had the *actual tree* to which the victim had been bound brought into the courtroom. She—the prosecutor was a woman, which certainly magnified the effects of what she did—then tied herself to the tree and spoke to the jury "from the perspective of the victim in her final moments of life." Whether the jury would have returned a death sentence anyway can be debated, but this particular demonstrative exhibit was "absolutely" persuasive in Lindsay's opinion—and it is difficult to argue against that opinion. In fact, the prosecutor's act was so prejudicial and lacking in evidentiary value that it is hard to imagine that the court would have allowed it even as a demonstrative exhibit during the trial phase.

Lindsay notes that public defenders rarely "have the opportunity to represent wealthy clients" and consequently face "very limited budgets when it comes to trial preparation." One easy, inexpensive, but nevertheless persuasive type of demonstrative exhibit he recommends is the diagram. In part this is because he sees them as "a wonderful way to get you up out of your seat, away from your podium, and close to the jury" given that "many jurisdictions require counsel to either remain at [the] counsel table or at a podium."[60]

Diagrams are also a method for enabling "a witness [to] tell his or her story more than once," which is important since "the more times the witness's version of the events is told, the more likely the jury is to believe what is said." He describes a "funnel approach" which involves multiple diagrams, the first covering a large area, then a second covering a smaller subsection of that area, and finally a third one that "focuses on the relevant location," thereby providing "multiple, legitimate opportunities to repeat the witness's version of the events."[61] In considering this tactic it is hard not to be reminded of Kevin Costner as prosecutor Jim Garrison in the 1991 movie *JFK*, as he shows the moment in the Zapruder film when the fatal shot hits President Kennedy over and over, each time repeating "Back, and to the left."

One potential problem with diagrams is that the other side can use them as well, often to the detriment of those who introduced them. Lindsay warns that "Prosecutors will often attempt to undermine your diagrams in a variety of ways"; in particular they "often mark up our exhibits and leave the exhibits looking like a doodle pad." He suggests covering the diagram with a piece of clear plastic so that the prosecutor and opposing witnesses are forced to write on the plastic instead, which can later be removed for use in closing arguments. His description of another public defender's tactic for avoiding this problem sounds rather less savory:

> Jon Sands uses PAM vegetable spray on his diagrams. He puts "Velcro" on the diagram where he wants to affix something. He then sprays the diagram with PAM. The magic of this is that you can't write on a diagram sprayed with PAM. The prosecutors usually don't have "Velcro" and when they try and write on the diagram the ink beads up. Even if the prosecutor does have some "Velcro," it doesn't stick to the PAM-covered diagrams either.[62]

One need not be an attorney to recognize that most judges would probably not tolerate such games were substantive evidence involved.

For using photographs, Lindsay recommends making slides and presenting a slide show. The problem with passing photos to the jury, he argues, is that as each one is passed along, each juror is taking in the contents of the picture and judging its significance separately. Furthermore, the trial proceedings will continue, and jurors may well be distracted or at best forced to divide their attention between the two. With a slide show, the entire jury sees the same photo and hears the description of its significance simultaneously, and that is the only thing they are doing.[63]

He recommends justifying a slide show to the trial judge "as a 'time-saving' procedure" in this way:

> If the witness has several photos to go through, put them in a single photo album. Have the witness identify each photo then offer the album into evidence. Advise the judge that there is only one set and rather than take the time for each juror to go through the album, you have made slides of each picture and they are merely copies of the actual exhibit. Then dim the lights, [and] go through the slides one at a time as the witness describes what is being shown.[64]

Another inexpensive technique is the use of an overhead projector. Lindsay recommends this especially when dealing with witness testimony if the witness has said conflicting things in the past. Rather than merely telling the jury, it is much more effective to put transcripts of the conflicting statements side-by-side on the overhead and walk the jury through the differences. Similarly, if a witness has entered into a plea deal in return for providing testimony, "during closing use the witness's plea agreement comparing it to how he/she testified about having no expectations from providing testimony."[65]

Paint chips are another cheap-to-free option recommended by Lindsay as useful demonstrative exhibits. If, for example, the car used in a crime was blue according to witness testimony and the defendant was apprehended in a blue car, the attorney can during cross-examination refer to a set of paint chips and ask the witness something along the lines of "Mrs. Smith, you said the car you saw was blue. Was it closer to this blue or to this blue?" Doing so—and doing so over and over—forces "the witness to select between options and make choices. This can create the appearance of uncertainty."[66]

The same technique is also an option with skin color. Lindsay sets up the scenario thus:

> "Officer Jones, the store clerk told you the robber was a black man. Did you understand the clerk to mean his skin tone was closer to this color or to this color ... ?" When you do the skin tone, paint chip cross with your police officer have him or her come down in front of the jury with his/her back to the defendant. When you start using the paint chips, nine times out of ten the police officer will [peek] over his or her shoulder to look at the defendant. This is a wonderful time to say "no cheating now." The point is brought home that even the officer isn't sure, and the point is brought home demonstratively, powerfully, and persuasively. Even if the officer does not sneak a [peek], you can still say to the officer "now don't peek."

Clearly both such uses of paint chips have nothing to do with determining the truth and everything to do with weakening the credibility of a witness, quite possibly a very competent witness, and/or on a point that is not really in contention. (Otherwise, after all, the attorney would directly attack the evidence.)[67] You may call these "dirty tricks," but attorneys call them "tactics," and with demonstrative exhibits they are generally permissible. Since as a law enforcement officer you could one day be subject to such a tactic, it is helpful to be able to anticipate it.

Lindsay's exploration of demonstrative exhibits goes even further, encompassing a very broad definition that includes what he terms "non-evidence demonstrative evidence." At its most basic this "includes how you dress, how you act, react, or respond, and your overall attitude." He goes on to provide examples from both his own experience and that of others.[68]

First, he recommends closely observing the demeanor of witnesses in order to see whether it includes anything that might be of value. For example, "in a sex offense case where you suspect the child is being coached by his or her parent," he suggests deliberately standing between the child and the suspected coach. If coaching is taking place, the child, the coach, or both will move in order to maintain eye contact, and the attorney can then move to block that contact once more. If this continues, "the jury will catch on and before long the jury will look like the gallery at a tennis match—left, right, left, right, turning first to the child and then to the parent/coach. The point is brought home that the child is being coached. However, nowhere in the trial transcript will that which was so persuasive be revealed."[69]

Next, returning to his theme of visually oriented jury pools, Lindsay suggests ways to better illustrate quantities that are key to testimony. With a witness who admits to having consumed alcohol prior to observing the event about which he or she is testifying, for example, it will probably already have been determined during depositions just how much the witness claims to have consumed. "If the witness says he or she had consumed about a case of beer that night, bring in a case of beer, count out the cans or bottles with the witness in front of the jury." The attorney can then refer to the exhibit again during closing arguments "to again bring home the point that the witness, by his or her own admission, had 'this much alcohol to drink.' "[70]

Similarly, if the weight or bulk of an item is at issue, that can also be illustrated for the jury. Lindsay's example is of a suspect accused of stealing $125 in quarters from a game machine; bringing that quantity of quarters into the courtroom will show the jury just how much weight and bulk is involved. This is particularly effective if a witness claims to have seen the defendant leaving the vicinity of the crime but observed nothing in his hands and no unusual bulges in his clothing.

A more abstract employment of this concept has been used by public defenders in rape cases in which the defense's assertion is that consensual sex occurred, not rape — what Lindsay refers to as the "this was not rape, it was regret" defense. He offers the example of Sheila Lewis, an attorney with the New Mexico Public Defender's Office, who during closing arguments presented the jury with two boxes, one labeled "Rape" and the other labeled "Regret." She had previously established through testimony that even under microscopic examination the alleged victim's clothing showed no damage — "not a thread was loose, not a button torn free, not a zipper out of line." Furthermore, physician testimony established that there was no evidence of trauma. Lewis then walked the jury through each piece of evidence during her close, dropping each one into the "Regret" box as she finished with it. This technique shows the jury "in a quantitative way that all of the evidence points to innocence."[71]

In some cases demonstrative exhibits may be aural rather than visual. Lindsay relates another case defended by Jon Sands in which the defendant was accused of sexual assault. Sands had established in the course of investigation that several people were at home and near the bed when the assault allegedly occurred, and furthermore that the bed springs were very squeaky, so he introduced that bed as a demonstrative exhibit during his closing argument. He sat on the bed, bouncing up and down, as he spoke to the jury — over the very loud squeak of the springs, illustrating that witnesses would have heard the bed had the assault actually occurred.[72]

Lindsay's second example of such aural exhibits is indirect and involves fingerprint evidence. Since fingerprint analysis involves establishing six to twelve matching points of identification out of about 150 possible such points, he describes a technique wherein he brings a metal pail and a jar of BBs before the jury during closing arguments, asking them to close their eyes when he reaches the discussion of the fingerprint evidence.

> This case boils down to whether this fingerprint is in fact the defendant's. But we know so little about the print. All we know is that it is supposedly the same in six places. (Slowly drop six BBs into the pail, one at a time). But there

are some two hundred places we know nothing about. (Slowly pour 150 BBs into the pail). I don't know how you define reasonable doubt, but I'd say you just heard it.[73]

He recommends similar techniques "in any situation where you have a large quantity versus a small quantity," even going so far as to suggest that steel shot is better than BBs since it "is heavier and makes a louder noise when the pellets hit the pail."[74]

Whether you like them or not, whether you consider them fair tactics or unfair trickery, and bearing in mind that these are not solely tools of the defense attorney, the fact remains that you will likely encounter such demonstrative exhibits more than once during your career as you testify in criminal cases. Forewarned, as the old saying tells us, is forearmed.

Relevance

Setting aside some of the techniques described by Stephen Lindsay that are strictly for use in closing arguments, it is important to remember that demonstrative exhibits must have a basis even though they are not admitted as substantive evidence. Bear in mind that such an exhibit "has no probative value itself, but merely serves as a visual aid to the jury in comprehending the verbal testimony of a witness or other evidence."[75] As such, in many cases the admissibility of a demonstrative exhibit is directly tied to the admissibility of the testimony or evidence that it supports, and essentially the same relevance standards apply. A law enforcement officer or forensic technician might testify to the scene he or she encountered at a murder, but whether explicit, gory photographs of the crime scene would be admitted as supporting exhibits to that testimony will depend on whether their potential prejudicial effects are outweighed by their value in proving the alleged events. The trial judge might determine, for example, that a diagram of the scene provides all of the relevant information needed by the jury.

Visual aids used to support testimony can also be excluded as merely cumulative, meaning that they are redundant and add little or nothing of value to that testimony. The attorney who attempts to introduce demonstrative exhibits to support every single facet of a witness's testimony, including facts that are simple, commonly known, or stipulated, will quickly have his or her reins pulled sharply by the trial judge. But within reason, "in practice ... the use of models, drawings, and charts is now almost universally permitted."[76]

The common law background of demonstrative evidence was not particularly illuminating for judges and attorneys. Brain and Broderick note that

> Under common law regulation of evidence, the propriety of a witness's use of some sort of demonstrative exhibit was simply assumed by most American trial judges and trial lawyers. Occasionally an objection would be made to the introduction of a particular demonstrative exhibit, but the early case law contains absolutely no discussion of what evidential standards governed the admissibility of demonstrative evidence as a separate category of proof.[77]

He goes on to add that "the assumed admissibility of this type of proof has not changed in the modern era of code-based evidence regulation," leading to judicial determinations on a case-by-case basis when opposing counsel objects to a particular piece of demonstrative evidence.[78]

However, Brain and Broderick also make a key point in their discussion regarding demonstrative evidence and relevance: " ... As a matter of definitional logic, demonstrative evidence does not and cannot meet the test of relevance required under modern evidence rules" because the basic standard for relevance (and therefore admissibility) is that a given "piece of evidence must make the existence of a fact of consequence in the action more or less probable than it would be without that evidence."[79] This is the same fundamental definition of relevance that we considered earlier in this text; Brain and Broderick are not offering any earth-shattering leaps of logic here, and it is thus surprising that courts have ever had cause to question the status of demonstrative evidence.

In order to address this gap in logic, Brain and Broderick propose a concept they call "derivative relevance." This is akin to the premise included in the first paragraph of this section, which is that a demonstrative exhibit derives its relevance from that of the substantive evidence or testimony that it is intended to clarify or explain. Standing alone, demonstrative evidence has no life of its own in the courtroom, let alone relevance. Still, demonstrative evidence can have a significant impact, since "making a piece of substantive evidence more comprehensible may ultimately change the perceived likelihood that a fact of consequence has occurred...."[80] Conversely, the use of some of the techniques described by Lindsay—such as the use of paint chips in the cross-examination of an eyewitness—may negatively affect the jury's perception of what was previously a rather solid fact.

Brain and Broderick's proposed definition is essentially the one we have arrived at in the course of our discussion in this chapter; they describe it as "any display that is principally used to illustrate or explain other testimonial, documentary, or real proof, or a judicially noticed fact. It is, in short, a visual (or other sensory) aid."[81] They divide demonstrative evidence into six categories:

- In-court demonstrations, re-creations, or experiments;
- Models and other tangible objects;
- Charts, diagrams, and maps;
- Photographs, movies, and videotapes;
- Jury views (*i.e.*, "when the jury visits a relevant site that has been or will be described by a witness"); and
- Computer-dependent animations and simulations.[82]

Not every piece of evidence or exhibit that falls into one of these categories is automatically a demonstrative exhibit, however. For example, photographs or video taken from a surveillance camera that captured a criminal act in progress are substantive evidence; a map might be documentary evidence (albeit normally in a civil matter); and we have previously discussed how some computer simulations can be substantive evidence as well.

Relevance of substantive evidence is established by what Brain and Broderick call the "tendency-to-prove relationship," the condition that a given piece of evidence proves or helps to prove a fact substantive to the case. But they extend that definition to the function of demonstrative evidence, which is to clarify or explain a piece of substantive evidence, and has a tendency to illustrate or explain a piece of relevant evidence.[83]

It is worth noting that Brain and Broderick's definition is narrower than that offered by Lindsay; they distinguish demonstrative exhibits used during opening and closing arguments (Lindsay's bucket and BBs or "Rape" and "Regret" boxes) from true demonstrative evidence. "To the extent that such exhibits are subsequently used as demonstrative evidence during the testimony of a witness, their status as demonstrative evidence is unchanged. On the other hand, if the exhibit principally repeats counsel's words and is not referenced by later [or prior] testimony, then the exhibit becomes part of the argument of counsel...."[84]

As mentioned in the opening paragraphs of this section, it is possible for a demonstrative exhibit to meet relevance standards based on the relevance of the evidence it explains yet not be permitted in court. Rule 403 of the Federal Rules of Evidence allows the court to "exclude relevant evidence if its probative value is substantially outweighed by a danger of one or more of the following: unfair prejudice, confusing the issues, misleading the jury, undue delay, wasting time, or needlessly presenting cumulative evidence."[85] The most common reasons for a judge to bar a demonstrative exhibit are unfair prejudice (for example, the aforementioned gory murder scene photographs) and needless presentation of cumulative evidence (redundancy).

Photographic Evidence

As previously noted, humans are strongly visually oriented. While models, diagrams, charts, and graphs are all potentially helpful visual aids in the courtroom, it is difficult to find anything that conveys a tremendous amount of information with as great efficiency as a photograph. We previously discussed photographs as substantive evidence as a subset of documentary evidence in Chapter 4; here we will briefly consider photographs as demonstrative exhibits.

Federal Rule of Evidence 1002 requires "an original ... photograph" for authentication purposes. However, "when [photographs are] used purely as demonstrative evidence, legal issues regarding authentication and chain of custody are somewhat relaxed so long as a competent witness can testify that the photograph accurately and fairly depicts the scene about which he or she is testifying."[86] Moreover, "over many years, the definition of an 'original' has been greatly expanded, particularly with regard to electronically stored information," and today duplicates "are typically admissible to the same degree as an original document unless admitting the duplicate would prove inaccurate or unfair."[87]

Naturally, authentication issues arise when the opposing side disputes the accuracy or authenticity of a given photograph. There is normally some tolerance for a degree of inaccuracy in a photograph so long as that inaccuracy is fully disclosed. The Alaska Supreme Court (which tends to mirror federal rulings) held in *Kaps Transport, Inc. v. Henry* (1977)[88] that the fact "that there are inaccuracies or defects in the photograph does not necessarily render it inadmissible so long as there is an explanation of these imperfections so that the jury is not misled."[89] With proper disclosure, opposing counsel has the opportunity to explore those imperfections during cross-examination of the witness whose testimony the photographs support.

However, the standards are significantly higher when a photograph is to be part of an expert witness's testimony. Kashi provides the example of *Kaps v. Henry*, in which an expert witness intended to use a photograph of the accident scene as part of an accident reconstruction technique called perspective analysis. An accurate perspective analysis requires that "the focal length used to take the photograph and the conditions under which the photograph was taken must be known with a substantial degree of precision," something the defendant in the case was unable to provide. Because "the photograph was to be used to provide actual data about the accident scene rather than merely illustrating the area," "it was subject to a more rigorous authentication process which it ultimately failed."[90] This is akin to the difference between a computer animation used as a demonstrative exhibit and a computer simulation that purports to reconstruct an event, as we discussed earlier.

Even wholly inaccurate photographs permitted as exhibits will generally not taint a verdict if they are countered by testimony or other evidence. In another Alaska Supreme Court ruling, the highway department, that was the defendant in a case stemming from an accident on an icy highway, submitted photographs showing that the roadway at the accident site was well-sanded. As it happened, those photographs were taken a significant amount of time after the accident (exactly how long was never established), raising the possibility that they did not reflect the actual condition of the road when the incident occurred. However, the state police officers who investigated the accident testified that the road was in fact poorly sanded and that the pictures did not accurately reflect conditions at the scene, thereby nullifying the impact of the inaccurate photographs.[91]

In order to keep photographs from crossing the line into undue prejudice, there are a few rules of thumb that should be observed. While enlargements are quite acceptable—Brain and Broderick quote a Vermont Supreme Court justice who in 1887 dismissed objections to enlarged photographs by noting that "one may 'as well object to the use of an eye-glass by one whose vision is defective, as to the use of enlarged illustrative photographs' "[92]—there are limits. Peterson advises against enlargements that are larger than life-size, especially when wounds, injuries, or other content with the potential to elicit a strong emotional response are the subject.[93]

Another good practice with gory—and therefore potentially prejudicial—photograph subjects is to take both color and black and white pictures. "Graphic injuries such as open wounds, severed limbs, and other gruesome injuries" tend to be perceived as less "real" and therefore have less emotional impact in black and white, and these may pass the potential prejudice threshold when a color photograph would not.[94] Finally, in order to avoid the sorts of technical issues that Kashi describes or outright poor quality, any of which can provide grounds for opposing counsel to object to the photographs even as demonstrative exhibits (or at the very least a basis to attack those exhibits if admitted by the trial judge), having photographs taken professionally is a good practice.[95]

We should note in closing that under the Federal Rules of Evidence, video (whether a videotape or digital video) is treated the same as photographs. Moreover, Rule 1001(3) holds that " 'any print' of a videotape is an 'original' and thus outside the scope of the best evidence rule."[96] From the attorney's perspective, video tends to be more persuasive than photographs and also can be edited if the version submitted is ruled inadmissible. But Peterson warns against overplaying videos because "a jury may become desensitized after several viewings, as evidenced by the jury's decision after viewing the video depicting the Rodney King beating."[97]

Digital Evidence

One driver of efforts to better define and establish rules for demonstrative evidence is the impact that computer technology has had, and continues to have, on the conduct of trials. Brain and Broderick—and bear in mind that they were writing in 1992—describe how "the advent of relatively low-cost but powerful computers and sophisticated computer graphics software" has changed demonstrative evidence "from the 'state-of-the-art' brightly colored charts and nascent day-in-the-life films of the early 1980s to professionally produced movies ... dramatically depicting, for example, an expert's opinion of what the pilot saw from the cockpit during the last fifteen minutes before an airplane crash...."[98] With commendable foresight, they predict that "Within the next decade or so, even these types of demonstrative exhibits will seem tame, as then-state-of-the-art demonstrative proof will be even more powerful," and go on to speculate that "Technology will soon be available for a witness to don a 'body suit' in the courtroom, step into a three-dimensional reconstruction of the scene, and illustrate exactly what she says occurred at the relevant locale by interacting in real time with the objects on the screen."[99] Of course, such technology is indeed available today, though thus far it is not exactly in common use in the courtroom.

Technology has in some respects raised concerns about tampering or outright falsification of evidence. While there is certainly some risk in this arena, in other ways technology has actually improved the ability to authenticate evidence. Kashi explains how the metadata that is built into every digital photograph can aid the discovery process and assist in the screening of evidence produced by opposing counsel. Photographic metadata includes a wealth of information about the photo—many smartphones, in fact, by default even include GPS tagging of the location where the picture was taken—that readily point to any alteration of the picture after the fact, and of course metadata that is missing entirely is a huge red flag. Metadata can show "use of a camera that the witness did not own or that the photograph was taken on date or time remote from the pertinent time frame."[100] Careful examination of metadata may also enable the impeachment of digital photographic evidence submitted by opposing counsel.

Metadata is associated with digital files other than photographs as well. To see a simple example, right-click on a Microsoft Word file and select "Properties." What appears is a subset of the metadata for that file; the "Details" tab will show such information as how many times the file has been revised; the total amount of time spent editing the file; the count of pages, words, characters, paragraphs, and lines; and the dates it was last accessed and modified. But metadata is far more powerful, and it is incorporated into a set of standards for what is collectively known as electronically stored information, or ESI.

Industry standards for forensic examination of ESI use a unique hash value that changes every time a file is accessed or modified. If a file is merely copied from a computer onto a USB drive or CD, for example, the hash value for the new file is different even though no alterations were made to the original file. Digital forensic analysts use a special process that includes use of a write blocker device on the source hard drive to prevent any changes to the source data and a bit-by-bit copy of the entire drive. This process also copies the blank space on the drive, where evidence of deleted files may linger.[101] This process allows the presentation of authenticated digital evidence as well as the ability to forensically recover deleted files.

Experiments

In most cases an experiment (or strictly speaking, the results of that experiment) constitutes substantive evidence. Experimental results typically "show the nature of a substance, cause and effect, characteristics, and the like. Common illustrations include ballistics tests, blood tests in paternity matters, and analysis of substances in narcotics cases."[102] Rarely will such types of experiments be intended merely as demonstrative evidence, instead being held to the higher standard of substantive evidence including when necessary evaluation based on the standards for scientific evidence discussed earlier in this chapter. Additionally, "the purpose of an experiment ... [may be] to determine how a particular event occurred or did not occur."[103] This form is more akin to the simulation intended to reconstruct an event, and similarly must meet higher standards.

In most cases experiments are conducted out of the courtroom, prior to trial—generally speaking we do not ask a laboratory technician to perform the testing necessary to identify a substance confiscated at a drug bust in front of the jury. Because the typical experiment requires carefully controlled conditions in order to provide valid feedback, to say nothing of the equipment often involved, it would not be practical to perform an experiment in court even if that were desirable. McCormick's *Evidence* points out that

> In addition to the limitations arising from the desirability of orderly and expeditious proceedings, in-court experiments are held to the same basic requirement of similarity of conditions which is applicable to experimental evidence generally. This requirement may be particularly difficult to meet under courtroom conditions, and many proposed courtroom experiments have been held properly excluded on this ground.[104]

Experiments intended to be only demonstrative naturally face a lower standard, though for the sake of strict accuracy the term "experiment" is probably not warranted; "demonstration" might be better. The infamous ladder in *Baugh* that we examined so thoroughly in this chapter may well spring to mind. The defense's expert witness manipulated the ladder in a number of ways in essence attempting to cause it to fail, which of course served to reinforce the expert's testimony that the design of the ladder was not in fact faulty, and this demonstration was presented to the jury by video. This was in some ways an experiment since the expert witness was arguably attempting to determine conditions that would cause the ladder to malfunction as the plaintiff alleged that it had, but the strict controls that would accompany a true experiment were not present, and in any event the absence of a design flaw in that model of ladder even if experimentally proven would not preclude a manufacturing flaw in the plaintiff's specific ladder. As a demonstration, however, it was adequate, and as it happened the plaintiff's counsel objected not to the demonstration mounted by the expert witness but by the sample ladder's presence in the jury room.

Sample State Treatments of Demonstrative Evidence

As we have seen, the Federal Rules of Evidence are nearly silent on the issue of demonstrative evidence. Federal court decisions have addressed the subject, though not always consistently as we saw with the rulings of the Seventh Circuit compared to some out of the Fifth and Tenth Circuits. Moreover, as a law enforcement officer you will typically deal with state, not federal, courts. For that reason, we will look at a sampling of states and how their rules address the concept of demonstrative evidence or exhibits.

Michigan: The Michigan Rules of Evidence generally echo the Federal Rules of Evidence on standards of admissibility and relevance. Michigan courts have held that "demonstrative evidence used to assist the testimony of a witness or to illustrate general principles only had to meet the 'substantial similarity' test of *Smith v. Grange Mutual Fire Insurance Co.* (1926)."[105] The state has in effect a three-tiered system; in addition to substantive evidence and demonstrative evidence as just described, it also recognizes "demonstrative aids," though the rules of evidence are "more vague and less developed" when it comes to "constraints on the use of demonstrative aids."[106] This class is essentially best described by the term "demonstrative exhibits" that we have adopted. From a legal standpoint, these aids are "intended to substitute for or complement a trial lawyer's spoken word. Thus, logically, if a trial lawyer can say it during the appropriate time at trial, he should also be able to show it."[107] As with the Seventh Circuit's holding in *Baugh*, demonstrative aids may not be taken into the jury room.

Missouri: Adding to the confused terminology surrounding demonstrative evidence, Missouri jurisprudence refers to demonstrative evidence and "true demonstrative evidence," which is "created by the attorneys which may be helpful in clarifying or illustrating information to the jury."[108] The Missouri Supreme Court established in *Vasseghi v. McNutt* (1991)[109] that trial judges may admit various aids intended "to aid the jury to understand the testimony, unless deemed so inaccurate as to engender confusion," which implies that a limited degree of inaccuracy is acceptable. (Specifically at issue in *Vasseghi* was a drawing of a motor vehicle accident scene that was not "drawn to scale or absolutely accurate.")[110] One form of demonstration addressed by the Missouri courts is the display of injuries in the courtroom, which are generally permitted unless "designed merely to arouse antipathy against the defendant and sympathy for the plaintiff." Of course, in most cases the presentation of an injury is substantive evidence since it is more direct than even a photographic or video presentation would be.[111] As for computer simulations, the Missouri Supreme Court rejected the admission of a computer simulation submitted by the State Highway and Transportation Commission in a motor vehicle accident case that was intended to show that one of the vehicles at issue could not have hydroplaned as claimed by the plaintiff. The ruling held that because so many factors of the accident were unknown that key variables in the simulation could not be determined, thereby destroying the reliability of the simulation as a whole.[112] Finally, as is common elsewhere, demonstrative aids may not be given to the jury during deliberations.

Texas: The state of Texas has not differentiated significantly between demonstrative evidence (*i.e.*, true evidence) and demonstrative exhibits or aids. Photographs, X-rays, and video face authentication requirements along the lines of those found in the Federal Rules of Evidence. Models and illustrations must "be helpful to the jury in understanding the evidence" and "an accurate representation of that which it is claimed to represent."[113] Charts and graphs "summarizing testimony are admissible subject to the trial court's discretion," while "charts utilized by an expert depicting data are admissible so long as the expert testifies to the truth and accuracy of the data." Timelines are treated similarly.[114] Computer animations must meet reliability and relevance tests; for reliability, the computer animator must be qualified and his or her testimony "grounded in the methods and procedures of science," and naturally for relevance the animation must be associated with the facts of the case. Reenactments, including experiments performed outside the courtroom, are permitted when used to summarize the testimony of an expert witness and when the conditions of the reenactment meet the "substantial similarity" standard.[115]

Idaho: Providing yet another alternative term, the Idaho Trial Handbook advises that "Courts interchangeably use the terms 'demonstrative evidence' and 'illustrative evidence' to refer to evidence which is offered to assist the jury in understanding the testimony of a witness or other evidence...."[116] As with other states we have considered, Idaho rules require that such aids supplement testimony or improve the jury's understanding of evidence presented or facts at issue, and exclusion is based on the classic balancing test between probative value and potential to prejudice or confuse the jury. As in Missouri, a diagram used as an illustrative aid "does not have to be shown to be precisely accurate or consistent with the testimony of other witnesses."[117] In-court demonstrations are acceptable "to show the feasibility or infeasibility of certain events," but if the "purported limitations are within the subjective control of the witness," the court must exercise care to ensure that the jury is not misled. (The case law reference is to an excluded demonstration of a witness's attempt to read from a book in order to establish that he did not understand English—the flaws in such a demonstration should be obvious.)[118] The criteria for allowing computer animations, simulations, and re-creations are similar to those applied in Texas.

Virginia: Virginia procedure uses "demonstrative evidence" to refer to both real evidence and what it, like Idaho, calls "illustrative evidence." Trial courts are permitted "very considerable latitude" in determining what is admissible and what is not, subject to the typical exclusions of evidence which is "highly prejudicial and without significant probative value," and appellate courts are not to interfere absent "an abuse of discretion" in this capacity.[119] Illustrative evidence is permitted in opening and closing arguments when it is supported by real evidence. The "Virginia courts have repeatedly admitted non-inflammatory photographs of murder victims into evidence over defendants' objections in order to illustrate malice, premeditation, and the degree of atrociousness of the crime."[120] Demonstrations of crimes for the jury are acceptable "if they are helpful to the jury in understanding testimony" even if the weapon used is not identical to the one used in a violent crime.[121]

The takeaway is that some states have gone further than others in defining demonstrative evidence, though some seem to have made little differentiation thus far. In general evidentiary standards are similar from state to state and in comparison to federal rules, but local specifics can vary in important ways, such as jurisdictions where demonstrative exhibits can be taken into the jury room. (Some authorities have even argued that this *should* be the case.) A review of your state's rules of evidence or, if available, a summary of how those rules are applied can prove quite useful in understanding the power and limitations of demonstrative exhibits for the sorts of cases in which you are likely to be involved.

Conclusion

Of all the topics covered in this text, demonstrative evidence is among the trickiest simply because overall it has been poorly defined and lacks clear rules governing its use. As we saw, even the terminology is fuzzy—"demonstrative evidence" is used to describe many different forms, including some that are formally admitted substantive evidence, and the term may well be used interchangeably within the same jurisdiction. Other terminology that is potentially clearer but not consistently used includes "demonstrative exhibits," "illustrative aids," and "illustrative evidence." Fortunately for the law enforcement officer, it is primarily the purview of the attorney, and on that note includes techniques that are less concerned with establishing objective truth than with influencing the jury's perception of a particular witness or piece of evidence. But as relevant technology, particularly computer animation, advances rapidly, and as more and more attorneys rely heavily on such aids, there is little doubt that demonstrative exhibits will only become more common.

Practicum

Practicum One

A plaintiff has brought suit regarding a motor vehicle accident in which he was injured. During the accident his nose was struck hard, and he bled profusely from it for a few minutes, soaking the front of his shirt in blood, though there was no significant injury. He also, however, suffered a broken leg that initially required external fixation. In the aftermath of the accident photographs were taken including some that showed the plaintiff sitting on the curb, looking stunned and seemingly covered in blood. The plaintiff's attorney proposes to submit these photographs as demonstrative exhibits to support medical testimony. He also plans to submit photographs of the plaintiff's leg after the external fixation was performed, showing the metal pins inserted into the leg to stabilize the broken bones, and a video showing how the injury affected the plaintiff's day-to-day life. Evaluate each of these three potential exhibits and decide whether or not each is likely to be admitted and why or why not.

Practicum Two

We considered some "demonstrative" trial techniques proposed by Lindsay. While none of these are substantive evidence, if properly employed they can have a material impact on the jury. Do you think such techniques should be permitted? Why or why not? If not, where should the line between acceptable and unacceptable be drawn?

Summary

- Typically, demonstrative evidence is used to explain or clarify some fact at issue, particularly one that is complex or otherwise potentially difficult for the jury to understand.
- Unlike real and documentary evidence, demonstrative evidence is the tool of the attorney.
- The purpose of the Federal Rules of Evidence as stated in Rule 102 is "to administer every proceeding fairly, eliminate unjustifiable expense and delay, and promote the development of evidence law, to the end of ascertaining the truth and securing a just determination."
- The general rule is that materials not admitted into evidence simply should not be sent to the jury for use in its deliberations.
- In limited instances, some courts have permitted demonstrative exhibits to be provided to the jury during deliberations.
- Not every demonstrative exhibit is purely demonstrative. Some are substantive evidence in and of themselves, such as a computer simulation or reconstruction of an accident where scientific and other factual data is entered into a computer that processes the data and generates a visual image of how the accident must have occurred.
- There is one narrow set of circumstances in which computer animations are generally held to be self-authenticating and almost automatically relevant and therefore admissible: aircraft accident reconstruction.
- What is generally considered the landmark case in scientific evidence admissibility standards came in 1993 with *Daubert v. Merrell Dow Pharmaceuticals, Inc.*
- Science and the law employ different methodologies and seek "truth" in different manners. Science seeks "descriptive general theories based on particular data," whereas the law needs "a system of normative general rules that are individualized to apply to particular cases"—working in opposite directions, as it were. Science also works to predict future events, while the legal system attempts to discover facts about unique past events.
- It is important to remember that demonstrative exhibits must have a basis even though they are not admitted as substantive evidence. Bear in mind that such an exhibit has no probative value itself, but merely serves as a visual aid to the jury in comprehending the verbal testimony of a witness or other evidence.
- One driver of efforts to better define and establish rules for demonstrative evidence is the impact that computer technology has had, and continues to have, on the conduct of trials.
- Technology has in some respects raised concerns about tampering or outright falsification of evidence.
- Metadata can show use of a camera that the witness did not own or that the photograph was taken on date or time remote from the pertinent time frame.
- Experimental results typically show the nature of a substance, cause and effect, characteristics, and the like. Common illustrations include ballistics tests, blood tests in paternity matters, and analysis of substances in narcotics cases.

- As relevant technology, particularly computer animation, advances rapidly, and as more and more attorneys rely heavily on such aids, there is little doubt that demonstrative exhibits will only become more common.

Questions in Review

1. What constitutes demonstrative evidence?
2. What scientific tests do the courts use before admitting the results of a scientific test?
3. Describe two factors that could cause a trial judge to rule a computer-animated reconstruction of an event inadmissible even as a demonstrative exhibit. Assume that there is no question about the basic science underlying the animation software.
4. Explain why, according to the Federal Rules of Evidence, technically no demonstrative exhibit could ever achieve the relevance needed for admissibility.
5. What constitutes metadata?
6. What are the issues involved in using demonstrative evidence in court?

Key Terms

Demonstrative Evidence: Demonstrative evidence is that evidence addressed directly to the senses without intervention of testimony.

Frye **Rule:** The *Frye* rule set general acceptance in the scientific community as a prerequisite for admitting scientific evidence in court.

Non-Evidence Demonstrative Evidence: Non-evidence demonstrative evidence includes how you dress, how you act, react, or respond, and your overall attitude.

Photographic Metadata: Photographic metadata includes a wealth of information about the photo—many smartphones, in fact, by default even include GPS tagging of the location where the picture was taken—that readily point to any alteration of the picture after the fact, and of course metadata that is missing entirely is a huge red flag.

Endnotes

1. Marks, Steven C. (March 2004). Trial Practice: The Admissibility and Use of Demonstrative Aids. GPSolo Magazine. Chicago: American Bar Association. Accessed online at http://www.american-bar.org/content/newsletter/publications/gp_solo_magazine_home/gp_solo_magazine_index/demon-stativeaides.html. (Accessed on March 1, 2015).

2. Ibid.

3. Peterson, Kathleen Flynn (September 2009). Enhanced persuasion: Effective use of demonstrative evidence at trial. Journal of Consumer Attorneys Associations for Southern California (January 2010). Accessed online at http://www.robinskaplan.com/~/media/PDFs/Enhanced%20Persuasion%20Effective%20Use%20of%20Demonstrative%20Evidence%20at%20Trial.pdf. (Accessed on March 12, 2015).

4. (September 18, 2013). Reversible Error in Providing Jury Access to Demonstrative Evidence. Federal Evidence Review Editor's Blog. Accessed online at http://federalevidence.com/blog/2013/september/demonstrative-evidence-and-substantive-evidence-cross-purposes. (Accessed on March 12, 2015).

5. Brain, Robert D. and Broderick, Daniel J. (1992). The Derivative Relevance of Demonstrative Evidence: Charting Its Proper Evidentiary Status. UC Davis Law Review, Vol. 25, pp. 959–60. Accessed online at http://papers.ssrn.com/sol3/papers.cfm?abstract_id=955011. (Accessed on March 12, 2015).

6. Lindsay, Stephen P. (n. d.) "Do You Hear What I Hear?" Why Demonstrative Evidence Makes a Difference. San Diego: Federal Defenders of San Diego, pp. 3–4. Accessed online at http://www.fd.org/pdf_lib/TS2011/Demonstrative_evidence.pdf. (Accessed on March 12, 2015).

7. Baugh v. Cuprum S.A. de C.V., F.3d (7th Cir. Sept. 13, 2013) (No. 12-2019).

8. U.S. Court of Appeals for the Seventh Circuit (September 13, 2013). No. 12-2019: John Baugh, by and through his Wife and Next Friend, Sharon Baugh, v. Cuprum S.A. de C.V. Washington, D.C.: Government Printing Office, p. 2. Accessed online at http://www.gpo.gov/fdsys/pkg/USCOURTS-ca7-12-02019/pdf/USCOURTS-ca7-12-02019-0.pdf. (Accessed on March 9, 2015).

9. Ibid, p. 3.

10. Ibid.

11. Ibid, pp. 4–5.

12. Ibid, p. 5.

13. Ibid, p. 6.

14. Ibid, p. 8.

15. Ibid, pp. 9–10.

16. Legal Information Institute (a) (n. d.) Rule 102: Purpose. Federal Rules of Evidence. Ithaca, NY: Cornell University Law School. Accessed online at https://www.law.cornell.edu/rules/fre/rule_102. (Accessed on March 12, 2015).

17. Legal Information Institute (b) (n. d.) Rule 403: Excluding Relevant Evidence for Prejudice, Confusion, Waste of Time, or Other Reasons. Federal Rules of Evidence. Ithaca, NY: Cornell University Law School. Accessed online at https://www.law.cornell.edu/rules/fre/rule_403. (Accessed on March 10, 2015).

18. Lindsay, p. 4.

19. U.S. Court of Appeals for the Seventh Circuit (a), p. 7.

20. Bankcard America, Inc. v. Universal Bancard Systems, Inc., 203 F.3d 477 (2000)

21. U.S. Court of Appeals for the Seventh Circuit (b) (February 1, 2000). Nos. 98-2528, 98-2529, 98-2530: Bankcard America, Inc., Plaintiff-Appellee/Cross-Appellant v. Universal Bancard Systems, Inc., Defendant-Appellant/Cross-Appellee, and Samuel Buchbinder and Paul Alperstein, Counter-Defendants/Appellees. Washington, D.C.: Government Printing Office, F.3d 482. Accessed online at https://scholar.google.com/scholar_case?case=12882935366132968326&hl=en&as_sdt=6&as_vis=1&oi=scholarr. (Accessed on March 2, 2015).

22. Artis v. Hitachi Zosen Clearing, Inc., 967 F.2d 1132 (1992).

23. U.S. Court of Appeals for the Seventh Circuit (b), 967 F.2d 1142.

24. United States v. Holton, 116 F.3d 1536 (D.C. Cir. 1997).

25. U.S. Court of Appeals, District of Columbia Circuit (June 27, 1997). Nos. 96-3013, 96-3049: United States of America, Appellee v. Bobby A. Holton, Appellant. Accessed online at http://caselaw.findlaw.com/us-dc-circuit/1058002.html. (Accessed on March 12, 2015).

26. United States v. Treadwell, 760 F.2d 327, 339 (D.C. Cir. 1985).

27. United States v. Downen, 496 F.2d 314 (10th Cir. 1974).

28. U.S. Court of Appeals for the Seventh Circuit (a), pp. 16–17.

29. Big John, B.V. v. Indian Head Grain Co., 718 F.2d 143 (5th Cir. 1983).

30. Marks.

31. Ibid.

32. Ibid.

33. Ibid.

34. Frye v. United States, 293 F. 1013 (D.C. Cir. 1923).

35. Van Orsdel, Joisah A. (1923). Frye v. United States, 293 F. 1013 (D.C. Cir. 1923). Washington, D.C.: Supreme Court of the United States. Accessed online at http://www.law.ufl.edu/_pdf/faculty/little/topic8.pdf. (Accessed on March 12, 2015).

36. Orofino, Suzanne (Summer 1996). Daubert v. Merrell Dow Pharmaceuticals, Inc.: The Battle over Admissibility Standards for Scientific Evidence in Court. Journal of Undergraduate Sciences 3(109–111), p. 109. Accessed online at http://www.hcs.harvard.edu/~jus/0302/orofino.pdf. (Accessed

on March 10, 2015).

37. Ibid.
38. Daubert v. Merrell Dow Pharmaceuticals, Inc., 509 U.S. 579 (1993).
39. Orofino, Suzanne.
40. Ibid.
41. Ibid, pp. 109–10.
42. Ibid, p. 110.
43. Ibid.
44. Ibid.
45. Ibid.
46. Ibid.
47. Ibid.
48. Ibid.
49. Ibid.
50. Ibid.
51. Ibid.
52. Ibid.
53. Ibid, p. 111.
54. Marks.
55. Lindsay, p. 6.
56. Ibid.
57. Ibid, pp. 7–8.
58. Ibid, p. 8.
59. U.S. Court of Appeals for the Seventh Circuit (a), p. 8.
60. Lindsay, p. 10.
61. Ibid, p. 11.
62. Ibid, p. 12.
63. Ibid, p. 13.
64. Ibid.
65. Ibid, p. 14.
66. Ibid.
67. Ibid, p. 15.
68. Ibid, p. 16.
69. Ibid, p. 17.
70. Ibid, pp. 17–18.
71. Ibid, pp. 18–19.
72. Ibid, pp. 19–20.
73. Ibid, p. 20.
74. Ibid, pp. 20–21.
75. Peterson.
76. Ibid.
77. Brain and Broderick, pp. 961–62.
78. Ibid, p. 962.
79. Ibid, p. 965.
80. Ibid, p. 967.
81. Ibid, pp. 968–69.
82. Ibid, pp. 969–70.
83. Ibid, p. 974.
84. Ibid, pp. 983–84.
85. Legal Information Institute (b).
86. Kashi, Joe (June 2006). Authenticating digital photographs as evidence: A practice approach using JPEG metadata. Law Practice Today. Accessed online at http://apps.americanbar.org/lpm/lpt/articles/tch06061.shtml. (Accessed on March 11, 2015).
87. Ibid.

88. Kaps Transport, Inc. v. Henry, 572 P.2d 75–76 (Alaska 1977).

89. Kashi, Joe.

90. Ibid.

91. Ibid.

92. Brain and Broderick, p. 992.

93. Peterson.

94. Ibid.

95. Ibid.

96. Ibid.

97. Ibid.

98. Brain and Broderick, p. 963.

99. Ibid.

100. Kashi.

101. Olson, Bruce A. (February 2010). Technology: Engage the jury: Presenting electronic and computer evidence at trial. Wisconsin Lawyer, Vol. 83, No. 2. Accessed online at http://www.wisbar.org/newspublications/wisconsinlawyer/pages/article.aspx?Volume=83&Issue=2&ArticleID=2029. (Accessed on March 1, 2015).

102. Graham, Michael H. (September 1, 2010). Real and demonstrative evidence, experiments and views. Criminal Law Bulletin, Vol. 46, No. 4, p. 23. Accessed online at http://papers.ssrn.com/sol3/papers.cfm?abstract_id=1885714. (Accessed on March 12, 2015).

103. Ibid.

104. Ibid.

105. Smith v. Grange Mutual Fire Insurance Co., 234 Mich. 119, 208 NW 145 (1926) and Young, Roger D. and Susser, Steven (n. d.). Effective use of demonstrative exhibits and demonstrative aids. Michigan Bar Journal, Vol. 13. Accessed online at http://www.michbar.org/journal/article.cfm?articleID=151&volumeID=13. (Accessed on March 10, 2015).

106. Ibid.

107. Ibid.

108. Monsees, Timothy W. (n. d.). Evidentiary foundations for demonstrative evidence. Monsees & Mayer, P.C. Accessed online at http://www.mmmpalaw.com/Articles/Evidentiary-Foundations-For-Demonstrative-Evidence.shtml. (Accessed on March 10, 2015).

109. Vasseghi v. McNutt, 811 S.W.2d 456 (Mo. App. 1991).

110. Monsees, Timothy.

111. Ibid.

112. Ibid.

113. Gilstrap, Jr., T. O. and Harmonson, S. Clark (n. d.). Demonstrative Evidence for the Texas Trial Lawyer. The Law Offices of T. O. Gilstrap, Jr., P.C. Accessed online at http://www.gilstraplaw.com/files/news11.pdf. (Accessed on March 12, 2015).

114. Ibid.

115. Ibid.

116. Lewis, D. Craig and Clark, Merlyn W. (September 25, 2013). Trial evidence for judges: Exhibits, demonstrative evidence and illustrative aids, tests, analyses, and experiments. 2013 Idaho Judicial Conference. Accessed online at www.isc.idaho.gov/judicialedu/judges/conferences/IJC_2013/Trial Evidence for Judges-Exhibits_etc.doc. (Accessed on March 12, 2015).

117. Ibid.

118. Ibid.

119. Tate, Mary Lynn et al. (October 23, 2008). Real and illustrative evidence in Virginia. Abingdon, VA: The Tate Law Firm. Accessed online at http://c.ymcdn.com/sites/www.vba.org/resource/resmgr/imported/29.%20TAB%2023%20DEMONSTRATIVE%20EVIDENCE.pdf. (Accessed on March 12, 2015).

120. Ibid.

121. Ibid.

Chapter 6

Eyewitness Testimony

Chapter Objectives

What you should know after studying this chapter:

- The issues involved with eyewitness testimony
- Qualifications of an eyewitness
- Difference between a lay witness and an expert witness
- The rule against the use of hearsay testimony
- The exceptions to the hearsay rule
- The order in which witness testimony is presented
- Purposes of cross-examination
- Issues involved in the impeachment of witness testimony
- How to prepare a witness to testify

Chapter Outline

Introduction
Examination of Witnesses
Impeachment
Accuracy of Witness Testimony
Hearsay Rule
Rape Shield Laws
Preparing a Witness to Testify
Practicum
Summary
Questions in Review
Key Terms
Endnotes

Introduction

Juries love eyewitnesses to a crime. As a veteran prosecutor once remarked: "One eyewitness is worth a ton of scientific evidence when prosecuting a defendant in a jury trial." However, as will be discussed later, eyewitness testimony is not infallible. In the majority of cases where individuals have been wrongly convicted, the guilty findings were based on mistaken or misidentified eyewitness testimony.

A lay witness, also known simply as an "eyewitness," is any person who gives testimony in a case, but who is not an expert. A lay witness is a person that gives testimony based on direct knowledge of the person or crime. A lay witness does not testify based on any education or specialized knowledge. Expert witnesses testify based on their specialized knowledge or expertise on a particular subject. Expert witnesses are discussed in Chapter 7.

Evidence in Action
Difference between an Expert and a Lay Witness

An expert witness is someone that testifies according to his or her knowledge on a subject that pertains to the evidence given. Their expertise is needed to identify, test, and explain the evidence and how it is useful in proving information for either the innocence or guilt of a suspect. Examples of this would be trace evidence, DNA evidence, fingerprint analysis or ballistics.

A lay witness, however, is a person that gives testimony based on direct knowledge of the person or crime. A lay witness does not testify based on any education, training or expertise.

Federal Rule of Evidence 701. Opinion Testimony by Lay Witnesses

If a witness is not testifying as an expert, testimony in the form of an opinion is limited to one that is:

(a) rationally based on the witness's perception;
(b) helpful to clearly understanding the witness's testimony or to determining a fact in issue; and
(c) not based on scientific, technical, or other specialized knowledge within the scope of Rule 702.

The words "within the scope of Rule 702" were added at the end of FRE 701 in 2000, to emphasize that the Rule does not require witnesses to qualify as experts unless their testimony is of the type traditionally considered as an expert witness within the purview of Rule 702. There are some situations in which lay witnesses are allowed to give opinion testimony. As noted by FRE 701, the general rule is that it must be based on the witness's perception and helpful to understanding the testimony. For example a lay witness who observed the defendant driving her car in a school zone will normally be allowed to present an opinion as to the speed of the car that the witness observed. As noted by FRE 602, the general rule is that a lay witness may testify only as to information that is within the personal knowledge of the witness. If the witness testifies that the defendant was traveling at a high rate of speed in the school zone, the defense may cross-examine the witness regarding the witness's knowledge as to what constitutes a high rate of speed.

Rule 602. Need for Personal Knowledge

A witness may testify to a matter only if evidence is introduced sufficient to support a finding that the witness has personal knowledge of the matter. Evidence to prove personal knowledge may consist of the witness's own testimony. This rule does not apply to a witness's expert testimony under Rule 703.

Examination of Witnesses

The side or party that calls a witness, examines the witness on direct examination. The opposing party then has the right to cross-examines the witness. After the cross-examination is complete, the witness may be subject to re-direct examination by the party that originally called the witness. Then the opposing party has the right to re-cross the witness. This exchange may last several times until each side has no more questions of the witness.

The trial judge has considerable latitude in determining the mode and order of examining witnesses and the presentation of evidence. FRE 611 reflects the general rule in almost all American court jurisdictions.

Rule 611. Mode and Order of Examining Witnesses and Presenting Evidence

(a) CONTROL BY THE COURT; PURPOSES. The court should exercise reasonable control over the mode and order of examining witnesses and presenting evidence so as to:
    (1) make those procedures effective for determining the truth;
    (2) avoid wasting time; and
    (3) protect witnesses from harassment or undue embarrassment.
(b) SCOPE OF CROSS-EXAMINATION. Cross-examination should not go beyond the subject matter of the direct examination and matters affecting the witness's credibility. The court may allow inquiry into additional matters as if on direct examination.
(c) LEADING QUESTIONS. Leading questions should not be used on direct examination except as necessary to develop the witness's testimony. Ordinarily, the court should allow leading questions:
    (1) on cross-examination; and
    (2) when a party calls a hostile witness, an adverse party, or a witness identified with an adverse party.

Direct Examination

On direct examination, generally the witness may not be asked leading questions except for introductory or basic questions. A leading question is one that suggests the

Photo 6-1

Charles Lindbergh testifying as an eyewitness regarding the kidnapping and death of his son on the night of March 1, 1932. Photo courtesy of the Library of Congress.

answer. When the witness first takes the stand, he or she may be asked his or her name. While this is a leading question it is also an introductory question and may be asked. The witness, on direct examination, may not be asked questions like "Did you see Joe hit Mary?" That is a leading question that goes to the essence of the testimony. In most cases, the calling party would have to ask the witness a question like, "On May 23, did you observe anything unusual? If so, what?"

Generally, the witness on direct is required to answer in the narrative rather than simple yes or no answers. In certain cases, the trial judge may allow the calling party to ask questions that can be answered with a short answer.

Cross-Examination

When the prosecution has called a witness, the U.S. Constitution, Amendment VI, provides that the defense has the right to confront the witness. This right of confrontation is a constitutional right that the courts tend to uphold. The right of confrontation includes the right to cross-examination. The key functions of cross-examination are to test the truth of the information presented on direct examination, to show that the witness may be mistaken, and to point out any prejudice or bias that a witness may have.

On cross-examination, a witness may be asked leading questions. If the defense presents a witness, the prosecution has a right to cross-examine the witness. In the courts systems in the United States, there are two views as to the permissible scope of cross-examination: the restrictive rule and the wide open rule.

Photo 6-2

British cartoon showing lawyer cross-examining a woman. Cartoon first published in 1818. Photo courtesy of the Library of Congress.

The restrictive rule confines the scope of the cross-examination to matters within the scope of the direct examination, whereas the wide open rule allows any material issue in the case to be explored on cross-examination. While FRE 611 appears to adopt the restrictive approach, many trial judges use a broad definition of "matters within the scope of the direct examination." Accordingly, the two approaches are very similar in actual practice. Also, in a jury trial frequently counsel will not object when the opposing party exceeds the scope of the direct examination because it may appear to the jury that the objecting party is trying to hide certain information.

Evidence in Action
Dangers of Cross-Examination

Jake Ehrlich was a noted trial lawyer in San Francisco. At the time of his death in 1971, he was noted as one of the greatest cross-examiners among trial lawyers. In his 1970s book, *The Lost Art of Cross-Examination*,[1] he states that the object of cross-examination is to test the truth of statements of a witness made on direct examination; to sift, modify, or explain what has been said; and to weaken or disprove the case of your adversary.

Ehrlich notes that cross-examination is a necessary art used to trap the unwilling or dishonest witness, but its use is dangerous for the trial lawyer. Ehrlich states that on cross-examination the attorney should never ask a question to which he or she does not know the answer.

Consider this script from an early London criminal case:[2]

> The accused is on trial for biting off the ear of the victim.
>
> (On cross-examination) Counsel for Defendant (CD): Did you see Mr. Ingram bite Mr. Maye on the ear?
>
> Witness: No.
>
> CD: Well then, what did you see?
>
> Witness: I saw Mr. Ingram spitting the ear out of his mouth.

Competency

At common law there were various kinds of witness incompetency. For example, in many jurisdictions a person who had been convicted of a serious crime was not permitted to testify because he or she could not be trusted. Young persons and sometimes even married women were forbidden to testify. Fortunately, all of these incompetencies are now of only historical significance. Under the Federal Rules of Evidence and in all U.S. Court jurisdictions the general rule is to allow all witnesses to testify, and the past incompetencies are deemed as only factors that may be used by the jury or trial judge to determine the weight to be given to any witness's testimony.

Under FRE 601, every person is competent to be a witness unless these rules provide otherwise. State court jurisdictions follow the same concept. The question of when is a child mature enough to testify has generated most debate regarding witness competency. In the federal system, 18 U.S. Code 3509 provides that children should be treated no differently from other witnesses. That statute creates a presumption that children are competent and allows the exclusion of an otherwise admissible child witness only for compelling reasons. In many state court jurisdictions, the trial judge may determine if the child witness understands the importance of testifying truthfully. If so, the trial judge will allow the child to testify. There is generally a three-step procedure that may be used when the witness is a child or a person whose mental capacity is in issue.

1. Does the witness understand the duty to tell the truth?
2. Can the witness distinguish fact from fantasy?

3. Does the witness have the ability to communicate to the jury in a meaningful manner?

As a general rule, children over the age of six are rarely found to be incompetent. There are cases where a trial judge has allowed children as young as four years old to testify. A few states have enacted statutes that allow children to testify in child abuse cases without any demonstration of competency.

FRE 610 and many state evidence codes provide that evidence of a witness's religious beliefs or opinions is not admissible to attack or support the witness's credibility. For example, an opposing counsel may not attack a witness's creditability merely based on the witness's religious or lack of religious beliefs.

Witnesses Sequestration

It is the normal practice in both criminal and civil cases for all witnesses to be excluded from the trial until they are called as a witness. In some jurisdictions, the practice of witness sequestration is known as "invoking the rule." The purpose of the sequestration of witnesses is to keep witnesses from being influenced by the testimony of other witnesses. If however, the witness is also the defendant or a party to the trial, then that person may not be excluded. In criminal cases, the defendant has a right to be present when any witness is testifying under the Sixth Amendment's right of confrontation. Most states also allow a representative of the government (the other party to the trial) such as the police officer who led the investigation to remain in the court while other witnesses testify.

Rule 615. Excluding Witnesses

At a party's request, the court must order witnesses excluded so that they cannot hear other witnesses' testimony. Or the court may do so on its own. But this rule does not authorize excluding:

(a) a party who is a natural person;
(b) an officer or employee of a party that is not a natural person, after being designated as the party's representative by its attorney;
(c) a person whose presence a party shows to be essential to presenting the party's claim or defense; or
(d) a person authorized by statute to be present.

Privileges

In regards to eyewitness testimony, there are certain communications that are privileged. In other words certain communications may not be admitted into evidence even though they may be very relevant to the issues before the court. For example, conversations between an accused and his or her counsel are privileged. Other privileges include spousal communications, physician-patient communications, and priest-penitent communications. Privileges are discussed in detail in Chapter 11 and are introduced in this chapter merely to alert the reader that privileges constitute limitations on testimony that may be presented in court.

Witness's Prior Statement

When a witness testifies, he or she may be cross-examined about prior statements the witness may have made that conflict with the present testimony presented by the witness. For example Joe tells the police he saw James steal the car and then testifies in court that he saw Tom steal the car. The defense may cross-examine Joe regarding this statement in an attempt to impeach Joe's testimony.

Court's Calling or Examining a Witness

A few states allow the jury members to ask witnesses questions. Most states require any questions that a jury member has to be submitted to the judge. If the judge agrees after notifying the government and the defense, the judge asks the questions.

While all states allow the trial judge to question witnesses, it is a touchy area because questions asked by the judge may give the jury an impression of how the judge thinks of the testimony or case. For example if the defense calls a witness and the trial judge asks certain questions of the witness, it may leave the jury with the impression that the witness is untruthful. This would be grounds for reversal of the verdict. Note that a party to the trial may object to the court's calling or examining a witness either at that time or at the next opportunity when the jury is not present.

Rule 614. Court's Calling or Examining a Witness

(a) CALLING. The court may call a witness on its own or at a party's request. Each party is entitled to cross-examine the witness.
(b) EXAMINING. The court may examine a witness regardless of who calls the witness.
(c) OBJECTIONS. A party may object to the court's calling or examining a witness either at that time or at the next opportunity when the jury is not present.

Impeachment

Impeachment is the term used to describe the attempt by the opposing party to discredit the witness. For example, Jerry testifies that Jim was with him when the car was stolen. The prosecution could attempt to discredit Jerry in order to reduce or eliminate his testimony by asking a question such as "Didn't you tell the police officer on Monday the 23rd that at the time when the car was stolen that you were at the movies with your girlfriend?"

Generally a witness may be impeached based on anything that may affect the worthiness of the testimony. Some common situations include:

- Witness's reputation for lack of truthfulness,
- Witness's bias may have shaded testimony,

- Witness's prior criminal convictions,
- Proof of witness's poor perception or memory,
- Prior inconsistent statement or statements by the witness, and
- Witness's lack of opportunity to observe the incident in question.

Note: evidence entered for impeachment purposes serves only to negate the testimony or evidence being impeached. It is generally not considered as evidence to establish any facts in issue in the case.

Rule 613. Witness's Prior Statement

(a) SHOWING OR DISCLOSING THE STATEMENT DURING EXAMINATION.
When examining a witness about the witness's prior statement, a party need not show it or disclose its contents to the witness. But the party must, on request, show it or disclose its contents to an adverse party's attorney.

(b) EXTRINSIC EVIDENCE OF A PRIOR INCONSISTENT STATEMENT.
Extrinsic evidence of a witness's prior inconsistent statement is admissible only if the witness is given an opportunity to explain or deny the statement and an adverse party is given an opportunity to examine the witness about it, or if justice so requires.

This subdivision (b) does not apply to an opposing party's statement under Rule 801(d)(2).

At common law, a party may not impeach a witness he or she called. There are two general exceptions to this rule: one where the witness is designated as a hostile witness and where the witness suddenly changes his or her testimony. Rule 607 and similar rules in some states allow all parties to impeach a witness.

Rule 607. Who May Impeach a Witness?

Any party, including the party that called the witness, may attack the witness's credibility

Hostile Witness

A hostile witness, also known as an adverse witness or an unfavorable witness, is a witness at trial whose testimony is either openly antagonistic or appears to be contrary to the legal position of the party who called the witness. For example, the prosecutor call a police officer who testifies that Jerry confessed. The defense then may call another police officer who was present when Jerry made the statement to establish that the first officer's testimony was incomplete or incorrect. The defense, prior to calling the second officer, will generally request that the trial judge designate the officer as a hostile witness, thus allowing the defense to question by using cross-examination techniques that include leading questions or impeachment evidence on the direct examination of the hostile witness.

Witness Credibility

Any time a witness testifies, his or her credibility for truthfulness is in issue and may be attacked on cross-examination. The party that calls a witness may not attack the witness's credibility or enter evidence that the witness is credible. There is an exception to this rule when on cross-examination the witness's credibility is attacked; then the party who called the witness may present evidence as to the witness's credibility or reputation for honesty.

Rule 608. A Witness's Character for Truthfulness or Untruthfulness

(a) REPUTATION OR OPINION EVIDENCE. A witness's credibility may be attacked or supported by testimony about the witness's reputation for having a character for truthfulness or untruthfulness, or by testimony in the form of an opinion about that character.

But evidence of truthful character is admissible only after the witness's character for truthfulness has been attacked.

(b) SPECIFIC INSTANCES OF CONDUCT. Except for a criminal conviction under Rule 609, extrinsic evidence is not admissible to prove specific instances of a witness's conduct in order to attack or support the witness's character for truthfulness. But the court may, on cross-examination, allow them to be inquired into if they are probative of the character for truthfulness or untruthfulness of:

(1) the witness; or

(2) another witness whose character the witness being cross-examined has testified about.

By testifying on another matter, a witness does not waive any privilege against self-incrimination for testimony that relates only to the witness's character for truthfulness.

Rule 609. Impeachment by Evidence of a Criminal Conviction

(a) IN GENERAL. The following rules apply to attacking a witness's character for truthfulness by evidence of a criminal conviction:

(1) for a crime that, in the convicting jurisdiction, was punishable by death or by imprisonment for more than one year, the evidence:

(A) must be admitted, subject to Rule 403, in a civil case or in a criminal case in which the witness is not a defendant; and

(B) must be admitted in a criminal case in which the witness is a defendant, if the probative value of the evidence outweighs its prejudicial effect to that defendant; and

(2) for any crime regardless of the punishment, the evidence must be admitted if the court can readily determine that establishing the elements of the crime required proving—or the witness's admitting—a dishonest act or false statement.

(b) LIMIT ON USING THE EVIDENCE AFTER 10 Years. This subdivision (b) applies if more than 10 years have passed since the witness's conviction or release from confinement for it, whichever is later. Evidence of the conviction is admissible only if:

(1) its probative value, supported by specific facts and circumstances, substantially outweighs its prejudicial effect; and

(2) the proponent gives an adverse party reasonable written notice of the intent to use it so that the party has a fair opportunity to contest its use.

(c) EFFECT OF A PARDON, ANNULMENT, OR CERTIFICATE OF REHABILI-TATION.

Evidence of a conviction is not admissible if:

(1) the conviction has been the subject of a pardon, annulment, certificate of reha-bilitation, or other equivalent procedure based on a finding that the person has been rehabilitated, and the person has not been convicted of a later crime punishable by death or by imprisonment for more than one year; or

(2) the conviction has been the subject of a pardon, annulment, or other equiva-lent procedure based on a finding of innocence.

(d) JUVENILE ADJUDICATIONS. Evidence of a juvenile adjudication is admissi-ble under this rule only if:

(1) it is offered in a criminal case;

(2) the adjudication was of a witness other than the defendant;

(3) an adult's conviction for that offense would be admissible to attack the adult's cred-ibility; and

(4) admitting the evidence is necessary to fairly determine guilt or innocence.

(e) PENDENCY OF AN APPEAL. A conviction that satisfies this rule is admissible even if an appeal is pending. Evidence of the pendency is also admissible.

Refreshing a Witness's Memory

Consider this situation—a police officer is called as a witness regarding a traffic stop on May 28. The officer states that he does not remember the situation. The officer tes-tifies that shortly after the time of the stop she made written notes about the traffic stop and that her notes were truthfully made. Generally these notes are admissible as past recollection recorded and may be used to refresh the officer's memory. When a past recollection recorded is used, the record is admitted into evidence. To qualify as a past recollection recorded, the record:

- is on a matter that the witness once knew about but now cannot recall well enough to testify accurately on,
- was made or adopted by the witness when the matter was fresh in the witness's memory, and
- accurately reflected the witness's knowledge.

Present Recollection Refreshed

There is a second technique for refreshing a witness's memory—present recollec-tion refreshed. Present recollection refreshed is not considered as hearsay evidence. In using this technique, the party calling the witness is allowed to stimulate the witness's present memory. For example, the party may ask the officer if seeing the incident re-port of that date would help her remember the circumstances. After the officer indicates yes, the party may show the report to the officer. The officer then testifies as to her present memory of the incident. If the officer testifies that after seeing the report she still does not remember the incident, then the present recollection refreshed technique may not be used. Generally, unlike past recollection recorded, the record that refreshed the witness's memory is not admitted into evidence.

In either of the two memory refreshing techniques, the opposing party has the right to inspect and object to the use of the document. If an objection is made, then the trial judge decides whether the technique may be used.

Rule 612. Writing Used to Refresh a Witness's Memory

(a) SCOPE. This rule gives an adverse party certain options when a witness uses a writing to refresh memory:

(1) while testifying; or

(2) before testifying, if the court decides that justice requires the party to have those options.

(b) ADVERSE PARTY'S OPTIONS; DELETING UNRELATED MATTER.

Unless 18 U.S.C. §3500 provides otherwise in a criminal case, an adverse party is entitled to have the writing produced at the hearing, to inspect it, to cross-examine the witness about it, and to introduce in evidence any portion that relates to the witness's testimony.

If the producing party claims that the writing includes unrelated matter, the court must examine the writing in camera, delete any unrelated portion, and order that the rest be delivered to the adverse party. Any portion deleted over objection must be pre-served for the record.

(c) FAILURE TO PRODUCE OR DELIVER THE WRITING.

If a writing is not produced or is not delivered as ordered, the court may issue any appropriate order. But if the prosecution does not comply in a criminal case, the court must strike the witness's testimony or—if justice so requires—declare a mistrial.

Rule 613. Witness's Prior Statement

(a) SHOWING OR DISCLOSING THE STATEMENT DURING EXAMINATION.

When examining a witness about the witness's prior statement, a party need not show it or disclose its contents to the witness. But the party must, on request, show it or disclose its contents to an adverse party's attorney.

(b) EXTRINSIC EVIDENCE OF A PRIOR INCONSISTENT STATEMENT.

Extrinsic evidence of a witness's prior inconsistent statement is admissible only if the witness is given an opportunity to explain or deny the statement and an adverse party is given an opportunity to examine the witness about it, or if justice so requires.

This subdivision (b) does not apply to an opposing party's statement under Rule 801(d)(2).

Accuracy of Witness Testimony

Studies have been conducted on human memory and on subjects' propensity to remember erroneously events and details that did not occur. Elizabeth Loftus performed some interesting experiments in the 1970s which demonstrate some of the effects of a third party's introducing false facts into memory.[3]

In one experiment, subjects were shown a slide of a car at an intersection with either a yield sign or a stop sign. Experimenters asked participants questions, falsely introducing the term "stop sign" into the question instead of referring to the yield sign participants had actually seen. Similarly, experimenters falsely substituted the term "yield sign" in questions directed to participants who had actually seen the stop sign slide. The results indicated that subjects remembered seeing the false image. In the initial part of the experiment, subjects also viewed a slide showing a car accident. Some subjects were later asked how fast the cars were traveling when they "hit" each other, others were asked how fast the cars were traveling when they "smashed" into each other. Those subjects questioned using the word "smashed" were more likely to report having seen broken glass in the original slide. The introduction of false cues altered participants' memories.[4]

Evidence in Action
A Classroom Experiment

Co-author Cliff Roberson was teaching an upper division criminal justice class at Washburn University and conducted an experiment. There were 26 students present in the class. Prior to the start of the class, Roberson placed his cell phone and briefcase on a table near the door. While he was lecturing to the class, an individual entered the room to pick up his briefcase and cell phone and quickly exited the room (the incident was prearranged).

After the incident, Roberson asked the class to remain seated and not talk to each other while he called the police. Within minutes two police officers arrived. (The presence of the officers were pre-arranged.) The officers individually interviewed all 26 students. Three students stated that they did not see what happened and were dismissed. Out of the remaining 23 students only 6 students selected the correct individual from a photo lineup. One student could not identify anyone and 16 students selected the wrong person in the lineup.

Each student was asked to describe the clothes that the individual was wearing. Only seven students correctly pointed out that the individual was wearing a red sweater and khaki shorts.

The U.S. Department of Justice published in 1999 a guide, "Eyewitness Evidence: A Guide for Law Enforcement."[5] The guide states on page iii:

The legal system always has relied on the testimony of eyewitnesses, nowhere more than in criminal cases. Although the evidence eyewitnesses provide can be tremendously helpful in developing leads, identifying criminals, and exonerating the innocent, this evidence is not infallible. Even honest and well-meaning witnesses can make errors, such as identifying the wrong person or failing to identify the perpetrator of a crime.

The guide states that the manner in which the investigating officer obtains information from a witness has a direct impact on the amount and accuracy of that information (page 15). The guide advises when interviewing a witness, the investigating officer should:

1. Establish rapport with the witness.
2. Inquire about the witness's condition.
3. Use open-ended questions (e.g., "What can you tell me about the car?"); augment with closed-ended questions (e.g., "What color was the car?"). Avoid leading questions (e.g., "Was the car red?").
4. Clarify the information received with the witness.
5. Document information obtained from the witness, including the witness's identity, in a written report.
6. Encourage the witness to contact investigators with any further information.

False Testimony

If a witness knowingly testifies falsely about a material issue, the witness commits the crime of perjury. Perjury is a crime, because lying under oath can subvert the integrity of a trial and the legitimacy of the judicial system. To be guilty of perjury, the witness must knowingly making a false statement. Merely misremembering or making a mistake is not a crime.

Hearsay Rule

Consider this scenario: You are testifying in a criminal case. The prosecutor asks you, "When were you born?" This is an apparent easy question to answer, but how do you know the answer to it? You do not remember the day you were born. Your parents informed you of the date when you were very young and you remember it because your parents held birthday parties for you each year on that date. Your answer to that question, however, is hearsay. Why? Because you do not remember the date. Your testimony is offered for the truth of the date of your birthday and is based on out-of-court statements made by your parents. Note: While it is hearsay, the statement would be admissible as an exception to the rule against hearsay evidence.

The rule against hearsay testimony is one of the most complicated rules involving evidence. Many practicing attorneys do not understand it. Hearsay is information that one person learns from another person, but the first person has no direct experience that would indicate that information is true or false. Hearsay cannot be used as evidence in most U.S. courts because the person testifying has no direct experience with the event he or she is testifying to. There are numerous exceptions to the hearsay rule which will be discussed later in this section.

FRE 801(c) states that:

"Hearsay" means a statement that:

(1) the declarant does not make while testifying at the current trial or hearing; and
(2) a party offers in evidence to prove the truth of the matter asserted in the statement.

Example 1: Joe attempts to testify in court that Beth told him that Jim admitted to her that he stole the car. Not admissible because it is hearsay. It is hearsay because the declarant (Beth) did not make it in court, and it is offered to prove that Jim stole the car.

The problem with hearsay evidence is that the right to confront the witnesses against you is violated when statements such as the one set forth in Example 1 is offered as evidence. There is no way for the defense to confront the real witness, Beth.

Under FRE 801(c) and most state evidence codes or rules, to be hearsay, the statement must be entered into evidence to prove the truth of the matter asserted in the statement. As in Example 1, if the statement by Joe is entered into evidence to help prove that Jim stole the car, then it is hearsay because it is entered to prove the truth of the statement.

A simple test to determine if the testimony is hearsay is:

1. Is an out-of-court statement being offered into evidence?
2. Is the statement being offered into evidence to establish the existence of facts contained in the statement?

If the answers to both of the questions are yes, then it is hearsay. The statement is hearsay if it is being put into evidence as evidence of the facts contained in the statement. Hearsay can consist of oral, written, or recorded declarations. Court decisions have held that assertive behavior may under the right circumstances be considered as hearsay. For example, the assertive behavior such as pointing or nodding may qualify as hearsay evidence. There are issues and disagreements among the court jurisdictions as to whether or not the absence of a statement or conduct by a defendant may constitute hearsay.

Testimony as to the reputation of a person is clearly hearsay because you are entering the statements to show the good or bad character of a person. The issues surrounding reputation and character testimony will be discussed in Chapter 10.

Confrontation Clause

The U.S. Constitution, Sixth Amendment states that an accused shall have the right "to be confronted with the witnesses against him." This right of confrontation has been applied to state criminal court preceding by the Fourteenth Amendment's due process clause.

In *Crawford v. Washington*,[6] the U.S. Supreme Court adopted its present approach regarding out-of-court statements. The Court generally bans all statements of declarants who do not take the stand when their statements are offered to prove objective facts contained in the statements, unless the declarant is unavailable and there was an earlier opportunity for cross-examination. Crawford does allow the admission of a statement if it is not testimonial or if the defendant has forfeited his right by his conduct such as killing the declarant. Presently under the *Crawford* rule, if the hearsay is testimonial, it is only admissible if the declarant takes the stand or is both unavailable and formerly subject to an opportunity for cross-examination on the statement or defendant has forfeited his or her right.

The Court decision in *Crawford* provides the definitions of testimonial statements and when the right to confrontation applies, as follows:

- The right to confrontation applies to "witnesses" against the accused—in other words, those who "bear testimony."
- Testimony is typically a solemn declaration or affirmation made for the purpose of establishing or proving some fact.
- Testimonial statements include material such as affidavits, custodial examinations, prior testimony, confessions, or similar pretrial statements that are expected to be used in court.

Out-of-Court Statements Offered to Show Only That the Statement Was Made

Frequently out-of-court statements are offered not to prove the facts in the statement, but to merely show that the defendant made the statement. For example, Beth testifies in court that Jim told her that he stole the car. The prosecutor may offer this evidence to show that Jim made the statement. Since the evidence in this example is not being used as an absent witness to an objective fact, but only to show that Jim made the statement, the evidence is not hearsay.

Tests for Admission of an Out-of-Court Declaration

Trial judges frequently approach the issues by using the following analysis:

1. Is it hearsay?
2. If so, does it fall within one of the hearsay exceptions?
3. In a criminal case, does the admission of the declaration violate the constitutional right of confrontation?

Exceptions to the Hearsay Rule

There are numerous exceptions to the hearsay rule. Generally the exceptions are divided into three types:

1. Exemptions which are defined as non-hearsay evidence.

2.   Exceptions that apply without regard as to whether the declarant is available as a witness.
3.   Exceptions that apply only when the declarant is unavailable as a witness.

FRE 801(d) provides that certain statements are not hearsay. One such statement is the rule that when the declarant is a witness and testifies, the witness is subject to cross-examination about any prior statements he or she may have made. Other exemptions include a statement which is inconsistent with the declarant's testimony and was given under penalty of perjury at a trial, hearing, or other proceeding or in a deposition; a statements that is consistent with the declarant's testimony and is offered to rebut an express or implied charge that the declarant recently fabricated it or acted from a recent improper influence or motive in so testifying; or identifies a person as someone the declarant perceived earlier. In addition, a statement made by a defendant generally may be admitted as exempt from the hearsay rule.

Statements That Are Not Hearsay

Under the federal rules and in almost all state jurisdictions, a statement that meets the following conditions is not hearsay:

*   **A Declarant-Witness's Prior Statement**. The declarant testifies and is subject to cross-examination about a prior statement, and the statement:
*   is inconsistent with the declarant's testimony and was given under penalty of perjury at a trial, hearing, or other proceeding or in a deposition;
*   is consistent with the declarant's testimony and is offered to rebut an express or implied charge that the declarant recently fabricated it or acted from a recent improper influence or motive in so testifying; or
*   identifies a person as someone the declarant perceived earlier.

*   **An Opposing Party's Statement**. The statement is offered against an opposing party and:
*   was made by the party in an individual or representative capacity;
*   is one the party manifested that it adopted or believed to be true;
*   was made by a person whom the party authorized to make a statement on the subject;
*   was made by the party's agent or employee on a matter within the scope of that relationship and while it existed; or
*   was made by the party's coconspirator during and in furtherance of the conspiracy.

Exceptions to the Hearsay Rule Regardless of Whether the Declarant Is Available as a Witness

The following are not excluded by the rule against hearsay, regardless of whether or not the declarant is available as a witness under FRE 803 and in most state jurisdiction:

(1)   **Present Sense Impression**. A statement describing or explaining an event or condition, made while or immediately after the declarant perceived it.

(2) **Excited Utterance**. A statement relating to a startling event or condition, made while the declarant was under the stress of excitement that it caused.

(3) **Then-Existing Mental, Emotional, or Physical Condition**. A statement of the declarant's then-existing state of mind (such as motive, intent, or plan) or emotional, sensory, or physical condition (such as mental feeling, pain, or bodily health), but not including a statement of memory or belief to prove the fact remembered or believed unless it relates to the validity or terms of the declarant's will.

(4) **Statement Made for Medical Diagnosis or Treatment.**
   • A statement that is made for—and is reasonably pertinent to—medical diagnosis or treatment; and
   • describes medical history; past or present symptoms or sensations; their inception; or their general cause.

(5) **Recorded Recollection.** A record that:
   • is on a matter the witness once knew about but now cannot recall well enough to testify fully and accurately;
   • was made or adopted by the witness when the matter was fresh in the witness's memory; and
   • accurately reflects the witness's knowledge.

(6) **Records of a Regularly Conducted Activity**. A record of an act, event, condition, opinion, or diagnosis if:
   • the record was made at or near the time by—or from information transmitted by—someone with knowledge;
   • the record was kept in the course of a regularly conducted activity of a business, organization, occupation, or calling, whether or not for profit;
   • making the record was a regular practice of that activity;
   • all these conditions are shown by the testimony of the custodian or another qualified witness, or by a certification that complies with Rule 902(11) or (12) or with a statute permitting certification; and
   • neither the source of information nor the method or circumstances of preparation indicate a lack of trustworthiness.

(7) **Absence of a Record** of a Regularly Conducted Activity. Evidence that a matter is not included in a record described in paragraph (6) if:
   • the evidence is admitted to prove that the matter did not occur or exist;
   • a record was regularly kept for a matter of that kind; and
   • neither the possible source of the information nor other circumstances indicate a lack of trustworthiness.

(8) **Public Records.** A record or statement of a public office if:
   • it sets out: the office's activities; a matter observed while under a legal duty to report, but not including, in a criminal case, a matter observed by law-enforcement personnel; or in a civil case or against the government in a criminal case, factual findings from a legally authorized investigation; and
   • neither the source of information nor other circumstances indicate a lack of trustworthiness.

(9) **Public Records of Vital Statistics.** A record of a birth, death, or marriage, if reported to a public office in accordance with a legal duty.

(10) **Absence of a Public Record.** Testimony — or a certification under Rule 902 — that a diligent search failed to disclose a public record or statement if:
  - the testimony or certification is admitted to prove that the record or statement does not exist; or a matter did not occur or exist, if a public office regularly kept a record or statement for a matter of that kind; and
  - in a criminal case, a prosecutor who intends to offer a certification provides written notice of that intent at least 14 days before trial, and the defendant does not object in writing within 7 days of receiving the notice — unless the court sets a different time for the notice or the objection.

(11) **Records of Religious Organizations Concerning Personal or Family History.** A statement of birth, legitimacy, ancestry, marriage, divorce, death, relationship by blood or marriage, or similar facts of personal or family history, contained in a regularly kept record of a religious organization.

(12) **Certificates of Marriage, Baptism, and Similar Ceremonies.** A statement of fact contained in a certificate:
  - made by a person who is authorized by a religious organization or by law to perform the act certified;
  - attesting that the person performed a marriage or similar ceremony or administered a sacrament; and purporting to have been issued at the time of the act or within a reasonable time after it.

(13) **Family Records.** A statement of fact about personal or family history contained in a family record, such as a Bible, genealogy, chart, engraving on a ring, inscription on a portrait, or engraving on an urn or burial marker.

(14) **Records of Documents** that Affect an Interest in Property. The record of a document that purports to establish or affect an interest in property if:
  - the record is admitted to prove the content of the original recorded document, along with its signing and its delivery by each person who purports to have signed it;
  - the record is kept in a public office; and
  - a statute authorizes recording documents of that kind in that office.

(15) **Statements in Documents** that Affect an Interest in Property. A statement contained in a document that purports to establish or affect an interest in property if the matter stated was relevant to the document's purpose — unless later dealings with the property are inconsistent with the truth of the statement or the purpose of the document.

(16) **Statements in Ancient Documents.** A statement in a document that is at least 20 years old and whose authenticity is established.

(17) **Market Reports and Similar Commercial Publications.** Market quotations, lists, directories, or other compilations that are generally relied on by the public or by persons in particular occupations.

(18) **Statements in Learned Treatises, Periodicals, or Pamphlets.** A statement contained in a treatise, periodical, or pamphlet if:
  - the statement is called to the attention of an expert witness on cross-examination or relied on by the expert on direct examination; and
  - the publication is established as a reliable authority by the expert's admission or testimony, by another expert's testimony, or by judicial notice.

If admitted, the statement may be read into evidence but not received as an exhibit.

(19) **Reputation Concerning Personal or Family History.** A reputation among a person's family by blood, adoption, or marriage—or among a person's associates or in the community—concerning the person's birth, adoption, legitimacy, ancestry, marriage, divorce, death, relationship by blood, adoption, or marriage, or similar facts of personal or family history.

(20) **Reputation Concerning Boundaries or General History.** A reputation in a community—arising before the controversy—concerning boundaries of land in the community or customs that affect the land, or concerning general historical events important to that community, state, or nation.

(21) **Reputation Concerning Character**. A reputation among a person's associates or in the community concerning the person's character.

(22) **Judgment of a Previous Conviction.** Evidence of a final judgment of conviction if:
- the judgment was entered after a trial or guilty plea, but not a nolo contendere plea;
- the conviction was for a crime punishable by death or by imprisonment for more than a year;
- the evidence is admitted to prove any fact essential to the judgment; and
- when offered by the prosecutor in a criminal case for a purpose other than impeachment, the judgment was against the defendant. The pendency of an appeal may be shown but does not affect admissibility.

(23) **Judgments Involving Personal, Family, or General History, or a Boundary.** A judgment that is admitted to prove a matter of personal, family, or general history, or boundaries, if the matter:
- was essential to the judgment; and
- could be proved by evidence of reputation.

Exceptions to the Rule Against Hearsay—When the Declarant Is Unavailable as a Witness

In this section, we will list the exceptions to the hearsay rule when the individual who made the declarant is unavailable as a witness. These exceptions are contained in FRE 804 and in most state evidence codes.

A declarant is considered to be unavailable as a witness if the declarant:

(1) is exempted from testifying about the subject matter of the declarant's statement because the court rules that a privilege applies;
(2) refuses to testify about the subject matter despite a court order to do so;
(3) testifies to not remembering the subject matter;
(4) cannot be present or testify at the trial or hearing because of death or a then-existing infirmity, physical illness, or mental illness; or
(5) is absent from the trial or hearing and the statement's proponent has not been able, by process or other reasonable means, to procure the declarant's attendance.

The following are not excluded by the rule against hearsay if the declarant is unavailable as a witness:

(1) **Former Testimony.** Testimony that:
- was given as a witness at a trial, hearing, or lawful deposition, whether given during the current proceeding or a different one; and
- is now offered against a party who had—or, in a civil case, whose predecessor in interest had—an opportunity and similar motive to develop it by direct, cross-, or redirect examination.

(2) **Statement Under the Belief of Imminent Death.** In a prosecution for homicide or in a civil case, a statement that the declarant, while believing the declarant's death to be imminent, made about its cause or circumstances.

(3) **Statement Against Interest.** A statement that:
- a reasonable person in the declarant's position would have made only if the person believed it to be true because, when made, it was so contrary to the declarant's proprietary or pecuniary interest or had so great a tendency to invalidate the declarant's claim against someone else or to expose the declarant to civil or criminal liability; and
- is supported by corroborating circumstances that clearly indicate its trustworthiness, if it is offered in a criminal case as one that tends to expose the declarant to criminal liability.

(4) **Statement of Personal or Family History.** A statement about:
- the declarant's own birth, adoption, legitimacy, ancestry, marriage, divorce, relationship by blood, adoption, or marriage, or similar facts of personal or family history, even though the declarant had no way of acquiring personal knowledge about that fact; or
- another person concerning any of these facts, as well as death, if the declarant was related to the person by blood, adoption, or marriage or was so intimately associated with the person's family that the declarant's information is likely to be accurate.

(5) **Statement Offered Against a Party That Wrongfully Caused the Declarant's Unavailability.** A statement offered against a party that wrongfully caused—or acquiesced in wrongfully causing—the declarant's unavailability as a witness, and did so intending that result.

Rule 805. Hearsay Within Hearsay

Hearsay within hearsay is not excluded by the rule against hearsay if each part of the combined statements conforms with an exception to the rule.

Attacking and Supporting the Declarant's Credibility

When a hearsay statement has been admitted in evidence, the declarant's credibility may be attacked, and then supported, by any evidence that would be admissible for those purposes if the declarant had testified as a witness. The court may admit evidence of the declarant's inconsistent statement or conduct, regardless of when it occurred or whether the declarant had an opportunity to explain or deny it. If the party against whom the statement was admitted calls the declarant as a witness, the party may examine the declarant on the statement as if on cross-examination.

Rape Shield Laws

Under FRE 412 and similar rules in all state jurisdictions, there are limits on the use of a victim's sexual behavior in sex-offense cases. Evidence is not admissible in a civil or criminal proceeding involving alleged sexual misconduct in the following circumstances:

- evidence offered to prove that a victim engaged in other sexual behavior; or
- evidence offered to prove a victim's sexual predisposition.

In criminal cases, the court may admit the following evidence:

- evidence of specific instances of a victim's sexual behavior, if offered to prove that someone other than the defendant was the source of semen, injury, or other physical evidence;
- evidence of specific instances of a victim's sexual behavior with respect to the person accused of the sexual misconduct, if offered by the defendant to prove consent or if offered by the prosecutor; and
- evidence whose exclusion would violate the defendant's constitutional rights.

If the defendant or prosecution, generally the party must:

- file a motion that specifically describes the evidence and states the purpose for which it is to be offered;
- do so at least certain number of days before trial unless the court, for good cause, sets a different time;
- serve the motion on all parties; and
- notify the victim or, when appropriate, the victim's guardian or representative.

Before admitting evidence, the trial judge must conduct a non-public hearing and give the victim and parties a right to attend and be heard. Unless the court orders otherwise, the motion, related materials, and the record of the hearing must be and remain sealed. A "victim" includes an alleged victim.

Preparing a Witness to Testify

Counsel for both the prosecution and the defense normally prepare their witnesses before the witnesses testify in court. First, when calling a witness to help your side, whether it's a prosecution or a defense witness, you want to know what the witness will testify to. For example, if you are the lead police investigator in a murder case, you want to be able to advise the prosecutor as to what each witness you recommend to her will testify to. As chief investigator, you want to help present all legally sufficient evidence to support the charges filed against the defendant. In addition, you want to convince the jury or judge (in a trial by judge alone) of the integrity of the evidence and the truth of the charges. Accordingly, you need to discuss and evaluate the expected testimony of each proposed witness.

Wallace and Roberson, in *Written and Interpersonal Communication Methods for Law Enforcement*, have developed a list of suggestions for witnesses.[7] A summary of their suggestions include:

- Impress upon the witness the need to tell the truth.
- Do not guess. If the witness does not know the answer to the question, then the witness should state that rather than guessing.
- Make sure that the witness understands the question before answering.
- The witness should take his or her time and think about the answer before answering.
- The witness should talk in a loud, audible volume when answering questions.
- Witness should never look at the counsel or other person for assistance when testifying.
- Be cautious of questions involving distance and time.
- Be courteous.
- Avoid making jokes or wisecracks.
- If the witness is asked if they have talked to the prosecutor or defense before being called, testify truthfully and admit it.

Practicum

Practicum One

Joe is called to the witness stand as a defense witness. The defendant is being tried for rape of Susan. Joe attempts to testify that he had sex with Susan two days before the alleged rape. The prosecution objects to this evidence. As trial judge, how would you rule and why?

Practicum Two

The prosecutor asks his witness, "Did you see Jerry hit Susan?" The defense objects to the question. As trial judge, how would you rule and why?

Practicum Three

A witness is asked on direct examination, "In what city were you born?" The opposing party objects stating that the answer to the question would be hearsay evidence. How would you rule as trial judge? Why?

Practicum Four

Mary was a witness to a robbery. She is called by the prosecution and asked if there were any statements made by the robber. She testifies: "Yes, the robber stated that if everyone would hand over their money, no one would be hurt."

Summary

- Juries love eyewitnesses to a crime, but their accuracy is questionable.
- A lay witness, also known simply as an "eyewitness," is any person who gives testimony in a case, but who is not an expert.
- An expert witness is someone that testifies according to their knowledge on a subject that pertains to the evidence given.
- Generally, a witness may testify to a matter only if evidence is introduced sufficient to support a finding that the witness has personal knowledge of the matter. Evidence to prove personal knowledge may consist of the witness's own testimony.
- The trial judge has considerable latitude in determining the mode and order of examining witnesses and the presentation of evidence.
- On direct examination, generally the witness may not be asked leading questions except for introductory or basic questions. A leading question is one that suggests the answer.
- Generally, the witness on direct is required to answer in the narrative rather than simple yes or no answers.
- Under the Federal Rules of Evidence and in all U.S. Court jurisdictions, the general rule is to allow all witnesses to testify, and the past incompetencies are deemed as only factors that may be used by the jury or trial judge to determine the weight to be given to any witness's testimony.
- It is the normal practice in both criminal and civil cases for all witnesses be excluded from the trial until they are called as a witness. In some jurisdictions, the practice of witness sequestration is known as "invoking the rule."
- In regards to eyewitness testimony, there are certain communications that are privileged. In other words certain communications may not be admitted into evidence even though they may be very relevant to the issues before the court.
- When a witness testifies, he or she may be cross-examined about prior statements the witness may have made that conflict with the present testimony presented by the witness.
- Impeachment is the term used to describe the attempt by the opposing party to discredit the witness.
- Any time a witness testifies, his or her credibility for truthfulness is in issue and may be attacked on cross-examination.
- Studies have been conducted on human memory and on subjects' propensity to remember erroneously events and details that did not occur.
- The rule against hearsay testimony is one of the most complicated rules involving evidence. Many practicing attorneys do not understand it. Hearsay is information that one person learns from another person, but the first person has no direct experience that would indicate that information is true or false.
- Under FRE 412 and similar rules in all state jurisdictions, there are limits on the use of a victim's sexual behavior in sex-offense cases.
- Counsel for both the prosecution and the defense normally prepare their witnesses before the witnesses testify in court.

Questions in Review

1. What does it mean to impeach a witness?
2. Define hearsay evidence.
3. How accurate is eyewitness testimony?
4. What is the difference between lay witnesses and expert witnesses?
5. Who determines the admissibility of evidence in a criminal trial?

Key Terms

Expert Witness: An expert witness is someone that testifies according to his or her knowledge on a subject that pertains to the evidence given.

Hearsay: Hearsay is information that one person learns from another person, but the first person has no direct experience that would indicate that information is true or false.

Hostile Witness: A hostile witness, also known as an adverse witness or an unfavorable witness, is a witness at trial whose testimony is either openly antagonistic or appears to be contrary to the legal position of the party who called the witness.

Impeachment of a Witness: Impeachment is the term used to describe the attempt by the opposing party to discredit the witness.

Lay Witness: A lay witness is a person who gives testimony based on direct knowledge of the person or crime.

Leading Question: A leading question is one that suggests the answer.

Present Recollection Refreshed: Present recollection refreshed is where the party calling the witness is allowed to stimulate the witness's present memory.

Witness Sequestration: The practice of witness sequestration is segregation of the jury and is known as "invoking the rule." The purpose of the sequestration of witnesses is to keep witnesses from being influenced by the testimony of other witnesses.

Endnotes

1. J.W. Ehrlich (1970). The Lost Art of Cross-Examination. New York: Dorset.
2. Francis L. Wellman (1903). The Art of Cross-Examination, New York: Simon & Schuster.
3. Elizabeth F. Loftus & J.C. Palmer (1978). Reconstruction of Automobile Destruction: An Example of the Interaction Between Language and Memory, 13 J. of VERBAL LEARNING & VERBAL BEHAVIOR 585 (1974); Elizabeth F. Loftus, D.G. Miller, & H.J. Burns, Semantic Integration of Verbal Information into a Visual Memory, 4 J. of Experimental Psych, 19.
4. As described by George Fisher and Barbara Tversky (1999). "The Problem with Eyewitness Testimony Commentary" *Stanford Journal of Legal Studies*, Vol. 1, No. 1.
5. National Institute of Justice, U.S. Department of Justice (1999, October). Eyewitness Evidence: A Guide for Law Enforcement. Washington, DC: GPO.
6. 541 U.S. 36 (2004).
7. Harvey Wallace and Cliff Roberson (2013). Written and Interpersonal Communication Methods for Law Enforcement, 5th ed. Columbus, OH: Pearson.

Chapter 7

Using Expert Witnesses

Chapter Objectives

After studying this chapter, you should understand the following concepts and issues:

- The need for expert testimony
- The qualifications needed to be considered an expert
- Restrictions on the use of expert testimony
- Difference between lay and expert witnesses
- Basis of an expert witness's testimony

Chapter Outline

Introduction

An expert witness is a person who because of specialized knowledge can provide the fact finders (jury or judge alone in trial by judge alone) with information to help the fact finders determine the essential facts in the case.

In this chapter we will examine why experts are used in trials, how witnesses are qualified as experts, what matters they can testify to, and what matters they may not testify about. Article VII of the Federal Rules of Evidence provides the ultimate guide on the qualifications and use of expert witnesses. The states' evidence codes are very similar to the federal rules. As noted in Chapter 6, a lay witness is essentially a person who was an eyewitness to some aspects or facts that a party is trying to establish. As noted above, an expert witness is a person who, because of specialized knowledge, can provide the fact finders (jury or judge alone in trial by judge alone) with information to help the fact finders determine the essential facts in the case.

There are situations that do not need an expert witness to help the jury or judge to determine an issue. For example, an expert witness should not have been allowed to testify in *United States v. Romo* on the question of whether a reasonable person would have foreseen that defendant's letter to the President would be viewed as threatening. The letter writer, a former White House employee, announced his intention to put a bullet through the President's head. The appellate court held that there was no need for expert testimony because it was clear that any judge or jury could determine that a statement of an intention to put a bullet through the President's head was a threat.[1]

Role of the Expert Witness

As one federal district court noted: "Expert's sole duty is to use his expertise honestly and fairly so that justice may be done."[2]

In *Davie v. Magistrates of Edinburgh*, Lord President Clerk Cooper pointed out that an expert witness's duty was to furnish the judge or jury with the necessary scientific criteria for testing the accuracy of their conclusions, so to enable the judge or jury to form their own independent judgment by the application of these criteria to the facts proved in evidence.[3] Lord Cooper also stated that the weight to be given to the evidence provided by the expert witness is a matter for the judge or jury. That expert witnesses are only required in order that certain facts can be assessed and understood in the specialist or scientific context.

Lord Cooper was correct in pointing out that the duty of expert witnesses was to assist the judge or jury in forming their opinions as to what facts have been proved. Applying Cooper's comments to an actual case, suppose expert witnesses testified that the tire tracks left by Ted's automobile at the scene of the accident indicated that Ted was traveling at a speed in excess of 60 miles per hour. Also assume that there are no other expert witnesses presented to rebut the expert's opinion that Ted was traveling at a high speed. As noted by Lord Cooper, the province of fact finding still belongs to the jury in a jury trial. Accordingly, the jury would not be required to find the fact that Ted was traveling at an excessive speed when he was involved in the automobile accident even though the only expert testimony seems to support that fact.

As noted in one U.S. Court Appeal's case, there is no fixed or general rule that requires expert testimony, but where a topic requires special experience, only the testimony of a person of that special experience will be received and, even here, admission of such testimony is within the sound discretion of the trial court.[4]

Another appellate court noted that while expert testimony is warranted where the facts are such that inexperienced persons are likely to prove incapable of forming a correct judgment without expert assistance, expert testimony is not necessary where the matter in issue is such that the jury can be expected to draw the correct inferences from the facts presented.[5]

One appellate court held that expert testimony was not needed where the Federal Bureau of Investigation (FBI) language specialist's testified as an expert witness and opined that the phrase "your old man," used in intercepted telephone conversation with defendant's wife, referred to defendant. The court held that the opinion was not proper subject of expert testimony and, therefore, was not admissible, since no specialized knowledge was necessary to understand the phrase "your old man."[6]

In another case, the offered testimony of a psychiatrist—that a defendant being prosecuted for criminal income tax evasion was obsessed with his beliefs—was properly excluded, although federal evidence rule makes admissible testimony by an expert that will assist the trier of fact to understand evidence or to determine fact in issue. The court held that there was nothing to indicate that the jury was unable to determine whether defendant's refusal to pay taxes was in good faith or was knowing and willful, that a jury was fully capable of resolving that question after hearing defendant testify concerning reasons for his refusal to pay tax, and that defendant made no allegation of insanity or any psychological disorder requiring an expert's explanation.[7]

What about a case where a former deputy chief of police of the Los Angeles police department testified that the use of force against arrestee by defendant police officer was reasonable under totality of circumstances test? The court noted that since police practices and procedures, including use of force/control/subject resistance matrix, continuum or graphic, involved a type of specialized knowledge attributable to expert that the use of an expert witness was proper.[8]

Consider the case where an expert witness, a law enforcement agent, testifies that drug smugglers never used unwitting couriers because that would create too great a risk of failed delivery given the value of the drugs. In this case, the appellate court held that the admission of the expert testimony was error and thus inadmissible. The court noted that in prosecution for importing narcotics involving drugs found during customs search of defendant's truck at the Canadian border, where defendant contended that he was not aware that the truck contained drugs, the issue of knowingly possessing the drugs was an issue that was within the reach of an average juror's common sense.[9]

From a review of the cases, it is clear that:

- The trial judge has considerable discretion in deciding whether or not to admit expert testimony and his or her decision will be reversed only when the appellate court determines that the judge abused his or her discretion.
- Expert testimony should not be admitted in those cases where the issues are such that they are within the common sense of the average juror or judge. In other words, if expert testimony is not needed then it should not be admitted.

Photo 7-1

Photograph of the witness waiting room in the U.S. Courthouse, La Crosse County, Wisconsin. Photograph taken in the 1960s. Photograph courtesy of the Library of Congress.

Evidence in Action
Expert Witness Fees

Reich & Binstock, LLP v. Scates

2014 WL 6851606 Tex.App.-Houston [14 Dist.], 2014.

In a Texas case, a chemical engineering expert brought suit regarding payments owed by a law firm pursuant to their payment agreement. The state district court held that the agreement to pay the expert witness to consult and testify violated Disciplinary Rules of Professional Conduct and was unenforceable as against public policy.

The parties agreed that the expert was to invoice the firm $40 per hour of work that would be paid in the ordinary course of business. The parties further agreed that the expert would be paid an additional $30 per hour for that same work upon "settlement" of the case. The parties also agreed that if the case did not settle, the expert would not receive the additional $30 per hour.

The Texas court of appeals noted that the payment of the additional fees of $30 per hour was contingent upon the success of the R & B case upon which he worked. As such, the additional sum payable to the expert is far more like the percentage payment "reward." The court held that it was a violation of public policy to base an expert's fee on the success of the law suit and in addition that the fee arrangement was an improper splitting of its fees with a non-lawyer.

This case points out that an expert witness fee may not be based on the success of the litigation. The fee should be set without regards to the success of the litigation to prevent encouraging the expert to testify more favorably for one party.

Note: The common law rule is that lay witnesses are prohibited from receiving pay for testifying as a witness. Although the common law rule survives in some jurisdictions, most states have now modified the rule to permit fact or lay witnesses to be reimbursed for expenses incurred and compensated for time lost with respect to litigation.

Limitations on Opinion Testimony by Lay Witnesses

At common law, lay (non-expert) witnesses were not allowed to testify as to their opinions. This prohibition has been modified by the federal and state rules. FRE 701 provides that a lay witness may not testify as an expert. And they may only present opinion testimony in three general areas. Those areas are opinions that are:

(a) rationally based on the witness's perception;
(b) helpful to clearly understanding the witness's testimony or to determining a fact in issue; and
(c) not based on scientific, technical, or other specialized knowledge within the scope of Rule 702.

For example, a lay witness may testify that, in addition to seeing Ted driving his 1999 Ford Thunderbird in a school, in the witness's opinion Ted's speed was excessive. The witness, in testifying that Ted was driving in a school zone, is testifying as to what she actually observed. Her testimony about his speed is an opinion. But since the opinion is rationally based on her perception it is admissible under modern rules.

In a different example, a witness could testify as to observations that she made of the defendant but may not testify as to the meaning of those observations. Consider a criminal case where the defense is using the insanity defense. The lay witness could testify that she observed Ted walking down the street on a cold day without wearing any clothes. In so testifying, she is explaining what she observed. Generally she would not be allowed to testify that in her opinion that Ted's actions indicated that his mental capacity was not normal because this would be an opinion that is prohibited under FRE 701.

When a witness is called as a lay witness and later testifies as an expert witness, the party calling the witness should qualify the witness as an expert before continuing with the expert testimony. For example a federal agent's testimony as to drug dealers' manner of using baggies to package drugs was improperly admitted as lay opinion and should have been subject to expert witness disclosures, because his testimony was not limited to what the agent observed during the case or to other facts derived exclusively from the particular investigation involved in the case.[10]

It is within the trial judge's discretion to allow law enforcement officials to testify as experts concerning the modus operandi of drug dealers in areas concerning activities which are not something with which most jurors are familiar; however, the probative value of the expert testimony must not be substantially outweighed by the danger of unfair prejudice, confusion of issues, or misleading the jury.[11]

Apparently if the witness is qualified as an expert, he or she can testify both as a lay witness and an expert witness. For example in one case, an appeals court held that a district court did not impermissibly restrict defendant's cross-examination of the detective, who testified both as eyewitness and as expert on methods used by narcotics traffickers; defendant was even allowed to ask the detective whether narcotics traffickers generally received assistance from their relatives in purchasing airline or train tickets, and was permitted to relitigate, almost in its entirety, the propriety of the original stop.[12]

Testimony by an Expert Witness

FRE 702 and state evidence rules provide that a witness who is qualified as an expert by knowledge, skill, experience, training, or education may testify in the form of an opinion or otherwise if:

(a) the expert's scientific, technical, or other specialized knowledge will help the trier of fact to understand the evidence or to determine a fact in issue;
(b) the testimony is based on sufficient facts or data;
(c) the testimony is the product of reliable principles and methods; and
(d) the expert has reliably applied the principles and methods to the facts of the case.

Qualification of an Expert

Assume that you are a defense counsel representing a defendant on illegal drug charges in a jury trial. The prosecution intends to call an expert witness who is a well-known expert on controlled substances. Would you consider stipulating that the expert witness is qualified and request that the prosecution not waste time in parading the witness's background and education before the jury? This is a frequent tactic that counsel often use, especially if the expert witness is well-qualified. The tactic is based on the premise that allowing the jury to hear the background and education of the witness would only booster the witness's creditably.

Who determines whether or not a proposed witness is qualified to testify as an expert witness? The answer to that question is within the sole discretion of the trial judge.[13] Generally, one may become qualified as an expert by practical experience, and professional education is not a required prerequisite.[14]

Does 30 years' experience as a heroin addict qualify a person to testify on the effects of heroin withdrawals? Apparently not according to one appellate court which held that the witness did not qualify as an "expert" on heroin withdrawals, despite his alleged 30 years' experience as a heroin addict.[15]

One court determined that a Kentucky state police officer with ten years active experience including high risk warrant service, experience as an instructor in operational tactics, recipient of several service awards, and extensive training in advanced tactics, was qualified to testify in the estate's action against Kentucky state police officer for excessive force, assault, and negligence after the officer shot and killed arrestee when arrestee pointed a gun at police officers when they attempted to serve an arrest warrant.[16]

Another appellate court held that a U.S. Marshal was qualified to give expert testimony, in a drug trafficking case brought after methamphetamine was found in the vehicle defendants were driving, that drug traffickers, as a tool of their trade, commonly prayed to "narco saints" for protection from law enforcement and prosperity in their drug dealings; the proffered testimony would be useful to the jury to explain the significance of a Santa Muerte statue and prayer found in the vehicle. The witness had spent thousands of hours in researching the subject, had instructed other officers, had written two books, and had developed a law enforcement training video on the subject.[17]

Another appellate court held that the trial court could qualify as an expert on organized crime families a Federal Bureau of Investigation (FBI) agent with 17 years of experience, 5 years of participation in FBI's organized crime program, and 2 years as supervisor of organized crime program, even though the agent was not qualified as an expert in linguistics, sociology of crime, tape recording technology, and voice analysis, and even though the agent had never before been qualified as an expert witness. The trial court held that the agent did not need expertise in linguistics or voice analysis to be able to recognize defendants' voices on tape and understand what was being said.[18]

In a Missouri case, the appellate court held that a police officer offered as an expert witness by arrestee was not qualified to offer testimony regarding strip-search procedures, officer motivations, or psychological impact of custody on arrestees, where there was no evidence that the officer had any experience with civil rights violations or strip searches, nor was there any evidence that the officer had any work experience pertinent to psychology.[19]

An expert testifying as to a match between a spent cartridge case and a firearm must be qualified through training, experience, and/or proficiency testing to provide expert testimony, and must follow the established standards for intellectual rigor in the tool mark identification field with respect to documentation of the reasons for concluding there is a match, including, where appropriate, diagrams, photographs or written descriptions, and with respect to peer review of the results by another trained examiner in the laboratory.[20]

A witness was determined to be qualified to testify in a prosecution for aggravated sexual abuse of a child. The witness was considered an expert on the emotional and behavioral characteristics often observed in sexually abused children, even though he lacked formal education or training in child psychology and child psychiatry; the witness was a board-certified pediatrician who had served as medical director for a child abuse evaluation center, regularly examining and evaluating sexually abused children, for more than seven years, and he testified that in one year he had personally examined approximately 200 children following allegations of sexual abuse.[21]

In a prosecution for sex trafficking offenses, the court held that the pediatrician was qualified to testify as an expert on the dynamics of pimp-prostitute relationships. The

pediatrician had extensive experience and training as a developmental and forensic pediatrician, and she had presented at numerous national and international conferences
in the area of child sexual exploitation and human trafficking, had authored multiple
chapters for books and training materials on sexual exploitation, and was lead editor
of a two-volume treatise on child sexual exploitation. She also taught a 40-hour class
on prostitution four to six times per year, training investigators, prosecutors, judges
and others on sexual exploitation through prostitution, including training related to
pimp-prostitute relationship dynamics.[22]

Cross-Examination of an Expert

An expert witness may be cross-examined concerning his or her testimony and background or specialized education on his or her expert field. The witness may also be
cross-examined as to any bias in the favor of one of the parties.

As a general rule, the expert witness may also be cross-examined on anything that
a lay witness may be cross-examined on. Generally the opposing party is allowed to
cross-examine the expert witness on his or her qualifications and experience before
presenting testimony on the issues in the case. After the expert witness has testified,
then he or she may be cross-examined on the substance of the witness's testimony.
However, one appellate court held that there is no absolute right to cross-examine a
fingerprint technician concerning his qualifications before the technician's testimony
is received, and qualification of an expert witness is within the trial court's discretion.[23]

Consider this scenario: the expert witness testifies as to a prevailing custom in her
profession. The opposing counsel, in an effort to impeach this statement, may then
question the witness on whether she has knowledge of certain textbooks, treatises, articles and other publications in the field and may be confronted with extracts from
them and asked whether she is familiar with them or agrees with them.[24]

Allowing FBI agents to give expert testimony concerning defendants' roles in various gambling operations, the agents testified on the structure and operations of La
Cosa Nostra, and each defendant's role in the criminal organization. The agents did
not disclose the informant information. The court held that the agents did not impli-
cate the Sixth Amendment or violate the rule stating that an expert witness may be required on cross-examination to disclose facts and data underlying his or her opinion,
where experts testified only that information from past cooperating witnesses had con-
tributed to their knowledge about La Cosa Nostra in general, and their opinions as to
the roles played by defendants were based solely on tape recordings presented at trial.[25]

When an expert partially relies on the reports of others to reach his or her opinion,
the criminal defendant must have access to hearsay information relied on.[26] The modern view in evidence law recognizes that experts often rely on facts and data supplied
by third parties, and these rules permit the disclosure of otherwise hearsay evidence
for the purpose of illustrating the basis of an expert witness's opinion.[27]

The trial court's failure to allow defense counsel to cross-examine a prosecution psychiatrist, who gave expert opinion that a key prosecution witness was able to distin-

guish reality from imagination and who had been informed of the witness's polygraph test results, was reversible error. The defense was entitled to cross-examine the expert witness regarding the basis for his opinion, even though it might require the expert to reveal otherwise inadmissible underlying information as to polygraph results subject to proper limiting instructions.[28]

A trial court did not abuse its discretion by allowing the government to cross-examine defendant's expert witness, who testified that the specific type of conduct behind defendant's prior conviction was taken into account in forming his diagnosis that defendant suffered from pathological gambling, concerning facts underlying defendant's prior conviction, particularly in light of facts that the government carefully avoided any reference to the outcome of defendant's prior trial and that the entire area of questioning could have easily been avoided by defendant.[29]

Bases of Expert Opinions

As the U.S. Supreme Court noted in *Williams v. Illinois,* an expert witness may voice an opinion based on facts concerning the events at issue even if the expert lacks first-hand knowledge of those facts.[30] A long tradition in American courts permits an expert to testify in the form of a "hypothetical question," where the expert assumes the truth of factual predicates and then offers testimony based on those assumptions. Modern evidence rules dispense with the need for hypothetical questions and permit an expert to base an opinion on facts made known to the expert at or before the hearing, though such reliance does not constitute admissible evidence of the underlying information.

In the Williams case, the Court held that defendant's confrontation right was not violated when the expert witness answered "yes" to a question about whether there was a match between the DNA profile found in semen from the vaginal swabs of the victim and the one identified as defendant's DNA.

The Supreme Court noted in the Williams case that trial courts can screen out experts who would act as conduits for hearsay by strictly enforcing the requirement that experts display genuine scientific, technical, or other specialized knowledge to help the trier of fact understand the evidence or determine a fact at issue, FRE 702(a). Experts are generally precluded from disclosing inadmissible evidence to a jury. If such evidence is disclosed, a trial judge may instruct the jury that the statements cannot be accepted for their truth, and that an expert's opinion is only as good as the independent evidence establishing its underlying premises. If the prosecution cannot muster independent admissible evidence to prove foundational facts, the expert's testimony cannot be given weight by the trier of fact.

Expert witnesses are allowed to posit alternate models to explain their conclusions where an expert's hypothetical explanation of the possible or probable causes of an event would aid the jury in its deliberations. The question of whether the expert's theory is correct given the circumstances of a particular case is a factual one left for the jury to determine.

Expert Testimony on Ultimate Issues

FRE 704 Opinion on an Ultimate Issue

(a) In General—Not Automatically Objectionable. An opinion is not objectionable just because it embraces an ultimate issue.

(b) Exception. In a criminal case, an expert witness must not state an opinion about whether the defendant did or did not have a mental state or condition that constitutes an element of the crime charged or of a defense. Those matters are for the trier of fact alone.

At common law, an expert witness could not testify as to an opinion on an ultimate issue. Therefore, the expert could not testify that in her opinion the defendant committed the crime or that the defendant was insane. The findings of guilty or not guilty and similar issues belong to the province of the fact finder, i.e., the judge or jury. Most states and the federal rules have slightly modified this rule regarding an opinion on the ultimate question. In probably no jurisdiction could an expert witness testify on his opinion that the accused is guilty or acted in self-defense or is insane.

The jury, not the witness, must draw inferences from evidence, and the government should not "spoon-feed" its theory of the case to the jury through a government agent with an aura of expertise and authority who might prompt the jury uncritically to substitute the agent's view of the evidence for its own.[31]

One court did not allow the admission of expert testimony in a human trafficking and domestic-worker exploitation case against hotel owners. The expert attempted to express opinion as to the guilt of the owners in a manner of stating that worker witnesses were telling the truth. The court correctly held that those issues should be left to the jury or judge.[32]

As a court noted, mere qualification as an expert is not license to invade the jury's function by telling the jury what result to reach, nor is it appropriate for the expert to supplant the judge's function to instruct the jury on law.[33] In a similar case, the arrestee's proffered expert witness's opinions regarding the reasonableness of evidence collection and strip search procedures were inadmissible in a civil action for police abuse, where such opinions were impermissible legal conclusions.[34]

Testimony by a "use of force" expert indicating that a police officer acted reasonably in discharging a firearm was, however, admissible in a § 1983 action wherein it was alleged that the police officer used excessive force when he shot and killed a youth, even though the question posed tended to call for an answer which would invade the province of the jury; questions leading up to the testimony, and the manner in which the expert answered the question, properly informed the jury that the expert was testifying regarding prevailing standards in the field of law enforcement.[35]

Expert testimony concerning modus operandi of individuals involved in drug trafficking, specifically on whether the amount and packaging of drugs found in a house was consistent with distribution or personal use, did not violate the rule prohibiting expert testimony as to whether defendant had the mental state or condition constituting an element of the crime charged.[36]

Defendant was not prejudiced by the admission of expert testimony, without objection, that the possession of items police found on and near defendant would be consistent with his intent to distribute cocaine, where the amount of cocaine found in his possession was itself sufficient to support the inference that he intended to distribute drugs.[37]

Testifying on the ultimate issue has always been an issue in cases involving whether or not the defendant is insane. Expert testimony on the issue of insanity must be accompanied by a presentation of facts and premises underlying the opinions and conclusions of the experts.[38] A trial court in its discretion may require expert medical witness to amplify his conclusions with respect to the sanity of defendant with an explanation of the basis for them, and such discretion should be exercised where evidence of either sanity or insanity appears inadequate.[39]

Unfair Prejudice

Expert opinion evidence may be excluded if its prejudicial impact substantially outweighs its probative value, if it wastes time, or if trial court determines that expert's specialized knowledge will not assist trier of fact to understand evidence.[40]

The trial court may deny admission of expert testimony if the trial judge determines that the information would unfairly prejudice the defense. For example a California defendant, Adan Albarran, was convicted of attempted murder, shooting at an inhabited dwelling and attempted kidnapping for carjacking. Prior to trial, Albarran sought to exclude evidence of his gang affiliation and the other expert testimony on gang evidence arguing it was irrelevant to the charges and would unfairly prejudice him. The trial court allowed the evidence, and the jury convicted Albarran.

The appellate court noted that California courts have long recognized the potentially prejudicial effect of gang membership. Given its highly inflammatory impact, the California Supreme Court has condemned the introduction of such evidence if it is only tangentially relevant to the charged offenses. In fact, in cases not involving gang enhancements, the evidence of gang membership should not be admitted if its probative value is minimal.[41]

Junk Science

An example of junk science that should be excluded under the Daubert standard as too unreliable would be the testimony of a phrenologist who would purport to prove a defendant's future dangerousness based on the contours of the defendant's skull.

Associate U.S. Supreme Court Justice John Paul Stevens, 1997[42]

Under Daubert, courts must engage in two-step inquiry to determine admissibility of expert opinion: (1) proffered "expert" must be qualified to express expert opinion, and (2) opinion must be reliable.[43]

The courts have struggled with formulating rules regarding the reliability of expert testimony involving scientific tests. In a 1923 case, a court of appeals devised the "Frye test" based on the case of *Frye v. United States*.[44] The Frye test stated that the proponent of novel scientific evidence must establish that the proffered test, theory, or principle must have gained general acceptance in the relevant scientific community.

The Frye test was displaced by the Federal Rules of Evidence 702–705. The Federal Rules of Evidence, however, placed no limits on the admissibility of purportedly scientific evidence. In 1993, the U.S. Supreme Court held in *Daubert v. Merrell Dow Pharmaceuticals* that the federal rules did not incorporate Frye's general acceptance test.[45] In addition, the Supreme Court held that the trial judge has the duty to screen such evidence. The Daubert case holds that the trial judge must ensure that any and all scientific testimony or evidence admitted is not only relevant, but reliable.

Evidence in Action
Daubert Test

Daubert v. Merrell Dow Pharmaceuticals sets forth a non-exclusive checklist for trial courts to use in assessing the reliability of scientific expert testimony. The specific factors explicated by the Daubert Court are:

(1) whether the expert's technique or theory can be or has been tested—that is, whether the expert's theory can be challenged in some objective sense, or whether it is instead simply a subjective, conclusory approach that cannot reasonably be assessed for reliability;

(2) whether the technique or theory has been subject to peer review and publication;

(3) the known or potential rate of error of the technique or theory when applied;

(4) the existence and maintenance of standards and controls; and

(5) whether the technique or theory has been generally accepted in the scientific community.[46]

The Supreme Court noted in Daubert that the primary locus of this obligation is Rule 702, which clearly contemplates some degree of regulation of the subjects and theories about which an expert may testify. The Court noted that if scientific, technical, or other specialized knowledge will assist the trier of fact to understand the evidence or to determine a fact in issue, an expert may testify thereto. The subject of an expert's testimony must be scientific and within the witness's knowledge.

According to the Advisory Committee on the Federal Rules of Evidence official notes, the courts both before and after Daubert have found other factors relevant in determining whether expert testimony is sufficiently reliable to be considered by the trier of fact. These factors include:

- Whether experts are "proposing to testify about matters growing naturally and directly out of research they have conducted independent of the litigation, or whether they have developed their opinions expressly for purposes of testifying."[47]
- Whether the expert has unjustifiably extrapolated from an accepted premise to an unfounded conclusion. Noting that in some cases a trial court may conclude

that there is simply too great an analytical gap between the data and the opinion proffered.[48]

- Whether the expert has adequately accounted for obvious alternative explanations[49] (the possibility of some unilluminated causes presents a question of weight, so long as the most obvious causes have been considered and reasonably ruled out by the expert).
- Whether the expert is being as careful as he would be in his regular professional work outside his paid litigation consulting.[50] The Daubert test requires the trial court to assure itself that the expert employs in the courtroom the same level of intellectual rigor that characterizes the practice of an expert in the relevant field.[51]
- Whether the field of expertise claimed by the expert is known to reach reliable results for the type of opinion the expert would give.

The trial judge should use all of these factors to determine the reliability of expert testimony under the federal rules. The cases appear to be clear that the trial judge has considerable leeway in deciding in a particular case how to go about determining whether particular expert testimony is reliable. There is no single factor that is necessarily dispositive of the reliability of a particular expert's testimony.[52] Not only must each stage of the expert's testimony be reliable, but each stage must be evaluated practically and flexibly without bright-line exclusionary (or inclusionary) rules. The fact that the expert has developed an expertise principally for purposes of litigation is not a substantial consideration.

A review of the case law after Daubert shows that the rejection of expert testimony is the exception rather than the rule. As the Court in Daubert noted, the vigorous cross-examination, presentation of contrary evidence, and careful instruction on the burden of proof are the traditional and appropriate means of attacking shaky but admissible evidence.

The trial judge has the discretion both to avoid unnecessary reliability proceedings in ordinary cases where the reliability of an expert's methods is properly taken for granted, and to require appropriate proceedings in the less usual or more complex cases where cause for questioning the expert's reliability arises.

An interesting case that was decided after Daubert was *United States v. Romo*. In that case, the issue involved the admission of a White House employee's expert testimony on the hypothetical question of whether a reasonable person would have foreseen that defendant's letter to the President would be viewed as threatening. The court held that given the explicitness of the threat language used, the question was one which laypeople were qualified to answer, and expert testimony was not needed.[53]

In determining the admissibility of scientific expert testimony, the district court must undertake a two-step inquiry. First, the district court determines whether the expert's testimony pertains to scientific knowledge and, second, the district court must determine whether the evidence or testimony assists trier of fact in understanding evidence or in determining the fact in issue, that is, suggested scientific testimony must "fit" the issue to which the expert is testifying.[54]

Preparing an Expert for Trial

Most expert witnesses have testified numerous times before a judge or jury. This does not mean that you forgo the preparation. Always prepare both lay and expert witnesses. Generally trial preparation of witnesses can be divided into four broad areas:

- Each witness should know what information is expected to be covered by the witness. For example, if the witness is going to testify that she saw the accused at a certain location at a certain time, the witness should be advised that this is why she is being called as a witness.
- Each witness should be familiar with the specific subject matter of his or her testimony. In the case of an expert witness, the witness should know the area that he or she will be examined on.
- The witness should be familiar with the expected demeanor of the witness when testifying. In other words, the witness should be advised on how to act during both direct and cross examinations.
- The witness should be advised of any issues or expected problems that may arise during the process of testifying.

In addition to the above general areas, the witness (especially the lay witness) should be advised to:

- Testify in an objective manner.
- Remain within your field of knowledge.
- Be prepared.
- Do not answer questions or provide information that is not asked for.
- Answer the question asked—no more, no less.
- Do not get angry.
- If you do not know the information, don't guess.
- Talk in a manner and with the choice of words that the jury will understand.

Many counsel will, during cross-examination, attempt to get the witness angry. As one veteran defense counsel once stated: "Those whom the gods wish to destroy, they first make angry."

Evidence In Action
An Expert Witness Makes a Mistake

Park Dietz, MD, PhD, was a forensic psychiatrist who consulted and testified in some of the highest profile criminal cases in the United States. As an assistant professor at Harvard Medical School in 1982, he testified in the case of John Hinckley, Jr., who was on trial for the attempted assassination of President Ronald

Regan. He testified that at the time of the shooting, Hinckley knew what he was doing, knew it was wrong, and had the capacity to control this behavior.

Dietz also testified as an expert witness in the trial of serial killer Jeffrey Dahmer who was alleged to have killed 17 boys and men from 1978 to 1991. Dietz was hired by the prosecutor to rebut Dahmer's claim that he was guilty but insane. Dahmer was convicted of 15 murders and received 15 life sentences.

Dietz also testified as an expert witness in the trial of the "Unabomber" terrorist, Ted Kaczynski. Kaczynski was charged with injuring 23 people and killing three more by using homemade bombs. Dietz testified as a prosecution witness to rebut Kaczynski's defense as a paranoid schizophrenic.

The Mistaken Testimony

In 2002, Dietz testified for the prosecution in the trial of Andrea Yates. Yates was charged with drowning her five children in a bathtub.

On June 20, 2001, Yates drowned her five children one by one, then called the police to her Houston home and showed them the bodies of Noah, 7, John, 5, Paul, 3, Luke, 2, and 6-month-old Mary.

Excerpts from court's decision:

> Five mental health experts for the defense testified that she did not know right from wrong or that she thought what she did was right …
>
> Dr. Park Dietz, who interviewed appellant and was the State's sole mental-health expert in the case, testified that appellant, although psychotic on June 20, knew that what she did was wrong. Dr. Dietz reasoned that because appellant indicated that her thoughts were coming from Satan, she must have known they were wrong; that if she believed she was saving the children, she would have shared her plan with others rather than hide it as she did; that if she really believed that Satan was going to harm the children, she would have called the police or a pastor or would have sent the children away; and that she covered the bodies out of guilt or shame …
>
> On cross-examination, appellant's counsel asked Dr. Dietz about his consulting work with the television show, "Law & Order," which appellant was known to watch. The testimony was as follows:
>
> > Q. Now, you are, are you not, a consultant on the television program known as "Law & Order"?
> >
> > A. Two of them.
> >
> > Q. Okay. Did either one of those deal with postpartum depression or women's mental health?
> >
> > A. As a matter of fact, there was a show of a woman with postpartum depression who drowned her children in the bathtub and was found insane, and it was aired shortly before the crime occurred.

The second mention of "Law & Order" came during Dr. Lucy Puryear's testimony. Dr. Puryear, a defense expert witness, was cross-examined by the State regarding her evaluation of appellant. The State specifically asked about her failure to inquire into whether or not appellant had seen "Law & Order." Dr. Puryear testified as follows:

> Q. You know she watched "Law & Order" a lot; right?
>
> A. I didn't know. No.
>
> Q. Did you know that in the weeks before June 20th, there was a "Law & Order" episode where a woman killed her children by drowning them in a bathtub, was defended on the basis of whether she was sane or insane under the law, and the diagnosis was postpartum depression and in the program the person was found insane, not guilty by reason of insanity? Did you know that?
>
> A. No.
>
> Q. If you had known that and had known that Andrea Yates was subject to these delusions, not that she was the subject of a delusion of reference, but that she regularly watched "Law & Order" and may have seen that episode, would you have changed the way you went about interviewing her, would you have interviewed whether she got the idea somehow she could do this and not suffer hell or prison?

Yates was convicted.

There was no such episode of Law and Order.

Yates' conviction was overturned by a Texas appellate court because no such Law & Order episode existed. The appellate court noted: "His testimony was critical to establish the state's case. Although the record does not show that Dr. Dietz intentionally lied in his testimony, his false testimony undoubtedly gave greater weight to his opinion."

[*Yates v. State*, 171 S.W.3d. 215 (2005)]

Practicum

Practicum One

Patricia Campbell Hearst was kidnapped. While she was held as a captive, she was involved in the robbery of a bank. She was later charged with armed robbery and the use of a firearm to commit felony. She claimed that she had been coerced by her kidnappers to participate in the robbery and offered expert testimony in the field of psycholinguistics. The defense stated that if the expert witness was allowed to testify, the witness would have testified that her expertise in this area enables her to conclude, from a stylistic comparison of known writings and utterances of the defendant with certain writings and tape-recordings of the defendant's voice offered into evidence by the Government, that these latter writings or utterances could not have been authored by the defendant.

As a trial judge: Would you allow the expert witness to testify in the field of psycholinguistics? Or would you disallow the testimony based on the fact that the science has not achieved such general acceptance among psychological and scientific authorities as to justify courts of law in admitting expert testimony on this subject?

[See: *U.S. v. Hearst*, 412 F.Supp. 893 (1973)]

Practicum Two

In a prosecution in the United States District Court for the Southern District of New York, defendants were convicted of conspiracy to distribute heroin and to possess heroin with intent to distribute, one defendant was convicted of conducting a continuing criminal enterprise and was required to forfeit the assets obtained therefrom, and another defendant was convicted of receiving and possessing an unregistered automatic rifle. On appeal, defendants claimed that the extensive use of expert testimony by agents involved in the investigation deprived defendants of a fair trial.

Was it proper for the government to elicit expert testimony from law enforcement officers who also testified as fact witnesses? The Trial Court had permitted the law enforcement officers to testify as experts as to the clandestine manner in which drugs are bought and sold. The officers were also fact or lay witnesses since they had arrested the defendants.

[See: *U.S. v. Young*, 745 F.2d 743 (1984)]

Summary

- A lay witness is essentially a person who was an eyewitness to some aspects that a party is trying to establish.
- An expert witness is a person who, because of specialized knowledge, can provide the fact finders (jury or judge alone in a trial by judge alone) with information to help the fact finders determine the essential facts in the case.
- An expert witness's duty is to furnish the judge or jury with the necessary scientific criteria for testing the accuracy of their conclusions, so to enable the judge or jury to form their own independent judgment by the application of these criteria to the facts proved in evidence.
- The trial judge has considerable discretion in deciding whether or not to admit expert testimony, and his or her decision will be reversed only when the appellate court determines that the judge abused his or her discretion.
- Expert testimony should not be admitted in those cases where the issues are such that they are within the common sense of the average juror or judge. In other words, if expert testimony is not needed then it should not be admitted.
- Generally, one may become qualified as an expert by practical experience, and professional education is not a required prerequisite.
- An expert witness may be cross-examined concerning his or her testimony and background or specialized education in his or her expert field. The witness may also be cross-examined as to any bias in favor of one of the parties.
- A long tradition in American courts permits an expert to testify in the form of a "hypothetical question," where the expert assumes the truth of factual predicates and then offers testimony based on those assumptions.
- Modern evidence rules dispense with the need for hypothetical questions and permit an expert to base an opinion on facts made known to the expert at or before the hearing, though such reliance does not constitute admissible evidence of the underlying information.

- At common law, an expert witness could not testify as to an opinion on an ultimate issue.
- Most states and the federal rules have slightly modified this rule regarding an opinion on the ultimate question. In probably no jurisdiction could an expert witness testify on his opinion that the accused is guilty or acted in self-defense or is insane.
- Expert opinion evidence may be excluded if its prejudicial impact substantially outweighs its probative value, if it wastes time, or if trial court determines that expert's specialized knowledge will not assist the trier of fact to understand evidence.
- The courts have struggled with formulating rules regarding the reliability of expert testimony involving scientific tests.
- The trial judge should use all of these factors to determine the reliability of expert testimony under the federal rules. The cases appear to be clear that the trial judge has considerable leeway in deciding in a particular case how to go about determining whether particular expert testimony is reliable.
- Most expert witnesses have testified numerous times before a judge or jury. This does not mean that you forgo the preparation. Always prepare both lay and expert witnesses.

Questions in Review

1.   What is the purpose of an expert witness?
2.   Who determines whether or not expert testimony is needed in a trial?
3.   How does a person become an expert in a certain field?
4.   What background should an expert witness have?
5.   Explain how the courts handle the issue of "junk science."

Key Terms

Daubert **Standard**: The Daubert standard is a check-list type test used in courts to determine if the scientific evidence offered into evidence was reliable. The test is based on the *Daubert v. Merrell Dow Pharmaceuticals* case.

Expert Witness: An expert witness is a person who, because of specialized knowledge, can provide the fact finders (jury or judge alone in trial by judge alone) with information to help the fact finders determine the essential facts in the case.

Junk Science: Scientific evidence that has not been accepted by the courts as based on issues of reliability.

Ultimate Issue: Generally the ultimate issue means the main issue in a trial. In a criminal case it would be the finding of guilty or not guilty.

Endnotes

1. United States v. Romo, C.A.9 (Mont.) 2005, 413 F.3d 1044.

2. U.S. v. 364.82 Acres of Land, More or Less, in Mariposa County, State of Cal., N.D.Cal.1965, 38 F.R.D. 411.

3. Davie v. Edinburgh Corporation Magistrates, 1953 S.C. 34 at 40, 1953 SLT 54 at 57.

4. Randolph v. Collectramatic, Inc., C.A.10 (Okla.) 1979, 590 F.2d 844.

5. United Telecommunications, Inc. v. American Television & Communications Corp., C.A.10 (Colo.) 1976, 536 F.2d 1310.

6. U.S. v. Garcia, C.A.10 (Okla.) 1993, 994 F.2d 1499.

7. U.S. v. Felak, C.A.8 (Minn.) 1987, 831 F.2d 794.

8. Hutchison v. Cutliffe, D.Me.2004, 344 F.Supp.2d 219.

9. U.S. v. Jobin, D.Vt.2004, 327 F.Supp.2d 310.

10. U.S. v. Oriedo, C.A.7 (Ill.) 2007, 498 F.3d 593.

11. U.S. v. Solorio-Tafolla, C.A.8 (Neb.) 2003, 324 F.3d 964.

12. U.S. v. Foster, C.A.7 (Ill.) 1991, 939 F.2d 445.

13. U.S. v. Green, C.A.2 (N.Y.) 1975, 523 F.2d 229.

14. Southern Cement Co. v. Sproul, C.A.5 (Ala.) 1967, 378 F.2d 48.

15. Pedraza v. Jones, C.A.5 (Tex.) 1995, 71 F.3d 194.

16. King v. Taylor, E.D.Ky.2013, 944 F.Supp.2d 548.

17. U.S. v. Goxcon-Chagal, D.N.M.2012, 885 F.Supp.2d 1118.

18. U.S. v. Locascio, C.A.2 (N.Y.) 1993, 6 F.3d 924, 127 A.L.R. Fed. 599.

19. Schmidt v. City of Bella Villa, C.A.8 (Mo.) 2009, 557 F.3d 564.

20. U.S. v. Monteiro, D.Mass.2006, 407 F.Supp.2d 351.

21. U.S. v. Roach, C.A.8 (S.D.) 2011, 644 F.3d 763.

22. U.S. v. King, D. Hawai'i2010, 703 F.Supp.2d 1063.

23. U.S. v. Braxton, C.A.5 (Fla.) 1969, 417 F.2d 878.

24. Stottlemire v. Cawood, D.C.D.C.1963, 215 F.Supp. 266.

25. U.S. v. Angiulo, C.A.1 (Mass.) 1990, 897 F.2d 1169.

26. U.S. v. Lawson, C.A.7 (Ill.) 1981, 653 F.2d 299.

27. Bryan v. John Bean Division of FMC Corp., C.A.5 (Tex.) 1978, 566 F.2d 541.

28. U.S. v. A & S Council Oil Co., C.A.4 (N.C.) 1991, 947 F.2d 1128.

29. U.S. v. Gillis, C.A.4 (Md.) 1985, 773 F.2d 549.

30. Williams v. Illinois, 132 S.Ct. 2221 (2012).

31. U.S. v. Miner, 2014 WL 7003763 C.A.6 (Tenn.), 2014.

32. U.S. v. Farrell, C.A.8 (S.D.) 2009, 563 F.3d 364.

33. Fund of Funds, Ltd. v. Arthur Andersen & Co., S.D.N.Y.1982, 545 F.Supp. 1314.

34. Schmidt v. City of Bella Villa, C.A.8 (Mo.) 2009, 557 F.3d 564.

35. Samples v. City of Atlanta, C.A.11 (Ga.) 1990, 916 F.2d 1548.

36. In re Sealed Case, C.A.D.C.1996, 99 F.3d 1175, 321 U.S.App.D.C. 324.

37. U.S. v. Glenn, C.A.D.C.1995, 64 F.3d 706.

38. U.S. v. Brawner, C.A.D.C.1972, 471 F.2d 969.

39. Rollerson v. U.S., C.A.D.C.1964, 343 F.2d 269.

40. U.S. v. Milton, C.A.5 (La.) 1977, 555 F.2d 1198.

41. People v. Albarran, 57 Cal. Rptr. 3d 92—Cal: Court of Appeal, 2nd Appellate Dist., 7th Div. 2007.

42. In a concurring opinion in General Electric Company v. Robert K. Joiner, 522 U.S. 136 (1997).

43. U.S. v. Jasin, E.D.Pa.2003, 292 F.Supp.2d 670.

44. Frye v. United States, 293 F. 1013 (DC Cir. 1923).

45. Daubert v. Merrell Dow Pharmaceuticals, 509 U.S. 579 (1993).

46. 119 S.Ct. at 1175.

47. Daubert v. Merrell Dow Pharmaceuticals, Inc., 43 F.3d 1311, 1317 (9th Cir. 1995).

48. General Elec. Co. v. Joiner, 522 U.S. 136, 146 (1997).

49. Claar v. Burlington N.R.R., 29 F.3d 499 (9th Cir. 1994).
50. Sheehan v. Daily Racing Form, Inc., 104 F.3d 940, 942 (7th Cir. 1997).
51. Kumho Tire Co. v. Carmichael, 119 S.Ct. 1167, 1176 (1999).
52. Heller v. Shaw Industries, Inc., 167 F.3d 146, 155 (3d Cir. 1999).
53. U.S. v. Romo, C.A.9 (Mont.) 2005, 413 F.3d 1044.
54. O'Conner v. Commonwealth Edison Co., C.A.7 (Ill.) 1994, 13 F.3d 1090.

Chapter 8

Evidence-Based Motions

Chapter Objectives

What you should know and understand after studying this chapter:

- Issues that are decided during pretrial motions
- Rules regarding discovery
- Requirements to submit notice in certain situations
- What constitutes a violation of the Brady rule
- What constitutes work product

Chapter Outline

Introduction
Form of Motion
Notice of Intent in Sex Offense Cases
Motion in Limine
Motion for the Production of Evidence
Alibi Evidence
Practicum
Summary
Questions in Review
Key Terms
Endnotes

Introduction

Present-day evidence codes encourage that evidence issues be settled prior to trial. This practice shortens the length of jury trials and provides parties with an understanding of what evidence is admissible prior to the start of the trial. This knowledge provides valuable information to the parties, especially to the defense, in determining whether or not to enter into pretrial agreements or to plead not guilty.

At common law, a motion to suppress evidence was a formal, written request to a judge for an order that certain evidence be excluded from consideration by the judge or jury at trial. Presently, the term "motion to suppress" typically encompasses motions in criminal cases where the proposed basis for exclusion arises from the United States Constitution, a state constitution, or a specific statute permitting the exclusion of certain types of evidence. In addition, evidence may be excluded by the trial judge if the evidence is unduly prejudicial to the defendant and does not contribute materially to the case.

Generally objections to illegally seized evidence or inadmissible confessions are handled by motions to suppress prior to the presentation of witnesses and evidence at trial. In addition, the offered evidence may be objected to when offered into evidence. Some state evidence codes require that when a motion to exclude evidence is denied at a pretrial hearing, that the objecting party must also object at the time the evidence is offered into evidence to preserve the issue for appeal. In those states, failure to object when the evidence is actually admitted waives the issue. Most modern evidence codes do not require the continuous objection to preserve the issue for appeal. The advantage of using a motion to suppress the evidence is that the parties know in advance whether or not the evidence is admissible and can plan their presentations in court in accordance with the rulings.

Rule 12 of the Federal Rules of Criminal Procedure and many state rules of evidence require that motions to suppress evidence be raised by pretrial motion if it is reasonably available and the motion can be determined without a trial on the merits. In addition, Rule 12 and similar state rules require that the government notify the defendant of its intent to use specified evidence at trial in order to afford the defense an opportunity to object before trial.

Evidence in Action
Federal Rules of Criminal Procedure

Excerpts from Rules 12 and 16

Rule 12 Pleadings and Pretrial Motions
(b) Pretrial Motions.
(2) Motions That May Be Made Before Trial. A party may raise by pretrial motion any defense, objection, or request that the court can determine without a trial of the general issue.
(3) Motions That Must Be Made Before Trial. The following must be raised before trial:
(A) a motion alleging a defect in instituting the prosecution
(B) a motion alleging a defect in the indictment or information — but at any time while the case is pending, the court may hear a claim that the indictment or information fails to invoke the court's jurisdiction or to state an offense
(C) a motion to suppress evidence ...

Rule 16 Motion For Discovery

(4) Notice of the Government's Intent to Use Evidence.
(A) At the Government's Discretion. At the arraignment or as soon afterward as practicable, the government may notify the defendant of its intent to use spec-

ified evidence at trial in order to afford the defendant an opportunity to object before trial.

(B) At the Defendant's Request. At the arraignment or as soon afterward as practicable, the defendant may, in order to have an opportunity to move to suppress evidence under Rule 12(b)(3)(C), request notice of the government's intent to use (in its evidence-in-chief at trial) any evidence that the defendant may be entitled to discover under Rule 16.

(e) Waiver of a Defense, Objection, or Request. A party waives any Rule 12(b)(3) defense, objection, or request not raised by the deadline the court sets under Rule 12(c) or by any extension the court provides. For good cause, the court may grant relief from the waiver.

If a party fails to submit a pretrial motion to exclude the evidence, the party may have forfeited his or her right to object later. The trial judge, however, may make a determination as to whether there was good cause for the failure to submit a pretrial motion and allow the party to object to the admission of the document or object. For example in trials involving organized crime, trial judges have allowed the government to withhold the names and addresses of the certain witnesses until the witnesses have testified at trial. This procedure has been used when the prosecution has established that the delayed disclosure is necessary to protect the witnesses.

At the arraignment or as soon afterward as practicable, the defendant may, in order to have an opportunity to move to suppress evidence request notice of the government's intent to use (in its evidence-in-chief at trial) any evidence that the defendant may be entitled to discovery. Discovery issues are discussed later in this chapter.

A trial court may, at the arraignment or as soon afterward as practicable, set a deadline for the parties to make pretrial motions and may also schedule a motion hearing. If the court does not set one, the deadline is the start of trial. At any time before trial, the court may extend or reset the deadline for pretrial motions. As noted earlier, if a party does not meet the deadline for making an evidentiary motion, the motion is untimely. But a trial judge may consider the defense, objection, or request if the party shows good cause.

Consider a case where the only evidence against a defendant is illegal drugs that were found in her car during a routine traffic stop. If the defense obtains a favorable motion to suppress the evidence, then the prosecution may drop the case. Conversely, if the defense's motion is denied and the evidence is admissible, the defense may then enter a guilty plea with or without a plea bargain. Frequently in the latter case, the defense will plead guilty while reserving the right to appeal the denial of the motion to suppress. An example of this is the case of *Heien v. North Carolina*.[1]

In the *Heien* case, following a suspicious vehicle, a police officer noticed that only one of the vehicle's brake lights was working and pulled the driver over. While issuing a warning ticket for the broken brake light, the officer became suspicious of the actions of the two occupants and their answers to his questions. Heien, the car's owner, gave the officer consent to search the vehicle. The officer found cocaine, and Heien was arrested and charged with attempted trafficking. The trial court denied Heien's motion to suppress the seized evidence on Fourth Amendment grounds, concluding that the vehicle's faulty brake light gave the officer reasonable suspicion to initiate the stop.

After the trial court denied the defense's motion to suppress the evidence, Heien pled guilty and reserved the right to appeal the trial court's ruling on the admissibility of the evidence.

The North Carolina Court of Appeals reversed the conviction, holding that the relevant code provision, which requires that a car be "equipped with a stop lamp," N.C. Gen.Stat. Ann. §20–129(g), requires only a single lamp—which Heien's vehicle had— and therefore the justification for the stop was objectively unreasonable. Reversing in turn, the State Supreme Court held that, even assuming no violation of the state law had occurred, the officer's mistaken understanding of the law was reasonable, and thus the stop was valid. The U.S. Supreme Court agreed with the state supreme court and upheld the Conviction.

Form of Motion

The party applying for a court order must generally do so by motion. A motion— except when made during a trial or hearing—must be in writing, unless the court permits the party to make the motion by other means. A motion must state the grounds on which it is based and the relief or order sought. A motion is generally supported by points of authority and affidavits explaining the need for the relief requested.

Evidence in Action
Sample Form of Motion to Suppress Evidence

STATE of FLORIDA
vs.   Case No:

_____ Defendant

DEFENDANT'S MOTION TO SUPPRESS EVIDENCE
COMES NOW the Defendant, _____ pursuant to Rule 3.190(h) Fla.R.Crim.P., and respectfully requests this Court suppress evidence seized by law enforcement in this case from Defendant's person, and as grounds therefore states as follows;
I. EVIDENCE TO BE SUPPRESSED:
The Defendant respectfully requests this Honorable Court to suppress any and all evidence of narcotics found as a result of the stop and search of Defendant's person, more specifically, a small baggie of white powder (field tested positive as

cocaine, approximately 1 gram), one large baggie (field tested negative as co-caine), and a small colored paper envelope which contained approximately 20 (twenty) pills.

II. GROUNDS FOR SUPPRESSION:

The Defendant was seized and searched in contravention of the Fourth and Fourteenth Amendments to the United States Constitution and Article I, Sections 9 and 12 of the Florida Constitution, and any evidence obtained because of the illegal seizure is the fruit of the poisonous tree and should be suppressed. Wong v. United States, 371 U.S. 471 (1963).

The evidence was obtained as a result of an illegal search, without a warrant, in violation of the Fourth and Fourteenth Amendments to the United States Constitution and Article I, Sections 9 1 and 12 of the Florida Constitution.

The evidence was obtained in violation of Defendant's right to privacy guaranteed by Article 1, Section 23, of the Constitution of the State of Florida.

III. FACTUAL BASIS: [At this point the facts surrounding the search would be inserted.]

IV. LEGAL AUTHORITY: [Counsel's legal argument as to why the evidence should be suppressed would be listed at this point.]

WHEREFORE, based on the forgoing facts and case law stated herein, the Defendant moves this Honorable Court to suppress all evidence seized by law enforcement.

Public Trial on Evidentiary Motions

The U.S. Supreme Court held, in *Waller v. Georgia*,[2] that defendant's Sixth Amendment right to a public trial included the right of the public to attend a hearing on the motion to suppress the evidence. The Court noted that any closure of a suppression hearing over the objections of the accused must meet the following tests:

- The party seeking to close the hearing must advance an overriding interest that is likely to be prejudiced;
- the closure must be no broader than necessary to protect that interest;
- the trial court must consider reasonable alternatives to closing the hearing; and
- it must make findings adequate to support the closure.

In the *Waller* case, after court-authorized wiretaps of telephones by Georgia police revealed a large lottery operation, the police executed search warrants at numerous locations, including petitioners' homes. Petitioners and others were then indicted for violating the Georgia Racketeer Influenced and Corrupt Organizations (RICO) Act and other state gambling statutes. Prior to trial, petitioners moved to suppress the wiretaps and evidence seized during the searches. The State moved to close the suppression hearing to the public, alleging that unnecessary "publication" of information obtained under the wiretaps would render the information inadmissible as evidence, and that the wiretap evidence would "involve" the privacy interests of some persons who were indicted but were not then on trial, and some who were not then indicted. The trial court agreed, finding that insofar as the wiretap evidence related to alleged offenders not then on trial, the evidence would be tainted and could not be used in future prosecutions. Accordingly, over petitioners' objections, the court ordered the suppression hearing closed to all persons other than witnesses, court personnel, the parties, and the lawyers. The suppression hearing lasted seven days, but less than 2 ½ hours were devoted to playing the tapes of the intercepted telephone conversations, and few of them mentioned or involved parties not then before the court. The case was then tried before a jury in open court, and petitioners were acquitted under the RICO Act but convicted under the other statutes. The Georgia Supreme Court affirmed.

The Supreme Court held that under the above tests, the closure of the entire suppression hearing here plainly was unjustified. The State's proffer was not specific as to whose privacy interests might be infringed if the hearing were open to the public, what portions of the wiretap tapes might infringe those interests, and what portion of the evidence consisted of the tapes. As a result, the trial court's findings were broad and general and did not purport to justify closure of the entire hearing. The Supreme Court noted that the trial court should have considered alternatives to immediate closure of the hearing.

Notice of Intent in Sex Offense Cases

Generally in sex offense cases, evidence of the victim's sexual behavior or predisposition is not admissible under "rape shield" laws. If the defense intends to offer such evidence, the defense must file a motion that specifically describes the evidence and states the purpose for which the evidence is to be offered. When such a notice is filed, generally the trial judge will hold a private hearing and give the victim and parties to the case a right to attend and to be heard on the admissibility of the evidence. The results of the hearing is generally sealed and kept private unless the trial judge orders otherwise. For purposes of this requirement, the victim includes an alleged victim.

A similar rule applies to child molestation cases. Under the federal rules, a child is defined as a person under the age of 14 years. Most states have similar rules. The shield laws are designed to protect the victim and prevent undue harassment of them by a cross-examination of their sexual history that has little or no bearing on the current charges. For the most part, the sexual history of the victim is immaterial to the question as to whether the defendant committed a sex crime.

Motion in Limine

A "motion in limine" is a motion that requests a decision from the trial court as to whether or not certain evidence may or may not be presented to the jury at the trial. The motion generally addresses issues which would be prejudicial for the jury to hear in open court, even if the other side makes a timely objection which is sustained, and the judge instructs the jury to disregard the evidence. For example, a defendant requests that the trial court rule that evidence of his prior convictions that occurred years earlier not be allowed into evidence at the trial because it would be more prejudicial than probative. If the motion is granted, then evidence regarding the conviction may not be mentioned in front of the jury, without first approaching the judge outside of the hearing of the jury and obtaining permission. The violation of a motion in limine may result in the court declaring a mistrial or in contempt sanctions.

There are three general types of Motions in Limine:

- Inclusionary—A motion asking the court to have something included in the trial.
- Exclusionary—A motion asking the court to have something excluded in the trial.
- Preclusionary—A motion asking the court to have something precluded in the trial.

In *United States v. Sanders*,[3] the defendant appealed his conviction for kidnapping and extortion. The defense filed a motion to suppress the prosecution's evidence that defendant was identified as the results of a "show up." He claimed that the identification was unduly suggestive and that the police presented only one suspect to the victim. After that motion was denied by the trial court, the government moved to limit the defense's cross-examination of one of the witnesses. The witness had been convicted in 2001 of theft and forgery in connection with her employment. As a general rule convictions over ten years old are not admissible for purposes of impeaching a witness. The trial judge had limited the defense from cross-examining the witness regarding her convictions in 2001.

The appellate court held that the trial judge had not abused his discretion by limiting the cross-examination of the witness. The court held that the jury had sufficient information to make a discriminating appraisal of the witness's motives and biases. The court noted that the defense was allowed to present to the jury with its entire theory of the witness's motive to lie. The fact that the prior convictions in 2001 would not have given the jury any further material information in appraising her credibility. The jury might not have possessed all the information defense wanted it to have, but it certainly had sufficient information to evaluate her testimony.

Evidence in Action
SAMPLE DEFENDANT'S MOTION IN LIMINE

COMES NOW Defendant, ___, and requests this Court to enter an Order in Limine, pursuant to sections 90.402, 90.403, and 90.404, Florida Statutes. It is requested that this Honorable Court exclude certain evidence at hearing and trial of this case and to prevent any discussion in opening statement, questioning of witnesses or in argument concerning any of the following matters:

Evidence to be excluded:

1. Any and all evidence regarding the commission of any alleged criminal conduct, prosecuted or otherwise, by the Defendant not charged in the above-captioned case.

2. Any and all evidence regarding any arrests of Defendant on or before the date of the alleged incident on April 11, 2013.

3. Any and all evidence regarding any prior arrest warrants issued for the Defendant before the date of the alleged incident on April 11, 2013.

4. Any and all evidence relating to any alleged drug use or alcohol abuse by Defendant prior to April 11, 2013.

5. Any and all statements relating to defendant's membership status in any gang or other organized group prior to April 11, 2013.

6. Any and all references to the status of the Defendant's attorneys as public defenders.

Grounds for Exclusion

7. Exclusion of the evidence is required due to lack of relevance. §90.402, Fla. Stat. (2010).

8. Exclusion of any or all of the evidence described above is required as the value of such evidence is substantially outweighed by the danger of unfair prejudice, confusion of the issues, misleading the jury, and would serve only to inflame the jury. §90.403, Fla. Stat. (2010).

9. Exclusion of any or all of the evidence described above is required as improper character evidence introduced to show propensity. See §90.404(2), Fla Stat. (2010); Carter v. State, 687, So. 2d 327 (Fla. 1st DCA 1997).

WHEREFORE, Defendant respectfully requests that this Honorable Court enter an Order excluding any and all evidence, testimony or references to the above-described information at the trial of this case.

Motions for Production of Evidence

As noted by other chapters, evidence comes in numerous forms such as eyewitness or expert testimony, documents, real objects and scientific tests. Under the modern day rules of evidence in all U.S. and state jurisdictions, the trial courts encourage the voluntary sharing of evidence in the advance of trial. In most trials, the prosecutor and defense informally share information and evidence. In many jurisdictions there are standard motion forms that the defense may submit demanding that the prosecutor disclose to the defense the evidence that the prosecutor has regarding the crime.

The use of ambush evidence is disfavored in all U.S. jurisdictions. Ambush evidence is evidence that one of the parties keeps hidden and is disclosed as a method of ambushing the other side during the trial. As one experienced prosecutor noted, there is no room for Perry Mason in our courtrooms.

Discovery

Generally motions for the production of evidence involve the issue of discovery. As will be discussed later in this chapter, in some cases, such as with the alibi defense, the party intending to offer the evidence for admission must provide notice of the intent to enter such evidence. The two leading cases on the rights of a defendant to discovery the prosecutor's evidence are *Brady v. Maryland* and *United States v. Agurs*.

In *Brady v. Maryland*,[4] John Brady and a companion were found guilty of murder in the first degree. Their trials were separate. Brady was tried first. At his trial, Brady took the stand and admitted his participation in the crime, but he claimed that the companion did the actual killing. And, in his summation to the jury, Brady's counsel conceded that Brady was guilty of murder in the first degree, asking only that the jury return that verdict "without capital punishment." Prior to the trial, Brady's counsel had requested the prosecution to allow him to examine the out-of-court statements made by the companion, Boblit. Several of those statements were shown to Brady's counsel, but one dated July 9, 1958, in which Boblit admitted the actual homicide, was withheld by the prosecution and did not come to the defense's notice until after Brady had been tried, convicted, and sentenced, and after his conviction had been affirmed.

Brady's counsel moved for a new trial based on newly discovered evidence that had been suppressed by the prosecution. The Supreme Court held that a prosecutor that withholds evidence on demand of an accused, which, if made available, would tend to exculpate him or reduce the penalty, helps shape a trial that bears heavily on the defendant. And that casts the prosecutor in the role of an architect of a proceeding that does not comport with standards of justice. The Court held that the actions of the prosecutor in withholding the statement was a violation of the due process clause of the Fourteenth Amendment. *Brady* established the rule that the prosecutor has a duty to disclose favorable evidence to the defense.

In *U.S. v. Agurs*,[5] Associate Supreme Court Justice noted that although the prosecutor has no duty to provide defense counsel with unlimited discovery of everything known by him, if the subject matter of defense counsel's request for evidence is material, or indeed if a substantial basis for claiming materiality exists, it is reasonable to require the prosecutor to respond either by furnishing information or by submitting the problem to the trial judge; and when the prosecutor receives a specific and relevant request, failure to make any response is seldom, if ever, excusable.

In the *Agurs* case, defendant Linda Agurs was convicted of second degree murder for killing the victim with a knife. The victim was repeatedly stabbed by Agurs. Agurs claimed that she was acting in self-defense. The prosecutor had in his possession evidence that the victim had a prior criminal record (including guilty pleas to charges of assault and carrying a deadly weapon, apparently a knife) that would have tended to support the argument that Agurs acted in self-defense. The prosecutor failed to disclose this information to the defense. The Supreme Court reversed defendant's conviction and held:

- A prosecutor does not violate the constitutional duty of disclosure unless his omission is sufficiently significant to result in the denial of the defendant's right to a fair trial.
- Whether or not procedural rules authorizing discovery of everything that might influence a jury might be desirable, the Constitution does not demand such broad discovery; and the mere possibility that an item of undisclosed information might have aided the defense, or might have affected the outcome of the trial, does not establish "materiality" in the constitutional sense.
- Nor is the prosecutor's constitutional duty of disclosure measured by his moral culpability or willfulness; if the suppression of evidence results in constitutional error, it is because of the character of the evidence, not the character of the prosecutor.

• The proper standard of materiality of undisclosed evidence, and the standard applied by the trial judge in this case, is that if the omitted evidence creates a reasonable doubt of guilt that did not otherwise exist, constitutional error has been committed.

General Rules on Discovery

In most states and the federal government, the court rules or evidence codes require that the prosecution share its evidence with the defense prior to trial. Often prosecutors comply with this requirement by allowing defense counsel to inspect the prosecutor's files. This is referred to as an "open file" policy. The requirement to disclose generally includes any and all statements made to the police by the defendant or any witness and any scientific or lab reports.

Following are some of the rulings on the duty to disclose:

• The reversal of a conviction on the basis of a *Brady* violation (failure of government to disclose information) is required upon a showing that the favorable evidence could reasonably be taken to put the whole case in such a different light as to undermine confidence in the verdict.[6]
• Undisclosed evidence is material under *Brady* if there is a reasonable probability that, had the evidence been disclosed to the defense, the result of the proceeding would have been different, although a showing of materiality does not require demonstration by a preponderance that disclosure of the suppressed evidence would have resulted ultimately in the defendant's acquittal.[7]
• The individual prosecutor has a duty to learn of any evidence favorable to the defense that is known to the others acting on the government's behalf in the case, including the police. Such evidence is material if there is a reasonable probability that, had the evidence been disclosed to the defense, the result of the proceeding would have been different.[8]
• There are three components of a true *Brady* violation: the evidence at issue must be favorable to the accused, either because it is exculpatory, or because it is impeaching; the evidence must have been suppressed by the State, either willfully or inadvertently; and prejudice must have ensued.[9]
• Criminal rule permitting defendant to discover material within the government's possession, which is material to the defense or intended for use by the government as evidence in chief at trial, authorizes defendants to examine government documents material to preparation of their defense against the government's case-in-chief, but not material to preparation of selective-prosecution claims.[10]
• After a witness other than the defendant has testified on direct examination, the court, on motion of a party who did not call the witness, must order an attorney for the government or the defendant and the defendant's attorney to produce, for the examination and use of the moving party, any statement of the witness that is in their possession and that relates to the subject matter of the witness's testimony.[11] While that is the rule in most jurisdictions, the trial courts encourage the prosecution or defense to bring issue before the trial court in a pre-trial hearing and to make any statements available before trial.

Evidence in Action
Excerpts from Texas Code of Criminal Procedure, Article 39.14

(A typical evidence code provision)

As practicable after receiving a timely request from the defendant the state shall produce and permit the inspection and the electronic duplication, copying, and photographing, by or on behalf of the defendant, of any offense reports, any designated documents, papers, written or recorded statements of the defendant or a witness, including witness statements of law enforcement officers but not including the work product of counsel for the state in the case and their investigators and their notes or report, or any designated books, accounts, letters, photographs, or objects or other tangible things not otherwise privileged that constitute or contain evidence material to any matter involved in the action and that are in the possession, custody, or control of the state or any person under contract with the state. The state may provide to the defendant electronic duplicates of any documents or other information described by this article. The rights granted to the defendant under this article do not extend to written communications between the state and an agent, representative, or employee of the state. This article does not authorize the removal of the documents, items, or information from the possession of the state, and any inspection shall be in the presence of a representative of the state.

Remedies for Discovery Violations

The sanctions for discovery violations generally depend on the nature and extent of the violation. A *Brady* violation is considered a violation of a constitutional right to discovery and can result in the reversal of a defendant's conviction. To obtain a reversal, however, it's not enough to show that information was withheld, but also that the information would have had material impact on the outcome of a defendant's case.

Material impact means that a defendant must show that the introduction of the evidence may have resulted in he or she being found not guilty or receiving a lesser sentence. For example, in some sexual assault cases, convictions have been reversed because defendants were not advised that DNA evidence existed that tended to establish that defendant was not the person who committed the act. The courts have held that the absence of this evidence probably had a direct impact on determining the identity of the offender and was considered *Brady* evidence that should have been turned over.

Material impact does not include withholding evidence that only shows that the defendant was more culpable than charged. For example, withholding evidence that the state had fingerprint evidence proving defendant was in the house during a burglary trial was not a *Brady* violation even though had the defendant known this evidence was in possession of the state, he may have chosen to accept a plea bargain and plead guilty.

Some appellate courts have suggested that the prosecutor should disclose all of the evidence ahead of time. The courts will not automatically consider the withholding of evidence a *Brady* violation just because a defendant would have made a different decision at or before trial. Evidence will only be considered material when it could have resulted in a defendant's acquittal or a reduction in the sentence.

Once a *Brady* violation has been established and it is considered as material, the appellate courts do not enter an acquittal. Instead, a *Brady* violation results only in a reversal on appeal. It does not result in an acquittal. The case will be returned to the trial court for a new trial or dismissal of the charges. For example in the famous case of *Miranda v. Arizona*, the Supreme Court reversed the conviction and returned the case to the state courts. Miranda was retried without the use of his statement and convicted.

Need for Discovery Request

As noted in both the *Brady* and *Agurs* cases, a prosecutor has a duty when demanded to provide to the defense any evidence that is favorable to defendant. What about the situation where the prosecutor has favorable evidence for defense but there is no demand by the defense for such evidence? That was the situation in the *Kimmelman v. Morrison* case.[12]

In *Kimmelman*, at defendant's trial by judge alone in a New Jersey court, he was convicted of rape. A police officer testified that a few hours after the rape she accompanied the victim to defendant's apartment where the rape had occurred; that he was not there but another tenant let them into defendant's apartment; and that the officer seized a sheet from respondent's bed. At such point in the testimony, defense counsel sought to suppress the introduction of the sheet and any testimony about it on the ground that the officer had seized it without a search warrant in violation of the Fourth Amendment, but the trial judge ruled that counsel's suppression motion was late under the applicable New Jersey Court Rule. The trial judge rejected defense counsel's attempt to justify his omission on the grounds that he had not heard of the seizure until the day before, when the trial began; that it was the State's obligation to inform him of its case, even though he made no pretrial request for discovery, which would have revealed the search and seizure; and that he had not expected to go to trial because he had been told that the victim did not wish to proceed. The Supreme Court noted that the prosecutor was not required absent a motion to disclose the evidence, but reversed the conviction based on ineffective assistance of counsel.

To prevent the issues that occurred in the *Kimmelman* case, as a general rule, defense counsel will submit a request for discovery at the start of the case. See the sample motion for discovery in this chapter. Some jurisdictions are moving toward requiring the prosecutor to disclose all evidence without a specific demand by the defense. The excerpt below of the California Penal Code on discovery is typical of most state evidence codes.

Evidence in Action
California Penal Code Sections on Discovery

§ 1054. Discovery.

This chapter shall be interpreted to give effect to all of the following purposes:

(a) To promote the ascertainment of truth in trials by requiring timely pretrial discovery.

(b) To save court time by requiring that discovery be conducted informally between and among the parties before judicial enforcement is requested.

(c) To save court time in trial and avoid the necessity for frequent interruptions and postponements.

(d) To protect victims and witnesses from danger, harassment, and undue delay of the proceedings.

(e) To provide that no discovery shall occur in criminal cases except as provided by this chapter, other express statutory provisions, or as mandated by the Constitution of the United States The disclosures required under this chapter shall be made at least 30 days prior to the trial, unless good cause is shown why a disclosure should be denied, restricted, or deferred. If the material and information becomes known to, or comes into the possession of, a party within 30 days of trial, disclosure shall be made immediately, unless good cause is shown why a disclosure should be denied, restricted, or deferred. "Good cause" is limited to threats or possible danger to the safety of a victim or witness, possible loss or destruction of evidence, or possible compromise of other investigations by law enforcement.

§ 1054.1. Information to be disclosed by prosecution.

The prosecuting attorney shall disclose to the defendant or his or her attorney all of the following materials and information, if it is in the possession of the prosecuting attorney or if the prosecuting attorney knows it to be in the possession of the investigating agencies:

(a) The names and addresses of persons the prosecutor intends to call as witnesses at trial.

(b) Statements of all defendants.

(c) All relevant real evidence seized or obtained as a part of the investigation of the offenses charged.

(d) The existence of a felony conviction of any material witness whose credibility is likely to be critical to the outcome of the trial.

(e) Any exculpatory evidence.

(f) Relevant written or recorded statements of witnesses or reports of the statements of witnesses whom the prosecutor intends to call at the trial, including any reports or statements of experts made in conjunction with the case, including the results of physical or mental examinations, scientific tests, experiments, or comparisons which the prosecutor intends to offer in evidence at the trial.

§ 1054.7.

Upon the request of any party, the court may permit a showing of good cause for the denial or regulation of disclosures, or any portion of that showing, to be made in camera. A verbatim record shall be made of any such proceeding. If the court enters an order granting relief following a showing in camera, the entire record of the showing shall be sealed and preserved in the records of the court, and shall be made available to an appellate court in the event of an appeal or writ. In its discretion, the trial court may after trial and conviction, unseal any previously sealed matter.

Work Product

Federal Rule of Criminal Procedure 16, which governs discovery in criminal cases, requires the Government to permit discovery of documents that are material to the preparation of the defense or intended for use by the government as evidence in chief. The rule does apply to the documents that are considered as "work product." Rule 16(a)(2) exempts from discovery the work product of Government attorneys and agents made in connection with the case's investigation.[13] The work product of all parties are exempt from discovery.

Generally "work product" includes the writings, notes, memoranda, which an attorney or her investigators (including the police) have developed while representing a client, particularly in preparation for trial. A "work product" may not be demanded or subpoenaed by the opposing party, as are documents, letters by and from third parties and other evidence, since the work product reflects the confidential strategy, tactics and theories to be employed by the attorney. Note: In criminal cases, the prosecutor is the attorney representing the client (state or federal government).

Alibi Evidence

The alibi defense is designed to prove that the accused, during the whole time that the crime was being committed, was so far from the place where the crime occurred that he could not have participated in it, or that he was so far away that he could not, with ordinary exertion, have reached the place in time to have done so.[14]

Most state courts and the federal courts require that before alibi evidence may be admitted the defense must file a motion of its intent to ender alibi evidence. According to a 1920 law review article, the alibi defenses were singled out perhaps because they are the quintessential "hip pocket" defense, easily manufactured for introduction in the final hours of trial. During the 1920s, the alibi defense in criminal trials became a target of criticism as "one of the main avenues for escape of the guilty." Alibi defenses were perceived as providing a means for defendants to surprise and outmaneuver prosecutors unprepared for evidence that the accused was elsewhere when the crime occurred. In response to this criticism, most states have promulgated rules requiring defendants to provide notice of an alibi defense sufficiently in advance of trial to permit prosecutors to investigate the alibi. An alibi notice rule was added to the Federal Rules of Criminal Procedure in 1975.[15]

Prior to the *Williams v. Florida* case, there were serious doubts about the constitutionality of requiring notice-of-alibi evidence. The *Williams* case upheld the requirement in Florida cases.[16] Associate Supreme Court Justice White stated in *Williams*:

> Florida law provides for liberal discovery by the defendant against the State, and the notice-of-alibi rule is itself carefully hedged with reciprocal duties requiring state disclosure to the defendant. Given the ease with which an alibi can be fabricated, the State's interest in protecting itself against an eleventh-hour defense is both obvious and legitimate. Reflecting this interest, notice-of-alibi provisions, dating at least from 1927, are now in existence in a substantial

number of States. The adversary system of trial is hardly an end in itself; it is not yet a poker game in which players enjoy an absolute right always to conceal their cards until played. We find ample room in that system, at least as far as due process is concerned, for the instant Florida rule, which is designed to enhance the search for truth in the criminal trial by insuring both the defendant and the State ample opportunity to investigate certain facts crucial to the determination of guilt or innocence.

While the *Williams* case upheld the constitutionality of the Florida notice-of-alibi statute, it left unresolved two important questions:

- The court said that it was not holding that a notice-of-alibi requirement was valid under conditions where a defendant does not enjoy "reciprocal discovery against the State."
- The court said that it did not consider the question of the "validity of the threatened sanction, had petitioner chosen not to comply with the notice-of-alibi rule."

FRE 12.1(e) provides that the trial judge may exclude the testimony of any witness whose name has not been disclosed pursuant to the requirements of the rule. The defendant may, however, testify himself. Prohibiting a witness from testifying whose name was not disclosed is a common provision in most state statutes. This sanction is probably essential if the notice-of-alibi rule is to have any practical significance. The use of the term "may" makes it clear that the judge may allow the alibi witness to testify if, under the particular circumstances, there is cause shown for the failure to conform to the requirements of the rules. This is further emphasized by subdivision (f) which provides for exceptions whenever "good cause" is shown for the exception.

One interesting question is whether or not, in a state where defense is required to give a notice of alibi evidence, the prosecution is also required to disclose its alibi rebuttal witnesses. While one state supreme court held that prosecution is not, this is an undecided issue.[17] Because the defense complied with the requirement, the court did not have to consider the propriety of penalizing noncompliance.

Failure to Enter Alibi Evidence after Giving Notice

In *People v. Brown*,[18] the defense counsel submitted a notice of intention to enter alibi evidence. Later at trial, defendant, testifying on his own behalf, acknowledged that he was present at the scene of the crime, but maintained that he was there for completely innocent purposes and was not involved in any drug transaction. The trial court then permitted the prosecutor to cross-examine defendant about the notice of alibi evidence which indicated that defendant was elsewhere when the drug sale took place.

The appellate court concluded that the prosecution should not be permitted to impeach a defendant who has elected not to present an alibi defense at trial with statements contained in a notice of alibi withdrawn before trial. A contrary rule would have the tendency to inhibit a defendant from abandoning a factually inaccurate defense posture and the choice of an accused to testify on his or her own behalf.

Practicum

Practicum One

Maryland's DNA Collection Act provides that all arrestees charged with serious crimes must furnish a DNA sample on a buccal swab applied to the inside of the cheeks. Alonzo King was arrested in 2009 on first- and second-degree assault charges. He was processed through a Wicomico County, Maryland, facility, where booking personnel used a cheek swab to take a DNA sample pursuant to the Maryland DNA Collection Act (Act). The swab was matched to an unsolved 2003 rape, and King was charged with that crime. He moved to suppress the DNA match on the grounds that Maryland's DNA collection law violated the Fourth Amendment. The Court of Appeals of Maryland, on review of King's rape conviction, ruled that the DNA taken when King was booked for the 2009 charge was an unlawful seizure because obtaining and using the cheek swab was an unreasonable search of the person. It set the rape conviction aside. The State appealed the decision to the U.S. Supreme Court.

As a Supreme Court Justice, how would you rule?

See: *Maryland v. King*, 133 S.Ct. 1958 (2013).

Practicum Two

On August 1, 2009, United States Border Patrol agents stopped a truck belonging to Chad Camou at a primary inspection checkpoint on Highway 86 in Westmorland, California. Camou was driving the truck, while his girlfriend, Ashley Lundy, sat in the passenger seat. Agents at the checkpoint grew suspicious when Lundy did not make eye contact, so they asked Camou if they could open the door to the truck. Once they opened the door, the agents saw Alejandro Martinez-Ramirez (Martinez-Ramirez), an undocumented immigrant, lying on the floor behind the truck's front seats. Consequently, at about 10:40 p.m., agents arrested and handcuffed Camou, Lundy, and Martinez-Ramirez. At the same time, agents also seized Camou's truck and a cell phone found in the cab of the truck. Agents then moved Camou, Lundy, and Martinez-Ramirez into the checkpoint's security offices for booking.

At 12:00 a.m., one hour and twenty minutes after Camou's arrest, an immigration officer searched Camou's cell phone. In his subsequent report, the officer claimed he was looking for evidence of "known smuggling organizations and information related to the case." The officer did not assert that the search was necessary to prevent the destruction of evidence or to ensure his or anyone else's safety.

At trial, Camou's attorney submitted a motion to suppress the evidence discovered as the results of the search of the cell phone.

As trial judge, how would you rule?

See: *United States v. Camou*, 2014 WL 6980135 (C.A. 9, 2014).

Summary

- Present-day evidence codes encourage that evidence issues be settled prior to trial.
- The term "motion to suppress" typically encompasses motions in criminal cases where the proposed basis for exclusion arises from the United States Constitution, a state constitution, or a specific statute permitting the exclusion of certain types of evidence.
- In addition, evidence may be excluded by the trial judge if the evidence is unduly prejudicial to the defendant and does not contribute materially to the case.
- Generally objections to illegally seized evidence or inadmissible confessions are handled by motions to suppress prior to the presentation of witnesses and evidence at trial.
- If a party fails to submit a pretrial motion to exclude the evidence, the party may have forfeited his or her right to object later.
- The trial judge, however, may make a determination as to whether there was good cause for the failure to submit a pretrial motion and allow the party to object to the admission of the document or object.
- The party applying for a court order must generally do so by motion. A motion— except when made during a trial or hearing—must be in writing, unless the court permits the party to make the motion by other means.
- A motion must state the grounds on which it is based and the relief or order sought. A motion is generally supported by points of authority and affidavits explaining the need for the relief requested.
- The U.S. Supreme Court held, in *Waller v. Georgia*, that defendant's Sixth Amendment's right to a public trial included the right of the public to attend a hearing on the motion to suppress the evidence.
- Generally in sex offense cases, evidence of the victim's sexual behavior or predisposition is not admissible under "rape shield" laws. If the defense intends to offer such evidence, the defense must file a motion that specifically describes the evidence and states the purpose for which the evidence is to be offered.
- There are three general types of Motions in Limine: Inclusionary—A motion asking the court to have something included in the trial. Exclusionary—A motion asking the court to have something excluded in the trial. Preclusionary—A motion asking the court to have something precluded in the trial.
- The two leading cases on the rights of a defendant to discovery of the prosecutor's evidence are *Brady v. Maryland* and *United States v. Agurs*.
- The reversal of a conviction on the basis of a *Brady* violation (failure of the government to disclose information) is required upon a showing that the favorable evidence could reasonably be taken to put the whole case in such a different light as to undermine confidence in the verdict.
- Most state courts and the federal courts require that before alibi evidence may be admitted the defense must file a motion of its intent to enter alibi evidence.

Questions in Review

1. What are the modern rules regarding discovery?
2. Why is the defense required to give notice of alibi defense?
3. If the prosecution fails to disclose a witness, what sanctions may the trial judge impose?
4. Why are there restrictions on the cross-examination of sex offense victims?
5. Why do the trial courts encourage that evidentiary issues be settled prior to trial?

Key Terms

Brady **Violation:** A *Brady* violation is the failure of the government to disclose information upon a showing that the favorable evidence could reasonably be taken to put the whole case in such a different light as to undermine confidence in the verdict.

Motion in Limine: A "motion in limine" is a motion that requests a decision from the trial court as to whether or not certain evidence may or may not be presented to the jury at the trial.

Public Trial: A public trial is a trial that includes the right of the public to attend all hearings in the trial.

Work Product: Generally "work product" includes the writings, notes, memoranda, which an attorney or her investigators (including the police) have developed while representing a client, particularly in preparation for trial.

Endnotes

1. Heien v. North Carolina, 135 S.Ct. 530 (2014).
2. Waller v. Georgia, 467 U.S. 39 (1984).
3. United States v. Sanders, 708 F.3rd 976 (2013).
4. Brady v. Maryland, 373 U.S. 83 (1963).
5. United States v. Agurs, 427 U.S. 97 (1976).
6. Youngblood v. West Virginia, 547 U.S. 867 (2006).
7. Supra note 6.
8. Strickler v. Greene, 527 U.S. 263 (1999).
9. Strickler v. Greene, 527 U.S. 263 (1999).
10. U.S. v. Armstrong, 517 U.S. 456 (1996).
11. Federal Rules of Criminal Procedure, Rule 26.2(a).
12. Kimmelman v. Morrison, 477 U.S. 365 (1986).
13. U.S. v. Armstrong, 517 U.S. 456 (1996).
14. People v. Terrell, 138 Cal.App. 2nd 35 (1956).
15. Robert W. Millar, (1920) "The Modernization of Criminal Procedure", Journal of Criminal Law & Criminology Vol. 11, pp. 344–350.
16. Williams v. Florida, 399 U.S. 78, (1970).
17. People v. Holiday, 47 Ill.2d 300, 265 N.E.2d 634 (1970).
18. People v. Brown, 98 N.Y. 2nd 226 (2002).

Chapter 9

Admissibility of Evidence

Chapter Objectives

What you should know and understand after studying this chapter:

- The role of presumptions and the burden of proof
- The types of presumptions
- Importance of judicial notice
- How rebuttal presumptions conflict with constitutional issues
- The special issues involved in the admissibility of evidence

Chapter Outline

Introduction
Presumptions
Judicial Notice
Admissibility of Evidence
Practicum
Summary
Questions in Review
Key Terms
Endnotes

Introduction

While several issues or items were briefly discussed in other chapters, in this chapter we will discuss presumptions, judicial notice and admissibility issues. Both presumptions and judicial notice are designed to streamline the judicial system. Under admissibility issues, we will discuss dying declarations, former testimony, oaths or affirmations, and stipulations. For the most part in this chapter we will use the federal rules to illustrate the issues involved. Most jurisdictions follow rules that are very similar to the federal rules, although there are some minor exceptions.

Presumptions

There are two types of presumptions: conclusive and rebuttal. A conclusive presumption is a presumption of law that cannot be rebutted by evidence and must be taken as true. For example, at common law it was conclusively presumed that a child under the age of seven years was not capable of committing a criminal offense. Rebuttable presumptions are discussed later in this section.

In criminal cases, for the most part, the burden of proof is on the government to prove the guilt of the defendant beyond a reasonable doubt. The presumption of innocence is an important tenet in our criminal procedure. The presumption of innocence is a rebuttal presumption. Another important but not as well-known presumption is the rebuttal presumption that applies on appeals. That presumption is that the trial court was correct in its rulings that are in issue on appeal. The presumption of innocence basically means that

- Regarding the critical facts of a case, the defendant has no burden of proof.
- The state must prove the essential elements of the charged crime beyond a reasonable doubt.
- The jury may not draw any inferences adverse to the defendant merely on the fact that he or she has been charged with a crime and is present in court.

The presumption in appellate cases is that the trial judge was correct in his or her rulings and that the party appealing the case has the burden of establishing error on the part of the trial judge.

A presumption may relieve the party with the burden of proof from having to prove a certain fact. For example, in a criminal case where the prosecution has the burden of proof in the majority of issues, a presumption may relieve the prosecutor from having to enter evidence on that issue. For example, it is presumed that the defendant was sane at the time of the criminal act. If no evidence is entered regarding that issue, then there is no duty on the prosecutor to prove the sanity of the defendant. If, however, the defense enters evidence of the lack of sanity of defendant sufficient to rebut the presumption of sanity, then the prosecutor has a duty to present evidence of sanity in order to convict the defendant.

Consider the following fact situation: Watertown, New York, police officer Maney testified that on October 19 at about 7:23 p.m. he parked his patrol vehicle about 25 feet off the road to observe traffic traveling along Coffeen Street. He stated that it was dark and he did not have his lights on. He observed a red vehicle traveling west pass before him. He could clearly see a cell phone held to the driver's right ear. And he could see the back light from the phone lighting the cheek of the driver. He stopped the driver, Anthony Campanaro, and issued the driver a ticket for violation of the statute which provided that no person shall operate a motor vehicle upon a public highway while using a mobile telephone to engage in a call while such vehicle is in motion. The trial court noted that the statute in question provided that there was a rebuttal presumption that when a driver has a cell phone in close proximity to his or her ear while driving that he or she was using the phone to make a call.[1]

The defendant admitted that he was handling the cell phone but claimed that he did not make a call, that he was simply viewing the phone to see if he had an incoming call. The appellate court noted that a presumption may be an inference drawn from known facts or created by legislative fiat. A presumption has the effect of evidence and, in the criminal law, is permissive and generally rebuttable. It is a time-honored mechanism to meet a practical prosecutorial need but does not relieve the People's burden of proving guilt beyond a reasonable doubt. In order to be constitutionally valid there must be a rational connection between the facts that are proved and the fact that is to be inferred.

The court concluded that the People had shown that the defendant was "engaged in a call" created by the rebuttable presumption and that the defendant had failed to rebut the same with credible evidence. The Court found the defendant guilty of violating the statute and fined him $100 and assessed a $45 surcharge and a $5 victim fee. A question that was not addressed in the court decision was the fact that a check with the telephone provider could ascertain whether or not a call was being made at the time of the incident.

Creation of Presumptions

Some presumptions exist at common law by custom or court decision. Others are created by statutes. For example one of the oldest presumptions of law is that a marriage, once being established, is presumed to be valid.

An example of a statutory presumption is contained in 18 U.S. Code, § 1469 (a), which provides that in any prosecution under this chapter in which an element of the offense is that the property in question was transported, shipped, or carried in interstate commerce, proof, by either circumstantial or direct evidence, that such property was produced or manufactured in one State and is subsequently located in another State shall raise a rebuttable presumption that such property was transported, shipped, or carried in interstate commerce.

Rebuttal Presumptions

The Campanaro case, discussed earlier in this chapter, involved a rebuttal statutory presumption of when a driver was using a cell phone. A rebuttable presumption is an assumption of fact that is accepted by a court until it is disproved. It is an assumption that is made by the courts and it will stand as a fact unless someone comes forward to contest it and prove otherwise. Rebuttable presumptions in criminal law may in certain cases be controversial because they may effectively reverse the presumption of innocence in some cases as was the case in the Campanaro case.

Note: In the Campanaro case, the defendant testified that he was not using the cell phone. The officer testified that Campanaro had the phone near his ear and that the phone was on. Campanaro did not dispute the officer's testimony. An undiscussed issue in the case was since the statute created a rebuttal presumption that the driver was using the cell phone when it was near his ear, did the sworn testimony of the driver that he was not using the cell phone overcome the presumption? There was no evidence to rebut the driver's statement that he was not using the phone. Apparently the trial judge, in a trial by judge alone, disregarded the testimony of the driver. Accordingly, the fact finder in this case, the trial judge, found the defendant's testimony unbelievable.

Generally when we discuss rebuttal presumptions we are discussing presumptions that remove the government's burden of proof in a criminal case. Sometimes, the burden of proof shifts to the defendant. For example, the burden of establishing an insanity defense or other affirmative in many jurisdictions shifts to the defendant.

Consider, for example, where a defendant contends that a criminal statute does not apply to her, the burden of establishing that it does not apply to her is with her. In such a case, a presumption may assist in meeting her burden of proof. Regarding this issue, consider the situation that occurred in the *Bond v. United States* case.

The U.S. Supreme Court held in *Bond v. United States* that certain presumptions exist in criminal law.[2] In *Bond*, the Court noted that there is the presumption that a criminal statute derived from the common law carries with it the requirement of a culpable mental state — even if no such limitation appears in the text. And there is also the presumption that federal statutes do not apply outside the United States. Both of those are, indeed, established interpretive presumptions that are (1) based upon realistic assessments of congressional intent, and (2) well known to Congress — thus furthering rather than subverting genuine legislative intent. To apply these presumptions, then, is not to rewrite clear text; it is to interpret words fairly, in light of their statutory context.

Carol Bond was convicted in a federal district court of possessing and using a chemical weapon. She appealed. The question on appeal was whether the statute forbidding the use or possession of a chemical weapon applied to an amateur attempt by a jilted wife to injure her husband's lover. The victim suffered only minor injuries to her thumb. The statute was enacted in accordance with the Convention on the Prohibition of the Development, Production, Stockpiling, and Use of Chemical Weapons of 1998. Bond sought revenge against her husband's lover by spreading chemicals on the lover's car, mailbox, and door knob in hopes that the lover would develop an uncomfortable rash.

The Court held that there was a presumption that the statute was not meant to apply to minor local crimes that could easily be handled by the Commonwealth of Pennsylvania. The Court held that the ambiguity in the statute derives from the improbably broad reach of the key statutory definition, given the term — "chemical weapon" — that is being defined, the deeply serious consequences of adopting such a boundless reading, and the lack of any apparent need to do so in light of the context from which the statute arose — a treaty about chemical warfare and terrorism, not about local assaults. Thus, the Court can reasonably insist on a clear indication that Congress did not intend to reach purely local crimes before interpreting the statute's expansive language in a way that intrudes on the States' police power.

A dissenting justice noted that there is nothing either (1) realistic or (2) well known about the presumption the Court shoves down the throat of a resisting statute. The dissenter stated:

> Who in the world would have thought that a definition is inoperative if it contradicts ordinary meaning? When this statute was enacted, there was not yet a "Bond presumption" to that effect — though presumably Congress will have to take account of the Bond presumption in the future, perhaps by adding at the end of all its definitions that depart from ordinary connotation "and we really mean it."

Presumption to Establish Intent

As noted in *United States v. Wilkinson*, the law provides a rebuttable presumption that every person intends the natural and probable consequences of his or her own acts.[3] Wrongful acts knowingly or intentionally committed can neither be justified nor excused on the ground of innocent intent. The color of the act determines the complexion of the intent. The intent to injure or defraud can be presumed when the unlawful act which results in loss or injury is proved to have been knowingly committed. It is a well-settled rule that the intent can be presumed and inferred from the result of the action. If a person knows that the act he or she is about to commit will naturally or necessarily have the effect of injuring or defrauding another, and he or she voluntarily and intentionally does that act, he or she may be chargeable in law with the intent to injure or defraud.

Burden of Persuasion

As noted earlier in the question of guilty or not guilty of the defendant, the prosecution has the burden of establishing the guilt of the defendant to each and every element of the crime beyond a reasonable doubt. In most civil cases, the party that has the burden of proof generally must only establish by a preponderance of evidence. Thus, the standard of proof in most civil cases is that the party with the burden must convince the jury or judge alone if no jury that the odds are better than 50-50 that its version of the facts is true.

In criminal cases there are certain instances where the burden of proof to establish certain facts rest on the defense. In affirmative defenses like self-defense and insanity, the burden to produce facts are on the defense. An affirmative defense is a defense where the accused admits the act but provides justifiable grounds that the accused is not guilty.

If the defense raises the issue of insanity, since there is a presumption that a person is sane, the defense must rebut this presumption. The defendant, however, does not have the burden of proof to establish beyond a reasonable doubt that he or she is insane. In most jurisdictions the defense only needs to rebut the presumption of sanity by a preponderance of evidence. Once the defense has rebutted the presumption, then the burden shifts to the prosecution and the prosecutor must establish beyond a reasonable doubt that the defendant is not insane. Not all states allow the defense of insanity. Kansas, for example, has abolished the insanity plea and that issue is considered during the punishment phase of a criminal trial.

Permissive Inferences

A court may instruct the jury that it may infer a presumed fact from proof of other facts. For example a person found in possession of stolen property may be presumed to have stolen the property. A jury or judge in a trial by judge alone may accept or reject this inference. To constitute a constitutional permissive inference the connection between the basic fact and the presumed fact must be rational and more likely than not to flow from the basic fact.

Conclusive Presumptions

Most presumptions that are involved in criminal cases are rebuttal presumptions. As noted by the U.S. Supreme Court in *Sandstrom v. Montana*, conclusive presumptions conflict with the overriding presumption of innocence with which the law endows the accused and which extends to every element of the crime.[4]

David Sandstrom was convicted in a Montana state criminal court of deliberate homicide. The U.S. Supreme Court reversed his conviction and remanded the case for the possibility of a new trial. The Court noted that the question presented on appeal was whether, in a case in which intent is an element of the crime charged, the jury instruction, "the law presumes that a person intends the ordinary consequences of his voluntary acts," violates the Fourteenth Amendment's requirement that the State prove every element of a criminal offense beyond a reasonable doubt.

The Supreme Court noted that the jury were not told that the presumption could be rebutted by the defendant's simple presentation of "some" evidence; nor even that it could be rebutted at all. Given the common definition of "presume" as "to supposed to be true without proof," and given the lack of qualifying instructions as to the legal effect of the presumption, the Court held that it could not discount the possibility that the jury may have interpreted the instruction in more stringent ways.

The Court stated that first, a reasonable jury could well have interpreted the presumption as "conclusive," that is, not technically as a presumption at all, but rather as an irrebuttable direction by the court to find intent once convinced of the facts triggering the presumption. Alternatively, the jury may have interpreted the instruction as a direction to find intent upon proof of the defendant's voluntary actions (and their "ordinary" consequences), unless the defendant proved the contrary by some quantum of proof which may well have been considerably greater than "some" evidence—thus effectively shifting the burden of persuasion on the element of intent. Numerous federal and state courts have warned that instructions of the type given here can be interpreted in just these ways.

The Court also stated that it did not reject the possibility that some jurors may have interpreted the challenged instruction as permissive, or, if mandatory, as requiring only that the defendant come forward with "some" evidence in rebuttal. However, the fact that a reasonable juror could have given the presumption conclusive or persuasion-shifting effect means that the Court cannot discount the possibility that Sandstrom's jurors actually did proceed upon one of these interpretations. And that means that unless these kinds of presumptions are constitutional, the instruction cannot be adjudged valid.

Permissible or Conclusive

Sometimes it is not clear whether a presumption is conclusive or permissive. New York State had a statutory presumption that presence of a firearm in an automobile was evidence of its illegal possession by all occupants. In the case of *County Court of Ulster County, New York v. Allen*, the U.S. Supreme Court looked at whether the New York State presumption was conclusive or permissive.

In the *Allen* case, the Court noted that a permissive presumption allows but does not require the trier of fact to infer elemental fact from proof by prosecutor of basic fact and which places no burden of any kind on defendant. It leaves the trier of fact free to credit or reject inference and does not shift burden of proof. A permissive presumption affects the application of "beyond a reasonable doubt" standard only if, under the facts of the case, there is no rational way the trier could make a connection permitted by inference, since it is only in that situation that there is any risk that the explanation of permissible inference to a jury or its use by a jury has caused the fact finder to make an erroneous factual determination.[5] In deciding what type of inference or presumption is involved in a case, jury instructions will generally be controlling, although their interpretation may require recourse to the statute involved and the cases decided under it.

The Court in *Allen* also noted that in case of a mandatory presumption, which a jury must accept even if it is sole evidence of an element of an offense, the prosecution, since it bears the burden of establishing guilt, may not rest its case on a presumption unless the fact proved is sufficient to support inference of guilt beyond a reasonable doubt, but in case of permissive presumption, the prosecution may rely on all the evidence in the record to meet the reasonable doubt standard and thus, as long as it is clear that the presumption is not the sole and sufficient basis for finding of guilt, presumption need only satisfy a "more likely than not" standard to be constitutionally valid.

In the *Allen* case, four persons, three adult males (defendants) and a 16-year-old girl (who was processed in juvenile court and was not involved in the primary case), were arrested on charges that they possessed two loaded handguns, a loaded machinegun, and over a pound of heroin found in a Chevrolet in which they were riding when it was stopped for speeding on the New York Thruway shortly after noon on March 28, 1973. The two large-caliber handguns, which together with their ammunition weighed approximately six pounds, were seen through the window of the car by the investigating police officer. They were positioned crosswise in an open handbag on either the front floor or the front seat of the car on the passenger side where the young girl was sitting. The girl admitted that the handbag was hers. The machine gun and the heroin were discovered in the trunk after the police pried it open. The car had been borrowed from the driver's brother earlier that day; the key to the trunk could not be found in the car or on the person of any of its occupants, although there was testimony that two of the occupants had placed something in the trunk before embarking in the borrowed car. The jury convicted the three defendants on the possession of the handguns and acquitted them of possession of the contents of the trunk.

At the close of the trial, the judge instructed the jurors that they were entitled to infer possession from the defendants' presence in the car. He did not make any reference to the "upon the person" exception in his explanation of the statutory presumption, nor did any of the defendants object to this omission or request alternative or additional instructions on the subject.

Defendants appealed in which they challenged the constitutionality of the New York statute as applied in this case. The challenge was made in support of their argument that the evidence, apart from the presumption, was insufficient to sustain the convictions.

The Supreme Court concluded that inferences and presumptions are a staple of our adversary system of factfinding. And it is often necessary for the trier of fact to determine the existence of an element of the crime—that is, an "ultimate" or "elemental" fact—from the existence of one or more "evidentiary" or "basic" facts. The value of these evidentiary devices, and their validity under the Due Process Clause, vary from case to case, however, depending on the strength of the connection between the particular basic and elemental facts involved and on the degree to which the device curtails the factfinder's freedom to assess the evidence independently. Nonetheless, in criminal cases, the ultimate test of any device's constitutional validity in a given case remains constant: the device must not undermine the factfinder's responsibility at trial, based on evidence adduced by the State, to find the ultimate facts beyond a reasonable doubt.

The Court in *Allen* held that as applied to the facts of this case, the presumption of possession is entirely rational. Defendants were not "hitchhikers or other casual passengers," and the guns were neither "a few inches in length" nor "out of defendants' sight." The argument against possession by any of the defendants was predicated solely on the fact that the guns were in the girl's pocketbook. But several circumstances—which, not surprisingly, her counsel repeatedly emphasized in his questions and his argument—made it highly improbable that she was the sole custodian of those weapons.

Even if it was reasonable to conclude that she had placed the guns in her purse before the car was stopped by police, the facts strongly suggest that the young girl was not the only person able to exercise dominion over them. The two guns were too large to be concealed in her handbag. The bag was consequently open, and part of one of the guns was in plain view, within easy access of the driver of the car and even, perhaps, of the other two respondents who were riding in the rear seat.

The Court held that the presumption was permissive and was constitutional. And that the trial judge's instructions make it clear that the presumption was merely a part of the prosecution's case, that it gave rise to a permissive inference available only in certain circumstances, rather than a mandatory conclusion of possession, and that it could be ignored by the jury even if there was no affirmative proof offered by defendants in rebuttal. The trial judge explained that possession could be actual or constructive, but that constructive possession could not exist without the intent and ability to exercise control or dominion over the weapons.

Judicial Notice

Judicial notice has been described as an evidentiary shortcut. Judicial notice allows courts to accept certain facts or propositions of law as true even when no evidence is admitted to establish their proof. Judicial notice is designed to save time and expenses in a trial. It also avoids disrespect for the court that may occur if the court were required to make finding of fact on those issues. For example a trial court may take judicial notice of the fact that the City of New York is located in the State of New York without requiring evidence on this fact and then making a finding that the city is located in New York State.

As a general rule, courts may take judicial notice of:

- legislative facts,
- adjudicative facts, and
- law.

Federal Rule of Evidence 201 reflects the general rule regarding judicial notice in almost all U.S. and state court jurisdictions. The rule states that a court may take judicial notice of a fact that is not subject to reasonable dispute because it is generally known within the trial court's general jurisdiction or it can be accurately and readily determined from sources whose accuracy cannot be reasonably questioned.

Rule 201 provides that a court may take judicial notice on its own and must take judicial notice if a party requests it and the court is supplied with the necessary information. A court may take judicial notice at any stage of the proceeding. If there is a question regarding whether or not the court should take judicial notice of a certain fact, any party to the proceedings is entitled to be heard on the issue. If the court takes judicial notice and a party to the proceedings objects, the party is permitted to be heard on the issue, and if appropriate the court may reverse its notice of taking judicial notice.

Once a trial court has accepted a fact by judicial notice in a civil suit, the trial judge must instruct the jury that it must accept the fact as conclusive. In a criminal case, however, the trial judge must instruct the jury that it may or may not accept the noticed fact as conclusive.

Legislative facts that a court may take judicial notice of are those facts that a court would consider in making decisions involving the interpretations of common law, statutes, codes, and constitutions. An example of this issue is set forth in the *United States v. Gould* case. In the *Gould* case the court stated: "Legislative facts are established truths, facts or pronouncements that do not change from case to case but apply universally, while adjudicative facts are those developed in a particular case."[6]

Joseph Gould was convicted of conspiring to import and importing cocaine into the United States. On appeal, the defense objected to the fact that the trial judge had taken judicial notice of the fact that cocaine hydrochloride is derived from coca leaves. The U.S. Court of Appeals for the Eighth Circuit held that while the federal rule provides in part that, "in a criminal case, the court shall instruct the jury that it may, but is not required to, accept as conclusive any fact judicially noticed," the rule extends only to adjudicative, not legislative, facts. Accordingly, the district court properly instructed the jurors that they had to accept as conclusive the court's judicial notice that cocaine hydrochloride is a schedule II controlled substance, since that was a legislative rather than an adjudicative fact under the Comprehensive Drug Abuse Prevention and Control Act of 1970, § 1001 et seq. Whether cocaine hydrochloride is or is not a derivative of the coca leaf is a question of scientific fact applicable to the administration of the Comprehensive Drug Abuse Prevention and Control Act of 1970.

Note that judicial notice, unlike a presumption, is not subject to the requirement that the jury must be instructed that they can accept or not accept the fact. As noted in the *Gould* case:

> The fact that cocaine hydrochloride is derived from coca leaves is scientifically and pharmacologically unimpeachable. It would be incongruous to instruct the jurors on this irrefutable fact and then inform them that they may disregard it at their whim. It would be similarly illogical if we were to conclude that trial judges could rely upon generally accepted, undisputed facts in interpreting the applicable statutory law, yet obligate them to instruct the jury that it could disregard the factual underpinnings of the interpretation in its discretion.

In the case of *People v. Glover*, the trial court took judicial notice of the fact that Facebook Inc. has international popularity and widespread influence and that it was, by some measurements, the most popular social network. The court also took notice of the fact that Facebook was one of the fastest-growing and best-known sites on the Internet.[7] In that case, Roger Glover was convicted of first degree murder in a Colorado state court. During the trial, the prosecution presented conversations recorded on Glover's Facebook account. In one of the posts from his account, he threatened to "beat the s— outta" the victim and told him "its over for u."

A court may notice only those adjudicative facts not subject to reasonable dispute. Fed.R.Evid. 201(b). When a court takes judicial notice of another court's opinion, it may do so not for the truth of the facts recited therein, but for the existence of the opinion, which is not subject to reasonable dispute over its authenticity.[8]

Admissibility of Evidence

Dying Declarations

For the most part, out-of-court statements that qualify as testimonial are not admissible, under the Confrontation Clause of the Sixth Amendment, unless the witness is unavailable and the defendant had prior opportunity to cross examine the witness, including, at a minimum, prior testimony at a preliminary hearing, before a grand jury, or at a former trial, and statements elicited during police interrogations.[9] Federal Rule of Evidence 804 makes an exception to this restriction. Rule 804 states, in part, that in a prosecution for homicide a statement that the declarant, while believing death to be imminent, made about its cause or circumstances is admissible.

To be admissible in a murder case, the dying declaration must be made when the victim is under immediate apprehension of death. In addition, in criminal cases the dying declaration is limited to cases where the defendant is charged with murder of the declarant. The restrictions on the admissibility of the declaration are based on the fact that the declaration violates the accused's right of confrontation guaranteed by the Sixth Amendment. The rule is more liberal in civil cases.

The Supreme Court has, as of this date, refrained from ruling on the status of dying declarations under the Confrontation Clause. In *Crawford v. Washington* and again in *Giles v. California*, the Supreme Court hinted that dying declarations may fall within an exception to the constitutional bar against testimonial hearsay. The *Giles* case is discussed later in this chapter.

In the case of *Walker v. Harry*, Juan Walker appealed his conviction of first degree murder and possession of a firearm during the commission on a felony. A jury convicted Walker in a Michigan state court of the murder of Tommie Lee Baines who died in a hospital several days after the shooting. Baines's mother visited him in the hospital the day before he died. The mother testified in Walker's trial that she asked Baines whether Walker was the shooter and that Baines nodded his head in the affirmative. Defense objected to the admissibility of this testimony. The trial court ruled that the nod fell within the "dying declaration" exception to the hearsay rule. The admission of the nod was affirmed on appeal.

Consider this fact situation: Dwayne Giles was convicted of murder in a California Superior Court for killing his girlfriend.[10] The evidence indicated that Giles shot his girlfriend outside her grandmother's home. The grandmother testified that she heard Giles and the victim speaking in loud conversational tones. The victim was shot six times. Giles claimed he killed her in self-defense. Prosecutors introduced statements that the victim had made to a police officer responding to a domestic-violence report about three weeks before the shooting. The victim, who was crying when she spoke, told the officer that Giles had accused her of having an affair, and that after the two began to argue, Giles grabbed her by the shirt, lifted her off the floor, and began to choke her.

Giles appealed his conviction claiming his right to confrontation set forth in the Sixth Amendment of the U.S. Constitution by the admission into evidence statements made by the victim about three weeks before she was killed by Giles.

The Supreme Court noted that two forms of testimonial statements were admitted at common law even though they were unconfronted: (1) declarations made by speaker who was both on brink of death and aware that he was dying, and (2) statements of witness who was detained or kept away by means or procurement of defendant. The latter doctrine of admissibility is commonly known as "forfeiture by wrongdoing." The Court noted that loss of the right of confrontation based on forfeiture by wrongdoing as applied at common law required that the unconfronted testimony would not be admitted in a criminal case without a showing that defendant intended to prevent the witness from testifying.

The Supreme Court held in the *Giles* case that it would not adopt California's Supreme Court's theory of "forfeiture by wrongdoing" as an exception to the Sixth Amendment's confrontation requirement; the proposed exception to right of confrontation was not one established at the time of founding of the Bill of Rights and, furthermore, was not established in American jurisprudence since that time. The Court reversed the conviction and held that there was no evidence that the killing of the victim was done with the intent to prevent the victim from testifying in a court case. The case was remanded to the trial court.

Consider the situation where a victim makes a statement to the police that was made not as a testimonial statement but to assist the police in an ongoing emergency. Is that statement admissible if the witness dies before the trial? In the case of *United States v. Joseph*, several defendants were convicted of various racketeering charges.[11] An appellate court held that the district court did not violate the Confrontation Clause by admitting the dying declaration of a deceased person, Taliese. The appellate court noted that the Confrontation Clause applies only to testimonial statements and that the statements that Taliese made to the police after he was shot were not testimonial because, objectively viewed, they were elicited to assist the police in responding to an ongoing emergency. Even if Taliese's statements were testimonial, the district court correctly ruled that they were admissible as dying declarations under Fed.R.Evid. 804(b)(2).

Former Testimony

In light of the history and purpose of the Confrontation Clause, the United States Supreme Court has held that a testimonial statement cannot be admitted against the accused at trial when the declarant does not testify at trial, "unless she is unavailable to testify, and the defendant has had a prior opportunity for cross-examination." The constitutional requirement that a witness be "unavailable" before her prior testimony is admissible stands on separate footing that is independent of, and in addition to, the requirement of a prior opportunity for cross-examination. (*Rawlins v. People*, 2014)[12]

Federal Rule of Evidence 804(b) provides an exception to the hearsay rule for testimony from a declarant who is unavailable at trial. The former testimony must have been given under oath and the witness must currently be unavailable. In addition, the defendant or his or her counsel must have had the opportunity to cross-examine the witness. For example the defendant is tried with a criminal offense and his conviction is over-turned on appeal. If on a re-trial on the same charges one of the witnesses is unavailable, the prosecution may be able to use in the re-trial a transcript of the witness's testimony in the first trial.

Under Rule 804(b), former testimony is admissible if the declarant is unavailable and the party against whom the testimony is offered had an "opportunity and similar motive" to examine the declarant. As noted in *United States v. Paling*, Rule 804(b) is therefore more restrictive than the Confrontation Clause.[13] In the *Crawford v. Washington* case, the Supreme Court held that testimonial hearsay from a now-unavailable declarant may be admitted against a defendant at a criminal trial if the defendant had a prior opportunity to cross-examine him.[14]

In the *Paling* case, Crystal Paling was convicted of wire fraud conspiracy and money laundering. On appeal she contended that the trial court erred in allowing in the criminal case a copy of a witness's testimony given in a previous civil case. The witness died before the criminal trial was held and was therefore unavailable to be called as a witness in the criminal trial.

Prior to admitting the transcript of the civil court testimony, the District Court determined (1) that the witness, having died, was indisputably unavailable to testify at trial, and (2) the defendant's counsel had cross-examined the deceased during the civil trial. The trial court held that the requirements for the admission of former testimony of an unavailable witness had been satisfied in conformance with the *Crawford v. Washington* rule.

The trial court noted that the motives in the civil and criminal trials were not precisely identical but that they were very close. Paling's attorney argued on appeal that she did not have a sufficiently similar motive at the civil trial because at the time no criminal charges were pending.

The trial court noted that in the civil suit Paling was alleged to have committed mortgage fraud. And that the question in both the civil suit and the present criminal trial was whether she knowingly engaged in fraudulent conduct. Her appeal was denied.

In *Crawford*, the Supreme Court noted that because Rule 804(b)(1) requires the party against whom the prior testimony is offered to have had a "similar motive" to develop the declarant's testimony, not merely the opportunity to do so, evidence that is admissible under Rule 804(b)(1) necessarily satisfies a defendant's Confrontation Clause rights.

The Court in *Crawford* noted that the text of Rule 804(b)(1) does not require that a party have an identical motive to develop the testimony, only that the party has a "similar" motive. Whether a party had a similar motive to cross-examine a witness at a prior proceeding is essentially a factual question.

As noted in the case of *United States v. Sklena*, the test is whether the motive of the United States, acting through a civil enforcement agency, is similar enough to its interests when it engages in criminal enforcement. For purposes of the hearsay exception for prior testimony when the party against whom the testimony is offered has had an opportunity and similar motive to develop the testimony by direct, cross, or redirect examination at the time that it was given, depends on a number of factors, including the substantive law that each is enforcing, the factual overlap between the two proceedings, the type of proceeding, the potential associated penalties, and any differences in the number of issues and parties.[15]

Oaths or Affirmations

Witnesses in criminal proceedings are required to take an oath or affirmation as to the truth of their testimony. In the *Adams v. Texas* case, Randall Adams was tried and convicted of capital murder.[16] On appeal he claimed that the trial judge erred in disqualifying a potential jury member because the jury member refused to take an oath to perform his duties as required by state law. Prospective jurors were informed that a sentence of life imprisonment or death was mandatory on conviction of a capital felony. They were also told that a prospective juror shall be disqualified from serving as a juror unless he states under oath that the mandatory penalty of death or imprisonment for life will not affect his deliberations on any issue of fact.

The Court concluded that a state may bar from jury service those whose beliefs about capital punishment would lead them to ignore the law or violate their oaths. But in the present case Texas has applied the oath requirement to exclude jurors whose only fault was to take their responsibilities with special seriousness or to acknowledge honestly that they might or might not be affected. What the case decision appears to hold is that the state may require a prospective juror to take an oath to perform his or her duties in accordance with the trial judge's direction, but the requirement that the fact that this is a death penalty case will not affect his or her deliberations is an unconstitutional requirement. Common sense would seem to think that a juror's deliberations would be affected by whether the case was a death penalty case or a minor theft case.

Stipulations

A stipulation is an agreement between the parties to a trial that certain facts exist or that the appropriate legal principle applies. In civil proceedings, one party may serve on the other party a demand for admission of certain facts. For example in an automobile wreck the plaintiff may serve a demand on the defense to admit that Mary an unlicensed driver was driving the vehicle involved in the accident. If the defendant does not respond to the stipulation within a certain number of days, the court may accept the stipulation as true. If the other party denies the truth of the stipulation and the facts contained in the stipulation are established in court, the trial court may place sanctions on the party that denied the truth of the stipulation.

Generally courts will accept stipulations of fact but may refuse stipulations of law.[17] For example the prosecution and defense may stipulate that the witness is qualified as an expert. This is a stipulation of fact and no further evidence is required on this fact. However, if the parties stipulate that a Miranda warning was required before the police questioned the defendant, this is a stipulation of law and the trial court may refuse to agree to it. Stipulations are designed to speed the process of a trial by eliminating the need to prove issues that both parties agree to.

An example of the use of stipulations involved a case where a confined prisoner was being tried for assault and battery on a correctional officer. If the prosecution could establish that the defendant had previously been convicted of at least two prior felonies, the minimum punishment set by statute was 25 years confinement. The defense stipulated that the defendant had been found guilty in an earlier trial of kidnapping but denied that the case was final and contended that an appeal was pending. This stipulation established the fact that the defendant had been found guilty and the prosecution was not required to prove that issue. The prosecution was, however, required to establish that the prior conviction was final and not on appeal before it could be used in the present trial.

Generally the parties may state in open court the substance of the stipulation. In some jurisdictions, however, stipulations are required to be presented to the court in writing or made part of the trial record. For example, Kansas Supreme Court Rule 163 states that a court is not required to give effect to a stipulation between counsel or an oral admission of counsel which is not: (a) in writing and signed by the counsel to be charged with the stipulation or admission; or (b) made a part of the record.

Practicum

Practicum One

In the Supreme Court case of *Purkett v. Elem*, Elem sought a writ of habeas corpus against the superintendent of the Farmington Corrections Center (Purkett).[18] Elem contended that his conviction in a Missouri state criminal court was unconstitutional because the prosecutor had used peremptory challenges to strike two black men from the jury panel. [Note: each party has a limited number of peremptory challenges which allows them to excuse prospective jurors without cause.] The record of the criminal trial indicated that during the trial, defense objected to the use of the peremptory challenges by the prosecutor against the only two black jurors. During the hearing, the defense attorney requested that the court take judicial notice of the fact that the two prospective jurors were black. The trial judge refused to take the requested judicial notice that the two persons were black.

Did the trial judge commit error by refusing to take judicial notice of the fact that the two prospective jurors were black? Justify your conclusion.

[See *Purkett v. Elem*, 514 U.S. 765 (1995).]

Practicum Two

Prisoner brought suit pursuant to the Federal Tort Claims Act (FTCA) against the United States and the United States Bureau of Prisons alleging that he was denied adequate medical treatment and a proper diet. The District Court dismissed complaint, and prisoner appealed. One issue on appeal was the failure of the trial court to take judicial notice of various medical "facts." The appellate court reviews a district court's refusal to take judicial notice for an abuse of discretion.

As an appellate justice, how would you rule on the appeal?
[See: *Friedman v. U.S.*, 87 Fed.Appx. 459 (C.A.6, 2003)]

Practicum Three

Jesús Bello appeals his conviction and sentence for assaulting a fellow prisoner in the Metropolitan Detention Center in Guaynabo, Puerto Rico ("MDC–Guaynabo"), in violation of 18 U.S.C. § 113(a)(6). Bello claims that the trial court erred in taking judicial notice of the jurisdictional element of the offense, namely, that MDC–Guaynabo was within the territorial jurisdiction of the United States.

How would you rule as an appellate justice regarding the issue of whether a trial court could take judicial notice that the prison was within the territorial jurisdiction of the United States?

[See *U.S. v. Bello*, 194 F.3d 18 (C.A.1 (Puerto Rico), 1999].

Practicum Four

Defendant was convicted in the Court of Common Pleas, Allegheny County of possession of a firearm by a person with a felony conviction, and he pled guilty to two additional charges, carrying a firearm without a license and resisting arrest. He appealed his sentence based on the fact that defense had agreed with the prosecution to stipulate that defendant had previously been convicted of a felony. The trial court refused to accept the stipulation and the prosecution entered evidence of his prior conviction. Defense on appeal claimed that defendant suffered unfair prejudice merely by the admission into evidence of his or her certified conviction of a specific, identified, predicate offense, which has been offered by the Commonwealth. Had the court accepted his proposed stipulation, the jury would not have known the details of his prior conviction.

As an appellate justice, how would you rule on the fact that the trial judge refused to accept the stipulation even though both the defense and prosecution agreed to the stipulation?

[See: *Commonwealth v. Jemison*, 98 A.3d 1254 (Pa., 2014)].

Summary

- There are two types of presumptions: conclusive and rebuttal. A conclusive presumption is a presumption of law that cannot be rebutted by evidence and must be taken as true.
- The presumption of innocence is a rebuttal presumption.
- The presumption on an appeal is that the trial court was correct in its rulings that are in issue on appeal.
- A presumption may relieve the party with the burden of proof from having to prove a certain fact.

- Some presumptions exist at common law by custom or court decision. Others are created by statutes.
- A rebuttable presumption is an assumption of fact that is accepted by a court until it is disproved. It is an assumption that is made by the courts, and it will stand as a fact unless someone comes forward to contest it and prove otherwise.
- In criminal cases there are certain instances where the burden of proof to establish certain facts rests on the defense. In affirmative defenses, like self-defense and insanity, the burden to produce facts are on the defense.
- A court may instruct the jury that it may infer a presumed fact from proof of other facts. For example, a person found in possession of stolen property may be presumed to have stolen the property.
- Most presumptions that are involved in criminal cases are rebuttal presumptions.
- As noted by the U.S. Supreme Court in *Sandstrom v. Montana*, conclusive presumptions conflict with the overriding presumption of innocence with which the law endows the accused and which extends to every element of the crime.
- Judicial notice has been described as an evidentiary shortcut.
- Judicial notice allows courts to accept certain facts or propositions of law as true even when no evidence is admitted to establish their proof. Judicial notice is designed to save time and expenses in a trial.
- The rule states that a court may take judicial notice of a fact that is not subject to reasonable dispute because it is generally known within the trial court's general jurisdiction or it can be accurately and readily determined from sources whose accuracy cannot be reasonably questioned.
- For the most part, out-of-court statements that qualify as testimonial are not admissible, under the Confrontation Clause of the Sixth Amendment, unless witness is unavailable and defendant had prior opportunity to cross examine witness, including, at a minimum, prior testimony at a preliminary hearing, before a grand jury, or at a former trial, and statements elicited during police interrogations.
- To be admissible in a murder case, the dying declaration must be made when the victim is under immediate apprehension of death. In addition, in criminal cases the dying declaration is limited to cases where the defendant is charged with murder of the declarant. The restrictions on the admissibility of the declaration are based on the fact that the declaration violates the accused's right of confrontation guaranteed by the Sixth Amendment.
- Under Rule 804(b), former testimony is admissible if the declarant is unavailable and the party against whom the testimony is offered had an "opportunity and similar motive" to examine the declarant.
- Witnesses in criminal proceedings are required to take an oath or affirmation as to the truth of their testimony.
- A stipulation is an agreement between the parties to a trial that certain facts exist or that the appropriate legal principle applies.

Questions in Review

1. What are the issues involved in accepting a presumption as a conclusive fact?
2. How are presumptions created?
3. What types of facts may a trial court take judicial notice of?
4. What is the presumption that an appellate court uses when reviewing an appeal?
5. Why would an opposing counsel stipulate that an expert witness is qualified to testify as an expert?
6. In criminal trials, what are the requirements before the court will admit a dying declaration?

Key Terms

Affirmative Defense: An affirmative defense is a defense where the accused admits the act but provides justifiable grounds that the accused is not guilty.

Conclusive Presumption: A conclusive presumption is a presumption of law that cannot be rebutted by evidence and must be taken as true.

Dying Declaration: A declaration made by a victim who is under immediate apprehension of death.

Judicial Notice: Judicial notice allows courts to accept certain facts or propositions of law as true even when no evidence is admitted to establish their proof.

Rebuttable Presumption: A rebuttable presumption is an assumption of fact that is accepted by a court until it is disproved.

Stipulation: A stipulation is an agreement between the parties to a trial that certain facts exist or that the appropriate legal principle applies.

Endnotes

1. People v. Campanaro, 862 N.Y.S.2d 816 (2008).
2. Bond v. United States, 134 S.Ct. 2077 (2014).
3. United States v. Wilkinson, 460 F.2d 725 (C.A. 5, 1972).
4. Sandstrom v. Montana, 442 U.S. 510 (1979).
5. County Court of Ulster County, New York v. Allen, 442 U.S. 140 (1979).
6. United States v. Gould, 536 F.2d 216 (C.A. 8, 1976).
7. People v. Glover, 2015 WL 795690 (Colo. App. 2015).
8. Lee v. City of Los Angeles, 250 F.3d 668, (9th Cir.2001).
9. Crawford v. Washington, 541 U.S. 36 (2004).
10. Giles v. California, 554 U.S. 353 (2008).
11. United States v. Joseph, 465 Fed. Appx. 690 (C.A. 9, 2012).
12. Rawlins v. People, 2014 WL 7366626 (V.I., 2014).
13. United States v. Paling, 580 Fed. Appx. 144 (C.A. 3, 2014).
14. Crawford v. Washington, 541 U.S. 36 (2004).
15. United States v. Sklena, 692 F.3d 725 (C.A. 7, 2012).
16. Adams v. Texas, 448 U.S. 38 (1980).
17. United States v. Games-Perez, 695 F.3d 1104 (C.A. 10, 2012).
18. Purkett v. Elem, 514 U.S. 765 (1995).

Chapter 10

Uncharged Misconduct and Character Evidence

Chapter Objectives

After studying this chapter, the reader should be able to discuss or explain:

* Why admissibility of uncharged misconduct evidence is restricted
* Purposes for which this evidence may be admitted
* When evidence of accused's bad character may be admitted
* When the admission of the evidence will unfairly prejudice the defendant

Chapter Outline

Introduction
General Rules on Uncharged Misconduct
Admission of Character Evidence
Restrictions on Admission of Uncharged Misconduct
Relevance
Remoteness
Exceptions
Prejudicial Effect of the Evidence
Flight or Concealment
Practicum
Summary
Questions in Review
Key Terms
Endnotes

Introduction

Federal Rule of Evidence 404(b) and most state evidence rules provide that evidence of other crimes, wrongs, or acts that a defendant has committed is not admissible for the purpose of proving either bad character or that the defendant has committed the charged crime.[1] As a general rule, uncharged misconduct may be admitted for purposes such as proving motive, opportunity, intent, preparation, plan, knowledge, identity or to rebut the defenses of mistake or accident. For example, there have been three bank robberies in the local area. In each case, the robber wore a blue ski mask. The defendant is charged with only one of the three robberies. The prosecutor may request permission of the judge to admit into evidence facts about the other two robberies which were connected to the defendant in order to help establish that the defendant was the person who robbed the third bank. This would be evidence that tends to establish identity. The terms uncharged "misconduct and extraneous" offenses are used to describe criminal acts that the defendant is not formally charged with.

Consider the 2014 case of *United States v. Clark*.[2] On April 27, 2010, a man robbed the Regions Bank in Indianapolis at gunpoint while wearing a two-tone hat, dark sunglasses, and a bandana covering the lower half of his face. He threw three plastic grocery bags at the teller and ordered him to fill the bags with money. The teller filled one, which the robber took and fled, leaving the other two behind. The robber was described as a "stockier" Caucasian male, approximately 5' 9" and between 40–50 years old. Surveillance video from the drive-thru showed a blue car drive away.

Early the next morning, police found a blue Ford Crown Victoria less than half a mile from the Bank. An eyewitness confirmed that it was the same car she had seen around the Bank right before the robbery. Both the car and the plastic bags at the Bank were swabbed for DNA.

Five days earlier, Larry England visited a Harvesters Credit Union in Indianapolis, asked for a deposit slip, and left without conducting any business. A few minutes later, England's friend, Clark, got out of his blue Ford Crown Victoria and went into the same Harvesters. Clark, then fifty-six years old, is a Caucasian male who was wearing a T-shirt with sunglasses hanging off it and a two-tone cap. He asked for a deposit slip, was told the Harvesters did not use deposit slips, and left without conducting any business. Finding the acts troubling, Harvesters investigated and reported the incident to the Sheriff's Department.

The similarities between the Harvesters incident and the robbery led the Sheriff to Clark. Clark identified himself on the Harvesters video, and it was later determined that some of Clark's DNA was in the car and on the plastic bags left at the Bank. He was arrested and charged with bank robbery and using, carrying, and brandishing a firearm during and in relation to a crime of violence.

To prove the identity of the bank robber, the prosecution entered the evidence of Clark's conduct at the Harvesters Credit Union. On appeal, Clark argued that the trial court erred in admitting, without analysis, the Harvesters Credit Union evidence. He contended it was not properly admitted to show his "identity," and the government violated Federal Rule of Evidence 404(b) by using it for improper propensity purposes. The court held that because the identity of the bank robber was the key determination at issue, the physical similarities between the man shown at Harvesters and the Bank matched up, the evidence was admissible to help establish identity.

Prior to the admission of uncharged misconduct generally the prosecutor must meet a three-part test:

- Is the evidence relevant to an issue **other** than the defendant's bad character or that he or she acted in conformity with the character of a bad person?

- Prosecution must establish by relevant evidence that defendant committed the extraneous offense or offenses.
- The probative value of the uncharged misconduct in proving that defendant committed the charged offense or offenses outweighs the prejudicial impact on the defendant.

Evidence in Action
Federal Rules of Evidence Rule 404, 28 U.S.C.A.

Rule 404. Character Evidence; Crimes or Other Acts

(a) **Character Evidence.**

(1) **Prohibited Uses.** Evidence of a person's character or character trait is not admissible to prove that on a particular occasion the person acted in accordance with the character or trait.

(2) **Exceptions for a Defendant or Victim in a Criminal Case.** The following exceptions apply in a criminal case:

(A) a defendant may offer evidence of the defendant's pertinent trait, and if the evidence is admitted, the prosecutor may offer evidence to rebut it;

(B) subject to the limitations in Rule 412, a defendant may offer evidence of an alleged victim's pertinent trait, and if the evidence is admitted, the prosecutor may:

(i) offer evidence to rebut it; and

(ii) offer evidence of the defendant's same trait; and

(C) in a homicide case, the prosecutor may offer evidence of the alleged victim's trait of peacefulness to rebut evidence that the victim was the first aggressor.

(3) **Exceptions for a Witness.** Evidence of a witness's character may be admitted under Rules 607, 608, and 609.

(b) **Crimes, Wrongs, or Other Acts.**

(1) **Prohibited Uses.** Evidence of a crime, wrong, or other act is not admissible to prove a person's character in order to show that on a particular occasion the person acted in accordance with the character.

(2) **Permitted Uses; Notice in a Criminal Case.** This evidence may be admissible for another purpose, such as proving motive, opportunity, intent, preparation, plan, knowledge, identity, absence of mistake, or lack of accident. On request by a defendant in a criminal case, the prosecutor must:

(A) provide reasonable notice of the general nature of any such evidence that the prosecutor intends to offer at trial; and

(B) do so before trial—or during trial if the court, for good cause, excuses lack of pretrial notice.

General Rules on Uncharged Misconduct

Co-author Cliff Roberson, in his attorney desk book, *Extraneous Offenses and Uncharged Misconduct* (11 ed.) summarizes the general rules regarding the admission of uncharged misconduct:

- The evidence of other crimes is not admissible to prove the defendant's character is such and that he or she acted in conformity therewith.
- While the evidence is inadmissible to prove the above, it may be admissible on other grounds. For example if defendant claims that when he had voluntary sex with the victim he thought she was over 18 years of age, then the prosecution may enter evidence that defendant has had sex with other minors.
- The evidence is generally admissible only when it is relevant to a fact other than propensity.
- The trial court should use a balancing test based on the prejudicial impact of the evidence, the tendency of the evidence to show a material fact, and the need of the prosecution for the evidence to prove a fact.
- Notice of the intent to use such evidence is normally required during the pre-trial motion stage of the proceedings.
- No notice is generally required if the evidence is admitted to rebut testimony presented by the defense.
- The evidence should be excluded if it is inherently prejudicial and inflammatory and creates the likelihood that the jury will convict the defendant because he or she is a bad person.
- The evidence should not be admitted if it tends to confuse the issues in the case or creates a likelihood that the jury will convict the defendant on insufficient evidence.
- Evidence may be admitted if it is necessary to establish the defendant's connection to the charged misconduct. For example, if the defendant is charged with receiving stolen property, evidence that the property was stolen is relevant.
- When the defendant enters evidence of his or her good character, the prosecution may enter the extraneous evidence to rebut the good character evidence. For example, if the defendant, while testifying in her defense, stated that she had never stolen anything, the prosecution may enter evidence of her thefts by her.
- Evidence to rebut other evidence entered by defense can be admissible. For example, the accused testified that he had not been involved with trafficking in illegal substance. Evidence that he had engaged in selling illegal drugs was admissible to rebut this statement by the accused.
- If the defendant raises the defense of entrapment or claims that he or she was tricked into committing the crimes by law enforcement, the prosecution may enter evidence of similar acts by defendant.
- In most states, certain criminal statutes expressly permit the admission of extraneous offenses for specific crimes. For example many states allow evidence of defendant having sex with other minors when he is charged with sexual assault on a minor.

Admission of Character Evidence

A popular exception to the rule against showing the bad character of the defendant is where the defense enters evidence of the accused's good character. The admission of this evidence by the defense "opens the door" for the prosecution to enter evidence of accused's bad character to rebut the defense evidence. In *Michelson v. United States*,[3] the Supreme Court noted that, under the general rule, the prosecution may not resort in its case in chief to any kind of evidence of the defendant's evil character to establish the probability of his or her guilt. And that in a criminal trial, there is no presumption of a defendant's good behavior. A defendant may introduce affirmative testimony that the general estimate of his character is so favorable that the jury may infer that he or she would not be likely to commit the offense charged.

When a character witness is called by the defendant, the witness may not testify about the defendant's specific acts or courses of conduct or his possession of a particular disposition or of benign mental and moral traits, nor can he or she testify that his or her own acquaintance, observation and knowledge of the defendant leads to his or her own independent opinion that the defendant possesses a good general or specific character, inconsistent with the commission of acts charged. But the witness may summarize what he has heard in the community, though much of it may have been said by persons less qualified to judge than him or herself.

When a defendant has put his or her reputation in issue, his or her own character witness is subject to cross-examination as to the contents and extent of the hearsay on which he or she bases his or her conclusions, and the witness may be required to disclose rumors and reports that are current even if they do not affect his own conclusion. The sufficiency of his or her knowledge may be tested by asking what stories were circulating concerning events, such as one's arrest, about which people normally comment and speculate.

In *Michelson*, the U.S. Supreme Court held that in a prosecution for bribing a federal revenue agent, where character witnesses called by the defendant had testified that the defendant's reputation for honesty and truthfulness and for being a law-abiding citizen was very good, asking the witnesses on cross-examination whether they had ever heard that the defendant was arrested for receiving stolen goods was permissible, though the offenses of bribery and of receiving stolen goods were dissimilar. In the case, two of the character witnesses called by the defendant testified that their acquaintanceship with the defendant extended over a period of 30 years. The defendant himself, on direct examination, voluntarily called attention to his conviction for an offense 20 years before. Three of the witnesses testified to the defendant's reputation for honesty and truthfulness and for being a law-abiding citizen was very good. This line of questioning permitted the prosecution to ask four of the witnesses on cross-examination whether they had ever heard that defendant had been arrested, on a date 27 years prior to trial, for receiving stolen goods. The question by the prosecutor was not an abuse of discretion, in view of fact that court satisfied itself that there was a basis for the inquiry, and that the court warned jury of the limited purpose for which the evidence was received.

Associate Supreme Court Justice Robert Jackson stated:

> Courts that follow the common-law tradition almost unanimously have come to disallow resort by the prosecution to any kind of evidence of a defendant's

evil character to establish a probability of his guilt. Not that the law invests the defendant with a presumption of good character … but it simply closes the whole matter of character, disposition and reputation on the prosecution's case-in-chief. The State may not show defendant's prior trouble with the law, specific criminal acts, or ill name among his neighbors, even though such facts might logically be persuasive that he is by propensity a probable perpetrator of the crime. The inquiry is not rejected because character is irrelevant; on the contrary, it is said to weigh too much with the jury and to so over persuade them as to prejudge one with a bad general record and deny him a fair opportunity to defend against a particular charge. The overriding policy of excluding such evidence, despite its admitted probative value, is the practical experience that its disallowance tends to prevent confusion of issues, unfair surprise and undue prejudice.

When the defendant elects to initiate a character inquiry, another anomalous rule comes into play. Not only is he permitted to call witnesses to testify from hearsay, but indeed such a witness is not allowed to base his testimony on anything but hearsay. What commonly is called "character evidence" is only such when character is employed as a synonym for reputation. The witness may not testify about defendant's specific acts or courses of conduct or his possession of a particular disposition or of benign mental and moral traits; nor can he testify that his own acquaintance, observation, and knowledge of defendant leads to his own independent opinion that defendant possesses a good general or specific character, inconsistent with commission of acts charged.

The witness is, however, allowed to summarize what he has heard in the community, although much of it may have been said by persons less qualified to judge than himself. The evidence which the law permits is not as to the personality of defendant but only as to the shadow his daily life has cast in his neighborhood. This has been well described in a different connection as the slow growth of months and years, the resultant picture of forgotten incidents, passing events, habitual and daily conduct, presumably honest because disinterested, and safer to be trusted because prone to suspect. It is for that reason that such general repute is permitted to be proven. It sums up a multitude of trivial details. It compacts into the brief phrase of a verdict the teaching of many incidents.

When Character Is at Issue

Another exception to the inadmissibility of character evidence is in cases where the accused's character is at issue. For example, in *United States v. Foster*,[4] the trial court allowed the testimony of the accused's wife regarding the physical and sexual abuse in the accused's trial for child pornography. The appellate court held that the testimony was not character assassination but was relevant to his wife's inconsistent pretrial statements and to rebut the anticipated defense that the wife rather than the defendant downloaded the pornography.

Rebuttal of Entrapment Defense

Frequently in undercover operations, the defense of entrapment will be raised by the accused. Under this defense, the accused claims that he or she would not have engaged in the criminal act except for the encouragement of the undercover officer. In *United States v. Hooker*,[5] an informant was allowed to testify that he had previously bought drugs from the defendant. The testimony was admissible to rebut the defense of entrapment in a case where the defendant was charged with aiding and abetting the distribution of crack cocaine.

In *United States v. Martinez*,[6] the defendant was charged with conspiracy and possession with the intent to deliver cocaine. He testified that he had never used cocaine and was entrapped by a law enforcement agent. The prosecution was allowed to enter evidence that when Martinez was arrested, he had cocaine in his possession.

Specific Statutes That Allow Character Evidence

Many state statutes allow the admissibility of character evidence in sexual misconduct or domestic abuse cases. For example, in *White v. State*,[7] a state appellate court held that the trial court did not commit error in allowing evidence of prior domestic assaults by the defendant in a case where defendant was charged with assault and battery on his common law wife. The admissibility of the prior assaults was based on a Texas statute.

Another example is 18 U.S. Code 894(b), which allows the prosecution to enter evidence of prior threats used by a debt collector in an attempt to collect a debt. The statute permits the introduction of this type of evidence also in cases where an implied threat is used to collect a debt.

Restrictions on Admission of Uncharged Misconduct

Generally for the admission of extraneous offenses or uncharged misconduct, the evidence must be relevant to a fact other than propensity and also meet a balancing test of probative value and prejudice. To be relevant the evidence must be:

- connected to the defendant,
- not too remote, and
- have a tendency to prove a material fact.

The balancing test is determined by:

- The prejudicial impact of the evidence.
- The tendency of the evidence to prove a material fact.
- The need of the party introducing the evidence to prove the fact.

Relevance

If the evidence is not relevant, it should not be admitted without consideration of the balancing test. Relevance is the concept of one fact being connected to another fact in a manner that makes it useful to consider the first fact when considering the second. For example, establishing that Jerry was at the crime scene prior to the criminal act being committed is relevant in attempting to prove that Jerry was the actor. However, if two days after the crime Jerry visited the city in which the crime took place, that probably is not connected with him being the person who committed the criminal act and therefore is not relevant to the question of whether or not he committed the crime.

Suppose that the prosecution wants to establish that Jerry has committed a similar crime in the past in order to establish that he committed the crime being charged. This evidence would be relevant to the question of whether or not he committed the crime since it establishes that he has committed a similar crime using very similar methods. For example, a bank is robbed by a masked, six-foot, overweight male, wearing a blue baseball cap, using a certain type of weapon, and giving the teller a note that orders the teller to place the money in the enclosed brown bag. In the note, the word "teller" is misspelled. Jerry was convicted as the bank robber and served a five-year sentence in prison. After Jerry was released, another bank was robbed under the same circumstances, and the note to the teller had the same misspelling. The evidence that Jerry robbed the first bank would be clearly relevant to establishing the identity of the second bank robber.

Evidence that Jerry was the robber in the first robbery would not be admitted in a trial for committing the second robbery unless:

- the commission of the first crime and the method by which it was committed are clearly established, and
- the accused is clearly established as the perpetrator of the first robbery.

Suppose in the previous scenario, the prosecutor only suspected that Jerry committed the first robbery but could not clearly establish that Jerry was the robber. The evidence of the similar robbery would probably not be admitted.

What if Jerry was in prison when the first robbery occurred and therefore could not have committed it? Should the defense be allowed to enter the evidence of the methods used in the first robbery as relevant to establishing that someone other than Jerry robbed the second bank? A trial judge would probably allow the entry of this evidence because it is relevant to the question of whether or not Jerry committed the second robbery.

In *Thompson v. State*,[8] Thompson's trial for robbing the store and stealing Timex watches, the trial judge allowed the prosecutor to admit evidence of subsequent burglaries of the same store in which only Timex watches were stolen. The appellate court held that the trial judge committed error in allowing the admission of this evidence because there was no evidence that Thompson was involved in the other robberies and that Timex watches are very common. A similar case is *United States v. Gilan*.[9] In the *Gilan* case, the U.S. Supreme Court held that where there was no evidence tying defendant to an earlier theft, evidence of the earlier theft was wrongly admitted by the trial judge. In that case, the Court noted that first the trial court must determine that the evidence is relevant to an issue other than the accused's character and that the evidence must possess probative value that is not outweighed by its undue prejudice, and it must be tied to the accused.

Remoteness

While there are no general rules on time-remoteness, the more remote in time of the extraneous offense, the more the need for it to have strong similarities to the charged offense. For example, evidence that Jerry committed a similar crime twenty years ago will probably not be admitted to establish his identity as the perpetrator of the present crime unless the prosecution can show very strong similarities between the two crimes.

In *United States v. Foley*,[10] the U.S. Court of Appeals held that it was not in error to admit evidence of the convictions of two prior crimes, one of which occurred eleven years prior to the present crime, on the issue of intent where the crimes involved similar fraudulent schemes and were relevant. But in *United States v. San Martin*,[11] the court held that evidence of nine- and ten-year-old prior assaults on police officers, when the accused was a minor, were too remote to be admissible in a trial involving assault on an FBI agent.

If the accused takes the stand in his or her trial and testifies to certain facts, then the accused's testimony generally may be rebutted by his remote misconduct. For example, in a drug case, if an accused testifies that he has never been involved with the trafficking of illegal drugs, then evidence of a remote conviction for trafficking is probably admissible because the remoteness limitation is not designed to protect an individual who testifies falsely.

Exceptions

As noted earlier, there are numerous exceptions to the rule regarding the admission of uncharged misconduct or extraneous offenses. Generally, this type of evidence may be admitted to establish intent, motive, and identity. Several of the exceptions have previously been discussed in this chapter. In *United States v. Miller*,[12] the U.S. Court of Appeals noted that rules on admission of uncharged misconduct were intended not to define the set of permissible purposes for which bad-acts evidence may be admitted, but rather to define the one impermissible purpose for such evidence. In other words, the Court is stating the general rule that bad-acts evidence may not be entered to show the accused's propensity to commit crime, but such evidence is admissible for other purposes. From a reading of the Court's decision, the general rule emerges that any admissible purpose for which bad-acts evidence is introduced is a proper purpose so long as the evidence is not offered solely to prove character.

Evidence Discovered at Arrest Scene

There are two general rules regarding the admission of evidence found at the scene of the arrest where the evidence is irrelevant to any issues in the case. For example, a defendant being tried for murder is arrested in his home. At the time of the arrest, the police discovered the defendant smoking marijuana. Should the fact that he was smoking marijuana be admissible in the murder trial? The majority rule and what seems to be the better rule is that where evidence found at the scene of the arrest is completely irrelevant to any issue in the case and its admission would risk unfair prejudice against the accused, the evidence should not be admitted. As noted in *United States v. Childs*,[13] evidence of other crimes is not admissible solely because the evidence was found at the scene of the accused's arrest.

The second rule holds that everything taken in an arrest is admissible under the legal theory that the jury had a right to know the entire context of the arrest.[14] In *United States v. Blanton*,[15] an appellate court held that evidence that defendant was carrying a shotgun and had marijuana in his possession when arrested was admissible since the accused was being tried for distribution of methaqualone, and the shotgun and marijuana evidence was part of the arrest.

If the evidence is relevant to any issue in the case, it probably will be admissible in all jurisdictions unless the trial judge determines that it will unfairly prejudice the accused. In *United States v. Royal*,[16] Royal, who was in prison, was charged with the crime of conspiracy to hand over drug business to a coconspirator while defendant was in prison. The appellate court ruled that evidence of defendant's prior arrest and imprisonment was inextricably intertwined with charged and, therefore, was admissible as intrinsic evidence despite the restriction on evidence of other crimes, wrongs, or acts. The court noted that the government could not have proven its case without establishing that defendant had ongoing drug business at the time he entered prison, and cautionary instruction was given.

Signature Theory

The courts frequently allow the use of the signature theory to justify the admission of evidence of other crimes to establish the identity of the individual who committed the crime. The signature theory relates to the admission of other offenses showing a distinctive modus operandi so similar to that used in the charged offense as to be highly probative of the fact that they were all committed by the same person. As noted in *United States v. Goodwin*,[17] the court noted that:

> Sometimes in criminal offenses, one's method of doing things, of painting a portrait, or of laying fancy brickwork or of committing a crime, the methods and artistry involved are so similar that you can almost say from looking at the two of them that the same hand did both of them.

The courts are uniform in holding that merely raising the issue of identity does not automatically render the evidence of other misconduct admissible. To be admissible, the evidence must be so similar to the charged offense that the offenses illustrate the defendant's distinctive and idiosyncratic manner of committing criminal acts.[18] Prior to admitting the other misconduct under the signature theory, the state must first show that the defendant was, in fact, the person who committed the act and that the misconduct was so similar to the charged offense as to be considered the accused's handiwork. For example, evidence of other crime was not admissible where the seminaries were that both the other crime and charged crime where committed in a neighborhood store on a sunny afternoon by an African-American wearing sunglasses.[19]

Voice Examples to Prove Identity

In *United States v. Tibbetts*,[20] the defendant was convicted of making a false bomb threat. He appealed his conviction because the trial court had admitted into evidence a tape recording of a prior telephone bomb threat made by the defendant almost six months earlier. While he was never charged with the earlier threat, he was put under surveillance by a private investigator that was employed by a company that was subjected to the threat. The appellate court upheld the admission and stated that, based on the particular facts of this case, identification of Tibbetts as the caller in the earlier bomb threat was proper.

Eyewitnesses

Another exception to the rule against admitting prior misconduct is, when the ability of an eyewitness to make a correct identification is questioned, prior conflicts between the defendant and the eyewitness may be admissible even if the prior conflicts involve early misconduct by the defendant. In *United States ex rel. Barksdale v. Sielaff*,[21] which was an aggravated kidnapping and rape case, a defense witness testified that the defendant had a long Afro and a mustache at the time of the crime in contradiction to the complaining witness's description of the defendant. The trial court correctly allowed the prosecution to call a rebuttal witness that testified that when she had a confrontation with the defendant shortly before the alleged crime he had short hair and no mustache.

In a Texas case, where the defendant was on trial for aggravated robbery, the state was allowed to introduce evidence of earlier robberies on the same day.[22] In that case, the robberies were conducted in a very similar manner, and the defendant had raised the issue of mistaken identity. On the evening of December 10, 2005, three separate incidents of robbery occurred at the Camden Station apartment complex in Houston, Texas. In the offense-at-issue, at approximately 9:45 p.m., a young man approached John Dufour as Dufour walked his two dogs and accompanied his wife, Janna Dufour, to her car. The man was running and repeating the phrase "come get me." As he ran past the Dufours, the dogs began to bark at him. He turned around and pointed a handgun at the dogs, threatening to shoot them if the Dufours did not make the dogs stop barking. He then threatened to shoot John and Janna if they did not give him their money. However, when a neighbor turned on his porch light and opened the front door, the assailant ran away without taking anything from the Dufours.

Robert Kelly and Carlos Cruz were also robbed that night at the Camden Station apartments. Kelly was accosted as he returned home from a Christmas shopping trip.

As he stepped out of his van, a man walked up to him, put a gun to his throat, and asked how much money he had. Before Kelly could retrieve his wallet, the man struck him twice in the head with the gun. After obtaining Kelly's wallet, the man demanded Kelly's cellular phone, and struck Kelly three times with the gun before Kelly relinquished the phone. The assailant proceeded to kick Kelly in the ribs before leaving. Similarly, Cruz was robbed as he walked towards his apartment. As Cruz approached his apartment door, a man addressed him, asking if he needed a woman. When Cruz declined his offer, the man walked past him and turned around, producing a handgun. He demanded Cruz's money. Before Cruz could turn over his wallet, the man struck him multiple times with the handgun. The assailant ran away after taking Cruz's wallet and cellular phone.

Each of the victims spoke with police the night of the robberies. Although their recollections of the assailant's description differed, all four concurred that the man was dark-skinned, about six feet tall, wore a coat or jacket with either a skull cap or the jacket hood up, styled his hair in braids or dreadlocks, and carried a handgun. However, the police identified no suspects at that time.

At Dickson's trial, he was tried for the robbery of the Defours. Defense contested the identification of the defendant as the robber. The appellate court noted that identity was a material issue in this case and was vigorously contested at trial. Three of the State's witnesses identified the appellant as their robber at trial. Additionally, the State presented evidence that John Dufour and Robert Kelly each positively identified appellant in a photo-lineup, as well as evidence that Janna Dufour and Carlos Cruz each made tentative identifications of appellant from a photo-lineup. Defendant had testified at trial and denied that he committed any of the robberies on December 10, 2005. The appellate court held that while evidence of extraneous offenses is inadmissible to show action in conformity with bad character, the rule provides that extraneous offense evidence may be admissible for some other purpose, such as proof of identity.

Rebuttal of a Defense Theory

Other misconduct evidence may be admitted to rebut a defense by the defense. For example, if a defendant is charged with an aggravated assault and claims that he was acting in self-defense, the prosecution is generally allowed to admit evidence of other assaultive acts by the defendant where the defendant was the aggressor.

In *United States v. Gilmore*,[23] Walter Gilmore was convicted by a jury of conspiring to distribute and to possess with the intent to distribute 500 grams or more of cocaine. Gilmore testified on his behalf that he had never sold drugs. The trial court allowed the prosecution to cross-examine Gilmore and to ask him if he had been convicted in 1992 of possession with the intent to distribute controlled dangerous substances within a thousand feet of a school. Gilmore appealed his conviction based on the alleged error of the trial court in allowing the prosecution to question him about a conviction that was over ten years old. The appellate court held that the cross-examination was proper to correct false testimony presented by the defense.

The prosecution may not generally rebut an insanity defense by establishing that the defendant was found insane in a prior murder trial. The courts appear to hold that the admission of a previous finding of not guilty by reasons of insanity is not admissible because it does not establish any inconsistency with the present claim of insanity.[24]

To Prove State of Mind

In *United States v. Wilson*,[25] Edwin Wilson was charged with illegally shipping plastic explosives to Libya. Wilson sought to justify his acts by claiming that he had no intent to commit the charged crimes and that he was duped by agents of the government. The prosecution was allowed to call the former Attorney General and former CIA employees who testified that they had no knowledge of defendant or of his association or involvement with the CIA. In addition, the prosecution was allowed to present evidence of defendant's commission of offenses and incidents involving terrorism to establish his true motive, intent and plan.

Wilson complained of the testimony that in 1976 he supported terrorist activities, including the building of booby traps, letter bombs and the shipment of explosives to England. He complained of evidence that in 1979 similar cans as were involved in the instant shipment were seen in a Rotterdam warehouse, and two such cans were recovered in 1982. He further complained of the use of a videotape showing the recovery of cans containing C-4 and detonation tests reflecting the explosive power of C-4. Wilson further complained of testimony by a co-actor about a contract the co-actor had to furnish personnel for production of certain "clandestine devices" in Libya. The appellate court held that the prosecution's evidence was probative of the essential element (state of mind), and the particular extrinsic acts were sufficiently proximate to the alleged offenses. The court also perceived the probative value was not substantially outweighed by the danger of unfair prejudice.

To Prove the Existence of a Larger Plan

If a defendant is charged with breaking and entering a motel to steal room keys, should the prosecution be allowed to establish that this was just the first step of a plan by the defendant to rob certain motel rooms? In *Lamar v. Steele*,[26] a civil rights case, Lamar, a prison writ writer, claimed that a correctional major sought to have another inmate kill him. To establish this plan, Lamar was allowed to enter evidence that the correctional major had given the other inmate a knife.

Narcotics Cases

The courts frequently admit evidence of prior narcotics involvement in narcotics cases with a minimal exploration of the rationale underlying the admission decision. This may be based on the general theory that individuals involved in narcotic trafficking are generally repeat offenders. In narcotics cases the courts appear to be less concerned with the similarity of the cases between the charged crime and the uncharged misconduct. In *United States v. Douglas*,[27] the defendant's prior arrest for the offense of possessing with the intent to distribute cocaine was allowed to be admitted. In the *Douglas* case, a federal officer testifying that as he pursued the defendant in a foot chase, the defendant abandoned the cocaine in a trash barrel.

Impeachment of a Witness

In a trial where the defendant was charged with filing false income tax statements, the defense called several witnesses who testified that defendant was an upstanding citizen. The prosecution rebutted the defense's character evidence with a witness who testified that the defendant did not have good character. The question before the appellate court was whether the defense should have been allowed to present evidence that the government witness had stolen money and lied to the IRS and had a motive to lie about the defendant to gain favor with the government. The appellate court held that the defense should have been given the opportunity to impeach the witness with the information.[28]

Prejudicial Effect of the Evidence

Probably any evidence of past or present misconduct by a defendant will be considered as prejudicial to the defense. The question is, at what point does the prejudicial effect outweigh the probative value of the evidence?

Consider the case of *United States v. Blackwell*.[29] Claude Blackwell was charged with the illegal possession of firearms by a convicted felon. Washington, D.C. police executed a search warrant at a hotel, in a room rented by Blackwell's common-law wife. Both the wife and Blackwell were present in the room when the search occurred. During their search, the police seized two guns hidden in the room, a .357 magnum Dan Wesson revolver and a .38 Smith & Wesson revolver; a brown canvas bag containing both live and spent .357 and .38 ammunition, weapon cleaning and breakdown tools, a Smith & Wesson box bearing the same serial number as that of the seized .38 revolver, Blackwell's birth certificate, and a pawnbroker's certificate with Blackwell's name and address on it; marijuana; and four color photographs of Blackwell with a revolver similar to the .357 magnum discovered during the search.

Blackwell's defense counsel objected to the introduction into evidence of the four color photographs stating that they were prejudicial and there was no date established as to when the photographs were taken. The defense also argued that the photographs were unauthenticated and irrelevant. The U.S. Court of Appeals noted that as a general rule tangible evidence such as photographs must be properly identified or authenticated before being admitted into evidence at trial. The court noted that the prosecution did not, however, present sufficient evidence to establish with any degree of certainty when the photographs were taken. Proper authentication requires not only that the government identify the scene depicted in the photographs, but also their coordinates in time and place.

The court noted that the probative value of the photographs would have been extremely high if it had been conclusively proven that the gun and room in the photographs were identical to the seized gun and the room at the hotel, and that the photographs were taken a short time before Blackwell's arrest. This, of course, was not the case. As a result, the probative value of the photographs is diminished, even though the gun and the room in the photographs closely resemble the seized gun.

In addition, the defendant may have been prejudiced by the admission of the photographs. One of the charges against Blackwell concerned possession of a firearm by a convicted felon. The photographs may have led the jury to believe that, even if Blackwell had not possessed the guns found at the hotel, he had had some guns in his possession since his felony conviction. There is also some likelihood that the jury, after viewing these photographs, may have been prejudiced by Blackwell's stance in one of them (holding a gun in firing position).

Flight or Concealment

The courts have generally allowed evidence of flight, concealment, false statements to police, destruction or concealment of evidence, bribing or threatening witnesses, or similar conduct, as some evidence of consciousness of guilt.[30]

In *United States v. Ceja*,[31] Jamie Ceja, an illegal immigrant, fled to Mexico when he discovered that he was being investigated in Georgia for conspiracy to distribute and possess with intent to distribute five kilograms or more of cocaine and less than 100 kilograms of marijuana with the intent to distribute. Could the evidence of his flight to Mexico be used as evidence of his guilt of the charged offenses? Ceja was arrested in Tijuana by a Mexican immigration officer. The officer took him to the Mexican-American border and turned him over to a U.S. immigration officer. He was then extradited to Georgia based on an outstanding arrest warrant.

The defense objected to the trial first based on the fact that he was illegally brought into the United States. After denying that objection, the trial court allowed the prosecution to enter evidence that Ceja had traveled to Mexico as soon as he learned that he was being investigated for the drug offenses. The trial judge allowed the evidence of flight as evidence of his guilt. The trial judge instructed the jury as follows:

> You are instructed that the flight of the defendant is a circumstance which may be taken into consideration with all other facts and circumstances in the evidence. And if you believe and find from the evidence beyond reasonable doubt that the defendant fled for the purpose of avoiding arrest and trial under the charges set out in the indictment, you may take this fact into consideration in determining guilt or innocence.

The U.S. Court of Appeals stated that flight is an admission by conduct that provides "circumstantial evidence of guilt." Jurors considering such evidence infer "(1) from the defendant's behavior to flight; (2) from flight to consciousness of guilt; (3) from consciousness of guilt to consciousness of guilt concerning the crime charged; and (4) from consciousness of guilt concerning the crime charged to actual guilt of the crime charged."

Practicum

Practicum One

Lambert was talking to Joseph, his friend. As they passed a bank, Lambert remarked that the bank would be a good target for a robbery. Later the bank was robbed, and Lambert was arrested and charged with the robbery. During Lambert's criminal trial, Joseph was called as a witness for the prosecution to testifying as to Lambert's statement that the bank was a good target for a robbery. As trial judge how would you rule on this proposed testimony?

[See *United States v. Lambert*, 995 F.2d. 1006 (10th Cir., 1993).]

Practicum Two

On the night of September 3, 2012, Angelica Martinez was working the cash register at the Dollar Tree store in Chico, California. She saw a thin woman enter the store, wearing a black tank top, jeans, and a wig, and carrying a large purse. The woman (later identified as defendant), selected an energy drink, then approached the register and handed Martinez two dollars.

As Martinez was making change, defendant pulled a gun from her purse. She told Martinez to give her the money. Martinez did not know if the gun was real and asked, "Are you serious?" Defendant replied, "Yes. I don't want to have to hurt you. Now put the money in the bag." Defendant pulled out a crumpled plastic bag from her purse and Martinez put the money in the bag. Defendant took it and left. Martinez called the police.

On September 13, 2012, a teller at U.S. Bank in Chico saw two suspicious people enter the bank. The man wore a red baseball cap and sunglasses, and the woman had an obvious black, choppy wig, a black tank top, sunglasses, and a beige purse. The teller had received information that a similar looking man had robbed the Colusa branch of the bank. She immediately notified the branch manager by instant messaging.

Sally Mendez, the branch manager, received the message and went to acknowledge the suspicious customers, asking, "So what's going on?" The man responded, but the woman did not; she was writing something at the deposit kiosk. The customers left and Mendez called the police.

Officer Scott Harris was on patrol that day. That morning, at the police briefing, he had learned of a BOLO (Be on the Lookout) flyer from the FBI about a series of bank robberies. When he saw the pending call from the U.S. Bank, he pulled up the description of the suspicious customers. He saw the description was similar to that in the FBI BOLO flyer. The flyer had listed the vehicle as a tan Suburban. He saw a tan Yukon, a similar vehicle, near the bank. The female driver was wearing dark glasses and an obvious wig. When the Yukon pulled into a parking lot, he activated his lights and waited for backup. When the male passenger got out of the car, something fell to the ground. It was a loaded gun.

Emily Clark was charged with second-degree robbery of the Dollar Tree Store. At her trial, the prosecution attempted to admit into evidence a copy of the BOLO flyer to establish a course of action. The BOLO flyer contained pictures of a man and woman and stated that they were wanted for "multiple robberies in Northern California."

As trial judge, would you allow the admission of the BOLO flyer? Justify your decision. [*People v. Clark*, 2015 WL 739794 (Cal. App. 3 Dist. 2015).]

Summary

- Federal Rule of Evidence 404(b) and most state evidence rules provide that evidence of other crimes, wrongs, or acts that a defendant has committed is not admissible for the purpose of proving either bad character or that the defendant has committed the charged crime.
- As a general rule, uncharged misconduct may be admitted for purposes such as proving motive, opportunity, intent, preparation, plan, knowledge, identity or to rebut the defenses of a mistake or accident.
- Prior to the admission of uncharged misconduct, generally the prosecutor must meet a three-part test: (1) Is the evidence relevant to an issue other than the defendant's bad character or that he or she acted in conformity with the character of a bad person? (2) Prosecution must establish by relevant evidence that defendant committed the extraneous offense or offenses. (3) The probative value of the uncharged misconduct, in proving that defendant committed the charged offense or offenses, outweighs the prejudicial impact on the defendant.
- A popular exception to the rule against showing the bad character of the defendant is where the defense enters evidence of the accused's good character. The defense's admission of this evidence "opens the door" for the prosecution to enter evidence of the accused's bad character to rebut the defense evidence.
- Generally, for the admission of extraneous offenses or uncharged misconduct, the evidence must be relevant to a fact other than propensity and meet a balancing test of probative value and prejudice.
- If the evidence is not relevant, it should not be admitted without consideration of the balancing test. Relevance is the concept of one fact being connected to another fact in a manner that makes it useful to consider the first fact when considering the second.
- While there are no general rules on time-remoteness, the more remote in time of the extraneous offense, the more the need for it to have strong similarities to the charged offense.
- The courts have generally allowed evidence of flight, concealment, false statements to police, destruction or concealment of evidence, bribing or threatening witnesses, or similar conduct, as some evidence of consciousness of guilt.

Questions in Review

1. Why are there restrictions on the admission of uncharged misconduct?
2. What is meant by the term "relevant"?
3. Who makes the initial decision on the admission of uncharged misconduct?
4. What are some of the exceptions that allow the admission of uncharged misconduct?
5. Explain when prior uncharged crimes may be admitted against a defendant to establish identity.

Key Terms

Entrapment: The defense of entrapment is raised when the accused claims that he or she would not have engaged in the criminal act except for government encouragement.

Extraneous Offenses: Extraneous offenses or uncharged misconduct are offenses for which the defendant is not presently charged with and the prosecution wants to enter to help establish his or her case.

Relevance: Relevance is the concept of one fact being connected to another fact in a manner that makes it useful to consider the first fact when considering the second.

Signature Theory: The signature theory relates to the admission of other offenses showing a distinctive modus operandi so similar to that used in the charged offense as to be highly probative of the fact that they were all committed by the same person.

Endnotes

1. Cliff Roberson (2015). *Extraneous Offenses and Uncharged Misconduct, 11ed.* Fort Worth: Knowles Publishing Co.
2. U.S. v. Clark, 2014 WL 7235648, C.A.7 (Ind. 2014).
3. Michelson v. United States, 335 U.S. 469 (1948).
4. United States v. Foster, 623 F.3d 605 (8th Cir. 2010).
5. United States v. Hooker, 997 F.2d 67 (5th Cir. 1993).
6. United States v. Martinez, 710 F.2d 1424 (10th Cir. 1992).
7. White v. State, 2010 WL 2803018 (Tex. App. 2010).
8. Thompson v. State, 615 S.W.2d 760 (Tex. App. 1981).
9. United States v. Gilan, 967 F.2d 776 (2d Cir. 1992).
10. United States v. Foley, 683 F.2d 273 (8th Cir. 1982).
11. United States v. Martin, 505 F.2d 918 (5th Cir. 1974).
12. United States v. Miller, 895 F.2d 1431 (D.C. Cir. 1990).
13. United States v. Childs, 598 F.2d 169 (D.C. Cir. 1979).
14. Smith v. State, 646 S.W.2d 452 (Tex. Crim. App. 1983).
15. United States v. Blanton, 730 F.2d 1425 (11th Cir. 1984).
16. United States v. Royal, 972 F.2d 643 (5th Cir. 1992).
17. United States v. Goodwin, 492 F.2d 1141 (5th Cir. 1974).
18. Page v. State, 213 S.W.3d 332 (Tex. Crim. App. 2006).
19. Drew v. United States, 331 F.2d 85 (D.C. Cir, 1964).
20. United States v. Tibbetts, 565 F.2d 867 (4th Cir. 1977).

21. United States ex. rel. Barksdale v. Sielaff 585 F.2d 288 (7th Cir. 1978).
22. Dickson v. State, 246 S.W.3d 733 (Tex.App.–Houston [14 Dist.], 2007).
23. United States v. Gilmore, 553 F.3d 266 (3rd Cir. 2009).
24. Sanders v. State, 604 S.W.2d 369 (Tex. Crim. App. 1981).
25. United States v. Wilson, 732 F.2d 404 (5th Cir. 1984).
26. Lamar v. Steele, 693 F.2d 559 (5th Cir, 1982).
27. United States v. Douglas, 482 F.3d 591 (D.C. Cir. 2007).
28. United States v. Skelton, 514 F.3d 433 (5th Cir. 2008).
29. United States v. Blackwell, 694 F.2d 1325 (D.C. Cir. 1982.)
30. Com. v. Cassidy 470 Mass. 201, 21 N.E.3d 127 (Mass., 2014).
31. United States v. Ceja, 543 Fed. Appx. 948 (11th Cir, 2013).

Chapter 11

Privileges

Chapter Objectives

After studying this chapter, the reader should understand the following concepts or issues:

- The two types of privileges that exist
- The scope of the attorney-client privilege
- The scope of the physician-patient privilege
- The scope of the marital privilege
- The scope of the clergy-believer privilege
- When a privilege applies
- Who may waive the privilege

Chapter Outline

Introduction
Attorney-Client Privilege
Physician-Patient Privilege
Marital Privilege
Clergy-Believer Privilege
Miscellaneous Privileges
Practicum
Summary
Questions in Review
Key Terms
Endnotes

Introduction

In this chapter we will not discuss the most important privilege in criminal justice. That is the privilege set forth in the Fourth Amendment to the U.S. Constitution—the privilege against self-incrimination. That privilege is examined in Chapter 9 and in a course on criminal procedure.

Privileges are generally divided into two broad areas: those that protect communications and a group of miscellaneous privileges. Probably less uniformity exists in the area of privileges than in any other aspect of evidence. The generally accepted communications privileges include:

- attorney-client
- physician-patient
- marital privilege
- clergy-believer

A few states also recognize confidential communications between an accountant and client, parent and child, and social worker and client.

The rules of confidential communications are based on the concept that guaranteeing confidentiality is necessary to foster goals that society deems important. For example, a patient should be able to talk freely to his or her doctor with the knowledge that any statements made will be kept confidential. A similar goal exists in the privilege between husband and wife where they are encouraged to communicate with each other.

The communications privilege is designed to protect the holder of the privilege to refuse to disclose and to prevent others from disclosing the privileged communication. As will be discussed later in this chapter, the holder of the privilege may waive it. The communications privilege applies to oral and written statements. It also applies to non-verbal communications such as nodding or pointing.

Consider the possibility that you are charged with an offense, and you, while in a public place, call and discuss the crime with your attorney. Unknown to you, someone else is listening to your conversation. The communications between you and your attorney were privileged at common law. But the person who overheard your conservation is not a part of the privilege and could testify in court as to the statements you made to your attorney. The same rules would apply to a husband and wife discussing a confidential matter in public. There are some jurisdictions now that hold that eavesdroppers are prohibited from disclosing the information as long as their presence was not expected and the parties were not negligent.

Attorney-Client Privilege

Consider the following situation: Two attorneys were appointed to represent Robert Garrow for the murder of an 18-year-old college student who was camping in the Adirondacks with three friends when Garrow attacked them and tied them all to trees. Two of the three escaped, but the victim did not. In discussing the case with his attorneys, Garrow admitted killing the victim. Garrow also admitted that in a separate incident, he had murdered another camper—and abducted, raped and murdered the man's female companion. Garrow also admitted that he had abducted, raped and murdered a 16-year-old girl. Garrow even told his lawyers where he had dumped the bodies of his two female victims—information the attorneys confirmed by photographing the remains at the locations Garrow had identified.

One of the attorneys conducted his own investigation based upon what his client told him and, with the assistance of a friend, the location of the body of one Alicia

Hauck was found in a cemetery in Syracuse, New York. The attorney personally inspected the body and was satisfied, presumably, that this was the victim that his client had told him that he murdered.

The two lawyers told nobody about their client's confession; nor did they reveal that they had located the bodies of his two missing victims—even after the father of one of the victims begged them for information about the fate of his missing daughter, and after the victims' bodies were accidentally discovered several months later in separate locations hundreds of miles apart.

This discovery became public during the trial of Mr. Garrow when, to affirmatively establish the defense of insanity, these three other murders were brought before the jury by the defense in the trial. The day after Garrow finished testifying, the attorneys acknowledged publicly that they had known all along about the murders and the locations of the victims' bodies. Public indignation reached the fever pitch; statements were made by the District Attorney of Onondaga County relative to the situation, and he caused the Grand Jury of Onondaga County, then sitting, to conduct a thorough investigation. As a result of this investigation, an indictment was returned against the lawyer who had investigated and found the body. The attorney was accused of having violated section 4200(1) of the Public Health Law, which requires that a decent burial be accorded the dead, and section 4143 of the Public Health Law, which requires anyone knowing of the death of a person without medical attendance to report the same to the proper authorities. The indicted defense attorney's counsel moved for a dismissal of the indictment on the grounds that a confidential, privileged communication existed between him and Mr. Garrow, which should excuse the attorney from making full disclosure to the authorities.

Garrow was convicted on one murder charge and sentenced to 25 years to life in prison. He was shot to death by police in September 1978, shortly after making a daring prison escape. Ensuing editorials expressed no mercy for Garrow. The Poughkeepsie Journal called him "a malignant cancer on the society that fostered him" and "less than useless to the human race."

While the two lawyers insisted that their duty of client confidentiality obliged them to remain silent, they were widely reviled outside the profession for withholding the information. Their once-thriving law practices withered. They received hate mail and death threats. Longtime friends stopped speaking to them. They had to move out of their homes. One attorney eventually gave up his law practice altogether.[1] The indictment was eventually dismissed.

The parents of one victim filed an ethics complaint against the two lawyers with state bar disciplinary officials. It took four years, but that complaint, too, was eventually dismissed. In its decision, the Committee on Professional Ethics of the New York State Bar Association said the assurance of confidentiality helps encourage proper representation, which requires full disclosure of all relevant facts by the client—even if those facts include the commission of prior crimes.[2]

At the time of the incident, lawyers in the State of New York were governed by the ABA Model Code of Professional Responsibility. The Code provided that a lawyer must reveal the intention of his or her client to commit a crime and the information necessary to prevent the crime. The Code did not permit the attorneys from providing information obtained from a client regarding prior crimes if those acts were admitted in confidence.

The New York Code of Professional Responsibility was replaced in 1983 by the Model Rules. Rule 1.6 allows an attorney to reveal client confidences to prevent the client from committing a criminal act that the lawyer believes is likely to result in imminent death or substantial bodily harm. But the modified rules still require an attorney to hold in confidence any information received from a client about the client's past conduct.

The New York Judge who dismissed the indictment stated:[3]

> A trial is in part a search for truth, but it is only partly a search for truth. The mantle of innocence is flung over the defendant to such an extent that he is safeguarded by rules of evidence which frequently keep out absolute truth, much to the chagrin of juries. Nevertheless, this has been a part of our system since our laws were taken from the laws of England and over these many years has been found to best protect a balance between the rights of the individual and the rights of society.
>
> The concept of the right to counsel has again been with us for a long time, but since the decision of *Gideon v. Wainwright,* 372 U.S. 335, 83 S.Ct. 792, 9 L.Ed.2d 799, it has been extended more and more so that at the present time a defendant is entitled to have counsel at a parole hearing or a probation violation hearing.
>
> The effectiveness of counsel is only as great as the confidentiality of its client-attorney relationship. If the lawyer cannot get all the facts about the case, he can only give his client half of a defense. This, of necessity, involves the client telling his attorney everything remotely connected with the crime.
>
> Apparently, in the instant case, after analyzing all the evidence, and after hearing of the bizarre episodes in the life of their client, they decided that the only possibility of salvation was in a defense of insanity. For the client to disclose not only everything about this particular crime but also everything about other crimes which might have a bearing upon his defense, requires the strictest confidence in, and on the part of, the attorney.
>
> When the facts of the other homicides became public, as a result of the defendant's testimony to substantiate his claim of insanity, members of the public were shocked at the apparent callousness of these lawyers, whose conduct was seen as typifying the unhealthy lack of concern of most lawyers with the public interest and with simple decency. A hue and cry went up from the press and other news media suggesting that the attorneys should be found guilty of such crimes as obstruction of justice or becoming an accomplice after the fact. From a layman's standpoint, this certainly was a logical conclusion. However, the constitution of the United States of America attempts to preserve the dignity of the individual and to do that guarantees him the services of an attorney who will bring to the bar and to the bench every conceivable protection from the inroads of the state against such rights as are vested in the constitution for one accused of crime. Among those substantial constitutional rights is that a defendant does not have to incriminate himself. His attorneys were bound to uphold that concept and maintain what has been called a sacred trust of confidentiality.

If this indictment stands, the attorney-client privilege will be effectively destroyed. No defendant will be able to freely discuss the facts of his case with his attorney. No attorney will be able to listen to those facts without being faced with the Hobson's choice of violating the law or violating his professional code of Ethics.

Scope of Attorney-Client Privilege

The attorney-client privilege protects only those communications that are intended to be confidential. It also extends to assistants to the attorney. For example, the paralegal who types your statement is covered by the privilege. The privilege does not apply to communications made to an attorney who is acting in a non-legal capacity. While the presence of a secretary, interpreter or consultant does not destroy the confidentiality, the presence of a third person, like a close friend who does not need to be there, destroys the confidentiality of the communications.

Observations made by an attorney during a meeting with his or her client probably will not be privileged. For example, if, when the attorney first met with his client, the client was bleeding, the attorney could probably be forced to provide that information to the court.

Any writing originated by a client that was not prepared as a confidential communication is normally not privileged. For example, if a client writes a letter to her customer and retains a copy for her records, that letter is not privileged since it was not written as a confidential communication.

Generally, any communication that a client intended to be confidential or to be only disclosed to the attorney is considered confidential. If the client makes the communication with the attorney with the request that the attorney disclose the communications to another person, generally that communication is not considered privileged communication.

Clark v. State

Consider the case of *Clark v. State*.[4] In Clark, the defendant's ex-wife had secured a divorce from him on March 25, 1952. That night she was killed, as she lay at home in her bed, as the result of a gunshot wound. From the mattress on her bed, as well as from the bed of her daughter, were recovered bullets which were shown by a firearms expert to have been fired by a .38 special revolver having Colt characteristics. Defendant was shown to have purchased a Colt .38 Detective Special some ten months prior to the homicide. On the morning of March 26, 1952, Marjorie Bartz, a telephone operator, stated that she received a call from a local motel. The caller told her he wanted to speak to his lawyer in Dallas. Contrary to the telephone company rules, Bartz listened to the entire conversation between Clark and his attorney. Clark admitted to his attorney that he killed his wife. The lawyer then asked: "Did you get rid of the weapon?" Clark answered: "No, I still have the weapon." The lawyer then said: "Get rid of the weapon and sit tight and don't talk to anyone, and I will fly down in the morning." Bartz was allowed to testify as to their conversation in the trial. Clark was convicted of murder.

The state appellate court noted that Texas was one of those jurisdictions that allowed eavesdroppers to testify, and any conversations overheard by an eavesdropper were not protected by the attorney-client privilege. (Note Texas is one of the minority jurisdictions that does not extend the attorney-client privilege to eavesdroppers.) The court noted the fact that a telephone conversation between a defendant charged with murder and his attorney had been overheard by an operator as a result of eavesdropping in violation of a company rule did not preclude the conversation from being testified to, if relevant to the issue, and not otherwise inadmissible.

Next, the court discussed the issue as to whether the lawyer was an accessory after the fact under state criminal statutes. The court noted that the lawyer, with knowledge that an offense had been committed, had helped the defendant by advising the defendant to dispose of the murder weapon. That advice was not protected by the attorney-client privilege because it was considered as encouragement to commit the offense of the willful destruction of evidence.

The appellate court noted that it was is in the interest of public justice that the client be able to make a full disclosure to his attorney of all facts that are material to his defense or that go to substantiate his claim. The purpose of the privilege is to encourage such disclosure of the facts. But the interests of public justice further require that no shield such as the protection afforded to communications between attorney and client shall be interposed to protect a person who takes counsel on how he can safely commit a crime.

The court opined that privilege does not extend to one who, having committed a crime, seeks or takes counsel as to how he shall escape arrest and punishment, such as advice regarding the destruction or disposition of the murder weapon or of the body following a murder. One who, knowing that an offense has been committed, conceals the offender or aids him to evade arrest or trial becomes an accessory. The fact that the aider may be a member of the bar and the attorney for the offender will not prevent his becoming an accessory.

The conversation, as testified to by the telephone operator, was not within the attorney-client privilege. When the attorney advised defendant to get rid of the weapon (which advice, the evidence shows, was followed), such aid cannot be said to constitute aid in making or preparing his defense at law. It was aid to the perpetrator of the crime in order that he may evade an arrest or trial.

Is such a conversation privileged as a communication between attorney and client? If the adviser had been called to testify as to the conversation, would it not have been more appropriate for him to claim his privilege against self-incrimination rather than that the communication was privileged because it was between attorney and client?

Defendant, when he conversed with the attorney, was not under arrest nor was he charged with a crime. He had just inflicted mortal wounds on his former wife and apparently had shot her daughter. The attorney had acted as his attorney in the divorce suit, which had been tried that day, and had secured a satisfactory property settlement. Defendant called the lawyer and told him that he had gone to extremes and had killed "her," not "the driver." The lawyer appeared to understand these references and told defendant to get rid of the weapon.

The appellate court was unwilling to subscribe to the theory that such counsel and advice should be privileged because of the attorney-client relationship that existed between the parties in the divorce suit. The court held that the conversation was admissible as not within the realm of legitimate professional counsel and employment.

The court noted that the rule of public policy, which calls for the privileged character of the communication between attorney and client, demands that the rule be confined to the legitimate course of professional employment. It cannot be applied here consistent with the high purpose and policy supporting the rule.

The murder weapon was not found. The evidence indicates that defendant disposed of it as advised in the telephone conversation. Such advice or counsel was not such as merits protection because it was given by an attorney. It was not in the legitimate course of professional employment in making or preparing a defense at law.

The court, in conclusion, noted that nothing was found in the record to indicate that defendant sought any advice from the lawyer other than that given in the conversation testified to by the telephone operator. The court concluded that it was not, therefore, dealing with a situation where the accused sought legitimate advice from his attorney in preparing his legal defense.

General Rules on Attorney-Client Privilege

- The attorney-client privilege is the oldest of the privileges for confidential communications known to the common law.[5]
- The purpose of attorney-client privilege is to encourage full and frank communications between attorneys and their clients and thereby to promote broader public interests in observance of the law and the administration of justice.[6]
- Attorney-client privilege rests on a need for advocate and counselor to know all that relates to his or her client's reasons for seeking representation if the professional mission is to be carried out.[7]
- The protection of the privilege extends only to communications and not to facts. A fact is one thing, and a communication concerning that fact is an entirely different thing. The client cannot be compelled to answer the question, "What did you say or write to the attorney?" but may not refuse to disclose any relevant fact within his knowledge merely because he incorporated a statement of such fact into his communication to his attorney.[8]
- Attorney-client privilege survives the client's death, given that knowledge that communications will remain confidential even after death encourages the client to communicate fully and frankly with counsel; while fear of disclosure, and consequent withholding of information from counsel, may be reduced if disclosure is limited to posthumous disclosure in criminal context, it is unreasonable to assume that it vanishes altogether.[9]
- The privilege applies only to communications that are made for the purposes of facilitating the rendition of professional legal services or advice.
- Any observations made by the attorney may be required to be disclosed. For example, the attorney may be required to testify that, when he met with the accused, the accused's face was bruised.
- The privilege does not apply to writing made by a client that did not originate as a privileged communication. For example if the client has written a letter to a

third person (non-legal person) regarding the matter in question, the attorney may be forced to turn over that letter.

- There is a split of authority regarding eavesdroppers. Most courts hold that if the lawyer-client communication is overheard by an eavesdropper, it retains its confidentiality so long as it was the client's intention that it be confidential.
- The privilege belongs to the client and not the attorney.
- The client may voluntarily waive the privilege by failing to assert it in a timely fashion or by disclosing it.
- The privilege does not apply to comments made regarding plans of future criminal actions or behavior.

Physician-Patient Privilege

Federal statutes do not create a physician-patient privilege; it is created only in state statutes. It usually applies to testimony at trials or in administrative actions. In *United States v. Bek*, a U.S. Court of Appeals case involving a conspiracy to distribute controlled substances prosecution, the court held that physician-defendant could not assert that the medical records of his patients were subject to a doctor-patient privilege because the federal courts do not recognize this privilege under FRE 501.[10]

In an earlier case by the U.S. Supreme Court, *Jaffee v. Redmond*,[11] the court held that there was a psychotherapist-patient privilege in federal court. It appears that while the federal courts do not recognize a physician-patient privilege, they do recognize a psychotherapist-patient privilege. In the *Jaffee* case, Redmond, a police officer, had shot and killed a victim named Allen. Allen's estate brought a civil rights action against Redmond and sought discovery of notes made by a psychotherapist. The Supreme Court held that the notes were privileged. The Court noted that recognition of the privilege would serve the public interest by helping to promote an atmosphere in which patients could confide in their therapists and thus foster the mental health of the citizenry.

In those states, like California, that have the physician-patient privilege, generally the patient must consult the doctor for purposes of diagnosis or treatment. The privilege extends between the patient and medical personnel who assist the doctor. The privilege applies only to communications and includes the protection of the identity of the patient. The privilege applies when a patient communicates with the doctor through an intermediary such as a family member.

While the physician may assert the privilege on behalf of the patient, the privilege belongs to the patient. It does not end on the death of the patient.

In some states, the privilege does not apply to criminal cases. It also does not apply to litigation between a patient and a physician. So if you sue your doctor, that generally acts as a waiver of the privilege. There is no privilege in cases where the patient has been examined by court-appointed medical personnel.

What if the medical records were released to the prosecution and defense inadvertently? Does that waive the medical privilege of the victim of a rape case? In the case of *Colorado v. Kobe Bryant*, the basketball player, was charged with rape. At a private hearing in the judge's office, it was noted that the medical records of the alleged victim were inadvertently released to the prosecution and defense. The court ordered the parties to destroy the records and held that the victim had not waived her physician-patient privilege. The court also held that the victim did not waive the privilege by testifying in court that she sought medical treatment.[12] In this case, the court also held that the presence of the victim's mother when the communications took place did not constitute a waiver of the privilege.

States vary as to their definition of physicians and whether or not psychotherapists and psychologists are included. In some states it has been extended to licensed social workers.

Marital Privilege

Federal Rule of Evidence 501 provides that the privilege of a witness or person shall be governed by the principles of the common law as they may be interpreted by the courts of the United States in the light of reason and experience. The Supreme Court has recognized two privileges that arise from a marital relationship. The first permits a witness to refuse to testify against his or her spouse. This is the testimonial privilege. The witness spouse alone holds the privilege and may choose to waive it. For example, if the husband is being tried for a criminal offense, the wife can refuse to testify or may waive the privilege and testify. Note: in a few states, both spouses must waive the privilege. The Court noted that the trend in state law toward divesting accused of privilege to bar adverse spousal testimony has special relevance because the law of marriage and domestic relations are concerns traditionally reserved to states. The Court also noted that, "when one spouse is willing to testify against the other in a criminal proceeding—whatever the motivation—their relationship is almost certainly in disrepair; there is probably little in the way of marital harmony for the privilege to preserve."

The second marital privilege recognized by the Supreme Court is the marital communication privilege.

In *Trammel v. United States*, the Supreme Court stated that a husband can request that his wife not tell a jury about contraband that she observed in their home or illegal activity to which she bore witness, but it is she who decides whether to invoke the testimonial marital privilege.[13]

The Supreme Court first recognized a confidential marital communications privilege in *Wolfle v. United States*.[14] In *Wolfle*, the Supreme Court noted that, "communications between the spouses, privately made, are generally assumed to have been intended to be confidential, and hence they are privileged; but, wherever a communication, because of its nature or the circumstances under which it was made, was obviously not intended to be confidential, it is not a privileged communication." And, when made in the presence of a third party, such communications are usually regarded as not privileged because they were not made in confidence.

An interesting issue in the *Wolfle* case was that the letter by defendant to his wife was dictated to a stenographer. The prosecution argued that the voluntary disclosure to the stenographer negates the confidential character of the communication. The Supreme Court disagreed and stated that the key issue was whether the defendant's letter to his wife was intended to be confidential. The Court noted that communications between husband and wife may sometimes be made in confidence even though in the presence of a third person, and that would seem especially to be the case where the communication is made in the presence of or through the aid of a private secretary or stenographer whose duties, in common experience, are confidential.

In *United States v. Irving Kahn and Minnie Kahn*,[15] a bookmaker and his wife were tried in a federal district court. Prior to the indictments, the government had obtained a court order to intercept wire communications of the Kahns. The prosecutor was allowed to present statements made between the husband and wife in court as evidence of their illegal activities. The Court noted that both parties were subject to the court order and that all intercepted conversations were admissible. The Court denied the Kahns' argument that the conversations between husband and wife were subject to the marital privilege. In denying their claim of a marital privilege, the Court failed to explain why, except that all intercepts that met the requirements under the Title III of the Omnibus Crime Control and Safe Streets Act of 1968 were admissible. Three associate justices dissented—Brennan, Marshall, and Douglas.

Exceptions to the marital privilege include cases in which one spouse brings an action against the other spouse, such as in a divorce proceedings. The *Kahn* case noted earlier seems to stand for the proposition that it does not apply to communications made by a spouse in furtherance of a crime or fraud in which both spouses participated.

For the marital privilege to apply, the parties must be legally married. The privilege survives a divorce between the parties. If a couple is living together in common law marriage, they are protected by the privilege if they would be considered legally married in that jurisdiction.

There are cases holding that communications made between spouses when the marriage is no longer viable are not protected by the privilege. For example, Jim and Sarah are married. During the marriage, the confidential communications between them are subject to the privilege, even after they obtain a divorce. But after they have separated and prior to an official divorce, their communications made after the separation are not privileged in many jurisdictions.

An interesting case involving the marital privilege is the *Puterbaugh v. Puterbaugh* case.[16] In this case, David Puterbaugh's former wife petitioned for an increase in child support and requested discovery. The former wife wanted the court to order David to disclose his antenuptial agreement with his present wife. David's counsel objected on the grounds that the agreement between him and his present wife were protected from disclosure by the marital privilege. The trial judge rejected his contention and ordered that the agreement be provided to the former wife. The Illinois appellate court agreed with the trial judge and held that since the agreement was made prior to marriage the privilege was inapplicable.

Clergy-Believer Privilege

The majority of states recognize a clergy-believer privilege. In a few states, the privilege is limited in scope and applies only to confessions made to a priest. As a general rule, to be protected by the privilege, the communication must be made when the believer seeks religious or spiritual guidance.

In *Commonwealth of Massachusetts v. Agustin Garcia*,[17] the defendant Garcia argued that the trial judge committed error by allowing the testimony of his pastor regarding Garcia's admission that he sexually abused his daughter. The facts indicate that after the daughter complained to the pastor of sexual abuse, the pastor called Garcia and arranged a meeting. At the meeting with the pastor, Garcia admitted that he had touched his daughter's breasts. The Massachusetts appellate court stated that whether communications made to a member of the clergy are privileged under state law is a question of law to be decided by the trial judge, and that the privilege applies only to disclosures made by a person who is seeking religious or spiritual guidance. The appellate court agreed with the trial judge that there was a lack of any indication to the pastor that Garcia was looking for spiritual advice, and therefore the disclosures were not privileged.

In *State v. Hancock*,[18] Billy Jason Hancock was convicted of murdering his wife. One of the issues on appeal was the admission in the criminal trial of testimony by a Methodist pastor. The pastor was allowed to testify of a conversation he had with Hancock on the day that Hancock's wife had disappeared. Hancock told the pastor that he and his wife had gotten into an argument and provided information on where the body could be found. The pastor testified that at the time of the conversation with Hancock, primary concern was not in counseling Hancock but in locating the victim. The appellate court held that since no spiritual counseling took place, the conversations were not privileged.

As noted in *State v. Schauer*,[19] the purpose of the clergy privilege is to allow individuals freedom to unburden themselves by seeking spiritual healing without the threat of incriminating themselves. An assertion of the clergy privilege requires proof of the following:

(1) the potential witness is a religious minister;
(2) the communicant intended the conversation to be private; and
(3) the communicant was seeking religious or spiritual help.

In determining whether the privilege applies, the trial court should look to the circumstances leading up to the communication. The burden is on the party asserting the clergy privilege to show he or she was seeking spiritual aid in a confidential conversation when he spoke with a member of the clergy.

Miscellaneous Privileges

Various states have allowed other privileges; those include accountant-client, journalist's privilege, parent-child, and executive privilege. These privileges vary by jurisdiction, and most are very restrictive in nature.

Journalist's Privilege

More and more jurisdictions are allowing a journalist's privilege, but it is a limited one. For example, in Florida there is a statutorily created journalist's privilege. In order to overcome the privilege in Florida, the party seeking to compel disclosure must demonstrate that the journalist's information is relevant to the case, that the information cannot reasonably be obtained from alternative sources, and that a compelling interest exists requiring the disclosure.[20]

In the Florida case of *Muhammad v. Florida*, Askari Muhammad was convicted of first-degree murder of a correctional officer.[21] In a motion for post-conviction relief, Muhammad sought the source of information that a reporter had used in an article on the lethal drugs used in Florida's execution process. The appellate court held that Muhammad had failed to satisfy the three-prong test for overcoming the qualified privilege because he failed to prove that the information was relevant to his case and that he could not obtain the information from another source.

Executive Privilege

In recent years, the executive privilege has been in the news. Probably the leading case on executive privilege is the case of *United States v. Richard Nixon*.[22] In that case, following indictments which alleged violations of federal statutes by certain staff members of the White House and political supporters of the President, the Special Prosecutor filed a motion for the production before trial of certain tapes and documents relating to precisely identified conversations and meetings between the President and others. President Nixon resisted the order and claimed executive privilege.

The U.S. District Court rejected the President's claim of privilege and ordered the production of the material. The court's order was appealed to the U.S. Supreme Court. The Supreme Court held that neither the doctrine of separation of powers nor the generalized need for confidentiality of high-level communications, without more, can sustain an absolute unqualified presidential privilege of immunity from judicial process under all circumstances. By the statement, the Supreme Court held that the executive privilege was only a qualified privilege.

The Supreme Court in the *Nixon* case noted that, to overcome the claim of executive privilege, the Special Prosecutor must clear "three hurdles." He must establish (1) relevancy; (2) admissibility; and (3) specificity. The Court held that, in this case, the Special Prosecutor had overcome his burden and held that the tapes were admissible for certain purposes. The Court in its opinion stated:

> However, neither the doctrine of separation of powers, nor the need for confidentiality of high-level communications, without more, can sustain an absolute, unqualified Presidential privilege of immunity from judicial process under all circumstances. The President's need for complete candor and objectivity from advisers calls for great deference from the courts. However, when the privilege depends solely on the broad, undifferentiated claim of public interest in the confidentiality of such conversations, a confrontation with other values arises. Absent a claim of need to protect military, diplomatic, or sensitive national security secrets, we find it difficult to accept the argument that even the very important interest in confidentiality of Presidential communications is significantly diminished by production of such material for in camera inspection with all the protection that a district court will be obliged to provide.[23]

The *Nixon* case was cited in an Oklahoma case, *Vandelay Entertainment v. Fallin*, involving the executive privilege of a state governor.[24] In *Vandelay*, the entertainment company brought action against the state governor requesting information under the Affordable Care Act. The state district court granted summary judgment for the governor. On appeal, one of the issues involved was the governor's claim of privilege to prevent the release of certain documents.

The appellate court noted that the sheer number, diversity and magnitude of discretionary decisions entrusted to the Governor demonstrate the public interest is best served by the Governor seeking and receiving advice to aid in deliberations and decision-making, and that the United States Supreme Court has observed those who assist executive decision-makers must be free to explore alternatives in the process of shaping policies and making decisions and to deal so in a way many would be unwilling to express except privately.

The appellate court further observed that the confidentiality of advisory conversations and correspondence is grounded in the necessity for the protection of the public interest in candid, objective, and even blunt or harsh opinions in executive decision-making, and that the United States Supreme Court concluded these considerations justify a presumptive privilege. The appellate court also concluded that such a privilege is fundamental to the operation of Government and inextricably rooted in the separation of powers under the Constitution. The court noted that the refusal to recognize the gubernatorial communications privilege would subvert the integrity of the governor's decision-making process, thereby damaging the functionality of the executive branch and transgressing the boundaries set by separation of powers.

The Oklahoma court also concluded that, in considering Governor Fallin's claim of privilege in the case at hand, it agreed with the United States Supreme Court's view that "complete candor and objectivity from advisers calls for great deference from the courts" in determining the scope of executive privilege. An Oklahoma Governor has no less need than the President of the United States to receive "candid, objective, and even blunt or harsh opinions" provided by "senior executive branch officials" as well as the need to refuse to disclose such advice that was solicited or received confidentially.

Parent-Child Privilege

A few jurisdictions have a statutorily created parent-child privilege. The State of Minnesota has this privilege. In *State v. Thompson*, Stafon Thompson, who was 17 years old, was convicted in a Minnesota district court of two counts of first-degree murder while committing an aggravated robbery.[25] One issue on appeal was the admission into evidence of a recording of Thompson's conversation, while in jail, with his mother and brother. During this conversation, Thompson admitted his presence at the robbery and claimed that the co-robber threatened him to keep him quiet. The appellate court noted that the police's action in recording his conversations with his mother violated the recognized parent-child privilege of confidentiality, but the error was harmless because of the other evidence.

It is noted that all federal courts of appeal have uniformly declined to recognize a parent-child privilege.[26] Even those states that recognize the parent-child privilege have limited it. There are numerous cases which hold that a third party cannot claim the privilege on behalf of the child or the parent.

In *Ahmad A. v. Superior Court*, a California court faced the question of whether the police violated Ahmad's rights by secretly recording conversations between him (a minor) and his mother.[27] The California appellate court held first that California did not recognize a parent-child privilege. The court also noted that although the officer had left the minor in the interrogation room alone with his mother after closing the door, no representations or inquiries were made as to privacy or confidentiality. The court noted that any such belief that the conversation was in private would not have been objectively reasonable. The court noted that in "the jailhouse, the age-old truism still obtains: 'Walls have ears.'"

Practicum

Practicum One

In 1840, an English nobleman, Lord William Russell, was murdered, his throat cut while he slept. Lord Russell's maid, Sarah Mancer, awoke to discover disorder in the house. She roused the cook, Mary Hannell, and the Swiss valet-butler, Benjamin Courvoisier. They soon discovered Lord Russell's dead body and summoned the police. The police discovered that a large amount of Lord Russell's property was missing and concluded that it was an inside job. The case generated intense public and media interest since the upper classes were terrified by the notion that a wealthy man could be murdered by a servant in his bed.[28] The police suspected Courvoisier, the valet-butler. The butler was represented by a leading British lawyer, Charles Phillips. At trial, Phillips aggressively cross-examined the maid and attacked every detail of her testimony. It was reported that the maid never recovered from the trauma of the trial and died in an insane asylum. Phillips also cross-examined other witnesses and did considerable damage to their reputations. He even suggested that several of the witnesses were dishonest and had lied on the stand. The jury found the butler guilty, and he was later hanged. It was later revealed that, prior to the trial, the butler had admitted to his attorney, Phillips, that he was guilty.

If you were a member of an ethics panel investigating the conduct of Attorney Phillips, would you consider that Phillips' conduct at trial was unethical?

[See: Michael Asimow (2009, Winter), "When the Lawyer Knows the Client is Guilty," Southern California Interdisciplinary Law Journal, vol. 18, pp. 229–261.]

Practicum Two

In San Diego, California, a seven-year-old girl was abducted from her home in the middle of the night. Neighbor David Westerfield was charged with her murder and kidnapping. During a plea bargaining session prior to trial, the prosecutor offered to not seek the death penalty if the defense counsel would agree to disclose the location of the girl's body. It was apparent from the negotiations that Westerfield knew the location of the body. Before a plea bargain could be completed, volunteers found the girl's body, and the plea bargain collapsed. When the case went to trial, the defense counsel conducted an all-out defense. He argued that there were serious doubts that Westerfield had killed the girl. Defense counsel, in cross-examining the girl's parents, brought out facts that the parents had a "swinging life style" and did considerable damage to their reputations. Defense also contested the testimony of expert witnesses regarding the time of death and suggested that their testimony was wrong. After Westerfield was convicted, a conservative TV commentator filed an ethics complaint with the bar association regarding the actions of the defense attorney during the plea bargaining and trial.

As a member of an ethics panel, would you condone the conduct of the counsel?

[Also discussed in Michael Asimow (2009, Winter), "When the Lawyer Knows the Client is Guilty," Southern California Interdisciplinary Law Journal, vol. 18, pp. 229–261; and Alex Roth, "Defenders in Eye of Public Storm," Copley News Serv., Sept. 18, 2002, quoted in Jeralyn Merritt, "On Westerfield's Lawyers' Conduct," Talkleft, Sept. 19, 2002, available at http://www.talkleft.com/story/2002/09/19/723/24550. Accessed on March 7, 2015.]

Practicum Three

The federal government was investigating the 1993 dismissal of White House Travel Office employees. Deputy White House Counsel Vincent Foster met with attorney Hamilton. Hamilton took notes of Foster's statements. Nine days later, Foster committed suicide. A federal grand jury issued subpoenas for the notes of Foster's statements from Hamilton. Hamilton moved to quash the subpoenas arguing that they were protected by the attorney-client privilege.

As a federal district court judge, how would your rule?

[See: *Swidler & Berlin v. United States*, 524 U.S. 399 (1998).]

Practicum Four

Defendant Jason Strauch, who is charged with criminal sexual contact of a minor in the second degree, filed a motion for protective order, seeking to bar disclosure of alleged confidential communications made by him to a licensed social worker for the purpose of diagnosis and treatment. The jurisdiction has a social worker-client privilege. The state also has a statute that mandates a social worker to report information on child abuse. The trial court denied Strauch's request for a protective order and ruled that the disclosures to the social worker were admissible in court. The trial court ruled that the mandatory reporting requirements overruled any privilege. Strauch's counsel appealed the denial.

As an appellate judge, how would you rule?

[See *State v. Strauch*, 2015 WL 1005021 (N.M. 2015).]

Summary

- Privileges are generally divided into two broad areas: those that protect communications and a group of miscellaneous privileges.
- Probably less uniformity exists in the area of privileges than in any other aspect of evidence.
- The rules of confidential communications are based on the concept that guaranteeing confidentiality is necessary to foster goals that society deems important.

- The communications privilege is designed to protect the holder of the privilege to refuse to disclose and to prevent others from disclosing the privileged communication.
- The communications between you and your attorney were privileged at common law. But the person who overheard your conservation is not a part of the privilege and could testify in court as to the statements you made to your attorney.
- The attorney-client privilege protects only those communications that are intended to be confidential. It also extends to assistants to the attorney.
- Observations made by an attorney during a meeting with his or her client probably will not be privileged.
- Attorney-client privilege rests on the need for advocate and counselor to know all that relates to a client's reasons for seeking representation if the professional mission is to be carried out.
- The protection of the privilege extends only to communications and not to facts. A fact is one thing and a communication concerning that fact is an entirely different thing.
- Attorney-client privilege survives a client's death.
- The privilege applies only to communications that are made for the purposes of facilitating the rendition of professional legal services or advice.
- Federal statutes do not create a physician-patient privilege; it is created only in state statutes. It usually applies to testimony at trials or in administrative actions.
- In those states, like California, that have the physician-patient privilege, generally the patient must consult the doctor for purposes of diagnosis or treatment.
- The Supreme Court has recognized two privileges that arise from a marital relationship. The first permits a witness to refuse to testify against his or her spouse. This is the testimonial privilege.
- The second marital privilege recognized by the Supreme Court is the marital communications privilege.
- Exceptions to the marital privilege include cases in which one spouse brings an action against the other spouse, such as in divorce proceedings.
- The *Kahn* case seems to stand for the proposition that it does not apply to communications made by a spouse in furtherance of a crime or fraud in which both spouses participated.
- The majority of states recognize a clergy-believer privilege. In a few states, the privilege is limited in scope and applies only to confessions made to a priest. As a general rule, to be protected by the privilege the communication must be made when the believer seeks religious or spiritual guidance.
- The burden is on the party asserting the clergy privilege to show he or she was seeking spiritual aid in a confidential conversation when he spoke with a member of the clergy.

Questions in Review

1. How did the attorney in the *State v. Clark* case exceed the scope of the attorney-client privilege?

2. What are the justifications for allowing certain parties to communicate without worry that their conversations may be admissible in a court proceeding?
3. Explain the scope of the clergy-believer privilege.
4. Who generally has the burden to establish that a privilege exists?
5. Explain the two types of marital privileges.

Key Terms

Attorney-Client privilege: Communications between an attorney and his or her client may not be disclosed unless the privilege is waived by the client. The attorney-client privilege protects only those communications that are intended to be confidential

Clergy-believer privilege: In a few states, the privilege is limited in scope and applies only to confessions made to a priest. As a general rule, to be protected by the privilege the communication must be made when the believer seeks religious or spiritual guidance.

Communications privilege: The communications privilege is designed to protect the holder of the privilege to refuse to disclose and to prevent others from disclosing the privileged communication.

Executive privilege: The right of the president of the United States or state executive to withhold information from legislatures or the courts.

Marital privilege: The marital or spousal privilege (also called husband-wife privilege) is a term used in the law of evidence to describe two separate privileges: the communications privilege and the testimonial privilege. Both types of privilege are based on the policy of encouraging spousal harmony and preventing spouses from having to condemn, or be condemned by, their spouses.

Endnotes

1. People v. Belge, 372 N.Y.S.2d 798 (1975).
2. Mark Hansen (2007), "The Toughest Call," American Bar Journal, posted online at www.aba-journal.com accessed on February 26, 2015.
3. People v. Belge, 372 N.Y.S.2d 798 at. p. 799 (1975).
4. Clark v. State, 261 S.W.2d 339 (1963).
5. Upjohn v. United States, 449 U.S. 383 (1981).
6. Fed. Rules Evid. Rule 501.
7. ABA Code of Professional Responsibility, EC4-1.
8. Philadelphia v. Westinghouse Electric Corp., 205 F.Supp. 830 (1982).
9. Fed. Rules Evid. Rule 501.
10. United States v. Bek, 493 F.3d 790 (7th Cir. 2007).
11. Jaffee v. Redmond, 581 U.S. 1 (1996).
12. State v. Bryant, 2004 WL 869618 (Colo. Dist. Ct. 2004).
13. Trammel v. United States, 445 U.S. 40, 53, 100 S.Ct. 906, 63 L.Ed.2d 186 (1980).
14. Wolfle v. United States, 291 U.S. 7, 54 S.Ct. 279, 78 L.Ed. 617 (1934).
15. United States v. Kahn, 415 U.S. 143 (1974).
16. Puterbaugh v. Puterbaugh 764 N.E. 582 (Ill. App. Dist. 3, 2002).
17. Com. v. Garcia 22 N.E.3d 178 (Mass. app. Ct. 2015).
18. State v. Hancock, 2014 WL 7006969 (Tenn. Crim. App. 2014).

19. State v. Schauer, 2014 WL 6608790 (Minn. App. 2014).

20. Florida Statute §90.5015 (1998).

21. Muhammad v. State, 132 So. 3d 176 (Fla. 2013).

22. United States v. Nixon, 418 U.S. 683 (1974).

23. Note 20, at page 707.

24. Vandelay Entertainment v. Fallin, 2014 WL 71570155 (Okla. 2014).

25. State v. Thompson, 788 N.W.2d 485 (Minn. 2010).

26. United States v. Red Elk, 955 F.Supp. 1170, 1178 (D.S.D. 1997).

27. Ahmad A. v. Superior Court, 215 Cal. App. 3d 528 (Cal. App. 2d Dist. 1989).

28. Michael Asimow (2009, Winter), "When the Lawyer Knows The Client is Guilty," Southern California Interdisciplinary Law Journal, vol. 18, pp. 229–241.

Appendix A

Federal Rules of Evidence
(As amended to December 1, 2014)

ARTICLE I. GENERAL PROVISIONS

ARTICLE II. JUDICIAL NOTICE

ARTICLE III. PRESUMPTIONS IN CIVIL CASES

ARTICLE IV. RELEVANCE AND ITS LIMITS

ARTICLE V. PRIVILEGES

ARTICLE VI. WITNESSES

ARTICLE VII. OPINIONS AND EXPERT TESTIMONY

ARTICLE VIII. HEARSAY

ARTICLE IX. AUTHENTICATION AND IDENTIFICATION

ARTICLE X. CONTENTS OF WRITINGS, RECORDINGS, AND PHOTOGRAPHS

ARTICLE XI. MISCELLANEOUS RULES

Rule 101. Scope; Definitions

(a) **Scope.** These rules apply to proceedings in United States courts. The specific courts and proceedings to which the rules apply, along with exceptions, are set out in Rule 1101.

(b) **Definitions.** In these rules:

(1) "civil case" means a civil action or proceeding;

(2) "criminal case" includes a criminal proceeding;

(3) "public office" includes a public agency;

(4) "record" includes a memorandum, report, or data compilation;

(5) a "rule prescribed by the Supreme Court" means a rule adopted by the Supreme Court under statutory authority; and

(6) a reference to any kind of written material or any other medium includes electronically stored information.

Rule 102. Purpose

These rules should be construed so as to administer every proceeding fairly, eliminate unjustifiable expense and delay, and promote the development of evidence law, to the end of ascertaining the truth and securing a just determination.

Rule 103. Rulings on Evidence

(a) **Preserving a Claim of Error.** A party may claim error in a ruling to admit or exclude evidence only if the error affects a substantial right of the party and:

(1) if the ruling admits evidence, a party, on the record:

(A) timely objects or moves to strike; and

(B) states the specific ground, unless it was apparent from the context; or

(2) if the ruling excludes evidence, a party informs the court of its substance by an offer of proof, unless the substance was apparent from the context.

(b) **Not Needing to Renew an Objection or Offer of Proof.** Once the court rules definitively on the record—either before or at trial—a party need not renew an objection or offer of proof to preserve a claim of error for appeal.

(c) **Court's Statement About the Ruling; Directing an Offer of Proof.** The court may make any statement about the character or form of the evidence, the objection made, and the ruling. The court may direct that an offer of proof be made in question-and-answer form.

(d) **Preventing the Jury from Hearing Inadmissible Evidence.** To the extent practicable, the court must conduct a jury trial so that inadmissible evidence is not suggested to the jury by any means.

(e) **Taking Notice of Plain Error.** A court may take notice of a plain error affecting a substantial right, even if the claim of error was not properly preserved.

Rule 104. Preliminary Questions

(a) **In General.** The court must decide any preliminary question about whether a witness is qualified, a privilege exists, or evidence is admissible. In so deciding, the court is not bound by evidence rules, except those on privilege.

(b) **Relevance That Depends on a Fact.** When the relevance of evidence depends on whether a fact exists, proof must be introduced sufficient to support a finding that the fact does exist. The court may admit the proposed evidence on the condition that the proof be introduced later.

(c) **Conducting a Hearing So That the Jury Cannot Hear It.** The court must conduct any hearing on a preliminary question so that the jury cannot hear it if:

(1) the hearing involves the admissibility of a confession;

(2) a defendant in a criminal case is a witness and so requests; or

(3) justice so requires.

(d) **Cross-Examining a Defendant in a Criminal Case.** By testifying on a preliminary question, a defendant in a criminal case does not become subject to cross-examination on other issues in the case.

(e) **Evidence Relevant to Weight and Credibility.** This rule does not limit a party's right to introduce before the jury evidence that is relevant to the weight or credibility of other evidence.

Rule 105. Limiting Evidence That Is Not Admissible Against Other Parties or for Other Purposes

If the court admits evidence that is admissible against a party or for a purpose—but not against another party or for another purpose—the court, on timely request, must restrict the evidence to its proper scope and instruct the jury accordingly.

Rule 106. Remainder of or Related Writings or Recorded Statements

If a party introduces all or part of a writing or recorded statement, an adverse party may require the introduction, at that time, of any other part—or any other writing or recorded statement—that in fairness ought to be considered at the same time.

ARTICLE II. JUDICIAL NOTICE

Rule 201. Judicial Notice of Adjudicative Facts

(a) **Scope.** This rule governs judicial notice of an adjudicative fact only, not a legislative fact.

(b) **Kinds of Facts That May Be Judicially Noticed.** The court may judicially notice a fact that is not subject to reasonable dispute because it:

(1) is generally known within the trial court's territorial jurisdiction; or

(2) can be accurately and readily determined from sources whose accuracy cannot reasonably be questioned.

(c) **Taking Notice.** The court:

(1) may take judicial notice on its own; or

(2) must take judicial notice if a party requests it and the court is supplied with the necessary information.

(d) **Timing.** The court may take judicial notice at any stage of the proceeding.

(e) **Opportunity to Be Heard.** On timely request, a party is entitled to be heard on the propriety of taking judicial notice and the nature of the fact to be noticed. If the court takes judicial notice before notifying a party, the party, on request, is still entitled to be heard.

(f) **Instructing the Jury.** In a civil case, the court must instruct the jury to accept the noticed fact as conclusive. In a criminal case, the court must instruct the jury that it may or may not accept the noticed fact as conclusive.

ARTICLE III. PRESUMPTIONS IN CIVIL CASES

Rule 301. Presumptions in Civil Cases Generally

In a civil case, unless a federal statute or these rules provide otherwise, the party against whom a presumption is directed has the burden of producing evidence to rebut the presumption. But this rule does not shift the burden of persuasion, which remains on the party who had it originally.

Rule 302. Applying State Law to Presumptions in Civil Cases

In a civil case, state law governs the effect of a presumption regarding a claim or defense for which state law supplies the rule of decision.

ARTICLE IV. RELEVANCE AND ITS LIMITS

Rule 401. Test for Relevant Evidence

Evidence is relevant if:

(a) it has any tendency to make a fact more or less probable than it would be without the evidence; and

(b) the fact is of consequence in determining the action.

Rule 402. General Admissibility of Relevant Evidence

Relevant evidence is admissible unless any of the following provides otherwise:

- the United States Constitution;
- a federal statute;
- these rules; or
- other rules prescribed by the Supreme Court.

Irrelevant evidence is not admissible.

Rule 403. Excluding Relevant Evidence for Prejudice, Confusion, Waste of Time, or Other Reasons

The court may exclude relevant evidence if its probative value is substantially outweighed by a danger of one or more of the following: unfair prejudice, confusing the issues, misleading the jury, undue delay, wasting time, or needlessly presenting cumulative evidence.

Rule 404. Character Evidence; Crimes or Other Acts

(a) Character Evidence.

(1) *Prohibited Uses.* Evidence of a person's character or character trait is not admissible to prove that on a particular occasion the person acted in accordance with the character or trait.

(2) *Exceptions for a Defendant or Victim in a Criminal Case.* The following exceptions apply in a criminal case:

(A) a defendant may offer evidence of the defendant's pertinent trait, and if the evidence is admitted, the prosecutor may offer evidence to rebut it;

(B) subject to the limitations in Rule 412, a defendant may offer evidence of an alleged victim's pertinent trait, and if the evidence is admitted, the prosecutor may:

(i) offer evidence to rebut it; and

(ii) offer evidence of the defendant's same trait; and

(C) in a homicide case, the prosecutor may offer evidence of the alleged victim's trait of peacefulness to rebut evidence that the victim was the first aggressor.

(3) *Exceptions for a Witness.* Evidence of a witness's character may be admitted under Rules 607, 608, and 609.

(b) **Crimes, Wrongs, or Other Acts.**

(1) *Prohibited Uses.* Evidence of a crime, wrong, or other act is not admissible to prove a person's character in order to show that on a particular occasion the person acted in accordance with the character.

(2) *Permitted Uses; Notice in a Criminal Case.* This evidence may be admissible for another purpose, such as proving motive, opportunity, intent, preparation, plan, knowledge, identity, absence of mistake, or lack of accident. On request by a defendant in a criminal case, the prosecutor must:

(A) provide reasonable notice of the general nature of any such evidence that the prosecutor intends to offer at trial; and

(B) do so before trial—or during trial if the court, for good cause, excuses lack of pretrial notice.

Rule 405. Methods of Proving Character

(a) **By Reputation or Opinion.** When evidence of a person's character or character trait is admissible, it may be proved by testimony about the person's reputation or by testimony in the form of an opinion. On cross-examination of the character witness, the court may allow an inquiry into relevant specific instances of the person's conduct.

(b) **By Specific Instances of Conduct.** When a person's character or character trait is an essential element of a charge, claim, or defense, the character or trait may also be proved by relevant specific instances of the person's conduct.

Rule 406. Habit; Routine Practice

Evidence of a person's habit or an organization's routine practice may be admitted to prove that on a particular occasion the person or organization acted in accordance with the habit or routine practice. The court may admit this evidence regardless of whether it is corroborated or whether there was an eyewitness.

Rule 407. Subsequent Remedial Measures

When measures are taken that would have made an earlier injury or harm less likely to occur, evidence of the subsequent measures is not admissible to prove:

- negligence;
- culpable conduct;
- a defect in a product or its design; or
- a need for a warning or instruction.

But the court may admit this evidence for another purpose, such as impeachment or—if disputed—proving ownership, control, or the feasibility of precautionary measures.

Rule 408. Compromise Offers and Negotiations

(a) **Prohibited Uses.** Evidence of the following is not admissible—on behalf of any party—either to prove or disprove the validity or amount of a disputed claim or to impeach by a prior inconsistent statement or a contradiction:

(1) furnishing, promising, or offering—or accepting, promising to accept, or offering to accept—a valuable consideration in compromising or attempting to compromise the claim; and

(2) conduct or a statement made during compromise negotiations about the claim—except when offered in a criminal case and when the negotiations related to a claim by a public office in the exercise of its regulatory, investigative, or enforcement authority.

(b) **Exceptions.** The court may admit this evidence for another purpose, such as proving a witness's bias or prejudice, negating a contention of undue delay, or proving an effort to obstruct a criminal investigation or prosecution.

Rule 409. Offers to Pay Medical and Similar Expenses

Evidence of furnishing, promising to pay, or offering to pay medical, hospital, or similar expenses resulting from an injury is not admissible to prove liability for the injury.

Rule 410. Pleas, Plea Discussions, and Related Statements

(a) **Prohibited Uses.** In a civil or criminal case, evidence of the following is not admissible against the defendant who made the plea or participated in the plea discussions:

(1) a guilty plea that was later withdrawn;

(2) a nolo contendere plea;

(3) a statement made during a proceeding on either of those pleas under Federal Rule of Criminal Procedure 11 or a comparable state procedure; or

(4) a statement made during plea discussions with an attorney for the prosecuting authority if the discussions did not result in a guilty plea or they resulted in a later-withdrawn guilty plea.

(b) **Exceptions.** The court may admit a statement described in Rule 410(a)(3) or (4):

(1) in any proceeding in which another statement made during the same plea or plea discussions has been introduced, if in fairness the statements ought to be considered together; or

(2) in a criminal proceeding for perjury or false statement, if the defendant made the statement under oath, on the record, and with counsel present.

Rule 411. Liability Insurance

Evidence that a person was or was not insured against liability is not admissible to prove whether the person acted negligently or otherwise wrongfully. But the court may admit this evidence for another purpose, such as proving a witness's bias or prejudice or proving agency, ownership, or control.

Rule 412. Sex-Offense Cases: The Victim

(a) **Prohibited Uses.** The following evidence is not admissible in a civil or criminal proceeding involving alleged sexual misconduct:

(1) evidence offered to prove that a victim engaged in other sexual behavior; or

(2) evidence offered to prove a victim's sexual predisposition.

(b) **Exceptions.**

(1) *Criminal Cases.* The court may admit the following evidence in a criminal case:

(A) evidence of specific instances of a victim's sexual behavior, if offered to prove that someone other than the defendant was the source of semen, injury, or other physical evidence;

(B) evidence of specific instances of a victim's sexual behavior with respect to the person accused of the sexual misconduct, if offered by the defendant to prove consent or if offered by the prosecutor; and

(C) evidence whose exclusion would violate the defendant's constitutional rights.

(2) *Civil Cases.* In a civil case, the court may admit evidence offered to prove a victim's sexual behavior or sexual predisposition if its probative value substantially outweighs the danger of harm to any victim and of unfair prejudice to any party. The court may admit evidence of a victim's reputation only if the victim has placed it in controversy.

(c) **Procedure to Determine Admissibility.**

(1) *Motion.* If a party intends to offer evidence under Rule 412(b), the party must:

(A) file a motion that specifically describes the evidence and states the purpose for which it is to be offered;

(B) do so at least 14 days before trial unless the court, for good cause, sets a different time;

(C) serve the motion on all parties; and

(D) notify the victim or, when appropriate, the victim's guardian or representative.

(2) *Hearing.* Before admitting evidence under this rule, the court must conduct an in camera hearing and give the victim and parties a right to attend and be heard. Unless the court orders otherwise, the motion, related materials, and the record of the hearing must be and remain sealed.

(d) **Definition of "Victim."** In this rule, "victim" includes an alleged victim.

Rule 413. Similar Crimes in Sexual-Assault Cases

(a) **Permitted Uses.** In a criminal case in which a defendant is accused of a sexual assault, the court may admit evidence that the defendant committed any other sexual assault. The evidence may be considered on any matter to which it is relevant.

(b) **Disclosure to the Defendant.** If the prosecutor intends to offer this evidence, the prosecutor must disclose it to the defendant, including witnesses' statements or a summary of the expected testimony. The prosecutor must do so at least 15 days before trial or at a later time that the court allows for good cause.

(c) Effect on Other Rules. This rule does not limit the admission or consideration of evidence under any other rule.

(d) Definition of "Sexual Assault." In this rule and Rule 415, "sexual assault" means a crime under federal law or under state law (as "state" is defined in 18 U.S.C. §513) involving:

(1) any conduct prohibited by 18 U.S.C. chapter 109A;

(2) contact, without consent, between any part of the defendant's body—or an object—and another person's genitals or anus;

(3) contact, without consent, between the defendant's genitals or anus and any part of another person's body;

(4) deriving sexual pleasure or gratification from inflicting death, bodily injury, or physical pain on another person; or

(5) an attempt or conspiracy to engage in conduct described in subparagraphs (1)–(4).

Rule 414. Similar Crimes in Child Molestation Cases

(a) Permitted Uses. In a criminal case in which a defendant is accused of child molestation, the court may admit evidence that the defendant committed any other child molestation. The evidence may be considered on any matter to which it is relevant.

(b) Disclosure to the Defendant. If the prosecutor intends to offer this evidence, the prosecutor must disclose it to the defendant, including witnesses' statements or a summary of the expected testimony. The prosecutor must do so at least 15 days before trial or at a later time that the court allows for good cause.

(c) Effect on Other Rules. This rule does not limit the admission or consideration of evidence under any other rule.

(d) Definition of "Child" and "Child Molestation." In this rule and Rule 415:

(1) "child" means a person below the age of 14; and

(2) "child molestation" means a crime under federal law or under state law (as "state" is defined in 18 U.S.C. §513) involving:

(A) any conduct prohibited by 18 U.S.C. chapter 109A and committed with a child;

(B) any conduct prohibited by 18 U.S.C. chapter 110;

(C) contact between any part of the defendant's body—or an object—and a child's genitals or anus;

(D) contact between the defendant's genitals or anus and any part of a child's body;

(E) deriving sexual pleasure or gratification from inflicting death, bodily injury, or physical pain on a child; or

(F) an attempt or conspiracy to engage in conduct described in subparagraphs (A)–(E).

Rule 415. Similar Acts in Civil Cases Involving Sexual Assault or Child Molestation

(a) Permitted Uses. In a civil case involving a claim for relief based on a party's alleged sexual assault or child molestation, the court may admit evidence that the party committed any other sexual assault or child molestation. The evidence may be considered as provided in Rules 413 and 414.

(b) **Disclosure to the Opponent.** If a party intends to offer this evidence, the party must disclose it to the party against whom it will be offered, including witnesses' statements or a summary of the expected testimony. The party must do so at least 15 days before trial or at a later time that the court allows for good cause.

(c) **Effect on Other Rules.** This rule does not limit the admission or consideration of evidence under any other rule.

ARTICLE V. PRIVILEGES

Rule 501. Privilege in General

The common law—as interpreted by United States courts in the light of reason and experience—governs a claim of privilege unless any of the following provides otherwise:

- the United States Constitution;
- a federal statute; or
- rules prescribed by the Supreme Court.

But in a civil case, state law governs privilege regarding a claim or defense for which state law supplies the rule of decision.

Rule 502. Attorney-Client Privilege and Work Product; Limitations on Waiver

The following provisions apply, in the circumstances set out, to disclosure of a communication or information covered by the attorney-client privilege or work-product protection.

(a) **Disclosure Made in a Federal Proceeding or to a Federal Office or Agency; Scope of a Waiver.** When the disclosure is made in a federal proceeding or to a federal office or agency and waives the attorney-client privilege or work-product protection, the waiver extends to an undisclosed communication or information in a federal or state proceeding only if:

(1) the waiver is intentional;

(2) the disclosed and undisclosed communications or information concern the same subject matter; and

(3) they ought in fairness to be considered together.

(b) **Inadvertent Disclosure.** When made in a federal proceeding or to a federal office or agency, the disclosure does not operate as a waiver in a federal or state proceeding if:

(1) the disclosure is inadvertent;

(2) the holder of the privilege or protection took reasonable steps to prevent disclosure; and

(3) the holder promptly took reasonable steps to rectify the error, including (if applicable) following Federal Rule of Civil Procedure 26 (b)(5)(B).

(c) Disclosure Made in a State Proceeding. When the disclosure is made in a state proceeding and is not the subject of a state-court order concerning waiver, the disclosure does not operate as a waiver in a federal proceeding if the disclosure:

(1) would not be a waiver under this rule if it had been made in a federal proceeding; or

(2) is not a waiver under the law of the state where the disclosure occurred.

(d) Controlling Effect of a Court Order. A federal court may order that the privilege or protection is not waived by disclosure connected with the litigation pending before the court—in which event the disclosure is also not a waiver in any other federal or state proceeding.

(e) Controlling Effect of a Party Agreement. An agreement on the effect of disclosure in a federal proceeding is binding only on the parties to the agreement, unless it is incorporated into a court order.

(f) Controlling Effect of this Rule. Notwithstanding Rules 101 and 1101, this rule applies to state proceedings and to federal court-annexed and federal court-mandated arbitration proceedings, in the circumstances set out in the rule. And notwithstanding Rule 501, this rule applies even if state law provides the rule of decision.

(g) Definitions. In this rule:

(1) "attorney-client privilege" means the protection that applicable law provides for confidential attorney-client communications; and

(2) "work-product protection" means the protection that applicable law provides for tangible material (or its intangible equivalent) prepared in anticipation of litigation or for trial.

ARTICLE VI. WITNESSES

Rule 601. Competency to Testify in General

Every person is competent to be a witness unless these rules provide otherwise. But in a civil case, state law governs the witness's competency regarding a claim or defense for which state law supplies the rule of decision.

Rule 602. Need for Personal Knowledge

A witness may testify to a matter only if evidence is introduced sufficient to support a finding that the witness has personal knowledge of the matter. Evidence to prove personal knowledge may consist of the witness's own testimony. This rule does not apply to a witness's expert testimony under Rule 703.

Rule 603. Oath or Affirmation to Testify Truthfully

Before testifying, a witness must give an oath or affirmation to testify truthfully. It must be in a form designed to impress that duty on the witness's conscience.

Rule 604. Interpreter

An interpreter must be qualified and must give an oath or affirmation to make a true translation.

Rule 605. Judge

The presiding judge may not testify as a witness at the trial. A party need not object to preserve the issue.

Rule 606. Juror

(a) **At the Trial.** A juror may not testify as a witness before the other jurors at the trial. If a juror is called to testify, the court must give a party an opportunity to object outside the jury's presence.

(b) **During an Inquiry into the Validity of a Verdict or Indictment.**

(1) *Prohibited Testimony or Other Evidence.* During an inquiry into the validity of a verdict or indictment, a juror may not testify about any statement made or incident that occurred during the jury's deliberations; the effect of anything on that juror's or another juror's vote; or any juror's mental processes concerning the verdict or indictment. The court may not receive a juror's affidavit or evidence of a juror's statement on these matters.

(2) *Exceptions.* A juror may testify about whether:

(A) extraneous prejudicial information was improperly brought to the jury's attention;

(B) an outside influence was improperly brought to bear on any juror; or

(C) a mistake was made in entering the verdict on the verdict form.

Rule 607. Who May Impeach a Witness

Any party, including the party that called the witness, may attack the witness's credibility.

Rule 608. A Witness

(a) **Reputation or Opinion Evidence.** A witness's credibility may be attacked or supported by testimony about the witness's reputation for having a character for truthfulness or untruthfulness, or by testimony in the form of an opinion about that character. But evidence of truthful character is admissible only after the witness's character for truthfulness has been attacked.

(b) **Specific Instances of Conduct.** Except for a criminal conviction under Rule 609, extrinsic evidence is not admissible to prove specific instances of a witness's conduct in order to attack or support the witness's character for truthfulness. But the court may, on cross-examination, allow them to be inquired into if they are probative of the character for truthfulness or untruthfulness of:

(1) the witness; or

(2) another witness whose character the witness being cross-examined has testified about.

By testifying on another matter, a witness does not waive any privilege against self-incrimination for testimony that relates only to the witness's character for truthfulness.

Rule 609. Impeachment by Evidence of a Criminal Conviction

(a) **In General.** The following rules apply to attacking a witness's character for truthfulness by evidence of a criminal conviction:

(1) for a crime that, in the convicting jurisdiction, was punishable by death or by imprisonment for more than one year, the evidence:

(A) must be admitted, subject to Rule 403, in a civil case or in a criminal case in which the witness is not a defendant; and

(B) must be admitted in a criminal case in which the witness is a defendant, if the probative value of the evidence outweighs its prejudicial effect to that defendant; and

(2) for any crime regardless of the punishment, the evidence must be admitted if the court can readily determine that establishing the elements of the crime required proving—or the witness's admitting—a dishonest act or false statement.

(b) **Limit on Using the Evidence After 10 Years.** This subdivision (b) applies if more than 10 years have passed since the witness's conviction or release from confinement for it, whichever is later. Evidence of the conviction is admissible only if:

(1) its probative value, supported by specific facts and circumstances, substantially outweighs its prejudicial effect; and

(2) the proponent gives an adverse party reasonable written notice of the intent to use it so that the party has a fair opportunity to contest its use.

(c) **Effect of a Pardon, Annulment, or Certificate of Rehabilitation.** Evidence of a conviction is not admissible if:

(1) the conviction has been the subject of a pardon, annulment, certificate of rehabilitation, or other equivalent procedure based on a finding that the person has been rehabilitated, and the person has not been convicted of a later crime punishable by death or by imprisonment for more than one year; or

(2) the conviction has been the subject of a pardon, annulment, or other equivalent procedure based on a finding of innocence.

(d) **Juvenile Adjudications.** Evidence of a juvenile adjudication is admissible under this rule only if:

(1) it is offered in a criminal case;

(2) the adjudication was of a witness other than the defendant;

(3) an adult's conviction for that offense would be admissible to attack the adult's credibility; and

(4) admitting the evidence is necessary to fairly determine guilt or innocence.

(e) **Pendency of an Appeal.** A conviction that satisfies this rule is admissible even if an appeal is pending. Evidence of the pendency is also admissible.

Rule 610. Religious Beliefs or Opinions

Evidence of a witness's religious beliefs or opinions is not admissible to attack or support the witness's credibility.

Rule 611. Mode and Order of Examining Witnesses and Presenting Evidence

(a) **Control by the Court; Purposes.** The court should exercise reasonable control over the mode and order of examining witnesses and presenting evidence so as to:

(1) make those procedures effective for determining the truth;

(2) avoid wasting time; and

(3) protect witnesses from harassment or undue embarrassment.

(b) **Scope of Cross-Examination.** Cross-examination should not go beyond the subject matter of the direct examination and matters affecting the witness's credibility. The court may allow inquiry into additional matters as if on direct examination.

(c) **Leading Questions.** Leading questions should not be used on direct examination except as necessary to develop the witness's testimony. Ordinarily, the court should allow leading questions:

(1) on cross-examination; and

(2) when a party calls a hostile witness, an adverse party, or a witness identified with an adverse party.

Rule 612. Writing Used to Refresh a Witness

(a) **Scope.** This rule gives an adverse party certain options when a witness uses a writing to refresh memory:

(1) while testifying; or

(2) before testifying, if the court decides that justice requires the party to have those options.

(b) **Adverse Party's Options; Deleting Unrelated Matter.** Unless 18 U.S.C. § 3500 provides otherwise in a criminal case, an adverse party is entitled to have the writing produced at the hearing, to inspect it, to cross-examine the witness about it, and to introduce in evidence any portion that relates to the witness's testimony. If the producing party claims that the writing includes unrelated matter, the court must examine the writing in camera, delete any unrelated portion, and order that the rest be delivered to the adverse party. Any portion deleted over objection must be preserved for the record.

(c) **Failure to Produce or Deliver the Writing.** If a writing is not produced or is not delivered as ordered, the court may issue any appropriate order. But if the prosecution does not comply in a criminal case, the court must strike the witness's testimony or—if justice so requires—declare a mistrial.

Rule 613. Witness

(a) **Showing or Disclosing the Statement During Examination.** When examining a witness about the witness's prior statement, a party need not show it or disclose its contents to the witness. But the party must, on request, show it or disclose its contents to an adverse party's attorney.

(b) **Extrinsic Evidence of a Prior Inconsistent Statement.** Extrinsic evidence of a witness's prior inconsistent statement is admissible only if the witness is given an opportunity to explain or deny the statement and an adverse party is given an opportunity to examine the witness about it, or if justice so requires. This subdivision (b) does not apply to an opposing party's statement under Rule 801(d)(2).

Rule 614. Court

(a) **Calling.** The court may call a witness on its own or at a party's request. Each party is entitled to cross-examine the witness.

(b) **Examining.** The court may examine a witness regardless of who calls the witness.

(c) **Objections.** A party may object to the court's calling or examining a witness either at that time or at the next opportunity when the jury is not present.

Rule 615. Excluding Witnesses

At a party's request, the court must order witnesses excluded so that they cannot hear other witnesses' testimony. Or the court may do so on its own. But this rule does not authorize excluding:

(a) a party who is a natural person;

(b) an officer or employee of a party that is not a natural person, after being designated as the party's representative by its attorney;

(c) a person whose presence a party shows to be essential to presenting the party's claim or defense; or

(d) a person authorized by statute to be present.

ARTICLE VII. OPINIONS AND EXPERT TESTIMONY

Rule 701. Opinion Testimony by Lay Witnesses

If a witness is not testifying as an expert, testimony in the form of an opinion is limited to one that is:

(a) rationally based on the witness's perception;

(b) helpful to clearly understanding the witness's testimony or to determining a fact in issue; and

(c) not based on scientific, technical, or other specialized knowledge within the scope of Rule 702.

Rule 702. Testimony by Expert Witnesses

A witness who is qualified as an expert by knowledge, skill, experience, training, or education may testify in the form of an opinion or otherwise if:

(a) the expert's scientific, technical, or other specialized knowledge will help the trier of fact to understand the evidence or to determine a fact in issue;

(b) the testimony is based on sufficient facts or data;

(c) the testimony is the product of reliable principles and methods; and

(d) the expert has reliably applied the principles and methods to the facts of the case.

Rule 703. Bases of an Expert

An expert may base an opinion on facts or data in the case that the expert has been made aware of or personally observed. If experts in the particular field would reasonably rely on those kinds of facts or data in forming an opinion on the subject, they need not be admissible for the opinion to be admitted. But if the facts or data would otherwise be inadmissible, the proponent of the opinion may disclose them to the jury only if their probative value in helping the jury evaluate the opinion substantially outweighs their prejudicial effect.

Rule 704. Opinion on an Ultimate Issue

(a) **In General—Not Automatically Objectionable.** An opinion is not objectionable just because it embraces an ultimate issue.

(b) **Exception.** In a criminal case, an expert witness must not state an opinion about whether the defendant did or did not have a mental state or condition that constitutes an element of the crime charged or of a defense. Those matters are for the trier of fact alone.

Rule 705. Disclosing the Facts or Data Underlying an Expert

Unless the court orders otherwise, an expert may state an opinion—and give the reasons for it—without first testifying to the underlying facts or data. But the expert may be required to disclose those facts or data on cross-examination.

Rule 706. Court-Appointed Expert Witnesses

(a) **Appointment Process.** On a party's motion or on its own, the court may order the parties to show cause why expert witnesses should not be appointed and may ask the parties to submit nominations. The court may appoint any expert that the parties agree on and any of its own choosing. But the court may only appoint someone who consents to act.

(b) **Expert's Role.** The court must inform the expert of the expert's duties. The court may do so in writing and have a copy filed with the clerk or may do so orally at a conference in which the parties have an opportunity to participate. The expert:

(1) must advise the parties of any findings the expert makes;

(2) may be deposed by any party;

(3) may be called to testify by the court or any party; and

(4) may be cross-examined by any party, including the party that called the expert.

(c) **Compensation.** The expert is entitled to a reasonable compensation, as set by the court. The compensation is payable as follows:

(1) in a criminal case or in a civil case involving just compensation under the Fifth Amendment, from any funds that are provided by law; and

(2) in any other civil case, by the parties in the proportion and at the time that the court directs—and the compensation is then charged like other costs.

(d) **Disclosing the Appointment to the Jury.** The court may authorize disclosure to the jury that the court appointed the expert.

(e) **Parties' Choice of Their Own Experts.** This rule does not limit a party in calling its own experts.

ARTICLE VIII. HEARSAY

Rule 801. Definitions That Apply to This Article; Exclusions from Hearsay

The following definitions apply under this article:

(a) **Statement.** "Statement" means a person's oral assertion, written assertion, or nonverbal conduct, if the person intended it as an assertion.

(b) **Declarant.** "Declarant" means the person who made the statement.

(c) **Hearsay.** "Hearsay" means a statement that:

(1) the declarant does not make while testifying at the current trial or hearing; and

(2) a party offers in evidence to prove the truth of the matter asserted in the statement.

(d) **Statements That Are Not Hearsay.** A statement that meets the following conditions is not hearsay:

(1) *A Declarant-Witness's Prior Statement.* The declarant testifies and is subject to cross-examination about a prior statement, and the statement:

(A) is inconsistent with the declarant's testimony and was given under penalty of perjury at a trial, hearing, or other proceeding or in a deposition;

(B) is consistent with the declarant's testimony and is offered:

(i) to rebut an express or implied charge that the declarant recently fabricated it or acted from a recent improper influence or motive in so testifying; or

(ii) to rehabilitate the declarant's credibility as a witness when attacked on another ground; or

(C) identifies a person as someone the declarant perceived earlier.

(2) *An Opposing Party's Statement.* The statement is offered against an opposing party and:

(A) was made by the party in an individual or representative capacity;

(B) is one the party manifested that it adopted or believed to be true;

(C) was made by a person whom the party authorized to make a statement on the subject;

(D) was made by the party's agent or employee on a matter within the scope of that relationship and while it existed; or

(E) was made by the party's coconspirator during and in furtherance of the conspiracy.

The statement must be considered but does not by itself establish the declarant's authority under (C); the existence or scope of the relationship under (D); or the existence of the conspiracy or participation in it under (E).

Rule 802. The Rule Against Hearsay

Hearsay is not admissible unless any of the following provides otherwise:

- a federal statute;
- these rules; or
- other rules prescribed by the Supreme Court

Rule 803. Exceptions to the Rule Against Hearsay

The following are not excluded by the rule against hearsay, regardless of whether the declarant is available as a witness:

(1) **Present Sense Impression.** A statement describing or explaining an event or condition, made while or immediately after the declarant perceived it.

(2) **Excited Utterance.** A statement relating to a startling event or condition, made while the declarant was under the stress of excitement that it caused.

(3) **Then-Existing Mental, Emotional, or Physical Condition.** A statement of the declarant's then-existing state of mind (such as motive, intent, or plan) or emotional, sensory, or physical condition (such as mental feeling, pain, or bodily health), but not including a statement of memory or belief to prove the fact remembered or believed unless it relates to the validity or terms of the declarant's will.

(4) **Statement Made for Medical Diagnosis or Treatment.** A statement that:

(A) is made for—and is reasonably pertinent to—medical diagnosis or treatment; and

(B) describes medical history; past or present symptoms or sensations; their inception; or their general cause.

(5) **Recorded Recollection.** A record that:

(A) is on a matter the witness once knew about but now cannot recall well enough to testify fully and accurately;

(B) was made or adopted by the witness when the matter was fresh in the witness's memory; and

(C) accurately reflects the witness's knowledge.

If admitted, the record may be read into evidence but may be received as an exhibit only if offered by an adverse party.

(6) **Records of a Regularly Conducted Activity.** A record of an act, event, condition, opinion, or diagnosis if:

(A) the record was made at or near the time by—or from information transmitted by—someone with knowledge;

(B) the record was kept in the course of a regularly conducted activity of a business, organization, occupation, or calling, whether or not for profit;

(C) making the record was a regular practice of that activity;

(D) all these conditions are shown by the testimony of the custodian or another qualified witness, or by a certification that complies with Rule 902(11) or (12) or with a statute permitting certification; and

(E) the opponent does not show that the source of information or the method or circumstances of preparation indicate a lack of trustworthiness.

(7) **Absence of a Record of a Regularly Conducted Activity.** Evidence that a matter is not included in a record described in paragraph (6) if:

(A) the evidence is admitted to prove that the matter did not occur or exist;

(B) a record was regularly kept for a matter of that kind; and

(C) the opponent does not show that the possible source of the information or other circumstances indicate a lack of trustworthiness.

(8) **Public Records.** A record or statement of a public office if:

(A) it sets out:

(i) the office's activities;

(ii) a matter observed while under a legal duty to report, but not including, in a criminal case, a matter observed by law-enforcement personnel; or

(iii) in a civil case or against the government in a criminal case, factual findings from a legally authorized investigation; and

(B) the opponent does not show that the source of information or other circumstances indicate a lack of trustworthiness.

(9) **Public Records of Vital Statistics.** A record of a birth, death, or marriage, if reported to a public office in accordance with a legal duty.

(10) **Absence of a Public Record.** Testimony—or a certification under Rule 902—that a diligent search failed to disclose a public record or statement if:

(A) the testimony or certification is admitted to prove that

(i) the record or statement does not exist; or

(ii) a matter did not occur or exist, if a public office regularly kept a record or statement for a matter of that kind; and

(B) in a criminal case, a prosecutor who intends to offer a certification provides written notice of that intent at least 14 days before trial, and the defendant does not object in writing within 7 days of receiving the notice—unless the court sets a different time for the notice or the objection.

(11) **Records of Religious Organizations Concerning Personal or Family History.** A statement of birth, legitimacy, ancestry, marriage, divorce, death, relationship by blood or marriage, or similar facts of personal or family history, contained in a regularly kept record of a religious organization.

(12) **Certificates of Marriage, Baptism, and Similar Ceremonies.** A statement of fact contained in a certificate:

(A) made by a person who is authorized by a religious organization or by law to perform the act certified;

(B) attesting that the person performed a marriage or similar ceremony or administered a sacrament; and

(C) purporting to have been issued at the time of the act or within a reasonable time after it.

(13) **Family Records.** A statement of fact about personal or family history contained in a family record, such as a Bible, genealogy, chart, engraving on a ring, inscription on a portrait, or engraving on an urn or burial marker.

(14) **Records of Documents That Affect an Interest in Property**. The record of a document that purports to establish or affect an interest in property if:

    (A) the record is admitted to prove the content of the original recorded document, along with its signing and its delivery by each person who purports to have signed it;

    (B) the record is kept in a public office; and

    (C) a statute authorizes recording documents of that kind in that office.

(15) **Statements in Documents That Affect an Interest in Property**. A statement contained in a document that purports to establish or affect an interest in property if the matter stated was relevant to the document's purpose—unless later dealings with the property are inconsistent with the truth of the statement or the purport of the document.

(16) **Statements in Ancient Documents**. A statement in a document that is at least 20 years old and whose authenticity is established.

(17) **Market Reports and Similar Commercial Publications**. Market quotations, lists, directories, or other compilations that are generally relied on by the public or by persons in particular occupations.

(18) **Statements in Learned Treatises, Periodicals, or Pamphlets**. A statement contained in a treatise, periodical, or pamphlet if:

    (A) the statement is called to the attention of an expert witness on cross-examination or relied on by the expert on direct examination; and

    (B) the publication is established as a reliable authority by the expert's admission or testimony, by another expert's testimony, or by judicial notice.

    If admitted, the statement may be read into evidence but not received as an exhibit.

(19) **Reputation Concerning Personal or Family History**. A reputation among a person's family by blood, adoption, or marriage—or among a person's associates or in the community—concerning the person's birth, adoption, legitimacy, ancestry, marriage, divorce, death, relationship by blood, adoption, or marriage, or similar facts of personal or family history.

(20) **Reputation Concerning Boundaries or General History**. A reputation in a community—arising before the controversy—concerning boundaries of land in the community or customs that affect the land, or concerning general historical events important to that community, state, or nation.

(21) **Reputation Concerning Character**. A reputation among a person's associates or in the community concerning the person's character.

(22) **Judgment of a Previous Conviction**. Evidence of a final judgment of conviction if:

    (A) the judgment was entered after a trial or guilty plea, but not a nolo contendere plea;

    (B) the conviction was for a crime punishable by death or by imprisonment for more than a year;

    (C) the evidence is admitted to prove any fact essential to the judgment; and

    (D) when offered by the prosecutor in a criminal case for a purpose other than impeachment, the judgment was against the defendant.

The pendency of an appeal may be shown but does not affect admissibility.

(23) **Judgments Involving Personal, Family, or General History, or a Boundary.** A judgment that is admitted to prove a matter of personal, family, or general history, or boundaries, if the matter:

    (A) was essential to the judgment; and

    (B) could be proved by evidence of reputation.

(24) [**Other Exceptions.**] [Transferred to Rule 807.]

Rule 804. Hearsay Exceptions; Declarant Unavailable

(a) **Criteria for Being Unavailable.** A declarant is considered to be unavailable as a witness if the declarant:

    (1) is exempted from testifying about the subject matter of the declarant's statement because the court rules that a privilege applies;

    (2) refuses to testify about the subject matter despite a court order to do so;

    (3) testifies to not remembering the subject matter;

    (4) cannot be present or testify at the trial or hearing because of death or a then-existing infirmity, physical illness, or mental illness; or

    (5) is absent from the trial or hearing and the statement's proponent has not been able, by process or other reasonable means, to procure:

        (A) the declarant's attendance, in the case of a hearsay exception under Rule 804(b)(1) or (6); or

        (B) the declarant's attendance or testimony, in the case of a hearsay exception under Rule 804(b)(2), (3), or (4).

    But this subdivision (a) does not apply if the statement's proponent procured or wrongfully caused the declarant's unavailability as a witness in order to prevent the declarant from attending or testifying.

(b) **The Exceptions.** The following are not excluded by the rule against hearsay if the declarant is unavailable as a witness:

    (1) *Former Testimony.* Testimony that:

        (A) was given as a witness at a trial, hearing, or lawful deposition, whether given during the current proceeding or a different one; and

        (B) is now offered against a party who had—or, in a civil case, whose predecessor in interest had—an opportunity and similar motive to develop it by direct, cross-, or redirect examination.

    (2) *Statement Under the Belief of Imminent Death.* In a prosecution for homicide or in a civil case, a statement that the declarant, while believing the declarant's death to be imminent, made about its cause or circumstances.

    (3) *Statement Against Interest.* A statement that:

        (A) a reasonable person in the declarant's position would have made only if the person believed it to be true because, when made, it was so contrary to the declarant's proprietary or pecuniary interest or had so great a tendency to invalidate the declarant's claim against someone else or to expose the declarant to civil or criminal liability; and

        (B) is supported by corroborating circumstances that clearly indicate its trustworthiness, if it is offered in a criminal case as one that tends to expose the declarant to criminal liability.

(4) *Statement of Personal or Family History.* A statement about:

(A) the declarant's own birth, adoption, legitimacy, ancestry, marriage, divorce, relationship by blood, adoption, or marriage, or similar facts of personal or family history, even though the declarant had no way of acquiring personal knowledge about that fact; or

(B) another person concerning any of these facts, as well as death, if the declarant was related to the person by blood, adoption, or marriage or was so intimately associated with the person's family that the declarant's information is likely to be accurate.

(5) [*Other Exceptions .*] [Transferred to Rule 807.]

(6) *Statement Offered Against a Party That Wrongfully Caused the Declarant's Unavailability.* A statement offered against a party that wrongfully caused—or acquiesced in wrongfully causing—the declarant's unavailability as a witness, and did so intending that result.

Rule 805. Hearsay Within Hearsay

Hearsay within hearsay is not excluded by the rule against hearsay if each part of the combined statements conforms with an exception to the rule.

Rule 806. Attacking and Supporting the Declarant

When a hearsay statement—or a statement described in Rule 801(d)(2)(C), (D), or (E)—has been admitted in evidence, the declarant's credibility may be attacked, and then supported, by any evidence that would be admissible for those purposes if the declarant had testified as a witness. The court may admit evidence of the declarant's inconsistent statement or conduct, regardless of when it occurred or whether the declarant had an opportunity to explain or deny it. If the party against whom the statement was admitted calls the declarant as a witness, the party may examine the declarant on the statement as if on cross-examination.

Rule 807. Residual Exception

(a) **In General.** Under the following circumstances, a hearsay statement is not excluded by the rule against hearsay even if the statement is not specifically covered by a hearsay exception in Rule 803 or 804:

(1) the statement has equivalent circumstantial guarantees of trustworthiness;

(2) it is offered as evidence of a material fact;

(3) it is more probative on the point for which it is offered than any other evidence that the proponent can obtain through reasonable efforts; and

(4) admitting it will best serve the purposes of these rules and the interests of justice.

(b) **Notice.** The statement is admissible only if, before the trial or hearing, the proponent gives an adverse party reasonable notice of the intent to offer the statement and its particulars, including the declarant's name and address, so that the party has a fair opportunity to meet it.

ARTICLE IX. AUTHENTICATION AND IDENTIFICATION

Rule 901. Authenticating or Identifying Evidence

(a) **In General.** To satisfy the requirement of authenticating or identifying an item of evidence, the proponent must produce evidence sufficient to support a finding that the item is what the proponent claims it is.

(b) **Examples.** The following are examples only—not a complete list—of evidence that satisfies the requirement:

(1) *Testimony of a Witness with Knowledge.* Testimony that an item is what it is claimed to be.

(2) *Nonexpert Opinion About Handwriting.* A nonexpert's opinion that handwriting is genuine, based on a familiarity with it that was not acquired for the current litigation.

(3) *Comparison by an Expert Witness or the Trier of Fact.* A comparison with an authenticated specimen by an expert witness or the trier of fact.

(4) *Distinctive Characteristics and the Like.* The appearance, contents, substance, internal patterns, or other distinctive characteristics of the item, taken together with all the circumstances.

(5) *Opinion About a Voice.* An opinion identifying a person's voice—whether heard firsthand or through mechanical or electronic transmission or recording—based on hearing the voice at any time under circumstances that connect it with the alleged speaker.

(6) *Evidence About a Telephone Conversation.* For a telephone conversation, evidence that a call was made to the number assigned at the time to:

(A) a particular person, if circumstances, including self-identification, show that the person answering was the one called; or

(B) a particular business, if the call was made to a business and the call related to business reasonably transacted over the telephone.

(7) *Evidence About Public Records.* Evidence that:

(A) a document was recorded or filed in a public office as authorized by law; or

(B) a purported public record or statement is from the office where items of this kind are kept.

(8) *Evidence About Ancient Documents or Data Compilations.* For a document or data compilation, evidence that it:

(A) is in a condition that creates no suspicion about its authenticity;

(B) was in a place where, if authentic, it would likely be; and

(C) is at least 20 years old when offered.

(9) *Evidence About a Process or System.* Evidence describing a process or system and showing that it produces an accurate result.

(10) *Methods Provided by a Statute or Rule.* Any method of authentication or identification allowed by a federal statute or a rule prescribed by the Supreme Court.

Rule 902. Evidence That Is Self-Authenticating

The following items of evidence are self-authenticating; they require no extrinsic evidence of authenticity in order to be admitted:

(1) *Domestic Public Documents That Are Sealed and Signed.* A document that bears:

    (A) a seal purporting to be that of the United States; any state, district, commonwealth, territory, or insular possession of the United States; the former Panama Canal Zone; the Trust Territory of the Pacific Islands; a political subdivision of any of these entities; or a department, agency, or officer of any entity named above; and

    (B) a signature purporting to be an execution or attestation.

(2) *Domestic Public Documents That Are Not Sealed but Are Signed and Certified.* A document that bears no seal if:

    (A) it bears the signature of an officer or employee of an entity named in Rule 902(1)(A); and

    (B) another public officer who has a seal and official duties within that same entity certifies under seal—or its equivalent—that the signer has the official capacity and that the signature is genuine.

(3) *Foreign Public Documents.* A document that purports to be signed or attested by a person who is authorized by a foreign country's law to do so. The document must be accompanied by a final certification that certifies the genuineness of the signature and official position of the signer or attester—or of any foreign official whose certificate of genuineness relates to the signature or attestation or is in a chain of certificates of genuineness relating to the signature or attestation. The certification may be made by a secretary of a United States embassy or legation; by a consul general, vice consul, or consular agent of the United States; or by a diplomatic or consular official of the foreign country assigned or accredited to the United States. If all parties have been given a reasonable opportunity to investigate the document's authenticity and accuracy, the court may, for good cause, either:

    (A) order that it be treated as presumptively authentic without final certification; or

    (B) allow it to be evidenced by an attested summary with or without final certification.

(4) *Certified Copies of Public Records.* A copy of an official record—or a copy of a document that was recorded or filed in a public office as authorized by law—if the copy is certified as correct by:

    (A) the custodian or another person authorized to make the certification; or

    (B) a certificate that complies with Rule 902(1), (2), or (3), a federal statute, or a rule prescribed by the Supreme Court.

(5) *Official Publications.* A book, pamphlet, or other publication purporting to be issued by a public authority.

(6) *Newspapers and Periodicals.* Printed material purporting to be a newspaper or periodical.

(7) *Trade Inscriptions and the Like.* An inscription, sign, tag, or label purporting to have been affixed in the course of business and indicating origin, ownership, or control.

(8) *Acknowledged Documents.* A document accompanied by a certificate of acknowledgment that is lawfully executed by a notary public or another officer who is authorized to take acknowledgments.

(**9**) *Commercial Paper and Related Documents.* Commercial paper, a signature on it, and related documents, to the extent allowed by general commercial law.

(**10**) *Presumptions Under a Federal Statute.* A signature, document, or anything else that a federal statute declares to be presumptively or prima facie genuine or authentic.

(**11**) *Certified Domestic Records of a Regularly Conducted Activity.* The original or a copy of a domestic record that meets the requirements of Rule 803(6)(A)-(C), as shown by a certification of the custodian or another qualified person that complies with a federal statute or a rule prescribed by the Supreme Court. Before the trial or hearing, the proponent must give an adverse party reasonable written notice of the intent to offer the record—and must make the record and certification available for inspection—so that the party has a fair opportunity to challenge them.

(**12**) *Certified Foreign Records of a Regularly Conducted Activity.* In a civil case, the original or a copy of a foreign record that meets the requirements of Rule 902(11), modified as follows: the certification, rather than complying with a federal statute or Supreme Court rule, must be signed in a manner that, if falsely made, would subject the maker to a criminal penalty in the country where the certification is signed. The proponent must also meet the notice requirements of Rule 902(11).

Rule 903. Subscribing Witness

A subscribing witness's testimony is necessary to authenticate a writing only if required by the law of the jurisdiction that governs its validity.

ARTICLE X. CONTENTS OF WRITINGS, RECORDINGS, AND PHOTOGRAPHS

Rule 1001. Definitions That Apply to This Article

In this article:

(**a**) A "writing" consists of letters, words, numbers, or their equivalent set down in any form.

(**b**) A "recording" consists of letters, words, numbers, or their equivalent recorded in any manner.

(**c**) A "photograph" means a photographic image or its equivalent stored in any form.

(**d**) An "original" of a writing or recording means the writing or recording itself or any counterpart intended to have the same effect by the person who executed or issued it. For electronically stored information, "original" means any printout—or other output readable by sight—if it accurately reflects the information. An "original" of a photograph includes the negative or a print from it.

(**e**) A "duplicate" means a counterpart produced by a mechanical, photographic, chemical, electronic, or other equivalent process or technique that accurately reproduces the original.

Rule 1002. Requirement of the Original

An original writing, recording, or photograph is required in order to prove its content unless these rules or a federal statute provides otherwise.

Rule 1003. Admissibility of Duplicates

A duplicate is admissible to the same extent as the original unless a genuine question is raised about the original's authenticity or the circumstances make it unfair to admit the duplicate.

Rule 1004. Admissibility of Other Evidence of Content

An original is not required and other evidence of the content of a writing, recording, or photograph is admissible if:

(a) all the originals are lost or destroyed, and not by the proponent acting in bad faith;

(b) an original cannot be obtained by any available judicial process;

(c) the party against whom the original would be offered had control of the original; was at that time put on notice, by pleadings or otherwise, that the original would be a subject of proof at the trial or hearing; and fails to produce it at the trial or hearing; or

(d) the writing, recording, or photograph is not closely related to a controlling issue.

Rule 1005. Copies of Public Records to Prove Content

The proponent may use a copy to prove the content of an official record—or of a document that was recorded or filed in a public office as authorized by law—if these conditions are met: the record or document is otherwise admissible; and the copy is certified as correct in accordance with Rule 902(4) or is testified to be correct by a witness who has compared it with the original. If no such copy can be obtained by reasonable diligence, then the proponent may use other evidence to prove the content.

Rule 1006. Summaries to Prove Content

The proponent may use a summary, chart, or calculation to prove the content of voluminous writings, recordings, or photographs that cannot be conveniently examined in court. The proponent must make the originals or duplicates available for examination or copying, or both, by other parties at a reasonable time and place. And the court may order the proponent to produce them in court.

Rule 1007. Testimony or Statement of a Party to Prove Content

The proponent may prove the content of a writing, recording, or photograph by the testimony, deposition, or written statement of the party against whom the evidence is offered. The proponent need not account for the original.

Rule 1008. Functions of the Court and Jury

Ordinarily, the court determines whether the proponent has fulfilled the factual conditions for admitting other evidence of the content of a writing, recording, or photograph under Rule 1004 or 1005. But in a jury trial, the jury determines—in accordance with Rule 104(b)—any issue about whether:

(a) an asserted writing, recording, or photograph ever existed;

(b) another one produced at the trial or hearing is the original; or

(c) other evidence of content accurately reflects the content.

ARTICLE XI. MISCELLANEOUS RULES

Rule 1101. Applicability of the Rules

(a) **To Courts and Judges.** These rules apply to proceedings before:

- States district courts;
- United States bankruptcy and magistrate judges;
- United States courts of appeals;
- the United States Court of Federal Claims; and
- the district courts of Guam, the Virgin Islands, and the Northern Mariana Islands.

(b) **To Cases and Proceedings.** These rules apply in:
- civil cases and proceedings, including bankruptcy, admiralty, and maritime cases;
- criminal cases and proceedings; and
- contempt proceedings, except those in which the court may act summarily.

(c) **Rules on Privilege.** The rules on privilege apply to all stages of a case or proceeding.

(d) **Exceptions.** These rules—except for those on privilege—do not apply to the following:

(1) the court's determination, under Rule 104(a), on a preliminary question of fact governing admissibility;

(2) grand-jury proceedings; and

(3) miscellaneous proceedings such as:

- or rendition;
- issuing an arrest warrant, criminal summons, or search warrant;
- a preliminary examination in a criminal case;
- sentencing;
- granting or revoking probation or supervised release; and
- considering whether to release on bail or otherwise.

(e) **Other Statutes and Rules.** A federal statute or a rule prescribed by the Supreme Court may provide for admitting or excluding evidence independently from these rules.

Rule 1102. Amendments

These rules may be amended as provided in 28 U.S.C. §2072.

Rule 1103. Title

These rules may be cited as the Federal Rules of Evidence.

Appendix B

[Reprinted with permission from *Journal of Behavioral Profiling*, January 2000, Vol. 1, No. 1.]

"Evidence Dynamics: Locard's Exchange Principle & Crime Reconstruction"

Authors: Chisum, W.J.,[1] & Turvey, B.[2] "Evidence Dynamics: Locard's Exchange Principle & Crime Reconstruction," *Journal of Behavioral Profiling*, January, 2000, Vol. 1, No. 1

Abstract: Conclusions regarding the circumstances and behaviors elicited from the physical evidence related to a crime (crime reconstruction) can infrequently be housed within the confines of absolute certainty. This paper discusses the development of Locard's Exchange Principle and historical and contemporary philosophies surrounding crime reconstruction. It further discusses the fallacy of assuming the integrity of physical evidence, and provides a logical foundation for the concept of Evidence Dynamics. Evidence Dynamics refers to any influence that changes, relocates, obscures, or obliterates physical evidence, regardless of intent. Evidence Dynamics, it is further argued, come into play during the interval that begins as evidence is being transferred, and ends when the case is ultimately adjudicated. A discussion of the various types of Evidence Dynamics is provided, followed up by demonstrative examples from the authors' case files.

---

[1]W. Jerry Chisum has been a criminalist since 1960. In October of 1998, he retired from 30 years of service with the California Department of Justice into private practice. He is currently serving as Vice-President of the Academy of Behavioral Profiling, and is a member of their Board of Directors. He can be reached for comment or consultation by contacting: URL: www.ncit.com; jchisum@pro-filing.org.

[2]Brent E. Turvey, MS, is a forensic scientist, criminal profiler, and a full partner of Knowledge Solutions, LLC. He is currently serving as Secretary of the Academy of Behavioral Profiling, and is a member of their Board of Directors. He can be reached for comment, consultation or reprints of this article by contacting: Knowledge Solutions, 1961 Main St., PMB 221, Watsonville, CA 95076; Phone (831)786-9238; bturvey@corpus-delicti.com.

Of all responsibilities shouldered by the forensic scientist, the reconstruction of the circumstances and behaviors involved in a crime is one of the most important. In conjunction with agreeable witness accounts, a crime reconstruction may be a powerful instrument of corroboration. In the face of conflicted witness accounts, it may provide an objective view that points to one possibility over another. In the absence of witness accounts, it may be used to investigate and establish the actions that occurred at the scene of a crime. The role that crime reconstruction can play investigatively and legally should never be underestimated.

Because of the varied evidence and circumstances involved, the ability to reconstruct crime requires broad forensic knowledge, an objective if not conservative disposition towards the examination and interpretation of evidence, and what the fictional Dr. Watson of *Sherlock Holmes* fame referred to as a "peculiar facility for deduction." [9]

Despite its importance to investigative and legal venues, crime reconstruction is often performed inappropriately by the unknowledgeable and overconfident. This includes those with little knowledge of, or training in, the peculiarities of physical evidence and the forensic sciences. Those testifying as experts in the area of crime reconstruction routinely cite as a premise, for otherwise unproven opinions, the sum of their education, training, and experience. It may be the case that this is offered in the place of facts from the case file. This practice is regarded as illegitimate for a forensic examiner. "Experience should not make the expert less responsible, but rather more responsible for justifying an opinion with defensible scientific facts." [12]

Conclusions regarding the circumstances and behaviors elicited from the physical evidence related to a crime can infrequently be housed within the confines of absolute certainty. It is often an intensive process with imprecise results containing evidentiary holes, sequential gaps, and alternate possibilities. This does not suggest that crime reconstruction efforts lack investigative or legal utility. The utility of crime reconstruction is by no means bound to any predisposition for certainty. Rather, its utility is more often found in establishing the general circumstances of a crime, demonstrating links between victims, suspects, and offenders, corroboration of witness statements, providing investigative leads, and identifying potential suspects. [8]

Further still, it is often the case that what the physical evidence excludes, fails to establish, or equivocates, is actually of great investigative and legal importance. Forensic analysis in general, and crime reconstruction in particular, is concerned with those conclusions that can be logically drawn from the evidence, as well as with those that cannot. As such, the consideration of both the strengths and limitations of available physical evidence are an important part of crime reconstruction. It is with these considerations in mind that we begin our discussion of the relationship between Locard's Exchange Principle, Crime Reconstruction, *Evidence Dynamics* and their implications to forensic examinations.

The Development of Locard's Exchange Principle

Alphonse Bertillon developed one of the first scientific systems of documenting personal identification in Paris in the late 1800s [3, 11]. In 1879, Msr. Bertillon began his career when he was appointed clerk in the Premier Bureau of the Prefecture of Police [10]. The sheer volume of the files required organization. He used the measurement system that his father, a physical anthropologist, used to organize skeletal material. Bertillon's genius was in adapting this method to living persons and establishing a record system. The method referred to ultimately as *Bertillonage* used the relatively simple procedure of taking a series of body measurements, noting other physical characteristics, and placing this information on a single identification card in a police file [3]. As the method developed he started adding photographs of the individual to the files. Bertillonage was a significant advancement in terms of providing a useful database of criminals for criminal investigators.

Bertillon was motivated to develop his methods not only by the desire to assist in the tracking of criminals and their behavior, but also by a personal belief that everything that "lived and moved under heaven" was somehow unique [10]. His was something of a radical notion in criminal investigation at the time: that science and logic should be used to investigate and solve crime. As Msr. Bertillon's biographer stated:

> The methods of the French police in that year of grace 1879 had changed very little in principle from those initiated by that criminal turned policeman, the brilliant and unscrupulous [Eugene] Vidocq. They consisted in the liberal use of the police informer, and agent provocateur. [10]

Bertillonage was employed to identify criminals by law enforcement for at least two decades, until it was replaced by the use of fingerprints. In 1891, *Dr. Hans Gross*, an Austrian Magistrate and Professor of Criminology, made the following observation, "The advantages of finger-prints over the Bertillon system have become so well established that the latter can with perfect safety be dispensed with altogether as unnecessary for the purposes of identification."[5]

However, Bertillonage was not the limit of Msr. Bertillon's contribution to the forensic sciences, nor was it his most significant. His dedication to precise measurements and the use of photography led to a combination of the two practices beyond criminal identification. Bertillon assisted in the development and practice of forensic photography by introducing a measuring scale with the persons and objects of evidence that he photographed [10]. The usefulness of this practice soon became apparent. He was routinely sent out with investigators to document crime scenes. He would photograph the bodies of victims, their relationship to significant items of evidence in the scene, as well as the position, size, nature and extent of other physical evidence including footprints, stains, tool marks, and points of entry [10]. Until the development of this practice, criminal investigators and the courts relied upon sketches and notes of varying precision for their understanding of the context of a crime. That is, if any record were made of a crime scene at all.

Bertillon also instructed and influenced several students, including *Dr. Edmond Locard*, whose work formed the basis for what is widely regarded as a cornerstone of the forensic sciences, *Locard's Exchange Principle* (for discussion, see: [3], [6] & [11]). Dr. Locard, like Dr. Hans Gross and Msr. Bertillon before him, advocated the application of scientific methods and logic to criminal investigation and identification [11]. As stated by *Dr. John Thornton*, a criminalist and a former professor of forensic science at the University of California, Berkeley:

> Forensic scientists have almost universally accepted the *Locard Exchange Principle.* This doctrine was enunciated early in the 20th Century by Edmund Locard, the director of the first crime laboratory, in Lyon, France. Locard's Exchange Principle states that with contact between two items, there will be an exchange ... [12]

Due in no small part to Mr. Bertillon's influence, it was Dr. Locard's belief and assertion that when any person comes into contact with an object or another person, a cross-transfer of physical evidence occurs [11]. By recognizing, documenting, and examining the nature and extent of this evidentiary exchange, Locard observed that criminals could be associated with particular locations, items of evidence and victims. The detection of the exchanged materials is interpreted to mean that the two objects were in contact. This is the cause and effect principle reversed; the effect is observed and the cause is concluded.

Forensic scientists also recognize that the nature and extent of this exchange can be used not only to associate a criminal with locations, items, and victims, but with specific actions as well [2, 3, 11, 13, 14].

Crime Reconstruction

Crime reconstruction is "the determination of the actions surrounding the commission of a crime." [1] Careful and competent examination of the physical evidence the documentation of the crime scene allows for this determination. The systematic documentation and recording of the crime scene is required for this analysis. The photographic documentation as established by Bertillon is a necessity for crime reconstruction. The veracity of statements by witnesses, victims, and suspects can be established by reconstruction.

Modern methods of crime reconstruction owe themselves to a strong history marked by rigorous analytical thought and forensic application. The collective work of Alphonse Bertillon, Dr. Hans Gross, and Dr. Edmond Locard are no small part of this history. Enduring themes include the importance of physical evidence, objectivity, the necessary employment of logic, and viewing witness, victim, and offender statements with suspicion.

Just before the turn of the century, Dr. Hans Gross, in discussing how a crime should be reconstructed, argued for strict objectivity and a logical, sequential, frame by frame analysis on the part of criminal investigators:

> Nothing can be known if nothing has happened ...
> ... in the profession of the criminal expert everything bearing the least trace of exaggeration must be removed in the most energetic and conscientious manner; otherwise, the Investigating Officer will become an expert unworthy of his service and even dangerous to humanity.
> ... all of the circumstances of the crime must be clearly taken into account and submitted to a strict logical examination from their commencement to their last stage. If at a given moment something has not been explained, suspicion is justified and a pause must be made at the point where the logical sequence is broken ... [5].

Dr. Gross also decried the heavy reliance of criminal investigators and the courts on witness accounts, strongly advocating the use of physical evidence, writing:

> The progress of criminology means less trust in witnesses and more in real proofs. [9]

Dr. Edmond Locard, in speaking similarly on the subject of physical evidence and crime reconstruction, maintained that:

> … the criminologist re-creates the criminal from traces the latter leaves behind, just as the archaeologist reconstructs prehistoric beings from his finds. [9]

Dr. Theodore Reik, a Professor of Psychoanalysis at Vienna University, an early disciple of Dr. Sigmund Freud, also argued for the use of objectivity and logic in the investigation of crime and criminals:

> The object of the criminologist's reasoning is knowledge of a material event and the finding of an unknown person …
> Cool, objective thought, re-examination of facts according to the rules of logic, *raisonnement* (Locard) is the pivot of the detectives mental process. [9]

In the second half of this century, the late Dr. Paul Kirk, Professor of Criminalistics at the University of California, Berkeley, shared the views of Drs. Gross and Locard regarding issues of witnesses, physical evidence, and crime reconstruction, arguing:

> … the utilization of physical evidence is critical to the solution of most crime. No longer may the police depend upon the confession, as they have done to a large extent in the past. The eyewitness has never been dependable, as any experienced investigator or attorney knows quite well. Only physical evidence is infallible, and then only when it is properly recognized, studied, and interpreted. [13]

Dr. Kirk further argued, supporting the validity of Locard's Exchange Principle, the importance of transfer evidence to crime reconstruction:

> Wherever he steps, whatever he touches, whatever he leaves, even unconsciously, will serve as silent witness against him. Not only his fingerprints or his footprints, but his hair, the fibers from his clothing, the glass he breaks, the tool mark he leaves, the paint he scratches, the blood or semen he deposits or collects. All of these and more bear mute witness against him. This is evidence that does not forget. [13]

However, Dr. Kirk also argued for caution in the interpretation of evidentiary exchanges. In this brief discussion on establishing the identification of an object's source, he makes it clear that it is an endeavor with inherent hazards under even the best conditions.

> In the examination and interpretation of physical evidence, the distinction between identification and individuation must always be clearly made, to facilitate the real purpose of the criminalist: to determine the identity of source.

That is, two items of evidence, one known and the other unknown, must be identified as having a common origin. On the witness stand, the criminalist must be willing to admit that absolute identity is impossible to establish. Identity of source, on the other hand, often may be established unequivocally, and no witness who has established it need ever back down in the face of cross-examination. It is precisely here that the greatest caution must be exercised. The inept or biased witness may readily testify to an identity, or to a type of identity, that does not actually exist. This can come about because of his confusion as to the nature of identity, his inability to evaluate the results of his observations, or because his general technical deficiencies preclude meaningful results. [13]

Dr. Henry Lee, former Director of the Connecticut State Police Crime Laboratory, also advocates a combination of both physical evidence and logic by forensic scientists engaging in reconstruction:

Reconstruction not only involves the scientific scene analysis, interpretation of scene pattern evidence and laboratory examination of physical evidence, but also involves systematic study of related information and the logical formulation of a theory. [7]

Dr. John Thornton, previously mentioned, a student of Dr. Kirk, describes the mechanics of the logic that should be employed by forensic scientists when undertaking a forensic examination:

Induction is a type of inference that proceeds from a set of specific observations to a generalization, called a premise. This premise is a working assumption, but it may not always be valid. A deduction, on the other hand, proceeds from a generalization to a specific case, and that is generally what happens in forensic practice. Providing that the premise is valid, the deduction will be valid. But knowing whether the premise is valid is the name of the game here; it is not difficult to be fooled into thinking that one's premises are valid when they are not. Forensic scientists have, for the most part, treated induction and deduction rather casually. They have failed to recognize that induction, not deduction, is the counterpart of hypothesis testing and theory revision.... too often a hypothesis is declared as a deductive conclusion, when in fact it is a statement awaiting verification through testing. [12]

Criminalist Dr. Richard Saferstein, retired Chief Forensic Scientist from the New Jersey State Police Lab, also argues:

The physical evidence left behind at the crime scene plays a crucial role in reconstructing the events that took place surrounding the crime ... The collection and documentation of physical evidence is the foundation of a reconstruction. [11]

One of the authors, also a student of Dr. Kirk, makes a cogent forensic argument regarding the potential value of crime reconstruction to the court in terms of establishing what has actually happened in a given case:

The prosecutor seeks to convict the defendant by making the crime more heinous in nature. The defense seeks to exonerate the defendant. Both theorize about how the crime occurred with different objectives. Both cannot be correct and, lacking a reconstruction, both are probably wrong. The theories are alternatives and should be examined against the evidence ...

Any theory of the crime must be based on logic—explaining the physical evidence and its location at the scene. It is through such analysis that the behavior of the perpetrator is revealed ... [1]

Crime reconstruction, as argued, involves examining the available physical evidence, those materials left at or removed from the scene, victim, or offender. These materials are used by the forensic scientist to establish contact between the suspect and victim or scene according to the principle proposed by Dr. Locard. These forensically established contacts are then considered in light of available and reliable witness, victim, and offender statements. From this, theories regarding the circumstances of the crime can be generated and falsified by logically applying the information of the established facts of the case. Left standing, ideally, will be legitimate, logical conclusions regarding the actions surrounding the commission of the crime or as put by the fictional Sherlock Holmes in the *Sign of Four*, "—when you have eliminated the impossible, whatever remains, however improbable, must be the truth."

The Assumption of Integrity

The process of crime reconstruction is often built on the assumption that evidence left behind at a crime scene, which has been recognized, documented, collected, identified, compared, individuated, and reconstructed, is pristine. This assumption involves the belief that the process of taping off an area, limiting access, and setting about the task of taking pictures and making measurements ensures the integrity of the evidence found within. Subsequently, any conclusions reached through forensic examinations and reconstructions of that evidence are assumed to be a reliable lens through which to view the crime. This assumption is not always accurate.

Even though a reliable *chain of evidence* may be established[1], physical evidence may have been altered prior to or during its collection and examination. Unless the integrity of the evidence can be reliably established, and legitimate evidentiary influences accounted for, the documentation of a chain of evidence, by itself, does not provide acceptable ground upon which to build reliable forensic conclusions.

Consideration of evidentiary influences, or *Evidence Dynamics,* is a necessary part of the crime reconstruction process.

Evidence Dynamics

Crime reconstruction efforts are concerned with examining the effects or results of actions done in the commission of the crime. As Dr. Gross was fond of saying, "What is effect and what is cause?" [9] This is answered by the use of logic and forensic axioms such as Locard's

Exchange Principle. However, often missing from that analysis is a consideration of those influences that can change physical evidence prior to or as a result of its examination.

The general term *Evidence Dynamics* has been developed by the authors to refer to any influence that changes, relocates, obscures, or obliterates physical evidence, regardless of intent. *Evidence Dynamics* comes into play during the interval that begins as evidence is being transferred, and ends when the case is ultimately adjudicated. For those who are familiar with such evidentiary influences, and account for them in their analysis, this terminology is intended to provide a necessary and useful descriptor. An appreciation of *Evidence Dynamics* on what can be concluded from the physical evidence is requisite, and often pivotal, to the reconstruction process.

In the interpretation of *Evidence Dynamics*, two questions require attention. First, is there an item of evidence that has been demonstrably influenced between the time of the crime and the time of examination? If an item of evidence has been moved, changed, or obscured, then this must be factored into the examiner's analysis in terms of when and how. Second, is there evidence of a circumstance that could have obliterated or influenced evidence? Forensic scientists can only include in their analyses those things for which evidence exists. However, if there is no reasonable suggestion of circumstances that could have influenced or obliterated evidence, then the examiner should not assume that they occurred.

There are many possible influences on *Evidence Dynamics* that should be considered as evidence is examined. A brief list, not meant to be all-inclusive, is provided below.

Offender actions: The actions of an offender during the commission of their crime and the post-offense interval influence the nature and quality of evidence that is left behind.

These can include *Precautionary Acts*, *Ritual* or *Fantasy*, and *Staging*. *Precautionary Acts* involving physical evidence are behaviors committed by an offender before, during, or after an offense that are consciously intended to confuse, hamper, or defeat investigative or forensic efforts for the purposes of concealing their identity, their connection to the crime, or the crime itself [15]. *Staging* of the crime scene is a specific type of precautionary act that is done to deflect suspicion away from the offender. *Staging* often involves the addition of, removal of, and manipulation of objects in the crime scene to change the apparent "motive" of the crime. [15]*Ritual* or *Fantasy* may also influence the offender's actions during a crime, and can include such things as postmortem mutilation, necrophilia, and purposeful arrangement of a body or items in a scene. [15]

Victim actions: The victim's activities prior to a crime may result in artifacts that are mistaken for evidence. The actions of a victim during an attack and in the post-offense interval can influence the nature and quality of evidence that is left behind. This includes defensive actions, such as struggling, fighting, and running, which can relocate transfer evidence, causing secondary transfer. The victim's actions may also include cleaning up a location or their person after an attack.

Secondary Transfer: Transfer evidence, as we have established, is produced by contact between persons and objects [2, 8]. Secondary transfer refers to an exchange of evidence between objects or persons that occurs subsequent to an original exchange, unassociated with the circumstances that produced the original exchange[2].

Witnesses: The actions of witnesses in the post-offense interval can influence the nature and quality of evidence that is left behind. This includes actions taken to preserve victim dignity, as well as the deliberate theft of items from the scene upon discovery of an incapacitated or deceased victim.

Weather/ Climate: The weather or climate of a crime can influence the nature and quality of all manner of evidence that is left behind. This includes the destruction or obliteration of evidence by all manner of weather, as well as the effects of weather and climate on rates of body and biological transfer evidence decomposition.

Decomposition: Naturally occurring rates of decomposition, over time, can obscure, obliterate or mimic evidence of injury to a body. The clothing from a decomposed body will normally receive less attention for trace or transfer evidence.

Insect Activity: The actions of flies, ants, beetles, and other insects can obliterate the wounds on a body. They may also move, remove or destroy the transfer evidence.

Animal Predation: The feeding activities of all manner of indigenous wildlife from mice to coyotes and bears can relocate evidence, obliterate patterns, and further obscure, obliterate or mimic evidence of criminal injury to a body.

Fire: In cases were fire is involved, intentional or otherwise, the result can be the obscuring of all manner of physical evidence related to criminal activities, as well as its potential destruction. The evidence showing the actions of the offender regarding the primary offense are obscured if not eliminated by the subsequent arson. Evidence of the arson may remain.

Fire Suppression Efforts: In cases were fire is involved, there may be suppression efforts made. These efforts typically involve the use of high-pressure water, heavy hoses, perhaps chemicals, and firemen. Any of these, alone or in concert, can relocate the evidence, obliterate patterns, cause potentially misleading transfers, and/or add artifact-evidence[3], to the scene.

Police: The duty of the first officer on the scene is to protect life, not to preserve evidence. They must establish that the scene is secure from further attacks. Their actions may relocate evidence, obliterate patterns, cause transfers, and add artifact-evidence to the scene.

Emergency Medical Technicians: The actions of emergency medical personnel engaged in life saving activities in a crime may relocate evidence, obliterate patterns, cause transfers, and add artifacts mistaken as evidence. As well, they can add therapeutic injuries to the victim.

Scene Technicians: The actions of technicians working in the physical evidence recognition, preservation, documentation, and collection phases in a crime scene are expected to remove evidence without obliterating patterns, causing potentially misleading transfers, and adding artifact-evidence to the scene. The technicians must thoroughly document the scene prior to entering so the changes that occur are obvious.

Forensic Scientists: The actions of forensic scientists will also remove evidence, obliterate patterns, may cause potentially misleading transfers, and add artifact-evidence to the scene. This can occur by virtue of improper storage or destructive analytical techniques, or the addition of transfer and/or pattern evidence to a victim's body or clothing during transport and/or storage.

Coroners: The actions of the coroner in removing the body from the scene can move evidence, obliterate patterns, cause potentially misleading transfer, and add artifact-evidence to the scene. This includes the physical removal of the body from the location where it was discovered, the placement of the body into a "body bag," and the process of transporting the body from the scene. These actions will change pattern evidence on the clothing of the victim and may destroy potential valuable transfer evidence.

Case Examples

The following case examples have been taken from the authors' case files:

Example #1 — Fire and Suppression Efforts

A young female arrived at her older boyfriend's home, where he lived with his elderly mother and two teenage children. A confrontation ensued. The boyfriend and his mother, who were the only ones home at the time, were both killed, dying of exsanguination from multiple gunshot wounds.

The boyfriend's body was found outside of the residence with an associated blood trail. After the girlfriend removed some items of value she set both the house and the body of the boyfriend on fire.

Some of the actions and circumstances involved in the crime were evident, given the body outside of the home, associated transfer evidence, and blood patterns. However, a sequential reconstruction of the shots fired within the house, as well as the relative positions of the shooter and the victims, was significantly impaired. This was due to the movement and destruction of walls, furniture, flooring, household items, the body of the mother, and blood evidence in the scene. A crime analysis of the case reads in part:

> … precise reconstruction efforts are hampered in this case due to the numerous destructive and evidence-altering variables that were imposed upon the scene in the interval after the deaths occurred and before it was safe for forensic efforts to take priority. These destructive and evidence-altering variables and elements, documented in part by a video made of this scene during and after suppression efforts were engaged, include, but are not limited to:
>
> - the destructive nature of the fire itself, which involved both stories and many rooms in the house;
>
> - the destructive nature of the suppression efforts, which involved water being pumped into the home at approximately 1000 gallons per minute, the destruction and movement of items in the home for

both suppression and salvage purposes, as well as unintentional damage that may have been caused by heavy fire hoses in various locations within the home;

- the number of personnel venturing in and out of the home during and after suppression efforts, which some estimate may have been more that 50 individuals.

Example #2 — Decomposition & Insect Activity

An adolescent female was missing for approximately two weeks before investigators found her body. It was located in a slightly concealed area of foliage behind an unoccupied residence. Her deceased body had been placed inside of a piece of recently discarded carpeting, beneath a heavy metal water tank, and then covered by several more layers of older discarded carpeting.

According to the autopsy report, and visible in the autopsy photos, the victim's underwear was found in her mouth. The cause of death was determined to be "asphyxia by gagging" possibly in combination with a violent blow to the victim's jaw as evidenced by a fracture to the mandible.

The question arose as to whether there was evidence of manual or ligature strangulation. Due to the overall advanced state of decomposition, and the fact that maggots had consumed the soft tissue associated with the neck, a determination on this issue was not possible. In the absence of evidence to examine, one cannot make a legitimate determination as to whether or not manual or ligature strangulation occurred. This did not exclude the possibility that it may have occurred; merely that it could not be established and therefore should not be assumed for the purposes of analysis.

Example #3 — Secondary Transfer and Scene Technicians

The body of an adolescent female was found on a couch in her home where she lived with her mother and younger brother. She was wearing only a shirt and bra at the time of discovery. She was determined to have died of "asphyxia secondary to manual strangulation." She had a history of sexual abuse, suggested by the absence of her hymen and numerous anal scars, as well as a history of promiscuity. The DNA of one of her mother's lovers was found on her perineum, in the form of sperm.

Given the location and circumstances of the crime, the precise conditions of this exchange could not be reliably established. One possibility is that the suspect was engaged in some form of sexual activity with the victim, and that sperm transferred to her perineum as a result. However, the suspect and the victim's mother had sexual relations in the mother's bed, where the victim had been playing previously with her brother. There were also reports that the suspect and the victim's mother may have had sexual relations on the couch, were the victim would have been sitting. Additionally, a review of the crime scene video shows several evidence technicians moving evidence around on the couch and other locations, and then touching the victim's body in multiple locations, examining her body as it is being photographed, with and without gloves.

Given these circumstances, and the victim's history, the following are potential evidence transfer relationships in this case:

- From the suspect to the victim during a forced sexual assault;
- From the suspect to the victim during a consensual (but unlawful) sexual encounter;
- From the couch to the victim's perineum;
- From the mother's bed to the victim's perineum;
- From the scene technician's fingers to the victim's perineum

Example # 4—Emergency Medical Technicians

A youth was stabbed several times by rival gang members. He ran for a home but collapsed in the walkway. A photo of the scene taken prior to the arrival of the EMT team shows a blood trail and that the victim was lying face down. Subsequent photos show the 5 EMTs working on the body on his back. He had been rolled over onto the blood pool. It became impossible for bloodstain pattern interpretation to be used to reconstruct the events leading to the death of the youth.

Example # 5—Coroner Activities

Photos taken of the deceased showed isolated bloodstain patterns on the clothing of the victim of a rape homicide. She had been sexually assaulted and her throat was cut. The patterns on her panties appeared to be bloody transfers from a hand. The coroner refused to remove the clothing at the scene. When the panties were submitted to the laboratory they were soaked in the victim's blood from transporting her in the body bag. The patterns were destroyed as well as making it impossible to isolate the stains for identification purposes.

Example # 6—Victim Activities

In this case the victim's actions prior to a crime caused "false evidence" to be present. A woman had sex with her boyfriend in his vehicle. He dropped her off at her apartment. As she enters her bedroom she surprises a burglar. A struggle ensued causing tears in her clothing before the burglar strangled her and fled. The boyfriend is suspected of the "rape/homicide." His DNA is found in her vagina. This would be considered proof of his guilt in many courts.

Fortunately, the boyfriend had an alibi; he was stopped for DUI a couple of blocks from the house. He was in police custody during the time the screams were heard by the neighbors.

Example # 7—Family Activities

> The body of an elderly man was found "in his bed." Upon examination, strangulation marks were found on his neck. These marks were consistent with a hanging. When questioned the family admitted that he had hanged himself. They didn't want the "shame on their family," so they had cut him down, changed his clothing and put him to bed. The evidence was destroyed for cultural reasons.

Conclusions

The failure to consider *Evidence Dynamics* as a part of any crime reconstruction process has the potential to provide for misinterpretations of physical evidence, and inaccurate or incomplete crime reconstructions. Any subsequent use of the reconstruction for investigations, trial or behavioral analysis would have a diminished foundation and relevance, compounding the harm in legal, investigative and academic venues. It is the responsibility of the forensic scientist to perform reconstructions of the circumstances and behaviors involved in a crime with care, and to be aware of the possibility of *Evidence Dynamics*, in order that opinions regarding reconstruction of the crime reflect the most informed and accurate rendering of the evidence.

Notes

1. For discussions, see: [3], [4], [7], & [11]

2. For example, an offender wearing a wool sweater kills a female in her home. The offender leaves a number of wool fibers behind on the victim's body. The victim's neighbor hears the struggle and discovers the body. While attempting to revive the victim, several of the wool fibers transfer onto his clothing. When the clothing is examined in the laboratory, wool fibers foreign to the location are found on both the victim and his clothing, causing investigators to suspect him of the crime. Unless the circumstances of the crime are thoroughly investigated, and the possibility of secondary transfer explored, the neighbor may be wrongfully charged with the crime.

3. Artifact-evidence is any change in crime scene evidence or addition to crime scene evidence that can mislead one into inferring that the "evidence" is related to the commission of the crime.

References

1. Chisum, J., "An Introduction to Crime Reconstruction," in Turvey B., *Criminal Profiling: An Introduction to Behavioral Evidence Analysis*, (London: Academic Press, 1999)

2. Cwiklik, C., "An Evaluation of the Significance of Transfers of Debris: Criteria for Association and Exclusion," *Journal of Forensic Sciences*, 1999: 44(6), pp.1136–1150

3. DeForest, P. & Gaensslen, R.E. & Lee, H., *Forensic Science: An Introduction to Criminalistics*, (New York: McGraw-Hill, 1983)

4. DeHaan, J., *Kirk's Fire Investigation, 4th Ed.*, (Upper Saddle River: Prentice Hall, 1997)

5. Gross, H., *Criminal Investigation*, (London: Sweet & Maxwell Ltd., 1924)

6. Inman, K., Rudin N., *An Introduction to Forensic DNA Analysis*, (New York: CRC Press, 1997)

7. Lee, H., Ed., *Crime Scene Investigation*, (Taoyuan, Taiwan: Central Police University Press, 1994)

8. Lee, H., Ed., *Physical Evidence*, (Enfield, CT: Magnani & McCormick, Inc., 1995)

9. Reik, T., *The Unknown Murderer*, (New York: Prentice Hall, 1945)

10. Rhodes, H., *Alphonse Bertillon: Father of Scientific Detection*, (New York: Abelard-Schuman, Inc., 1956)

11. Saferstein, R., *Criminalistics: An Introduction to Forensic Science, 6th Ed.*, (Upper Saddle River: Prentice Hall, 1998)

12. Thornton, John I., "The General Assumptions And Rationale Of Forensic Identification," in David L. Faigman, David H. Kaye, Michael J. Saks, & Joseph Sanders, Editors, *Modern Scientific Evidence: The Law And Science Of Expert Testimony*, Volume 2, (St. Paul: West Publishing Co., 1997)

13. Thornton, J. I., (Ed.) Kirk, P., *Crime Investigation, 2nd Ed.*, (New York: Wiley & Sons, 1974)

14. Taupin, J.M., "Hair and Fiber Transfer in an Abduction Case—Evidence from Different Levels of Trace Evidence Transfer," *Journal of Forensic Sciences*, 1996: 41(4), pp. 697–699

15. Turvey, B., *Criminal Profiling: An Introduction to Behavioral Evidence Analysis*, (London: Academic Press, 1999)

About the Authors

Cliff Roberson, LLM, Ph.D., is an Emeritus Professor of Criminal Justice at Washburn University, Topeka, Kansas, and a retired Professor of Criminology at California State University, Fresno, California. He has authored or co-authored numerous books and texts on legal subjects.

His previous academic experiences include Associate Vice-President for Academic Affairs, Arkansas Tech University; Dean of Arts and Sciences, University of Houston, Victoria; Director of Programs, National College of District Attorneys; Professor of Criminology and Director of Justice Center, California State University, Fresno; and Assistant Professor of Criminal Justice, St. Edwards University.

Dr. Roberson's non-academic experience includes U.S. Marine Corps service as an infantry officer; trial and defense counsel and military judge as a marine judge advocate; and Director of the Military Law Branch, Headquarters, U.S. Marine Corps.

Other legal employment experiences include Trial Supervisor, Office of State Counsel for Offenders, Texas Board of Criminal Justice, and judge pro-tem in the California courts.

Cliff is admitted to practice before the U.S. Supreme Court, U.S. Court of Military Appeals, U.S. Tax Court, Federal Courts in California and Texas, Supreme Court of Texas and Supreme Court of California.

Educational background includes: Ph.D. in Human Behavior, U.S. International University; LLM in Criminal Law, Criminology, and Psychiatry, George Washington University; J.D., American University; B.A. in Political Science, University of Missouri; and one year of post-graduate study at the University of Virginia School of Law.

Robert Winters holds a Juris Doctorate degree and is a Professor with Kaplan University. He is also a member of the National Criminal Justice Association and serves as a Western Regional Representative, a member of their National Advisory Board and their National Elections Committee. Robert has taught courses at both the graduate and undergraduate levels in a wide range of areas of criminal justice including Criminal Evidence, Criminal Procedure, Constitutional Law, Criminology, Ethics, Terrorism, Cyber Crime, Domestic Violence and Criminal Law. In addition to being a serial entrepreneur from the age of 7, Robert has held senior management positions in the aerospace, international logistics and legal industries in Southern California. Robert resides in the southwest with his wife and son.

Index of Cases

Index of Statutes and Rules

Index